—
INSIDE
DEVELOPMENT
IN LATIN
AMERICA

—
INSIDE
DEVELOPMENT
IN LATIN
AMERICA

A REPORT FROM
THE DOMINICAN REPUBLIC,
COLOMBIA, AND BRAZIL
BY JAMES LANG

The University of North Carolina Press
Chapel Hill and London

Library of Congress Cataloging-in-Publication Data

Lang, James, 1944–
Inside development in Latin America.

Includes index.
1. Rural development projects—Brazil.
2. Rural development projects—Dominican Republic.
3. Rural development projects—Colombia.
4. Agricultural development projects—Brazil.
5. Agricultural development projects—Dominican
Republic. 6. Agricultural development projects—
Colombia. 7. Public health—Brazil. 8. Public
health—Dominican Republic. 9. Public health—
Colombia. I. Title
HN290.Z9C647   1987   307.1'4'0981   87-5950
ISBN 0-8078-1753-8
ISBN 0-8078-4195-1 (pbk.)

The paper in this book meets the guidelines for
permanence and durability of the Committee on
Production Guidelines for Book Longevity of the
Council on Library Resources.

Printed in the United States of America
92 91 90 89 88   5 4 3 2 1

● FOR ELIOT ROSEWATER

"What are people for?" I asked Eliot.
"To put out fires," he said.

CONTENTS

TABLES, FIGURES, AND MAPS

TABLES

FIGURES

MAPS

PREFACE

• Fourth Grade

"Lake Titicaca," said Sister Pancretia, "is the highest in the world; it is the lake closest to God." In the fourth grade, we learned simple virtues: to feed the hungry, to care for the sick, to clothe the naked. Experience has overturned the truth of the fourth grade. God's plan was one thing, man's was another.

When John Gunther took a generation *Inside Latin America* in 1941, he described nations that "as everyone knows live by the export of raw materials; they are basically one-crop or one-product countries."[1] His index had no entries for manufacturing, hydroelectric power, or industrialization. To travel through Latin America today is to see a land much changed since Gunther's journey. Brazil is one of the world's top ten automakers, turns out 14 million metric tons of steel a year, and exports jet aircraft to the United States. Brazil can no longer be described by sambas, carnival, and coffee. And Brazil is not alone. To track the industrial sector in Argentina, Mexico, or Venezuela is to tally petrochemicals, steel output, automobile production, and cement.

Despite the achievements, aspects of the "old" Latin America Gunther knew persist. "Dictatorship," "poverty," and "illiteracy" were prominent categories in his index; today's Latin America cannot be described without them. Brazil's new democratic government, for example, follows twenty years (1964–85) of military rule. It has inherited the legacy the old regime left behind: the poorest 40 percent of Brazil's families get by on only 10 percent of the national income; half the country's school children drop out before the fourth grade. Based on gross national product (GNP), Brazil ranks as an upper-middle-income country. Based on infant mortality rates, it belongs in the low-income class.

Gunther's book warned against Nazi infiltration. A new enemy, of course, has replaced the old one. The region's turmoil, however, may still rest on the same basis as before: on recurrent dictatorship, and on persistent poverty and illiteracy. Perhaps ideology is only the symptom. The United Nations Bill of Rights defines an adequate standard of living, basic health care, and education as economic rights. It also specifies civil liberties: the right to security and privacy, freedom from arbitrary arrest and torture, and the liberty of conscience and association. Combining economic and political rights is the path to freedom; one alone, or neither, leads to tyranny.

Regimes in Poland, the Soviet Union, and China cite economic rights as their justification. Rebellion takes the shape of civil liberties. In the United States, the interdependence of both has long been acknowledged, if only implicitly. In the nineteenth century, no country educated ordinary people with the tenacity of the United States. That freedom of the press was an expendable liberty for the illiterate seemed self-evident. The property qualifications states once had for voting also recognized the convergence. People without decent incomes and property of their own provided an unstable basis for democracy. This truth, apparent in the United States, has not been applied to Latin America. South of the Rio Grande, rebellion is premised on economic rights.

In the 1980s, most Latin American countries returned to democracy. This has meant the restoration of civil liberties. The task ahead is to address the needs of the majority in a productive fashion. The alternative is familiar enough. Empty promises discredit democracy; inaction rallies the poor against the rich. "Instability" then becomes a pretext for another round of military intervention.

Today, the haves and the have-nots are analyzed in development theory. That was less true in 1940; Gunther's book did not bother to index the concept. One can now take courses in it and choose between textbooks. Some claim that development is impossible because the rich hog everything and run the machinery of state. Others claim that development occurs when a "hidden hand" is allowed to distribute resources. So the poor must wait for revolution or the benefits that are presumed to trickle down. To study orthodox theory is to wade through comparative advantages, competing "engines" of growth, and import-substitution industrialization. Whether people have an education becomes "human capital theory," whether they eat is called "basic needs fulfillment," and whether the sick are cared for is "health delivery." It might be better to stay closer to the fourth grade.

This report does not ask whether exports or domestic demand should be the engine of economic growth. There is no mention of dependency theory, the Kuznets curve, or models that "trade off" growth for inequality. The report does not quarrel with GNP, and it does not attack capitalism, business, or investment. The premise is simply this. In a country like Brazil, functional literacy, decent health care, and gainful employment require more than computer chips and General Motors executives. Regardless of which theories make the economy grow, the benefits do not reach most people fast enough. The hidden hand will not fill the shopping carts in Santo Domingo, Bogotá, or Rio de Janeiro anytime soon. This does not mean Brazil should abandon the computer. It means that for poorer citizens "development" has to be something more than superhighways and petrochemicals.

This report is about what that "something more" is. It tells the story of health and rural development projects in the Dominican Republic, Colombia, and Brazil. Gunther interviewed politicians; this book talks with physicians and agronomists, with farmers and midwives. My part was to listen. People explained what they did in community health and rural extension, how they organized their work, and why they did it. I asked questions and wrote down what they told me. I file this report more as a journalist than as a political analyst. I do not know how to end inequality or how to reconcile liberty with economic rights. The people I met did not know either. Nonetheless, they had set out to do what they could, where they were, and with what they had.

They offered no prepackaged remedies, only localized ones. That is a small truth for modern times when solutions must be big ones. Still, how they accomplished things preserved peoples' dignity and strengthened their self-respect. A project had a way to work with the poor on the problems they considered of importance; it reached into the neighborhoods where people lived. Community development was a good school for self-reliance, and a good way to turn democracy from promise to practice.

The people I met believed in such truths. The lesson was not just for Latin America either. In the United States, social policies have been short on consistency and self-reliance. If the United States worked with the poor in the spirit of the Dominican Republic's Plan Sierra, it might find new possibilities within itself and understand better the contentious Third World at its borders.

Twenty-five years later, I did get to Lake Titicaca. It was as deep, blue, and clear as Sister Pancretia promised.

• Starting Out

I had logged thousands of miles on the bus in Mexico, Brazil, and Peru, documenting the telltale signs of colonial history. Besides looking out the bus window, the closest I got to the Third World was a year in Vista and a summer with Crossroads Africa. In 1980, I applied for a Kellogg Fellowship.

The application was a troublesome one; it asked how my research could be applied. I told them I had compared colonization in Spanish, English, and Portuguese America. The best path to contemporary Latin America, I said, was to start with the Spanish conquest and colonial Brazil's sugar trade. Because I had done that already, I was qualified for the next step. I proposed to turn reporter and file exciting background stories on political economy, sketching "the broad trends on-the-spot coverage missed."

My application was accepted—because of Vista and Crossroads Africa, not because of colonial history. I got the fellowship, but not the project. The purpose of the award, it turned out, was to divert professors from their accustomed rut. Most applicants were like me: they proposed to dig in the same spot. The Kellogg Foundation kept on my case until I gave ground. I was expected to shift from Latin America entirely. Fortunately, the Foundation's *Annual Report* listed health and rural projects it contributed to. So I compromised on political economy to visit development projects.

I still wanted the big picture however, not the fragmented world of midwives and small farmers. I planned to dabble in projects just enough to be credible, and then get back to serious analysis. Anyway, a project patronized by a U.S. foundation could not be worth much; I did have my principles to consider.

The Kellogg grant provided $30,000 over three years: from September 1981 through August 1984. During the first year, I had leave from Vanderbilt University. Subsequently, I traveled in the summer. I began in Costa Rica in November 1981. The flight left from Miami, where I had arranged to meet Jim Hampton, editorial chief for the *Miami Herald*. My background reports had not been totally abandoned.

In Costa Rica, I started at the rural extension office in Cartago. I went with the agronomists to the region's towns and farms. They talked about potatoes and carrots, explained the credit system, and took me to the cooperative. I never looked back.

So I owe an apology. The Kellogg Foundation insisted I give way, and I am grateful it did. And I was wrong about how and what the Foundation accomplished in Latin America. People did not view their work as Kellogg projects. In health, most originated as local initiatives; only later did Kellogg support add to the budget. For agriculture too, Foundation assistance was but one aspect of a project's funds. The Foundation did not have an agenda that it imposed on projects; on the contrary, a project had objectives to which the Foundation contributed.

Between 1981 and 1984, I visited thirty-four projects in six countries: Costa Rica (6), Brazil (16), the Dominican Republic (2), Colombia (7), Paraguay (1), and Argentina (2). Of these, fourteen were rural development projects and twenty were health projects. I did not draw a sample from a universe that was hypothetical, but from one I knew firsthand. The projects selected were diverse enough to portray the problems involved and the solutions devised.

This report is a journey through three countries: the Dominican Republic, Colombia, and Brazil. The people who do the work tell the story. They explain how credit is organized and describe the routines at a health post; they tell us about crops and cooperatives, about nutrition and public health; they show us not only what has to be done, but how to do it. What they have to say is more compelling than any theory I could impose. Hernando Linero, a Colombian agronomist in Pamplona, explained his job this way. "When engineers build a road," he said, "they can blast out a path. In extension we work with the terrain as it is. Rural development means less blasting."

I did not bring a tape recorder. The machine, I admit, is accurate, but it records everything in a "great, gluey blob."[2] Instead, I compiled my report as Gunther did, with pad and pen. I took down information immediately and then reconstructed it at night. The next day, I clarified what I had not understood. This was not always possible, but I rarely left a project with my notes incomplete. Some quotes are almost verbatim, but most are summaries of what people said. I plead guilty to interpretation, to putting Señor Jorge on one bus when he belonged on another, and to concentrating incidents in one place. Nonetheless, the people are real and not composites; they would recognize each other.

My month in Costa Rica came to forty-three typed pages. Twelve days at Plan Sierra netted seventy pages. The difference was experience, not the quality of the projects. In Costa Rica, I got my bearings. I needed time to understand the significance of what people told me, and to learn what questions I should ask. With great patience, agronomists described the characteristics of winged beans, and explained programs in credit, firewood production, and dairy farming. Health workers took me to hospitals "without walls" that depended as much on community action as on physicians. Given the background acquired in Costa Rica, when I went to Plan Sierra in the Dominican Republic, I knew what I wanted and what to ask.

Details I could not get on the spot I got from project documents, manuals, and brochures. When possible, I cross-checked information with World Bank data and government statistics. For example, the story people told about agriculture in Minas Gerais, Brazil's *Agricultural Census* confirmed in detail.

One project by itself was insufficient. Each had an aspect that distinguished it from the others. There was repetition involved, but it seemed worthwhile. To understand the principles behind community health, I had to visit clinics in both cities and villages, attend community meetings, and talk with midwives and medical students. I learned different things in different places, not everything all at once. So too with agriculture, and so too in this report.

The book begins in the Dominican Republic. It asks why more factories, paved highways, and bank loans have not been matched by enough gainful employment, enough schools, and decent health care. To benefit the majority, development requires more than additions to capital stock; it requires parallel efforts that address the basic problems of ordinary people in ways they understand. How this can be done is shown by Plan Sierra's approach to rural development.

In Colombia, the report takes a closer look at community health. It explains what nutrition, risk assessment, and research mean when applied to poor neighborhoods and families. It also describes how new technology has transformed Latin America's agriculture and why small farmers were so often the last to benefit. Agronomists explain how credit and technical assistance can be reorganized on the small farmer's behalf.

The section on Brazil returns to the question first sketched for the Dominican Republic: why does big development so often shortchange the majority? This time the answer is pursued with more determination. It spells out the priorities a tight-fisted military regime imposed, and the impact its policies had on factories and farms, on jobs and wages. It explains how Brazil built up Latin America's most diversified industrial economy along with the world's largest external debt. It examines Brazil's remarkable record on GNP growth, and its abysmal record on primary education, nutrition, and infant mortality. Projects under way in different regions of the country show how community-centered development can help repay the debt Brazil owes to the majority of its citizens.

The book's analysis of Brazil is the most comprehensive. In part, this reflects firsthand experience acquired over thirteen years. Brazil, however, is also Latin America's best case. If industrial expansion has not countered poverty fast enough there, it is unlikely to do so in the Dominican Republic or Colombia.

The conclusion is not a rehashed summary. It discusses how the debt crisis has undercut Latin America's prospects for rapid growth. Whether the banks and their clients muddle through, however, is not the point. Even in good times, there is no substitute for community-based development. With this in mind, the conclusion spells out the principles successful projects have in common, and it asks what the projects tell us about alternative paths to development.

Readers will want to know how the projects described fared subsequent to my accounts. As of 1987, all were still active and many had expanded. The report's validity, however, does not rest on the fortunes of a specific project. For every project included, five were left out. I do not lack alternatives. If Plan Sierra folded tomorrow, it would not prove rural development is untenable, any more than abandoned highways prove that road building is impossible. The point is not so much the individual projects, as it is the collective enterprise they represent.

Not everyone will find this report satisfactory. For new ways to tackle old problems, Latin America ought to be the last place to look, not the first. Pragmatism is the Yankee virtue, othodoxy the Latin vice. The stereotypes now seem oddly reversed. Latin America is the region that questions the old certainties and the packaged solutions. The United States has turned to slogans and recipes from the past.[3]

This report does not present a model, it does not specify predictor variables, and it assigns no probabilities.[4] There is no theory of the state or a comparative analysis of health systems. Instead, *Inside Development* is faithful to the vision of those who worked on projects. They believed their work was about people and local situations, about values and choices, about hopes and aspirations. I believed that too.

ACKNOWLEDGMENTS

My greatest debt is to those who patiently explained their work. This book belongs more to them than to me.

I sent versions of what came to be my Kellogg project to foundations and research councils. I wish to thank all those who wrote on my behalf: Roberto Beltrán, Mario Chaves, Bill Christian, Lewis Wolf Goodman, Jim Hampton, Robert Kramer, Riordan Roett, Thomas Skidmore, Charles Tilly, Charles Vance, and Eric Wolf.

At the Kellogg Foundation, Robert Kramer and Mario Chaves advised me on which projects to visit and sent letters of introduction; they gave me encouragement and kept me on the right track. Barbara Bartholomew forwarded project summaries prior to visits. Special thanks are due John Kornacki, Karen Hellenbeck, and Larraine Matusak who organized the fellowship program, as well as members of the advisory committee: Glen Taggart, Ralph Smuckler, Rozella Schlotfeldt, Joseph Volker, and John Peoples.

At the Foundation's office in Rio de Janeiro, I relied on Marcos Kisil and Vera Sabino.

The Kellogg Foundation is not responsible for this report, but it is responsible for investing in people.

At the University of Michigan, Charles Gibson directed my work on Latin America's colonial history. When I set aside historical research for projects, I had to tell him. "It is best to work on faith," he told me, "and far preferable to someone else's goal."

Ted Newcomb founded the Residential College at the University of Michigan. He taught me that every classroom must have a sandbox. So I put some in my book.

• Acknowledgments

Bill Christian read the first version. "What's wrong with it?" I asked, "I've already done my best." "Well, do your best again," he insisted.

Charles Tilly told Lewis Bateman at the University of North Carolina Press about my report. It was not the first time Chuck had intervened on my behalf. Thank you, Chuck.

Lew Bateman called about the book. "It's not very academic," I warned him, "it's about people." "Send it anyway," he said. Thank you, Lew.

Sharon Lobert always thought I could write this book, and she was right. I always thought she could make heavy atom derivatives, and I was right.

Special thanks go to my research assistant, colleague, and friend, Paulo Calmon. He was an expert on sources, government budgets, and Brazilian music. The facts and figures on Brazil's income distribution I owe to the research done by my friend, Carlos Mauro Benevides. Jonathan Hartlyn shared his work on contemporary Colombia and provided documentation.

Stevie Champion copyedited the manuscript. She combined attention to detail with common sense and an eye for substance. Managing Editor Sandra Eisdorfer set up the production schedule and held me to it. Executive Editor Lewis Bateman stood by the project, reduced author anxiety, and always answered his telephone.

My parents, William and Arline Lang, have never been to Latin America, they do not speak foreign languages, and they did not check the manuscript for mistakes. They corrected my spelling and arithmetic homework, hoping I could correct my own mistakes in the future.

At Vanderbilt University, the Center for Latin American Studies supported my first trip to Brazil in 1975. In 1981–82, a year of leave got my project visits off to a good start. Dean David Tuleen allowed more leeway than he had to on my Kellogg budget. Dean Jacque Voegeli and my chairman, Richard Peterson, granted a semester leave in the fall of 1985 so I could finish the report. With a small grant from Vanderbilt's Research Council, I returned to Brazil and revisited projects in 1986.

Steve Smartt at Grants Accounting and Trudy Masic kept track of expenditures. Doris Davis put most of the manuscript on the word processor; Linda Willingham, Laurie Alioto, Mamie Padget, and Shannon Mann made revisions. At the Latin American Center, Norma Antillón prepared the tables.

Gillian Murrey, Henry Murrey, Virginia Murrey, Jim Tuck, Sara Tuck, Bill Christian, Lew Bateman, Paulo Calmon, and Norma Antillón all read versions of the manuscript and made suggestions.

Hank Murrey and Wade Oakely built me a place to write in Fairview, Tennessee. They put a picture window in the study that faces Rio de Janeiro. In winter, when the view turns to frost, there is Christmas brunch with John and Virginia Murrey, and Forty-Two with Jack and Sylvia Gibbs. For those of us without color television, there is National Public Radio, Jane Austen, and Dorothy Sayers.

PART I
THE
DOMINICAN
REPUBLIC

I
PLAN SIERRA

I wrote to Plan Sierra for permission to visit the project. The director, Señor Blas Santos, requested my flight and time of arrival. I sent the information, but explained I could find my way to the project well enough. That was the last of our correspondence.

• Arriving

I did not expect a reception at the Santo Domingo airport, and, besides, how would anyone recognize me? With black hair, brown eyes, and modest stature, I fancied myself Latino in appearance.

"Señor Jaime?" called a voice behind me. I turned around in disbelief. Señora Sandra Mancebo had not been fooled. She was in her thirties, and calm despite the throng at the airport. Sandra worked in Santo Domingo; Blas had asked her to find me. She denied I could have escaped her vigilance. "I once headed up a Dominican team that worked with the Peace Corps," she told me. "You have an eye for Americans then," I noted, "that's how you spotted me." "Perhaps, but look at your T-shirt," she grinned. I had forgotten that. "Music City USA" was splashed across the front in red, white, and blue letters; "Nashville" was on the back. "I haven't seen one like that in Santo Domingo yet," she added. "And your shoes!" "What's wrong with them?" I replied, "they're made in Brazil." "Exactly," she said. "That's what all the Americans wear now. You might pass for a Dominican in other circumstances, but you arrived with almost no luggage; Dominicans bring back an incredible collection of merchandise. Your jeans are too worn, your hair doesn't look right, and your duffel bag probably has $500 worth of camera equipment." "You're

Map 1.1   The Dominican Republic

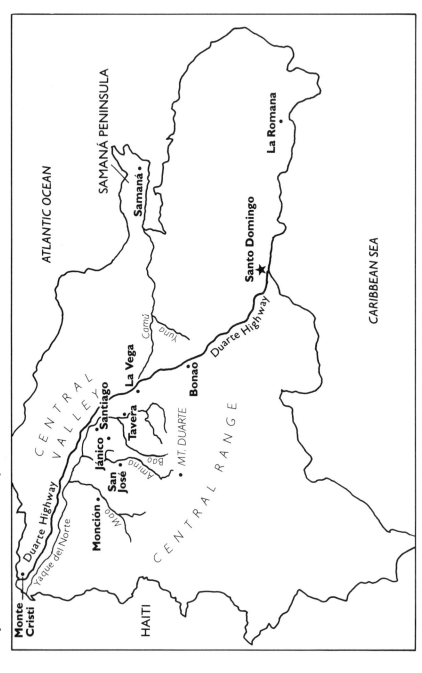

wrong about that," I announced, "I never bring a camera. And another surprise, I don't have reservations at the Sheraton." "I gathered that," she said. "They wouldn't let you in."

The Dominican Republic. A tropical island, south of Miami, small, and probably flat. I was right about one thing: tropical. The average temperature in February, the coolest month, is 74 degrees. From Miami, a flight to the Dominican Republic goes as much west as south. Sharing the island of Hispaniola with Haiti, the Dominican Republic is landlocked along its western border, and hence is not, strictly speaking, an island. Covering some 18,700 square miles, it is as large as Maryland and Massachusetts combined. And it certainly is not flat. Mt. Duarte, the highest peak in the central range, exceeds 10,000 feet.

Dictators. I had a recollection of a U.S. intervention (1916–24); the Marines built a lot of roads. They also trained a constabulary to protect democracy and maintain political stability. In 1930, Rafael Trujillo, backed by the U.S.-trained police force, turned the country into a kind of fief with himself as feudal lord. He kept "order" there until assassinated in 1961. "Disorder" followed, and so did another U.S. intervention, this time disguised as a peacekeeping mission under the Organization of American States (OAS). Joaquín Balaguer, a holdover from the Trujillo era, won the 1966 election. His regime did well at counting votes in 1970 and 1974, but less well in 1978 when the OAS sent observers. The opposition Dominican Revolutionary Party (PRD) won, purged the military, and retained the presidency again in the 1982 elections. The Dominican Republic somehow found its way through dictators, interventions, and transitions to democratic politics—both because of the United States and in spite of it.

Santo Domingo. Set amidst gardens and plazas, the capital's colonial quarter is one of the great treasures of Spanish America. And the new city expanded with an eye for parks. The broad avenues of suburban Santo Domingo suggest Miami much more than Mexico City or Bogotá. Along the waterfront, cafés and restaurants line one side of spacious George Washington Avenue; broad sidewalks, palm trees, and the Caribbean, the other. When the offshore breeze stirs in the evening, Santo Domingo turns out along the waterfront; people wear their best, if only a T-shirt and a neatly pressed pair of jeans. It was Christmastime. Strings of colored lights made the great obelisk at the Plaza de los Héroes look like a Christmas tree. Bands played in the adjoining park, while children scampered from carousel to Ferris wheel with parents in tow. Paintings done in Haitian style lined the streets: "clandestine imports and cheap copies destroying Dominican art," griped the newspaper critics of *El Caribe*. But there was an artistry in families meandering along the waterfront. In Santo Domingo, one could walk alone at night.

The Dominican Republic keeps one eye on its Yankee neighbor. The United States is the destination for most of the country's exports, and U.S. banks own most of the country's debt. Self-interest keeps Dominican politics in line with the U.S. State Department. Still, the affinity runs deeper. If Dominicans have traveled anywhere, it has been to the United States where they have half a million relatives living in "Nueva York." Dominicans apply the designation liberally: it includes most of New Jersey, eastern Pennsylvania, and all of Connecticut. The weather report on Dominican television covers the Caribbean plus New York City, the country's second capital. In winter, it highlights the latest blizzard, which attests to the good sense of those who stayed behind. The obituaries in *El Caribe* reflect the country's divided loyalties; the deceased are remembered in masses offered simultaneously in Santo Domingo and Nueva York. In 1984, Dominicans living in the United States remitted over $600 million to relatives back home.[1]

Like Cuba in the 1950s, the Dominican Republic is drawn to American culture, whether the latest fashion in jeans, or baseball, the country's national pastime. When Juan Marichal was voted into baseball's Hall of Fame, it was front-page news for a week. TV includes a Dominican version of Sesame Street, down to the Cookie Monster. Even Ma Bell recognizes the Dominican Republic as a network offspring, and includes it as a local area exempt from the zero applied to most foreign nations.

• Developments

My previous trips to Latin America had never included the Dominican Republic. I preferred big countries like Mexico and Brazil, which I considered more important. So I went to the library for two weeks of study prior to departure. Once in Santo Domingo, I tracked down my friend José del Castillo, a journalist and historian. I hoped to bring some good questions to Plan Sierra, lest they tire of me in two days rather than the proposed two weeks.

The Dominican Republic is a young country. In 1985, 40 percent of its inhabitants were under fifteen years of age, compared to 23 percent in the United States. The country's population of 6.4 million increases at an annual rate of approximately 2.6 percent.[2] The government is hard put to provide employment, adequate housing, sufficient food, and basic medical services.

Between 1968 and 1974, the gross national product (GNP) expanded by 11 percent a year, keeping ahead of population growth. A new manufacturing sector replaced imported shoes, textiles, processed food, and cosmetics with locally made products. In addition, industries took advantage of duty-free zones where they assembled or processed goods for reexport abroad; firms, many of them foreign, produced cigars, leather goods, garments, and electronics. Hotel construction for tourism expanded too, bolstered by a ten-year tax holiday and duty-free status for imported equipment and materials. High prices for sugar, the country's chief export, kept expansion going through the late 1970s.[3]

Despite the achievements, the benefits were slow to reach most Dominicans. The more prosperous 20 percent earned over half the national income, whereas the bottom fifth got by on only 4 percent.[4] Even in good years unemployment in Santo Domingo was 20 percent, not to mention the underemployed with only part-time jobs.[5] The infant mortality rate in 1983 was 63 per 1,000 live births, compared to 20 in Cuba and 11 in the United States.[6]

"Why didn't the gains of the 1970s generate sustained growth?" I asked José, over coffee. "The remedies that work in the States," he noted, "don't apply in such a small country. Industries that produce basics like clothing and shoes pay dearly to import machinery and raw materials. The Dominican Republic doesn't have the capacity or the market to produce the equipment itself. The duty-free zone allows industries to assemble prefabricated, imported ingredients with cheap labor; it has not stimulated much by way of related, local production. Tourism has some of the same limitations. Despite an investment of $700 million, its contribution to the Dominican economy is much less than might be expected. Although it means jobs for local construction firms, the materials used are imported: from bulldozers and cement mixers to steel girders, flush toilets, and light fixtures. Manufacturing and tourism create jobs, but not fast enough to absorb the country's expanding labor force at anywhere near acceptable levels. Modern industry is technology-intensive rather than labor-intensive; it employs relatively few workers per unit of output. And with tourism, once the hotels are up the jobs left are mostly unskilled minimum wage work for waiters, maids, and cooks."

The development of the 1970s benefited the cities, especially Santo Domingo, which also cashed in on the tourist trade. Even though the modern sector expanded rapidly, it did not outpace migration to the cities. In 1960, 70 percent of the country's population lived in rural areas. Two decades later a major shift had transferred over half the population to the cities. Santo Domingo alone had mushroomed to the point that one out of every four Dominicans lived there.[7] The remedy was to continue expansion as rapidly as possible: more import substitution, more free-zone exports, more hotels. Eventually, output reached the saturation point. With half of all Dominican families near or below the poverty line, the country had little capacity to consume apparel, shoes, and cosmetics. Exporting ran up against opposition by protectionists in foreign markets. And hotel accommodations expanded faster than the available tourist supply. As such nasty realities converged, the boom ran out of money.

Where had domestic entrepreneurs obtained the capital to finance their investments? They borrowed it from the country's Central Bank, often at subsidized rates. The Central Bank, in turn, had built up capital for loans by borrowing funds from U.S. and European banks. A substantial share of the

Dominican Republic's $2.8 billion debt (1985) was acquired during the boom years. When the debt crisis of the 1980s hit, even the modest growth of the late 1970s went bust. Between 1982 and 1985, the country's GNP expanded by an average of only 1.4 percent, less than population growth.[8] Oil prices led the way to the crisis.

Modernization meant improved highways for a growing number of trucks, buses, and passenger cars. New industries were also heavy users of fossil fuels. Because the country had no oil deposits of its own, it fell prey to OPEC's price hikes; the bill for fuel increased from only $48 million in 1972 to almost $500 million in 1981.[9] The cost of oil was partially offset by high sugar prices, which reached a decade high of 29 cents a pound in 1974; sugar accounted for half the country's exports. High prices, however, only spurred the movement away from sugar by U.S. consumers, food processors, and soft drink manufacturers. Sugar's share of the U.S. sweetener market dropped from almost 90 percent in 1960 to less than half in 1984. Substitution and oversupply drove sugar prices down to 10 cents a pound in 1980, and they kept dropping—to a rock-bottom 4 cents in 1984.[10] At the same time that sugar prices dropped, interest rates reached an unprecedented 18 percent during 1980–81.[11] Since most of the country's foreign debt carried an interest charge that fluctuated with international rates, loans contracted at 9 percent became twice as costly almost overnight. Then in 1982 Mexico's near default virtually halted bank loans to Latin America. Under the circumstances, the Dominican Central Bank had to cut back loans to entrepreneurs. Available capital shrank, and, anyway, it cost so much to borrow that the risks had increased appreciably. The Dominican Republic had "taken off" but was forced into a crash landing.

Like most countries of Latin America, the Dominican Republic had two economies. A modern sector of light industries, construction, transportation, and sales supported a consumption-oriented life-style of TV sets, automobiles, beauty aids, and toilet paper. Workers in the modern sector, as long as they were employed full-time, participated in this well-advertised collective fantasy, even if only marginally. Then there was the world most Dominicans lived in, a subsistence economy of underemployment and low productivity where families struggled to provide food, makeshift shelter, and a modicum of health care to their members. This indigent army included most of the rural work force plus those underemployed in the cities. That the modern sector has the dynamism to absorb the rest of the economy is a suspect proposition even in the best of times. In the worst of times, as the first half of the 1980s proved to be, it was a losing proposition. Investment capital netted the country a decent transportation system, a workable industrial base, ample tourist accommodations, and a credible increase in better jobs. But it did not create prosperity for the majority of families.

I like new cars and gadgetry, and keep my bathroom stocked with squeezable toilet paper. I only note that investment at the top has its limitations if the objective is adequate housing, sufficient food, and productive work for the majority. With two economies, different strategies are required: invest at the top, but also at the bottom; that is, address peoples' problems with solutions that are visible. A new textile plant in Santo Domingo is fine, but its relevance to a small farmer in the Sierra is far from obvious.

Plan Sierra, a project in the Dominican Republic's mountainous interior, provides a good example of investing at the bottom. No one has claimed that it is "the solution," that the Dominican Republic should distribute cows to rural families instead of building textile mills. Nonetheless, the project illustrates a practical approach to meeting the immediate needs of Dominican rural families. In the 1980s, given the financial constraints on costly, capital-intensive schemes, Plan Sierra provided a locally based option for development.

When a Planning Ministry talks about "development," it usually has new industries or infrastructure like roads and hydroelectric power in mind. When it considers agriculture, it means commodity exports like sugar and coffee. The most ignored aspect of development is typically the agricultural sector, and in particular, food for domestic consumption. About half the Dominican Republic's labor force is still in agriculture. Per capita rural incomes are only about 25 percent of urban incomes. Guesses as to rural underemployment run as high as 60 percent. Infant mortality rates are higher in rural areas, malnutrition more widespread, educational opportunities fewer. Between 1970 and 1980, while industrial growth averaged 8 percent a year, agriculture barely kept pace with the increase in population.[12] Small wonder Dominicans left the countryside.

Are people pushed out of agriculture by poor living conditions, or are they pulled to the cities by the lure of better jobs? Both propositions are true. In cities like Santo Domingo, the modern sector's growth attracted migrants much faster than the urban economy could employ them. Why did not word get back to the country's villages—stay put? Because families also faced a bleak future in agriculture. Stemming the disastrous flow to the cities requires a direct improvement in rural life.

To achieve a rough semblance of balance, the Dominican Republic has much at stake in rural development. Ignoring rural poverty eventually exacts its price in urban slums. It also shows up in the country's food deficit: the import bill for staples such as corn, beans, wheat, and cooking oil rose from about $70 million in the mid-1970s to over $120 million a year in the 1980s.[13] Finally, the methods employed by subsistence farming damage the country's ecology, threatening irrigation and hydroelectric projects.

What is the rationale for rural development? Stability in the countryside appeals to the Dominican military and the U.S. State Department. Social justice draws support from humanitarians and the Catholic church. Security in the cities makes sense to the middle class in Santo Domingo. Reducing the country's bill for imported food has validity for economists. Environmentalists

Map 1.2   Plan Sierra

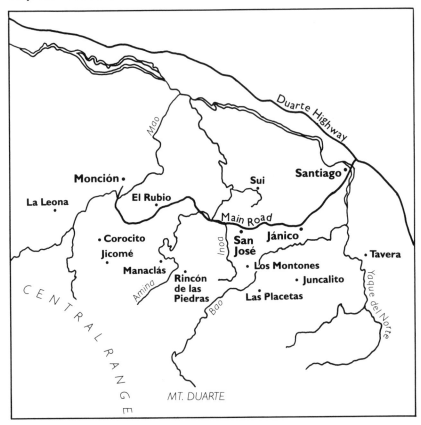

want to protect forests and reduce erosion. Common sense is not fashionable anywhere, so it can be safely disregarded. Nonetheless, that leaves a surplus of justifications in favor of rural development. Plan Sierra is a good example of how to do it.

• Plan Sierra

On Sandra's instructions, I took an express bus from Santo Domingo to Santiago, and then transferred to a local one that stopped in San José. From the guest house on the town square, I walked over to project headquarters a few blocks away. The buildings were simple but attractive with verandas and gardens. Señor Blas Santos was in his forties, casually dressed, and relaxed.

He had once served on the Dominican equivalent of the Federal Reserve Board, a position he abandoned for a thousand and one community meetings. Blas had no time to spare on a briefing. I apologized for arriving a day early. "You won't get in the way," he said. "Since you speak Spanish, I can send you out to the substations. And I won't have to waste time explaining what you can read for yourself." He took me to an office, piled the desk with project reports, and handed me a pad. "Go through these and you'll understand what we're trying to do; you can ask questions later. How we do things, and why, you can find out in the field from those who do the work."

I followed his advice. I have drawn some of my information from project documents: for example, the credit limits and repayment schedules for various crops. But I learned most from the explanations of agronomists and farmers, health workers and club members. My report begins with an overview of the project and then examines each facet: credit, crops, reforestation, and health care. The attention to detail reflects the careful work of those involved.

The Sierra

Plan Sierra covers a zone of small valleys and rugged mountains of approximately 730 square miles on the northern slopes of the Central Range. Three river systems traverse the region: the Bao, the Amina, and the Mao. San José, a picturesque town of about 5,000, is centrally situated within the project area. It is the Sierra's largest town, located about 20 miles from the provincial capital of Santiago.

"To me," Blas observed, "Plan Sierra is justified by what it contributes directly to people's lives. For the country as a whole, the rationale is mostly strategic. The Sierra has a direct impact on irrigation in the Central Valley, and it affects the hydroelectric grid."

The Dominican Republic has abundant water resources, both for generating hydroelectric power and for irrigation. The Central Valley, one of the richest agricultural zones in the country, stretches from the Samaná Peninsula on the East Coast to the Atlantic port of Monte Cristi in the Northwest. Two great rivers flow through the valley: the Camú-Yuna, which drains toward Samaná, and the Yaque del Norte, which passes through Santiago and then flows northwest toward Monte Cristi. Rainfall is heaviest near Samaná, over 80 inches annually. From Santiago, in the heart of the Central Valley, and on toward Monte Cristi, the valley gets progressively drier. The far western corner receives only 25 inches. The Yaque del Norte and its tributaries rise in the Sierra, making it the country's most important watershed. To provide hydroelectric power and extend irrigation to the western half of the Central Valley, dams were constructed on the Yaque del Norte and the Bao, a tributary. Additional projects are planned for the Mao and Amina rivers, which like the

Bao rise in the Sierra and feed the Yaque del Norte on its westward path. The Yaque Basin has over 40,000 irrigated acres, about 70 percent devoted to wet rice.[14]

Efficient management of the country's water resources is vital for irrigation and increased food production. It is also essential to replace imported fossil fuels with hydroelectric power—gas turbines currently supply the bulk of Santo Domingo's electricity. In 1982, fuel and food accounted for half of the Dominican Republic's import bill.[15]

"In the Sierra," Blas explained, "deforestation and hillside farming created erosion of such magnitude that it now threatens the useful life of dams and irrigation canals. Watershed deterioration has reduced the soil's capacity to absorb water; rivers hover between flash flooding and a trickle. At the Tavera dam, on the Yaque del Norte, sedimentation is three times greater than originally projected. At San José, the power plant built on the Inoa River in the 1950s is abandoned; a dependable depth of forty feet is now so shallow you can walk across it with your pants rolled up. To harness the region's water resources, the Sierra's ecosystem has to be protected and restored. By an ironic twist of fate, small farmers hold hydroelectric development hostage."

Until the 1930s, the Sierra's farmers exploited the pine forests, which provided firewood and timber for local construction. Subsequently, the lumber business moved in. Furniture making became an important cottage industry, but clear cutting soon depleted the Sierra's forests. In 1966, the newly elected Balaguer regime closed the sawmills and placed what forests remained under military protection. Today, the Dominican Republic imports wood both for construction and for furniture. The 3 million Dominican families that depend on firewood for cooking must glean what they can from their own land, cut wood illegally in protected forests, or purchase imported charcoal, which adds significantly to household expenses. Overall, the bill for imported timber and its derivatives runs around $100 million a year.[16]

"Most of the Sierra's families," Blas said, "live in conditions of absolute poverty. Inadequate income leads to deficient nutrition, which increases the susceptibility to disease. Contaminated water and crude waste disposal make the situation worse. Human misery goes hand in hand with the degradation of the environment. Incursions into protected forests to cut wood for household needs or extra income are constant. Agriculture, such as it is, jeopardizes human potential and compromises the region's water resources, soil, and forests."

As Blas explained, Plan Sierra's objective was to add to farm incomes and improve living conditions. The project provided credit for crops and introduced production methods that reduced soil erosion. Reforestation included timber, fruit trees, and coffee. The project planted pine trees at its own expense, starting with public lands along watersheds. Work in public health began with latrines, a safe water supply, and vegetable gardens for family nutrition. Within each program, training and participation strengthened the project's work. At its community center just outside San José at Los Montones, Plan Sierra held workshops with farmers, midwives, and the women's clubs.

Meeting the needs of rural families and protecting the environment are compatible and relevant beyond the Sierra. Less soil erosion will extend the life of hydroelectric projects and irrigation works. Food production contributes to eventual self-sufficiency; reforestation will ensure an adequate wood supply. A single Plan Sierra will not stem urban migration, but it is a start. Such factors have been recognized in the Dominican Republic. The World Bank did not create Plan Sierra. Quite the contrary, Dominican agronomists who lived and worked in the Sierra designed it; Dominican health workers, agronomists, and community groups managed it; and the Dominican Congress provided most of the project's funds.

Getting Things Done

The Dominican Republic has different agencies for rural credit, water resources, roads, cooperatives, and extension.[17] Rather than duplicate this structure, and the problems it presented for coordination, Plan Sierra was established with a single board of directors, one budget, one set of managers, and one mandate. As a result, it had autonomy to design and execute its own plans. Plan Sierra began its work in 1979; it was approved for ten years. The bishop of Santiago, Roque Adams, was chairman of the board. Permanent members included the dean of the Medical School from Santiago's Catholic University, the secretary of health for the Sierra, a representative from the Agricultural Institute in Santiago, plus community leaders from the region's main towns.

Plan Sierra had a target population of 17,000 families. Because the average size of a rural household was around six, the total number of beneficiaries was potentially over 100,000. The project area was divided into three zones within reach of Jánico, San José, and Monción—the Sierra's largest towns. Each had an Extension Center that served as a regional headquarters. Six substations provided extension in remote areas. (See Figure 1.1.) Given the Sierra's diversity of crops and microclimates, the centers and substations had to modify general objectives to suit local circumstances.

A substation usually had three agronomists who supervised programs in reforestation and crop production.[18] Many were recent graduates of the Agricultural Institute in Santiago. Assisting them were two or three extensionists trained for six months at Los Montones prior to their assignment. A substation also had a home educator who worked directly with the women's clubs. There was a cook, and sometimes a secretary to keep records. The local health clinic was situated near the substation, if not right next to it.

A substation was a modest, two-storied cement-block structure. A central

Figure 1.1 Extension Network: Plan Sierra

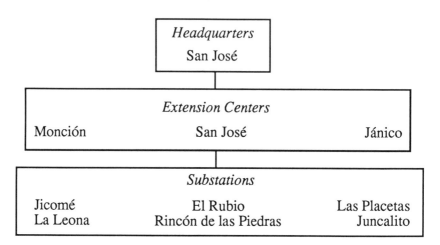

rectangular room doubled as dining and sitting area. Adjoining it were small offices, the kitchen, and showers. The upstairs had a large dormitory for the men; there were spare rooms downstairs for the women. The substations were in settlements too small to provide accommodations. Juncalito, El Rubio, and Las Placetas, for example, qualified as towns, but Jicomé was primarily defined by its cantina. La Leona strung out its makeshift housing along a rutted dirt road. Rincón de las Piedras was something between town and hamlet. Of the above localities, none had electricity except El Rubio. By contrast, the Extension Centers in Jánico, San José, and Monción were in larger towns with more amenities, including electricity; housing was also available.

Each substation had an impressive garden, terraced if necessary. Fruit trees dotted the grounds. The gardens were practical, providing fresh vegetables, but they were also demonstration plots for the community. And they showed that extension workers practiced what they preached.

The road from Santiago to San José was paved. From San José to Monción, a distance of about twenty miles, the passageway was wide enough, but the road was a mess of dirt, gravel, jagged rocks, and ruts. The trip took from one and a half to two hours, depending on the vehicle's durability and the driver's nerve. The trails that led to the substations were impassable to cars and qualified as roads only because of the persistence of jeeps and small trucks. When I visited Juncalito with Blas, the twenty-five-mile trip took an hour and a half; Blas said that his last trip there, in the rain and mud, took three. After a bout with the Sierra's roads, I returned to San José with a splitting headache. My main out-of-pocket expense, after cigarettes, was aspirin.

I readily admit a preference for asphalt over mud. The agenda of a project like Plan Sierra, however, necessarily placed credit for farmers, safe water, and the family cow before roads. To the extent that funds went to infrastructure, it was at the behest of localities. They provided community labor; Plan Sierra provided materials like cement and gravel. Bridges were particularly popular. During the rainy season, streams flooded and isolated towns even from mule traffic. At El Rubio and Jicomé, admiring the town's bridge was a way to show respect for community action.

Credit and Coffee

Iván Scarfullery, a specialist in coffee production, worked with the credit program. Tall, slender, and good-humored, he had moved to San José with his family. I accompanied him for two days, inspecting coffee fields, meeting extension workers at the substations, and attending community meetings.

To increase production, farmers need credit to buy better seeds, purchase fertilizer, and prepare the soil properly. A good credit system is the mainstay of an effective project. "Most of the Sierra's farms," Iván noted, "are too small and unproductive to justify bank loans; farmers lack collateral, and they don't know how to budget funds or fill out forms. They are high-risk clients wanting tiny sums, not exactly what the banks call preferred customers. Plan Sierra has a line of credit from the Agricultural Bank, which, in turn, it extends to farmers. We process the loans and help farmers fill out forms. And we provide technical assistance for erosion control and crop production. Unless credit is backed up by extension, it won't work; you end up with bad loans. Loans must be paid back with interest. Plan Sierra does not give handouts, and, anyway, people do not respect what they get for free."

The agronomists reviewed requests and inspected an applicant's land before approving funds. Most loans were worked out collectively with a farmers' association; nonetheless, each member had a specified amount depending on the acreage planted. Once a loan was approved, the association's members attended a three-day training program at Los Montones. They arrived at noon on Monday and stayed through Wednesday morning. Sessions went over the credit system; they also stressed the importance of reforestation, soil conservation, and new production methods geared to the crop in question. Because more credit had gone to coffee than to any other crop, it is a good place to begin.

On the mountain slopes around Juncalito, coffee had long provided a cash crop. The cool climate with abundant rainfall is ideal. The trees, however, were old and of an inferior quality. Plan Sierra was replacing older trees with better varieties and encouraging production in new regions, as about 20 percent of the Sierra has a microclimate suited to coffee. And when planted with top varieties, the Sierra produces some of the best coffee in the Dominican Republic. There were over forty associations of coffee producers, most of them concentrated around Juncalito, Rincón de las Piedras, Jicomé, and La Leona.

"Why coffee rather than food crops?" I asked Iván. "Because it provides a dependable cash crop for families," he replied. "In the Sierra, where coffee is confined to mountain slopes, production can't be mechanized and the land is too steep for crops. Coffee farms are of modest acreage; the family itself provides much of the labor, keeping costs down. Even when prices fall in New York, the Sierra's small coffee farms can still make a profit; they don't have the fixed costs for machinery and labor that characterize Brazilian production. Equally important, coffee trees help conserve the soil. When properly tended they produce for over twenty years. Planting coffee, in fact, is reforestation in disguise. We preserve the region's water and soil resources at the same time farmers net a cash crop. Coffee exports also contribute to the country's trade balance—the kind of positive result that gets attention in Santo Domingo."

Each crop financed, from coffee and fruit trees to beans and cassava, carried a specific credit limit per *tarea* (approximately one-sixth of an acre). The allowance for coffee was 100 pesos per tarea or about $66 (1.5 pesos = $1). The allocation did not cover all of a farmer's expenses. Over the loan cycle, borrowers added small amounts of their own capital; in the case of coffee, 8 pesos in the first year, 3 in the second, for a total of 32 pesos over five years. Thus, the working capital per tarea came to 132 pesos. Funds were apportioned to cover required inputs: so much for coffee seedlings, for preparing the land, for pesticides. The total capital per tarea was released over a five-year period until trees reached maturity. The first year, when seedlings were planted, claimed the largest investment—44 pesos. Subsequently, what remained of the 132-peso limit went mostly to fertilizer and pesticides. To the extent a farmer did all the work himself, he could reduce the amount of credit needed. He could plant the coffee seedlings himself, for example, or hire someone trained to do it. Repayment of loans started in the third year, when the trees yielded a small first crop. The bulk of the funds, however, would be repaid after the trees reached full production in the fifth and sixth years. Once a coffee grove was established, it was relatively easy to maintain.

"Extension work in coffee," said Iván, "stresses the care and planting of seedlings, proper weeding, and shading. To prepare a tarea for coffee, the land has to be properly contoured; on steep hillsides it has to be terraced. Trees should be planted about nine or ten per tarea in a diamond pattern to prevent erosion.

"Trees need adequate fertilization and constant weeding. Farmers purchase small seedlings from Plan Sierra, and maintain them in temporary nurseries until ready to plant. The coffee varieties favored in the Sierra require shade. If not protected from overexposure, the seedlings wilt and mature trees are less productive." Consequently, a succession of shade trees accompanies the coffee tree's life cycle. Since it grows rapidly and has large, elongated leaves, banana trees are usually interspersed among the seedlings. Later on, taller trees such as the mimosalike guama or the oil-seed hiquera take over. During the first years, while coffee and shade trees are short, beans and cassava can be planted in between. Once the trees are mature, pruning, pest control, and proper harvesting are the keys to high-quality coffee.

"Only ripe, red berries should be picked," Iván noted. "Dry ones are discarded, green ones left for successive gleanings. On the day harvested, the beans are shelled, allowed to ferment for twenty-four hours, and then washed. Then they are dried in the sun until ready for sacking. We stress selective picking and careful curing; it produces a premium grade of coffee that sells for up to 15 percent above the regular price."

Agronomists from the substations conducted evaluations: did farmers plant the number of tareas agreed upon? Were seedlings properly spaced and shaded, was the land terraced, were the trees healthy? If farmers did not fulfill their part of the bargain, additional credit could be withheld. At Rincón de las Piedras, I went to an assessment session held with one of the coffee associations. We met in the storage shed adjoining the local bar. It was stacked with old lumber and cases of empty beer bottles, and had a wobbly wooden table and rustic benches. The serious way that people conducted business gave the setting an inscrutable dignity. Iván reviewed each person's contract. Overall, the trees were in good condition but some had died, which led to a discussion of inadequate shading and poor contours. Iván summed up, pointing out that the local substation had only two agronomists to serve thirteen associations. "Two people can't do everything," he said. "Those who have experience with coffee have to help the others—that's what makes a strong association." He reminded the group to support other projects like family gardens, the women's clubs, and poultry production. Iván then left for other meetings in the district; he worked until late that night.

Rounds

Eight-hour workdays may apply to some office personnel at headquarters, but when I made rounds with agronomists like Iván or Leonardo Reynosa, we were on the road at 6:00 A.M. and returned at 8:00 or 9:00 P.M. We went by jeep to the substations, the heat and dust relieved by strategic stops for soft drinks. The best was the local lemonade, served up in recycled *Barceló* rum bottles for 10 centavos each. Along the way, I had noticed the shabby palm trees everywhere; only a few scrawny branches stuck out incongruously at the top. Anxious to display my expertise, I asked Reynosa if they suffered from the notorious palm blight. He was older than Iván, shorter, and serious by disposition; his specialty was crop production. "That's not precisely what I'd identify as palm blight, Jaime," he replied with the trace of a grin. "No, I'd identify that as *palma cana*, a species harvested for thatch." I should have known. Neat stacks of thatch lined the roadside. And trucks with mountainous piles swayed their loads at every rut and pothole. Here and there a capsized vehicle cautioned against tailgating.

Besides the thatch truck, we had to deal with the chicken. The local breed was fearless. The sound of an oncoming vehicle released some inner switch that sent them dashing across the road at the last possible second. There was no braking for chickens, but I never saw a casualty. Once off the main road, mule traffic took over. Saddles were of soft wood and resembled a short-legged stool; they were bound in layers of sisal and then covered by a quilt fringed with colorful knotted bows. Even the smallest hamlet had its hitching post, which marked the shop that doubled as general store and cantina. Painted palmwood siding, preferably in bright pink or blue, meant a family had relatives in the United States who paid for improvements back home.

Each substation had a rack for Toyota motor scooters. They were great for rough trails and the mule's only competitor. At La Leona, I abandoned the jeep for the back of a motor bike—the practical way to visit the region's farms.

Given poor market conditions and economies of scale, Plan Sierra did not encourage growing sugarcane. Production survived mainly as a curiosity, for the Sierra's old-fashioned techniques had long since been eclipsed by an industry modernized for export. We detoured to an old-fashioned mill several miles from La Leona. The first step in processing is to squeeze the cane juice from the stalk. The ancient press in use had three vertical cylinders hewn from tree trunks four feet in diameter; they looked like huge inverted wringers from an old-style washing machine. Two hefty, fifteen-foot poles extended horizontally from the top of the cylinders, so that oxen could be harnessed to rotate the press. Workers positioned on each side of the press passed cane back and forth through the wringers. The juice collected in a large run-off trough, from whence it was ladled into kettles for cooking. As it boiled, the juice turned a brackish color, signaling the cooling stage for *guarapo*, a popular local beverage and the mill's mainstay. Despite its murky appearance, the result was delicious, especially served cold after a long day.

A by-product of sugar refining is molasses, which leads to rum. The Dominican version is aged at least five years; served on ice it will delight the connoisseur of fine brandy or bourbon. In the United States rum suffers the indignity of the modifier "demon"—the consequences of a cheap, unmellowed imitation closer to raw alcohol. Such unaged variants are denied the distinction "rum" in the Dominican Republic.

I always returned to San José with pages of hastily scratched notes in my pad. People loved their work at the substations; talking about it was never enough, and a jaunt to coffee groves, cassava fields, gardens, and nurseries was obligatory. Nonetheless, keeping good agronomists more than a couple of years was difficult. Most were in their early twenties and single. Work at a substation did not stop for weekends, so it exacted a toll in girlfriends and night life. And there was always the lure of better pay elsewhere, which their experience soon warranted. Consequently, retaining personnel was a constant struggle.

I asked Blas about staff turnover. "Having to replace good people," he said, "adds to our training costs, but at least we provide practical experience. Our people learn how to implement programs and not just talk about theories. The problem is, development is shot through with double standards and contradictions. For a dam, a luxury hotel, or a textile factory, you don't try to hire engineers and managers at a cut rate. But for a project like Plan Sierra, it's just assumed people won't earn what they're worth. Work for the poor, and you're paid accordingly. If you manage money, you get your fair share. Men and women of equal skill who work to develop human potential get the spare change. The truth is, the agronomists at the substations subsidize the project and they know it. They stay as long as they can afford to. Of course, it's unfair. Engineers aren't asked to subsidize dam construction. But if the world were fair," he laughed, "we wouldn't need Plan Sierra in the first place."

Food Crops

Mother Nature apportioned an astounding array of microclimates to the Sierra. Valleys are staggered at different altitudes, each with its own distinguishing ecology. Temperate vegetables such as carrots and potatoes thrive in one place while pineapples, bananas, and cassava do well nearby. Coffee-producing Juncalito is drenched by seventy inches of rain annually, but Monción is arid with sisal a major crop. Imposed on nature's handiwork is man's. Deforestation and erosion were most serious in eastern valleys at lower elevations that had been settled the longest. In the Sierra's western corner, by contrast, rivers were still clear and the land densely forested. Given such diversity, Plan Sierra worked with a wide assortment of crops, fruit trees, and timber.

Loans were not restricted to coffee. The Sierra's farmers also favored food crops like green beans, cassava, and gandul—a bushy Caribbean pea variant. Loans were apportioned to soil preparation, the purchase of seeds, pesticides, fertilizer, and harvesting. Compared to coffee, the credit cycle for crop farmers was shorter; interest and principal were paid off each year when the crop was sold. Production costs were also less, so credit limits were lower: 32 pesos for a tarea of green beans, 17 pesos for cassava and gandul. As with coffee, farmers covered part of the production costs on their own.

Rubén, the chief agronomist at Jicomé, was only twenty. "He's young to be a director," Reynosa had told me, "but he has a way with people; he was the logical choice." An Afro-Dominican, thoughtful and deliberate, Rubén did not fit my stereotype of the flashy community organizer. He went over the details of the substation's credit program. "We keep a copy of each farmer's contract on file," he said, taking out some samples. "As you can see, many are signed with an X. And look through the cash box." It was filled with bills in denominations of 1, 5, and 10 pesos, with notes attached: "for my gandul," "for my coffee." "Farmers don't like debts," Rubén explained. "They pay up when they have a few extra pesos." The repayment rate for crop loans like gandul was well over 90 percent; an impressive record, as interest charges ranged from 9 to 11 percent—below market rates, but no giveaway. The results on coffee were still pending, given the crop's six-year repayment cycle.

When using credit for the first time, there is much to learn. The Sierra's farmers, for example, had little experience using fertilizer. Nothing to it? I once bought some *Grow Right* for my flower garden. The instructions specified one tablespoon per gallon of water. Because I have a Ph.D., I am not bound by anything so mindless as a set of directions; so I improved the formula. If one tablespoon was good, I thought, six tablespoons could only be that much better. My impatiens never lived to tell the tale. Although the Sierra's farmers were more impressed by instructions, Plan Sierra introduced novelties cautiously. An overdose, whether of fertilizer or pesticides, does more harm than good.

Like the coffee growers, crop farmers had training sessions at Los Montones. Erosion control was a basic requirement for credit. When planted in columns up and down a steep hillside—the traditional practice—the bottom of the slope was next to useless. "In heavy rains," Rubén pointed out, "the water gains velocity as it washes down, cutting gaps that grow in size and destructiveness near the bottom. A vertically planted hillside is actually very beautiful but it's no longer practical. In the old days, when the Sierra was forested, people planted only small, scattered patches. Now the district is heavily populated and the trees are gone. The old techniques have turned into the farmer's enemy. When I look at a hillside I realize the farmer is a kind of artist; my job isn't to destroy that expression, it's just to rearrange the materials."

Horizontal plots fortified by ditches helped prevent erosion and washing out. Effectiveness increased when a ditch's upper rim was planted with a strong barrier grass. This was more work and added to production costs as it required renting an ox team. On occasion associations kept oxen to rotate among members. The rewards were substantial. A farmer could devote more of his hillside to crops, and the losses from rainstorms and erosion declined dramatically. What a farmer gained with a larger harvest covered his initial investment. And once properly ditched and terraced, the cost for subsequent crops was much less. "When I get discouraged," Rubén told me, "I walk through a terraced field. Sometimes I just sit and admire what people have accomplished."

Reynosa and I lunched with the agronomists at Jicomé, and then went on to

Monción. "For most small farmers," Reynosa explained, "the value of long-term investment is zero. Survival is the main thing, making it from one year to the next. Farmers do not trench hillsides to please agronomists or because three days at Los Montones makes them conservationists. They do so because their own experience, or that of their neighbors, shows it pays off and quickly. Goodwill is important, but results everything."

Success could be dramatic. Near Sui, a relatively dry region, green beans provided the cash crop. The traditional time to prepare the soil was in October. Given the region's peculiar ecology, however, the rainy season came earlier, so it was possible to plant in September before anyone else. A new schedule was worked into the credit system; four associations participated. Their early harvest reached the market at a time when green beans were scarce. Instead of the 90 pesos per load they had made the year before, they got 280 pesos—precisely the kind of success that builds a project's reputation.

In January 1983, Plan Sierra had 838 loans on its books that totaled 3.9 million pesos ($2.6 million); of this, 2.2 million pesos ($1.5 million) was in coffee. Sixty of the loans were to associations with an average of about 50 members each: a total of 3,000 families. The remaining 758 loans were to individuals. The impact can be gauged by multiplying the 3,758 families with credit by 6, the average family size. Around 22,000 people benefited directly.

Once a farmer had experience in the credit program, he could apply new production methods on his own. He learned how to terrace his land, how to maintain a small nursery, how much fertilizer to apply. And, of course, farmers learned from each other. Plan Sierra did not need to keep hiring agronomists to expand credit; extension workers concentrated on the newcomers, letting the old hands manage on their own. Of Plan Sierra's total budget request, only 9 percent was for administration.[19]

Plan Sierra would have expanded the credit program if it had had more funds. The ten-year budget submitted to the Dominican Congress designated 75 percent for credit.[20] Once a capital base was built up, a credit program could keep going on its own: funds were gradually replenished with repaid loans. Eventually, Plan Sierra could even pay back the government. The main obstacle was that the working capital allocated did not cover the number of loans Plan Sierra wanted to make.

Agroindustries

"Increasing production won't help much," Reynosa pointed out, "if the farmer is left with a surplus he can't unload. Small farmers cannot afford risks. They prefer a low-profit crop they're sure to sell to an alternative whose potential return is higher but whose market is uncertain."

To strengthen the market for local staples, Plan Sierra encouraged small industries for food processing. Gandul is a case in point. A canning factory was constructed near Monción with a loan secured by Plan Sierra for the Farmers Federation of Guaraguano. Given the Sierra's microclimates, gandul can be planted in different zones almost all year-round. In slack periods, other pea varieties can be substituted with only minor changes in equipment. Consequently, the canning plant had a dependable supply to keep it operating at near capacity. And local farmers had a predictable outlet for their crops, which meant more to them than high profit margins. In addition, everyone knew what the going price at the canning plant was, so farmers could bargain better with truckers.

Small agroindustries may well be essential to rural development; they provide an outlet for local production and employment for those without enough land to farm full-time. Who owns the business does not really matter; the overall effect is the same. Sisal provided another example. Extracting the fiber required a relatively simple technology; industrial credit to local entrepreneurs brought hemp and pulp factories to the Sierra.

My favorite industry, however, was the humble *casabe* bakery. Cassava, a common tuber that resembles a yam, can be processed both for consumption and industrial use. In the Sierra, its most popular transformation is into *casabe*: a thin unleavened bread that is coarse, crusty, and granular. It comes out in all shapes and sizes from crackerlike squares to round pieces bigger than pie plates. The circular ones, if shipped any distance, are quartered and sold in stacks. Casabe comes in flavors, too: plain, garlic, and peanut. The small bakeries I visited in Monción were divided into two sections: one for processing cassava, the other for cooking casabe. The cylindrical cassava tuber is peeled, ground up, and put through a press to remove the water. In the kitchen, the sticky mass—a bit like thick cornmeal mush—is scooped into forms and baked on top of large, woodburning stoves, then cut and packaged. Casabe is excellent when fresh, less so if allowed to grow stale on supermarket shelves. Dominicans in New York City get casabe turned almost inedible during shipment.

Cassava can also be made into a granular white flour. As such, it is less popular in the Dominican Republic than in Brazil. For their part, Brazilians are strangers to casabe. Both countries, however, are likely to have cassava flour in their bread. When wheat flour is more expensive than the cassava variant, bakers cut corners by mixing the two. The stratagem is difficult to detect and provides an outlet for the wholesome cassava tuber.

The eighteen-month production cycle for cassava is longer than that of its cousins, the potato and the yam. For fresh boiled cassava, the roots should be harvested while still tender: between eighteen and twenty months after planting. Up to twenty-four months, cassava can be used in casabe. Thereafter, the crop's value as food declines. For industrial purposes, it can be left unharvested for as long as two and a half years after germination. The longer the cassava stays in the ground, the higher its starch content. Starch extraction could be a local industry in the Sierra just as it is in Colombia. The product has a market in the Dominican textile industry, which has to import it. Because cassava does well in poor soils, has dependable yields, and is relatively disease resistant, it was the kind of low-input crop Plan Sierra liked. To expand production beyond the current 40,000 tareas, however, would have required a starch industry to prevent a cassava glut.[21] Few results can be more damaging to a project's reputation than a financed crop without a market.

Cassava, gandul, and green beans were only some of the crops worked into Plan Sierra's credit schedule. The king of vegetables, the potato, was not ignored. Others were the ever-present banana, garlic and eggplant—two worthy but much maligned vegetables—plus tomatoes, radishes, carrots, and lettuce. A pilot project with pineapples yielded excellent results, but as the region's farmers had little experience with the crop, it would take time to promote. Although dry rice was grown locally, low yields made it an inefficient alternative, so it was not on Plan Sierra's list. Expanding the country's rice crop depended on irrigated production in the lowlands. Outside San José, along the road to Monción, one of the valleys had switched to tobacco. In this case, the government divided up the land and a tobacco company provided financing. Given the wide range of possibilities, Plan Sierra had to choose carefully. Priorities depended on the crops farmers already favored (green beans, cassava, gandul, potatoes), opportunities for processing, and suitability to each microclimate. Introducing new crops took patience and careful testing, as farmers did not like unproven alternatives.

Reforestation

Protect watersheds! Reduce sedimentation at the Tavera dam! To farmers, such appeals were not convincing. They did not care about pine trees, irrigation on the Yaque del Norte River, or hydroelectric power for Santo Domingo. Farmers wanted a cash crop that year; if they had to wait, they wanted something dependable like coffee that would produce income every year. As Reynosa said, "waiting thirty to forty years for a pine tree runs contrary to common sense. Anyway, farmers consider the pine trees useless, since it's illegal to cut them down." Plan Sierra would have preferred a more flexible option that permitted supervised cutting; at the time, however, the project was faced with a blanket prohibition.

Native to the region, pine trees are adapted to the Sierra's poorest soils. They thrive where only meager crops can be gleaned, even in the best of times. The pine does not compete with other permanent crops like coffee; it does well in a different niche. Farmers know from experience which hillside slopes are useless, erosion having long since taken its toll. Pines are accepted as a kind of last resort, and they are free.

Preparing the terrain, planting seedlings, and maintaining the pines until they took root was at Plan Sierra's expense. During the off-season, extensionists promoted reforestation both with individual farmers and with local associations. Then, during the planting season, they led brigades of about ten workers each. The labor force was contracted locally, which provided a source of income for farmers whose plots were too small for anything but subsistence crops. The brigades planted in a scattered fashion on private farms, but concentrated full-scale reforestation on the watersheds, which were considered public property and fell under the state's protection.

When the planting season ended, Plan Sierra was usually out of seedlings. This once coincided with a visit from the Inter-American Development Bank. "We considered restocking," Blas told me, "but decided an empty nursery made the point better than one filled with unplanted pines."

How can reforestation mesh with a farmer's top priorities, food production and cash crops? In the Sierra, the definition of "reforestation" included fruit trees in addition to timber. Coffee was the prototype. The grower saw a profitable commodity, Plan Sierra saw the contribution that shaded coffee trees make to soil conservation. The orange tree was also a popular choice because it bears fruit by the second year. Mangoes, avocados, and coconut palms were likewise favored, although they take longer to mature. Macadamia nuts, highly prized for export, yield little for the first ten years, putting them beyond the reach of most farmers. Introduction of the apple tree proved disappointing, but, given the wide variety available, alternatives were far from exhausted. In regions where dry conditions prevailed, viticulture was under study; the vines safeguard a hilly terrain and have a long, productive life cycle.

Farmers planted fruit trees where they did the most good. If erosion control alone was not a persuasive argument, a supply of oranges and avocados usually was. Nonetheless, farmers would not turn to a crop like oranges on a scale comparable to coffee until they were confident the harvest could be marketed. Given the Sierra's poor roads, exporting fresh oranges to Santo Domingo was impractical. The obvious solution was a juice processing plant. Businessmen, however, would not invest until orange production increased, and farmers would not risk expansion until the factory was built. Plan Sierra, of course, wanted to encourage processing, but it did not have the capital or authority to undertake such ventures independently.

A Farm

A successful farm that practiced what Plan Sierra preached did much to propagate the faith. Farmers may respect agronomists, but they trust each other more. What works for a neighbor or a friend speaks for itself. I visited such a farm outside Corocito. Serafín spoke a clear, melodic Spanish, his face was deep brown and leathery, his manner was engaging; we set off talking about his farm.

Serafín had seven children; they bunched around, close to his touch. Their modest dwelling was nestled on a hilltop with commanding views in all directions. The cooking area was set apart from the rest of the house to reduce the risk of fire. Orange trees shaded an earthen patio; the garden was fenced against chickens, a pig, and a cow. A contoured hillside was given over to gandul, with avocado seedlings to shore up the terracing. At the edge of each horizontal trench, he had alternated two tough barrier grasses, Super Merker and Pachulí; they held the soil and soaked up the runoff that collected at the bottom after a rain. Both improved the soil's organic composition. Rapidly growing, Super Merker somewhat resembles sugarcane. Cutting it back at intervals does no damage to the root system, and it makes excellent cattle fodder. Growing in thick clumps, Pachulí makes an even better barrier. Serafín illustrated its resistance by giving me sixty seconds to pull up a clump—a test I failed to everyone's delight. When harvested, Pachulí roots yield a high-quality perfume, although, of course, it destroys the barrier. On ridges too steep for gandul, Serafín had planted small coffee groves shaded with banana trees. His makeshift nursery was similarly protected from the sun, filled as it was with coffee and orange seedlings.

Increasing Access

Plan Sierra helped some farmers more than others. Scarce credit went where it had the greatest impact—to those farms with sufficient land. In the Sierra, "sufficient" may be only five tareas, but many families with less than that did not benefit from credit. What could be done? Plan Sierra designed alternatives that maximized participation but had the greatest impact on the poorest households. Notable examples included family gardens, the distribution of chickens, milk production for household consumption, and fisheries.

Keeping a vegetable garden adds to the family's diet and reduces food expenses. Plan Sierra supplied the first seeds and cuttings, sometimes from the model garden maintained at the substation. Thereafter, families held over seeds for the next crop or obtained them at the community nursery. Extension was also part of the program, because experience with gandul and cassava did not directly transfer to tomatoes and eggplants. Preparing a garden involved the whole family. Working the soil fell to the men, planting and maintenance to mothers and children. The Sierra's women's clubs actively promoted family gardens. The local repertoire included lettuce, radishes, cabbage, green tomatoes, beets, onions, garlic, assorted melons, and the infamous eggplant. Where a permanent water supply was available, gardens produced all year. Fruit trees were part of the gardening principle; oranges and avocados were especially popular. As to the number of gardens, 2,000 was the round figure most often cited. They certainly seemed to be everywhere, spreading by example. Children even planted them at school as class projects sponsored by the substation. And a brief stop at someone's house meant a tour of the garden—as essential to hospitality as handshakes and embraces.

Plan Sierra maintained an incubation unit for poultry. Once hatched, chicks were raised in coops for seven to ten weeks until they were big enough to be distributed to families—a task managed by the Sierra's women's clubs. As was true of gardens, the poultry project had the greatest impact on the poorest families. Ten chickens required minimal space and produced enough eggs for a family's needs. Those who already had chickens could cross their stock with a better breed from Plan Sierra, thus improving egg production.

When Plan Sierra began in 1979, it emphasized dairy farming: improved breeding, restoration of pastures, and animal health. It was a failure. Transporting bulls from place to place was unmanageable. The investment required to control erosion, plant a balanced pasture, and maintain it with the right mixture of soil supplements exceeded the return. The only impact the project had was on animal health. For now, developing the Sierra's dairy industry was beyond the project's capability.

Plan Sierra still had its own farm for cattle breeding, but the objective was now restricted to milk production for household consumption. The distribution of cows favored families with young children. The project worked through the women's clubs. Cows were either impregnated before distribution or families arranged to borrow a bull. To repay Plan Sierra, either one cow or two bulls had to be recycled back to the project. The main forage was Super Merker, which did well on the roadside, by fences, or along trenches. Half a tarea of this hardy, prolific grass sufficed. To prevent damage to the family's garden, the cow was tethered.

Plan Sierra's rule was to use resources efficiently. An illustration is the emphasis placed on nurseries. By producing its own seeds, saplings, and cuttings, Plan Sierra reduced costs and achieved an element of self-sufficiency—precisely the approach it fostered with families. Throughout the region, communities maintained thirteen nurseries supplied by Plan Sierra. I visited three: at Rincón de las Piedras, La Leona, and San José—the largest. They consisted of terraces in the open air that covered about an acre. Materials were simple and inexpensive as there was no danger of frost. To filter sunlight for germinating plants, netting was suspended over part of the nursery. Pines, coffee, and fruit-tree seedlings predominated. The main nursery at San José also produced vegetable seeds for family gardens.

Stocking the Sierra's ponds with fish had great potential for improving the local diet. Sixteen fish ponds were established, some of them in production. Maintaining a fishery was a community effort managed by the women's clubs. The goal was to set up about five hundred: one for every twenty families.

I once asked Reynosa what the most rewarding aspect of his job was. "How hard people work when they see it pays off," he replied. One can assess Plan Sierra by the acreage in coffee and pines, by gandul production, by the number of gardens, chickens, and cows. But there are things that cannot be counted. Using credit to advantage, planting gardens, and working together create confidence and self-respect. Development is more than production statistics for it also speaks to hopes and aspirations, to what people believe is possible.

Juncalito

I visited Plan Sierra in 1983, not long after a presidential election. Party slogans appeared on walls, bridges, and rocks. The main square in San José looked a bit like the inside of a New York City subway car. The propaganda war I judged a standoff; Bosch, Balaguer, and Blanco smiled broadly from their posters with roughly equal frequency, if not affability. The degree to which politics raised passions in the Sierra varied with proximity to Santiago and its organizers. Towns closest to the provincial capital or along paved roads were more politicized. Plan Sierra tried to keep out of the fray, working with appropriate groups regardless of their political orientation. In 1982, the ruling PRD candidate, Jorge Blanco, lost the Sierra, if only by a small margin. This irked the PRD, which supported Plan Sierra from the start and expected it to be a bastion of support. "Plan Sierra," Blas warned me, "has to justify itself on what it accomplishes for people, not politicians. Tampering in local politics endangers a project; it exposes it to reprisals and subverts its objectives."

Whenever possible, Plan Sierra worked directly with the farmers' associations. They were known by the crops they produced and by locality: the Gandul Association of Jicomé, the Coffee Association of Las Placetas. Part of Plan Sierra's mandate was to organize new groups and strengthen those already active. Las Placetas had twenty-one associations of about thirty farmers each; Rincón de las Piedras, thirteen; Jicomé, ten. A strong association formed a nucleus for development. It arranged credit and technical assistance for its members; promoted programs with a community-wide impact, such as vegetable gardens and household milk production; and supported the work of the women's clubs and the health clinics. At Jicomé, Rubén termed two of the town's ten associations "ideal." An additional four he characterized as "independent": working with minimum supervision on projects directly related to the association's welfare. Of the remaining four, two managed specific tasks like arranging credit, but they did not initiate plans; the others he considered "paper organizations." "A training session at Los Montones," he said, "is the best cure for complacency."

By local standards, coffee growers were a well-off lot; they had more land than most farmers and active associations to back them up. I attended a group meeting in Juncalito with Blas Santos. The town nestles between two mountain

27

peaks, easily visible from San José. The road, I was told, was "much improved," the apparent criterion being width; it was still impassable to cars. Our four-wheel-drive Toyota truck seemed unstoppable until we reached a near vertical incline. A mountain spring had detected a weakness in the road's defenses and jumped track, gleefully converting fifty yards of compacted dirt into a muddy morass. On the first try we narrowly escaped the ditch that had already trapped a pickup truck. By the third try I was out pushing. Our final sortie scraped upward, wheels spinning. As they say of Juncalito in San José, "so easy to see, so hard to get to."

Juncalito sits atop a mountain precipice affording spectacular views. There was no electricity, and the substation contacted San José by short-wave radio. Hitching posts lined the town's narrow streets. The mule held out in Juncalito, despite the motor scooter. Coffee was spread out everywhere to dry in the sun, taking over even the flagstone courtyard in front of the church. It was Sunday; worshippers walked around the coffee.

We met in a tin-roofed hall filled with benches. The turnout was excellent: over seventy members in their Sunday best of neatly pressed sportshirts and jeans. The Juncalito Association bought coffee and sold it at a profit; the previous year it was in the black by some 30,000 pesos. Not that the association did not offer good prices to growers—it did, often buying at above-market rates. But it had taken to speculation, borrowing 300,000 pesos to build up coffee stocks. If prices dropped, the association would take a beating. Blas counseled caution and the liquidation of stocks each year at the going rate.

As at any committee meeting, the discussion circled: from the state of the road, to the quality of this year's coffee crop, and back to prices and stocks. Blas was impatient. A young man in the back finally came to the point that had brought us to Juncalito in the first place. Would the association pay for the services of an agronomist? The question was bandied about inconclusively. The farmers asked Blas to speak.

"An association," he began, "should do more than make money; it should provide services to its members and foster the community's development. Plan Sierra supplied credit and supported the association. Now you're haggling over paying an agronomist. The association is supposed to improve coffee production, and that's what an agronomist does; he helps everybody. Members of the association should be sent for training at Los Montones so they can help the others. This is what an association means, that all the members progress together, helping each other and the community. Making a profit isn't enough; you have to show the development of the organization, training your members, providing services. Some people have as much as 500 tareas. Plan Sierra just distributed cows to fifteen families around Juncalito, benefiting ninety people. This is a subsidy to people who work for you; you ought to be willing to pay an agronomist.

"The roads are bad; we all know that. What you don't know is what your rights are—how to work with the Coffee Commission, who you should pressure on roads. The association should be educating its members; that is what Los Montones is for.

"The directors of the association are supposed to carry out the decisions of the members; they shouldn't make decisions for them. It's not so bad if you don't want to pay for an agronomist, as long as that's what the members want."

Decisions followed. The farmers selected members for orientation at the Los Montones training center. Blas offered a compromise on extension. Plan Sierra would assign an agronomist to work directly with the association for six months. If it wanted his services to continue, the association would pay for another six months, followed by an evaluation.

Why did Blas haggle over who paid the agronomist? When costs were covered locally, Plan Sierra could divert the savings to other priorities. An agronomist paid at Juncalito meant another one in Monción working with cassava farmers. Plan Sierra had a ten-year mandate. In the long run, the associations would have to do their share, would have to invest in training and extension.

Juncalito waited hesitantly at the threshold of modernization. Next to me was a heavyset man in his fifties; muddy boots with spurs betrayed a loyalty to the mule. His bright red cap with Coca-Cola in white letters across the top suggested the lure of another world. When the dam on the Bao is completed, electricity will find its way to Juncalito; the road will be paved, freed at last from the tyranny of mountain springs. Such improvements clear the way for conspicuous consumption. At Juncalito, the symbols of wealth electrified— telephones, stereos, and television—will set apart the haves from the have-nots, accentuating differences in new and unforeseen ways.

The incongruity between worlds is both subtle and blatant. I recalled the bargains hawked in the *New York Times* travel section—beginning at $70 a day at the Gulf-Western resort at La Romana. I managed to get by on $15 a day in Santo Domingo and $2 in San José. The exchange between the city and the campesino is inherently unequal. As Blas put it, "the cost of Coca-Cola in terms of gandul or cassava is astronomical." Mules and Coke. We all know where the future lies. For Plan Sierra, however, credit and extension, family cows, and associations must take precedence. Jeeps and trucks can share the roads with mules and motor scooters, at least for now.

We made our way back to San José. Blas was exhausted. "You have a right to be tired," I said. "I have the right," he laughed, "what I need is a chance to sleep."

Training

At Jicomé, Rubén called Plan Sierra the best school he ever attended: "A month here is worth a year in a University." Youthful enthusiasm no doubt. Nonetheless, Plan Sierra was like a dispersed campus. In one way or another, training crosscut every program. At Los Montones, for example, workshops took place almost weekly. A training center and retreat house combined, it had a meeting hall, cafeteria, kitchen, and two dormitories with twenty cots each. The grounds were spacious and laid out in gardens. Community groups sent their associations and clubs. A workshop concentrated on a group's specific task, but it also stressed the importance of related efforts. With coffee growers, sessions emphasized the work done by the women's clubs and clinics, not just the credit program. At Los Montones, Plan Sierra trained its extension workers and health assistants. For grade school teachers and midwives, it provided continuing education.

Plan Sierra wanted vocational training to impart skills to as many people as possible. Because it had no budget for this purpose, it lobbied the Ministry of Education. "Vocational schools in the Sierra," Blas said, "should admit anyone with a basic capacity to learn. They should be exceptionally practical, teach by application, and lead to employment." A center for carpentry and mechanical arts was near completion in San José. Others would emphasize sewing and domestic crafts. Students would receive a certificate of attendance, and courses would be short. "Degrees," Blas noted, "require longer programs and more classroom work. The result is better training, but restricted access."

Women's Clubs

Plan Sierra's ten-year timetable underscores the role that training and local organization must play in the project's success.[22] As Plan Sierra winds down, community groups will have to assume more responsibility. Strengthening participation is a practical necessity. The local Development Council, for example, drew leaders together to plan community projects. Members included the parish priest, the town's schoolteacher, and representatives from local associations, clubs, and health committees. The councils could claim credit for projects like water wells, bridges, and road improvements. At La Leona, the community built the pipeline that now provided the town with a common source of safe water. El Rubio's council, set up only three months earlier, already had a bridge to its credit, as did Jicomé. Plan Sierra's goal of a safe water supply for the region's towns depends substantially on the councils.

The Sierra had over one hundred women's clubs; La Leona, a typical hamlet, had thirteen. Señora Marta Fernández, an outgoing woman in her thirties, worked with the clubs and the health program. A tireless worker, she was always headed somewhere, but let me come along, enduring my many questions. "Plan Sierra," she said, "can talk about gardens, milk production, and safe water all it wants. We won't get results unless women take the lead. Promoting the clubs is a practical, obvious step. Gardens and fruit trees contribute to a family's nutrition and overall self-sufficiency. Careful circulation of water through the household reduces the risk of disease. Families can control basic aspects of their own welfare, if they choose to do so. And that choice rests with women who manage the household."

The clubs taught skills that could be applied at home with a minimum of expense. Family gardens, household milk production, poultry, and fisheries all depended on the clubs and practical training. From each substation, for example, the home educator organized extension sessions. In addition, the clubs sent members to Los Montones for workshops on gardening and poultry production. Because I have never planted a vegetable garden, the "expertise" involved was not readily apparent. Marta set me straight. "To keep a garden producing all year, Jaime, you have to stagger your vegetable selection over proper intervals. Then you have to guard against molds, fungi, and insects. You need to apply fertilizer or cycle animal compost into the garden, and you have to learn how to select seeds to hold over for the next planting. You can't neglect thinning and weeding, and you need to fence against marauding farm animals. A good garden is a great achievement, and the clubs are very good at it."

Women produced goods at home for household consumption. Clubs relied on skilled members to teach sewing and handicrafts to others. Women made brooms and kitchen utensils; they purchased machines and organized sewing centers. The home educator coordinated cooking classes. Cooking? A rural housewife certainly knew how to prepare local dishes. What she learned was to work more vegetables into traditional meals, or to prepare new dishes in a way her family found acceptable. And she had to cook with an eye to sanitation: food preparation was often the culprit in disease transmission.

Health

Human and animal wastes transmit parasitic infections, either through direct contact or indirectly through fecally contaminated water. When waste is not properly disposed of, children end up stepping in it, rubbing it in their eyes, and carrying it into the house. Contaminated water causes a host of ailments from typhoid fever to dysentery. Reducing such risk requires that families apply public health measures at home; prevention is at root a family affair. "Adding an extra doctor at the clinic," Marta said, "won't make the water safe to drink."

The health strategy followed by Plan Sierra was twofold: treatment, which depended on the region's clinics, and prevention, which depended on health education.[23]

Figure 1.2 Health System: Plan Sierra

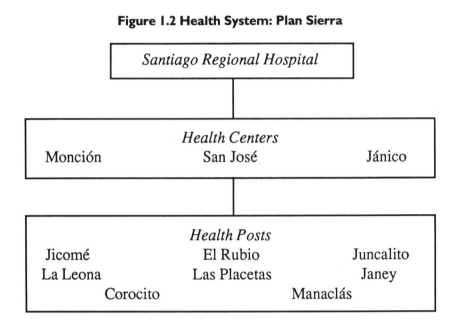

The health centers at Jánico, San José, and Monción were equipped for minor surgery; they had small infirmaries with about twenty beds each, a lab, and a pharmacy. Before 1979, they were the only facilities in the Sierra, geared primarily to the needs of townspeople. The Health Department had trained over two hundred women to work as health promoters (*promotoras de la salud*) in rural areas, but the two-week sessions were not followed up. *Promotoras* had little supervision and no supplies for basic programs like infant vaccinations. Since then, Plan Sierra, in conjunction with the Health Department, had built and staffed eight rural health posts. Much as the substations were a focus for extension work in agriculture, the posts provided basic health services and education. The communities that had substations likewise had a health post. In addition, Janey, Manaclás, and Corocito had health posts only. Supervision came from the health centers, which also handled referrals from the local clinics. The Regional Hospital in Santiago provided specialized treatment. (See Figure 1.2.)

"The division between the Health Department and Plan Sierra," Marta explained, "depends on whether a program is permanent or temporary. The clinics are permanent, so staff appointments and salaries are the Health Department's responsibility. Training programs, however, are defined as temporary and fall to Plan Sierra. The division looked neat on paper, but created conflict in practice. The Health Department resented Plan Sierra's intrusion, and Plan Sierra thought it had all the answers. After personnel changes on both sides, cooperation improved. Overall, I think the service the posts now provide is a solid achievement."

Each post had a physician who held regular office hours. A nurse auxiliary was responsible for vaccinations, patient histories, and administering the clinic. The auxiliaries either lived in small quarters at the posts or made arrangements in town. In addition, mobile health units from each of the health centers made rounds to the posts and peripheral communities on a regular basis. The units had simplified equipment for dentistry and lab tests.

Intestinal parasites and dysentery were the ailments most frequently treated at the clinics. Prevention depended in large part on the work of communities and households. Once again, the women's clubs were in the forefront. "Mothers confront the effects of poor health on their children every day," Marta said, "so they're especially receptive. When the local club goes to Los Montones, it finds health on the agenda." Cycling water through the household so it did not pose a threat to the family's health was particularly important. "Only Monción, Jánico, and San José have running water," Marta noted, "and when a community has a public spring or well, families still have to lug the water back. Once home, they need an arrangement of barrels and jugs based on the water's intended use: that destined for drinking, cooking, and washing dishes must be kept covered against flies and dirt; for washing clothes or bathing, less caution is required—but they can't mix up the two batches. If the community doesn't have safe water, it has to be boiled before it is used. This is extra work and an added expense; the temptation not to bother is great. When families have safe water on hand to begin with, the process is simplified and they save on fuel."

Providing a community with a source of safe water has an immediate impact on health conditions. So too does the installation of an inexpensive latrine. The women's clubs encouraged the use of safe water and household latrines, for which Plan Sierra provided materials. They emphasized cleanliness of the house and yard, personal hygiene, and child health, which included nutrition and vaccinations. Fencing farm animals to keep excreta beyond the reach of children was the kind of precaution every family could take. As for family gardens, household milk production, and poultry, they pertained as much to health as they did to agriculture.

The region's farmers planted gandul and cassava long before Plan Sierra arrived on the scene. But the credit program improved cultivation methods, and a better harvest spoke for itself. The benefits derived from boiling water, installing latrines, and fencing farm animals were less demonstrable in the short run; to be effective, they required systematic application and reinforcement from as many credible sources as possible. The women's clubs tried to hold the line on health. The men did not escape either. When they went to Los

Montones for a session on credit they also got a good dose on health. "When they claim they can't boil water," Marta laughed, "I take them to the kitchen for training."

Completing the health scheme were the region's 231 promotoras and over 100 midwives. The promotoras made home visits, referred patients to the clinics, and gave vaccinations. The clinics and mobile health units provided supervision. To strengthen the promotoras' skills, Plan Sierra organized continuing education over a three-year period: a month the first year, twenty days the second, ten days the third. The same scheme was followed for midwives, although the sessions were somewhat abbreviated: twenty days the first year, ten days the second, and five days the third. Plan Sierra only worked with women who were already respected as midwives in their communities; it reinforced their skills, furnished supplies, and enlisted their support for other aspects of the health program. Childbirth in the Sierra occurs almost exclusively at home with a local midwife. "If Plan Sierra expects mothers to lug back safe water and make sure kids are vaccinated," Marta said, "it needs the midwife's backing."

In the Sierra, women pay more attention to midwives than to doctors, which is fortunate. Medical training is geared to hospitals; doctors prefer the city's technology and fees. Although a year of public service is obligatory for medical students, most opted for Santo Domingo or a respectable provincial capital. Assignment to the Sierra often reflected a lack of connections. The doctor at Las Placetas was notorious for his sporadic office hours and "weekends" spent in Santiago: they began on Friday and spilled over into Monday. When he thought of colleagues he did not have promotoras in mind. There were exceptions. The doctor at Jicomé chose the Sierra for his year of service. He worked as hard on gardens as any agronomist, was a staunch water-boiling advocate, and a booster of the women's clubs—skills he did not acquire in medical school.

Every aspect of the health program could not be uniformly applied everywhere, any more than each facet of the agricultural program could be. Communities varied with respect to the leadership they provided in public health. At Manaclás, for example, the health committee had taken the lead, promotoras were assertive, and the doctor was cooperative. How strong a health committee was depended on the vitality of other community groups, as representatives from the clubs, associations, and the Development Council were de facto members.

When a break-in occurred at El Rubio's clinic—water stolen, beds occupied at night—the health committee called a community meeting to resolve the crisis. Participants included the newly arrived, shell-shocked clinic doctor, the supervisor from San José's Health Center, two of El Rubio's schoolteachers, a member of the town's Development Council, the president of the local women's club, two promotoras, a representative from the farmers' association, an agronomist from the substation, and Blas—with me in tow. The culprits were known to be El Rubio's teenagers. The discussion wandered inconclusively: were windows properly secured, who had the keys, who locked up at night? They called on Blas who was intent on keeping quiet: "If you're too directive," he told me beforehand, "it takes responsibility away from the community; if you talk too much, people won't listen." To the extent the break-in reflected the community's passive attitude toward the clinic, it was a serious, if symbolic, violation.

"The clinic," he said, "belongs to the community, which is responsible for its maintenance. People think the government is responsible for curing people; but it's the community that has to look after health. The government in Santo Domingo can't be responsible for a clinic in El Rubio—you have to do it. You can't rely on doctors to solve all your health problems—you have to take the initiative. Plan Sierra works for the development of the community, a community that is aware of its responsibilities, that can take action on its own. Plan Sierra will last a short time; it will fail without greater community support. Farmers have land, but they don't know how to use it effectively. El Rubio has a health clinic, but people aren't taking advantage of it as they should. Tell the groups you represent that the clinic belongs to the community, that you have to work together to use it for everyone's benefit."

Hotel

The sign over the entranceway to my lodgings in San José read "hotel," but "rooming house" would have been more accurate. On the first day I received guest treatment from Señora Lourdes. Americans had preceded me, leaving behind a reputation for fickle dietary habits. She asked not what I wanted to eat but what I could eat, offering me "vegetariano" with hopeless resignation. My preference for fried eggs, fried potatoes, and refried beans reassured even the skeptical Señora Lourdes I was not to be a troublesome guest. In fact, these are my favorite foods; I consent to salads only under duress. My room was in the back; other guests held the better spots up front. Or so she said. The hotel's veranda faced the square and a cantina with a stereo. Subsequent offers to move me "up front" were gratefully declined. My bed had a mosquito net suspended above it, which I used regularly despite assurances the insect was not currently in season. The hotel was like a community center: kids packed in for television, teens took over the porch after school, guests moved in at night. No matter how late I got back, I could not avoid the porch without being considered antisocial.

The hotel's bathroom was equipped with a pink commode, tiled walls, and faucets marked hot and cold for tub and sink. All it lacked was running water. Assorted pails and containers, including a bright red plastic barrel, filled in for the awaited running water. The spigot behind the hotel tapped an icy cold spring; I considered growing a beard, and cut back dramatically on the sponge bath.

A short walk from the square landed me in the cassava fields. Where the Saturday night supply of teenagers came from still escapes me. Motor scooters jammed the street around the square. In groups of three to five, the girls held the sidewalk, circulating at a leisurely, dignified pace. The boys, by contrast, bunched up on the corners, engaging in just enough horseplay to get attention. The square's center belonged to couples, who had priority on the benches. In the Sierra, the small town is not yet an endangered species.

Two blocks from my hotel a monument marked the spot where General Mella gathered troops to fight the Haitians in 1844. A great mango tree shaded the grounds, its huge roots making benches for those who watched the volleyball game across the way. Europe has real history, I thought, and some big countries like the United States. Little countries do not. The pecking order in a history department reflects this. There is an elite club devoted to the Renaissance or Louis XIV, an American history lobby, and then a motley sort specializing in Latin America with a marked preference for Brazil and Mexico. Small fry like the Dominican Republic are ignored. The obscure details of American history have a knack for writing chapters somewhere else. Who remembered Sumner Welles?—the Cubans did; the intervention against Sandino?—the Nicaraguans. If the Dominican Republic wants its history taught in American universities, it will take a revolution. That is what Fidel Castro did, and the United States now has "Cubanists" with their own scholarly journals. Nicaraguan specialists are not far behind.

• Going Home

It was my last morning in San José. The hotel got its daily scrub with mops and rags wielded by Señora Lourdes and her children. Paulito, one of the youngest, lugged water backward to the plastic barrel in the bathroom. While I packed my bags, an ill-tempered chair caught Paulito from behind; boy, pail, and water crashed to the floor. Señora Lourdes rushed in from the kitchen, and siblings dashed out from the bedrooms, mops in hand. They ran for rags laughing, Paulito included. The chair got a well-deserved reprimand and banishment to the porch.

I got a lift back to Santo Domingo with Ernesto, one of Plan Sierra's chauffeurs; he had a scheduled trip for materials. Ernesto directed the conversation to Plan Sierra. He had a garden, had not bought an orange in two years, and his beets were excellent. "What is your job like?" I asked. "I don't have a schedule," he replied. "I can be done at 4:00 P.M. but sometimes I'm not home until 9:00 P.M. I don't mind, everybody works hard. When I'm late for supper, so is Señor Blas, or the agronomists." He summed up his opinion of Plan

Sierra: "not a cent passes through the hand to the pocket," a point he illustrated by taking one hand from the steering wheel just as a truck barreled by. Ernesto was in his fifties, had started working when he was twelve, and knew the score. The project's honesty was an exceptional thing to him, a kind of fringe benefit he collected with pride.

Two-lane Duarte Highway was the country's main street. Heavy traffic was the rule from Santiago to the capital, and roadside stands added to the congestion. They sold just about everything: from bananas to pots and pans, clothing, and even used cars. Between La Vega and Bonao, carefully tended rice patties flanked the highway; irrigation had made the Dominican Republic self-sufficient.[24] Closer to the capital came sugarcane. At four cents a pound, the country's chief export had turned into a disaster.

Why did U.S. consumers pay $1.69 for 5 pounds of Dixie Crystal? Because Congress protected the sugar beet. An import quota split up among contenders covered the shortfall in U.S. production. The Dominican Republic's 1984 allotment came to 471,000 tons.[25] U.S. refiners mixed cheap imported sugar with a domestic product that cost $0.21 a pound. Add in retail markups, and it does not take long to get the Dixie Crystal price.

The quota system paid a premium price of twelve cents a pound. But the Dominican Republic was still left with a surplus that earned only the world price of four cents. Given the drop in U.S. consumption, the Dominican industry depended on quotas and subsidized prices. Why was sugar not abandoned? Because production was a state-owned agroindustry; the country had a tremendous investment tied up in refineries, equipment, and jobs.[26]

Back to Santo Domingo: traffic, pulsating energy, the city. I took a long hot shower and watched TV nonstop. Commercials that featured *Barceló* rum sophisticates, packs of Marlboro men, and housewives expunging odors drove me outside to the waterfront and the bar.

The city's wealth and power command all. Women's clubs and Development Councils can never match the political clout of Santo Domingo. Budgets reflect the tremendous pressure urban classes exert on priorities: from public works projects to subsidized food prices. The cure the International Monetary Fund (IMF) had for a debtor like the Dominican Republic was to cut domestic spending, freeze wages, and dismantle price controls. Enforcement led to political warfare. In April 1984, three days of rioting in Santo Domingo left sixty people dead, hundreds wounded, and thousands arrested.[27] Austerity measures divided and discredited the PRD. In 1986, it lost the presidency to its old adversary, Joaquín Balaguer, who was seventy-eight. People forgot repression but remembered past prosperity.

Given the depressed conditions in Santo Domingo, and unemployment at 30 percent, Plan Sierra's budget has always been up for grabs.[28] The original estimate for its ten-year program came to only $87 million, but the total has never been allocated. In 1983, for example, the hard-pressed Blanco administration reduced it by half, although Congress restored support to 1982 levels. Consequently, Plan Sierra had to decide which aspects of its "global plan" it could implement. Land reform, for example, had been one of the project's initial objectives. The global plan estimated that eight acres divided between marketable crops and household consumption could support a family. The Dominican Agrarian Institute, which monitors land reform, controlled enough real estate in the Sierra to make distribution feasible. To be successful, however, would require careful supervision at every step from the selection of families to credit and extension. With its budget trimmed, Plan Sierra was in no position to undertake land reform. So it started with programs that had an immediate impact. Credit, household gardens, health care, and the women's clubs all stressed participation and reached some of the poorest households. Nonetheless, those families with sufficient land and more skills benefited the most.

The realpolitik that shackles the Sierra's development can be traced to Santo Domingo and from there to the international banks; it is also lodged in the mind. Those in the Planning Ministry will always prefer big development. To build a road, a bridge, or a dam is a matter of cash and contracts. When complete, the planners have something public to display at ribbon-cutting ceremonies. A rural clinic, by contrast, is a small-change affair; there are no cost overruns for big contractors. And construction is the easy part, using it effectively, the hard part. One must train promotoras, court midwives, and push health education. Small-scale projects are messy: long on community meetings, short on champagne ceremonies. Results are cumulative, rarely sudden or dramatic. Whether it is credit or clinics, training and community education are fundamental. Rural development is necessarily a labor-intensive activity that depends on a project's human resources every bit as much as it does on a sum of money. To invest at the bottom is to confront people directly: their hopes and skills, their fears and limitations. Big development is clear-cut, easier, less intractable; it fits so much better into flow charts and accounting ledgers.

E. T.

My last day in Santo Domingo, I went to see *E.T.*—again. *El Caribe* claimed it drew 125,000 people in two weeks: the greatest box office success in Dominican history. *E.T.* had stolen the record from *Jaws*, a fact I noted with some satisfaction.[29] Seeing American films abroad is always a treat. *Stripes*, for example, was particularly appreciated in Brazil as a chance to laugh at the military. *E.T.* spells kids, a resource the Dominican Republic has in some abundance. The child-to-adult ratio in the theater I estimated at about five to two. It was Sunday, so both parents tagged along. Big heads stood out here and there, separated by a string of little heads, which popped up and then disappeared behind seats. Few parents had an empty lap, the average youngster being about four years old. There was no harried buying of popcorn; families brought homemade batches in big plastic bags. The show began. Spanish subtitles darted in and out at the bottom of the screen, a futile gesture for an audience still unacquainted with the first grade. Somehow, *E.T.* worked its magic: silence, apprehension, sorrow, and reprieve stirred young hearts, even without words. Humanheartedness is the thing in itself, the doing, the action—not the words.

PART II
COLOMBIA

2
COMMUNITY HEALTH

Nature forged Colombia in youth and vigor, kicking up mountains, clearing the way for rivers, flattening the coasts. The towering Andes enter Colombia to the south from Ecuador and then diverge hydralike into three distinct chains: the Coastal, Central, and Eastern ranges. Colombia is the only Andean country whose rivers flow south to north, paralleling the mountains. The Cauca River cuts between the Coastal and Central ranges: it opens up into a fertile plain near Cali, but narrows into a steep valley as it squeezes between the mountains farther north. Not to be outdone, the Magdalena River clears the way between the Central and Eastern ranges; as it approaches the coast it broadens out into swamplands, and then picks up the Cauca River before reaching the Caribbean. Of Colombia's three ranges, the Eastern is the most insistent; one branch forks east into Venezuela near Cúcuta, while the other continues north to a spectacular finish near the Caribbean coast: snowcapped Mt. Colón, at 19,000 feet, Colombia's highest peak.

• Geography

Traveling east or west in Colombia defies the country's geography. To reach the river port of Honda from Bogotá—only 90 miles away—requires a 10,000 foot descent from towering passes down to near sea level at the floor of the Magdalena Valley. To continue west to Cali (240 miles) is to face a climb out of the Magdalena Valley across the passes of the Central Range, followed by a spectacular drop down to the Cauca Plain. Colombia's Pacific port, Buenaventura, is only 90 miles from Cali—but still a mountain chain away.

Map 2.1 Colombia

Mother Nature packed an astounding diversity into the mountainous tropics. A descent from Bogotá to Honda passes from the cold country to the moderate *páramo*, through the subtropics and down to the hot country all in a couple of hours. Combining abundant rainfall with altitude variations means new flora at every turn. For unlike the parched altiplano shared by Peru and Bolivia, Colombia's verdant mountains are awash in rain. Bogotá averages almost 40 inches a year. Even the North Coast, despite a four-month dry season, counts on 30 inches—fairly wet by North American and European standards. The driest place in Colombia is the Guajira Peninsula; it juts out into the Caribbean, but misses the trade winds and ends up with less than 20 inches.

With almost 28 million inhabitants, Colombia's population is approximately the same size as that of Argentina.[1] A little chopping and cutting fits all of Texas, California, and most of Ohio within Colombia's borders. Half of the national territory is beyond the Eastern Range: great plains extend toward Venezuela, while the tropical forests of the Amazon Basin lie to the southeast. Both regions are sparsely settled. By contrast, a line drawn northeast from Bogotá to the city of Bucaramanga (270 miles) and thence west to Medellín (540 miles), south to Cali (270 miles), and back northwest to Bogotá marks off a densely populated core with 60 percent of Colombia's inhabitants but only 25 percent of the country's territory.

Colombia borders both on the Pacific and the Caribbean, the Isthmus of Panama jutting out between. The Coastal Range, however, virtually isolates the Pacific provinces from the rest of the country.* The port of Buenaventura is an enclave on the Pacific linked to populous Cali by the railroad. The province of Chocó, which extends north from Buenaventura to the border with Panama, is Colombia's poorest province.

Most Colombians live in the more temperate basins and valleys. The North Coast is an exception. Atlántico Province, for example, is the most densely populated in Colombia. The capital, Barranquilla, has over a million inhabitants: it is Colombia's principal port and the shipping point for most of the country's coffee. Cartagena is the focus for the region's distinctive culture. Along the North Coast an Afro-Colombian world predominates in contrast to the country's "Spanish" heritage.

• Politics

In Colombia, political affiliation is fixed at birth and reflects family loyalty and local history. The civil wars of the nineteenth century bequeathed an

---

*Colombia is divided into departments, but, for semantic reasons, I have referred to them as "provinces." This reduces repetition and avoids confusion between health departments, university departments, and geographic departments.

entrenched allegiance to the Liberal and Conservative parties that the twentieth century has not dislodged. To map the country by party allegiance is to crosscut the divisions geography has imposed. Although each party has a regional stronghold, even a Conservative province like Antioquia has Liberal townships that defy the majority. Consequently, political loyalty cannot be neatly predicted by geography. And it does not adhere to class divisions. Each party has support among the country's diverse occupational groups: from small coffee farmers and ranchers to construction workers and bankers.[2]

Colombian politics did not follow the pattern characteristic of many Latin American countries. Elsewhere, as factories and export agriculture transformed the old order, new parties took shape. They mirrored the divisions between industrialists and urban workers, between small businessmen and foreign investors, between landowners who exported and small farmers who produced for consumption. An era of rapid change engendered a succession of political parties with unstable constituencies. An electoral victory by populist reformers was often followed by armed intervention. Once in power, the military disbanded political parties, undercut past reforms, and forcibly imposed its own vision of development.

Modern Colombia, by contrast, has escaped the radical shift in priorities that a cycle of democratic politics and military repression has so often implied. To end the terrible partisan strife of *La Violencia* (1948–53), and to prevent displacement by the military, Liberal and Conservative leaders agreed on coalition government. The National Front pact, approved by plebiscite in 1957, pledged both parties to accept a joint presidential candidate for each election until 1974. Thereafter, the parties competed for the presidency but continued to share power. Positions at every level of government had to be distributed equitably: from cabinet posts and judicial appointments to the selection of governors and mayors.[3]

The result, as my colleague Jonathan Hartlyn put it, was a country "that disappointed the optimists and confounded the pessimists." The National Front was not full-fledged democracy, but it avoided the dogmatism of Brazil's military regime and the sterility of Mexico's one-party state.

Coalition government discouraged dramatic changes in economic policy. Nonetheless, the National Front set the stage for modest gains. Colombia did not have the rapid economic growth that characterized Brazil, nor did it benefit from the kind of export boom oil created in Mexico. Its accomplishments were gradual and less flamboyant, but they were more likely to benefit ordinary Colombians. Between 1970 and 1980, for example, Colombia's economy expanded at a solid, if unspectacular, 5.6 percent annually. Despite gains for industrial exports, coffee still dominated the country's trade.[4] Brazil's economy, on the other hand, grew by 8.7 percent a year, and its exports became much more diversified.[5] Yet Brazil's growth benefited the majority less. The value of the country's minimum wage declined and the income distribution got worse.[6] In Colombia, the earnings of unskilled workers, agricultural laborers, and small farmers improved.[7]

Whether or not development benefits ordinary people is not just a question of wages and income shares; it is also a matter of education, health care, and public services. During the 1970s, the percentage of Colombian children who completed basic schooling was about 40 percent. For Brazil, which had a much higher gross national product (GNP) per capita and a more dynamic economy, the figure was only 30 percent. Brazil today has its own computer industry, but in primary education it is still behind Colombia.[8] Because education changes the aspirations people have, it is not surprising that the birthrate has dropped further and faster in Colombia than in Brazil. Infant mortality is also lower in Colombia, which suggests better access to health care. With respect to public services, the urban population of both countries grew rapidly during the 1970s, but Colombia did a better job of providing poor households with water, electricity, and waste disposal.[9]

Brazil's military regime mortgaged the country's future to its fantasies of greatness; Mexico borrowed to pump out its petroleum as fast as possible. They ended up the world's largest debtors, owing a combined $153 billion in 1981. Colombia, by contrast, showed greater restraint and selectivity. Its foreign debt in 1981 was a manageable $7.8 billion. Argentina, roughly equivalent in population, owed $36 billion, and Chile, with one-third the population of Colombia, owed twice as much.[10] The composition of Colombia's debt also underscored its more cautious approach: over 40 percent was owed to development agencies like the World Bank.[11] Compared to most Latin American countries, which borrowed at their discretion from commercial banks, Colombia preferred specific projects whose objectives and management requirements followed World Bank guidelines. When the debt crisis hit in 1982, Colombia got by without one of the "rescue packages" of the International Monetary Fund (IMF). Although it did not escape recession, the impact the debt crisis had was less severe than in other countries.

Whether the restraint coalition government imposed on Colombia was a "modest success" or a "modest failure" depends on one's point of view.[12] The kind of land reform Liberals once advocated was never carried out. On the other hand, the loans made by the country's Agrarian Bank reached some of the country's poorest rural households—in contrast to how Brazil's credit policies so often excluded them.[13] Colombia's infant mortality rate was lower than Brazil's, but much higher than Costa Rica's or Cuba's.[14] If the income share of Colombia's poorest families increased during the 1970s, it was still a slim allocation. The most optimistic estimate left the poorest 40 percent of the country's households with only 15 percent of the national income. Still, that was better than in Brazil or Mexico.[15] In Colombian cities like Cali, it took a decade for poor neighborhoods to get electricity, piped water, and sewerage. In Brazil, it takes forever.[16]

To judge from the *New York Times*, the only Colombian story worth filing was about drug trafficking or guerrilla warfare. There is, of course, some truth in this. The drug trade that politicians once considered benign has created an underworld powerful enough to challenge the government.[17] Colombia, in fact, has reached a turning point. The National Front had reduced the animosity between Liberals and Conservatives, but the way the parties shared power left no room for disgruntled outsiders. But in 1986, the last of the old National Front agreements ended. To take advantage of competitive, local elections, Colombia's largest guerilla group signed an amnesty, organized its own party, and went into politics. Whether Colombian democracy can absorb the Left without reprisals on the Right will now be tested.[18]

This report, however, is not for the *New York Times*. It is about health posts and promotoras, about nutrition and risk assessment. That Colombia has a story to tell about community health is not consistent with its media image, but it is consistent with the modest success profile previously sketched.

In Colombia, the government's commitment to community health had both a legal and a financial basis, and it respected the country's regional loyalties. Colombia's approach left room for local initiatives and regional planning in a way Brazil's overly centralized administration discouraged. Nonetheless, for Colombia's poorest families, access to health care still depended on where they lived: it was better in the cities than in the countryside, better in a province like El Valle than in a poor, isolated one like the Chocó.

The government endorsed community health, but it left implementation to others. This report is about those who have worked on application and what they have accomplished. It explains how health care has to be organized to reach poor families. The report does not discuss every aspect of each project. Instead, it illustrates different facets of community health that specific projects typified. Thus, Bogotá is about nutrition and local health committees. Medellín demonstrates what "risk assessment" means in the context of poor neighborhoods. Cali shows how decentralized health care is applied to an entire province; it also explains how a research project can strengthen the promotoras' work at the clinics. The story begins with an orientation at a health conference in Cartagena.

• Cartagena

The great walled port of Cartagena once defended the Caribbean against the buccaneers. To Cartagena came Peru's silver for shipment back to Spain; from Cartagena Spanish merchandise reached a thousand shops, some as distant as Santiago in Chile. The old city's fortifications still encircle a labyrinth of streets that block the sun's intensity; overarched with balconies on both sides and decked out in flowers, the passageways wind between churches and squares. The past hangs heavy in Cartagena: the cathedral and the Inquisition, the merchant guild, and the governor's palace—God, mammon, and the state allied in Hispanic tradition, born again in the New World's arrogance. Under the great arched gateway that leads from the Plaza of the Coaches beyond the walls, pass the city's people, vehicles, and vendors. Outside are old quays lined with ramshackled wooden boats, stacks of bananas, and produce stands. From every transistor radio comes salsa music. Cartagena still belongs to people, not to museum curators. Past and present rub shoulders, stalk the same streets.

Bocagrande, a narrow peninsula to the city's south, separates the Caribbean Sea from the tranquil Bay of Cartagena. The Caribbean side has Cartagena's beaches. Most of the hotels are small family affairs except for the Hilton, fortified against the natives at Bocagrande's southernmost tip.

I splurged and checked into the Hilton. The management did not trust my duffel bag, so I had to cough up the equivalent of a night's lodging. At $60, I had a bargain: central air conditioning, a shag carpet, color TV, and a bathroom with space for a double bed. I took a swim in the Olympic-size pool, followed by a $2 beer. I had all the comforts a hotel could offer. I did not like it.

The last thing Bocagrande's Hilton wanted admitted to its chambers was Colombia. Like a feudal castle, it considered itself superior to the clutter down below. Standardized down to the sanitized paper seal stretched across the toilet seat, the Hilton's appeal was nondescript luxury.

I walked from the Hilton back to the center of town past exchange houses, a supermarket, a long-distance telephone office, and a dozen ticket agencies for Avianca, Colombia's national airline. If I wanted service, it was available along Bocagrande's Main Street. I did not need the Hilton and regretted the corporate accommodations.

"Cigarettes, señor?" asked a boy, as I waited to cross the street. I bought a pack, along with some matches. "Americano?" he asked. "Yes," I replied. "At the Hilton?" he ventured. "Yes," I said, "but it's too expensive and I don't like it. It's too far from town and there aren't any people around." "Why not stay here, señor," he said, pointing to a small hotel on the corner. "At night there's music and it's right on the beach, lots of people all the time. Señora Teresa," he called out before I could stop him, "a customer."

Señora Teresa walked me around the corner to the hotel's entrance, which was separate from the office and restaurant. The room was on the second floor. It had two cots, an overhead fan, a spotless tiled floor, and a tiny bathroom with a cold shower. A balcony in front overlooked the beach. It was perfect. I offered to pay the first night's charge of $12, which Señora Teresa refused to accept. "Like everyone else," she said, "pay when you go." I never did sleep in the Hilton; I went back to get my bag.

On weekends, all of Cartagena cycles, buses, or walks to the beach. Most families come early, stay late, and bring their lunch. It is not the Caribbean fantasy of a secluded beach for two. At Bocagrande, radios, kids, and soccer games take over, backed up by vendors of everything from stolen watches to sausages and T-shirts. After sunset, tables are set up on the sidewalk. The open-air bands always attract a crowd; tables are packed with customers; a cold beer, served in a glass, is the preferred drink. At sunrise, clean-up crews set the stage for the next day. .

Naïf Caribbean art fills the canvas with people: at the market, at work, at play; it favors repetition as if everyday life had redeeming value. As critics note, primitive art lacks "perspective." Modern art features the soup can, the bull's-eye, and broken glass.

A Conference

I had come to Cartagena to attend a conference on the country's health system sponsored by the Colombian Medical Association. Actually, the beach was first on my agenda, with Cartagena's colonial architecture a close second. These I interspersed with Ursula LeGuin's *Earthsea Trilogy*. I found myself more interested in wizards than in physicians. I decided to take in only the opening session and cut the rest.

Dr. Ricardo Galán Morera, the Medical Association's executive director, was a tall, impressive man in his late forties. From the podium, he conveyed the dignified aura characteristic of the profession he represented. What he had to say, however, diverged sharply from the party line I had naively attributed to medical authorities. "The conference's objective," he said, "is to make medical training realistic, that is, geared to the health needs of most Colombians." When doctors take the plight of the indigent as the starting point for health care, I thought, it is time to listen. I stayed.

At Cartagena, medical schools from Colombia's five largest cities reported on community health. They did not claim they had solved Colombia's health problems. Nonetheless, the work of each project, and the collective experience it represented, pointed the way to solutions. What follows combines presentations made at Cartagena with background research of my own. While at the conference, I arranged to visit projects in Bogotá, Medellín, and Cali, which are described below.

Realities

Between 1970 and 1985, Colombia's population increased by 36 percent, compared to 16 percent in the United States. Colombia is a young country: in 1985, 36 percent of its people were under fifteen years of age and only 4 percent were over sixty-five. In the United States, by contrast, only 22 percent of the population was under fifteen and 12 percent was over sixty-five.[19] The typical American family had just over three members.[20] In Bogotá's low-income neighborhoods, the typical wage earner had five dependents.[21] In the United States, the leading causes of death are malignant tumors and diseases of the circulatory system that strike during the adult years. For most of Latin America, Colombia included, parasitic and bacterial diseases predominate, and they strike the newborn to tragic effect. Colombia's infant mortality rate in 1984 was 48 per 1,000: dysentery, respiratory ailments, and malnutrition being the main causes. In poor barrios of Bogotá, about a third of all deaths occur among children less than five years old. In the United States, the infant mortality rate in 1984 was 11 per 1,000; less than 3 percent of all deaths occurred among children under age five. Among Colombia's adult population, skin, eye, and gastrointestinal diseases are endemic, a result of unsafe water and exposure to improperly treated human waste. "Enteritis," which covers a variety of diarrheal infections and parasitic diseases, kills more people in Colombia than "malignant neoplasmas" (cancer). Enteritis is not one of the five leading causes of death in the United States.[22]

In 1960, 48 percent of Colombia's population was classified as urban; in 1985, the figure was 67 percent. Three out of every ten Colombians now live in one of the country's five largest cities: Bogotá, Medellín, Cali, Barranquilla, and Bucaramanga.[23] Urban growth has outstripped the provision of basic services such as regular garbage collection, waste disposal, and safe water. As a consequence, poor urban dwellers are faced with a "high-risk health environment."

The United States has long since flushed public enemy number one down the toilet; it continues to do so at an astounding rate: the commode siphons off a third of domestic water use at five gallons a flush. In Colombia, only the more affluent benefit from the flush toilet. The cramped barrios of the poor are notorious for untreated sewage. Even when families install a septic tank, waste mixes with groundwater during the rainy season. Potable water, if available, only partially compensates for inadequate sewerge; children carry fecal contamination into the house where it gets into the food and the water supply.

The pathogens carried by human excrement include viruses, bacteria, protozoa, and parasitic worms. The viral group transmits poliomyelitis and Hepatitis A. The bacterial pathogens carry typhoid fever, paratyphoid, and cholera, although vaccinations make outbreaks infrequent. Bacillary dysentery and the various strains of diarrhea-inducing bacterium, however, have no comparable preventive remedy. With respect to protozoal diseases, amoebic dysentery is the most common. Both bacterial and amoebic infections occur through ingestion. Children play near open sewers and privies, they slosh barefoot through contaminated groundwater; their hands get in it, they suck their fingers, rub their eyes, carry it into the house. Dogs, cats, and chickens circulate in the living quarters spreading pathogens. Human excrement is also tied to the life cycle of intestinal worms. The eggs of roundworms and whipworms are carried in feces; infection spreads from exposed hands, food, and water. When a person is barefoot, hookworm larvae can penetrate the skin, usually between the toes or around the ankles.[24]

Dysentery and parasitic infections are debilitating rather than deadly—at least for adults. The health hazard posed by parasites, for example, depends on sheer quantity, what the textbook calls the "worm burden." Adults have learned to live with a battery of chronic ailments that wax and wane in their intensity, but children have not. What is merely debilitating for adults is often fatal for the young. How serious the hazard is can be illustrated by data from Cartagena, Medellín, and Cali. Fifteen years ago, 40 percent of the deaths recorded for children under five were related to inadequate waste disposal.[25]

In poor barrios, urban housing is cramped, short on both ventilation and sunlight. When families have to lug water from a neighborhood spigot, or do not have a tub, bathing is infrequent. Such conditions are a breeding ground for irritating rashes, scabies, and trachoma. Tuberculosis is spread by respiratory droplets; chronic parasitic infections, aggravated by poor nutrition, lower resistance and heighten susceptibility.

To the extent a disease has a quick fix, its incidence can be reduced rapidly. Diphtheria, tetanus, and whooping cough, along with measles, mumps, and rubella, can be controlled with vaccinations given during infancy. In Colombia, especially in urban areas, outbreaks are relatively rare, for vaccinations are effective regardless of a family's income or the quality of housing. Between 1965 and 1984, Colombia's infant mortality rates dropped from 99 per 1,000 to 48.[26] Further reduction, however, depends on long-run strategies rather than stopgap measures.

The notion that health can be left to the marketplace will not work in Colombia because the distribution of wealth is too skewed: 60 percent of the population has to get by on 29 percent of the national income.[27] "Health care," Dr. Galán observed, "doesn't trickle down to poor neighborhoods from the hospitals. To be effective, Colombia has to build health care from the bottom up, creating a strong, community-based system. The first rule of community health is prevention, not treatment. Families have to cope with the health hazards uncollected garbage and raw sewage pose; they must understand the role vaccinations play in infant health. Hospitals are too removed from the community to worry about garbage collection, rabid animals, or the evil eye. Unless backed up by a strong clinic network, we're merely trading in symptoms."

The fact that most Colombians cannot afford the pay-as-you-go system creates a sense of urgency. The cost of doing nothing is too high. Clinics and promotoras express the commitment Colombia has to poorer citizens; neglect conveys indifference. For health care in Colombia, the realistic borders on the pragmatic.

Strategies

A middle-class housewife in Bogotá does not need a promotora to encourage vaccinations. When pregnant, she consults her pediatrician, stops smoking, watches her diet, and cuts down on alcohol. The family's house or apartment will be reasonably spacious and well ventilated; there is no raw sewage near the childrens' play area. Middle-class Colombia purchases health care in the private sector, goes to specialists, and worries about fitness; it tends to ulcers, heart disease, and cancer rather than to enteritis or tuberculosis. For the majority, however, clinics and community medicine are more important than hospitals. The issues at Cartagena were public health and primary care.

In the United States, medical training and health care rely on the hospital. During the 1950s and 1960s, Colombia took a similar approach, but it turned out to be too expensive and overly centralized. The hospital's role was treatment, not primary care or public health. Recognizing the deficiency, Colombia opted for a more decentralized, clinic approach. The National Health Law approved by the Colombian Congress in 1975 was the symbol of reform.

Each province now has a relatively autonomous health department; it determines local priorities, but has to take federal guidelines into account. Over half of a health department's funds come from federal taxes set aside for health care and allocated on the basis of population; the rest comes from local taxes and the profits made on a province's lottery. Colombia's social security system also has its own health budget. Its coverage includes only a minority of the labor force, and it often subcontracts its obligations to the health department. So overall, the majority of Colombia's families depend on the services a province's health department provides.[28]

The 1975 law stressed primary care and decentralization. It subdivided provinces into health regions composed of contiguous counties. Within each county, health posts make referrals to a health center, which also provides supervision. Health centers, in turn, can send patients to the region's local hospital. Treatment for cancer or heart disease occurs at specialized hospitals in the provincial capital. (See Figure 2.1.)

The health post was the mainstay of Colombia's new strategy. It was expected to promote health and not simply be a passive dispenser of medications. The promotora managed the health post and was responsible for primary care: risk assessment and referrals, prenatal exams, vaccinations and infant health, and home visits. She also worked with local committees on public health campaigns. The health team's role was to rotate regularly to the clinics and attend to referrals. The team's members changed periodically, so continuity depended on the promotora. Consequently, too much supervision on the health team's part was counterproductive.

"The health team," Dr. Galán emphasized, "has to cooperate with the

---

53

Figure 2.1 Colombian Health System: Provincial Level

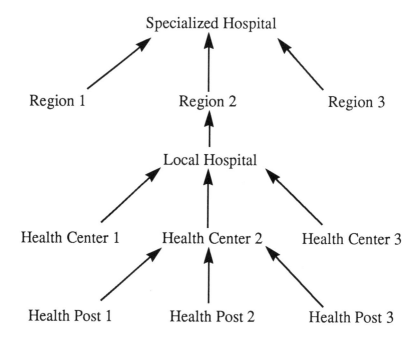

Specialized Hospital

Region 1   Region 2   Region 3

Local Hospital

Health Center 1   Health Center 2   Health Center 3

Health Post 1   Health Post 2   Health Post 3

promotora and back up her work. When team members take over the promotora's assigned tasks, they undermine her effectiveness. To prevent this, the team has to be trained in community medicine and not just in hospital specialties." The 1975 reform incorporated university hospitals into the public sector. Clinic internships became standard in many of Colombia's medical schools, an innovation that had the outspoken support of the Medical Association. First, however, the old curriculum had to be revised.

As in Spain and the rest of Latin America, Colombian students concentrate on the liberal arts during high school. University training implies immediate specialization; students apply for entrance to a particular "Faculty," be it medicine, law, economics, or foreign languages. The comparable equivalent in the United States would be the "Schools" available to undergraduates such as engineering, nursing, or architecture: when they finish, they are engineers, nurses, and architects, even without the addition of graduate work.

Medical school in Colombia lasts six years; about 40 percent of those enrolled are women, compared to roughly 25 percent in the United States.[29] Colombian students do not face distribution requirements. From the start, they concentrate on the biological sciences: anatomy, physiology, biochemistry, genetics; followed by clinical studies: internal medicine, surgery, obstetrics, gynecology, and pediatrics. When they finish, students are physicians; further specialization—cardiology, oncology, endocrinology—can be acquired in postgraduate residencies.

To upgrade clinic services, train personnel, and improve administration, medical schools signed agreements with local health departments. The starting point was to revise the curriculum so that medical training included work at the clinics. Because most projects started with maternal-child care, the frontline departments were obstetrics, pediatrics, and gynecology. Other departments like surgery and internal medicine came later. Student teams, supervised by faculty members, made rounds to the clinics and attended patients referred by the promotoras. As a project gained momentum, the schools of dentistry and nursing joined in, expanding the services the student team provided. The curriculum included courses in preventive medicine, primary health care, and even anthropology. Eventually, new concentrations appeared in community medicine or family health.

The health post's function was primary care. Health centers did diagnostic tests and were equipped for childbirth, dentistry, and minor surgery. The distinction did not always hold in practice; in Bogotá, for example, most clinics provided both primary care and the services of a health center. To as great an extent as possible, however, the clinics handled initial consultations and treatment; hospitals concentrated on specialized care.

A successful project stressed health education. Doctors purged parasites, but they did not collect the garbage or cover the sewers. Health promotion required community action and depended on the measures families took at home. Local health committees, backed by the clinic staff, organized rat control programs, improved garbage disposal, and sponsored health fairs. Student teams gave courses in first aid, sanitation, and nutrition. In addition, most projects provided continuing education for promotoras and midwives.

"The attention provided at clinics," Dr. Galán emphasized, "can't be haphazard or third-rate. Urban dwellers may be poor, but their lives are still shaped by the city's sophisticated milieu. If clinics are shabby, disorganized affairs, families will gravitate to the hospital, which is glorified on television. A clinic in disarray can't keep tabs on such basic facts as which infants have been vaccinated, and it can't deliver on health education. To strengthen the clinic system we have to begin with basics: who does what, and how. Preaching 'participation' won't get us very far if the clinic is a patchwork of inconsistent services of doubtful value."

The projects presented at Cartagena involved student internships, treatment of patients at the appropriate level, and community participation. The gains for the public sector were considerable, and for the university as well. In practical terms, the increase in student enrollments overtaxed the hospital's capacity for clinical teaching; internships at community clinics reduced the burden at the hospital. The principal benefit stressed at Cartagena was how community work reshaped medical training and research. It corrected the bias introduced by the confining experience of the hospital. Hospitals pointed to heart disease and cancer, clinics pointed to dysentery and hookworm; hospitals said to install plastic hearts, clinics said to install sewage systems. In Colombia, medical school pulled students into the vortex of the country's urban poor.

Not all projects were equally strong on health extension. Some, for example, never got beyond services at the clinic. They were isolated affairs, disliked and distrusted by higher-ups. But despite opposition, the teaching-service approach was well entrenched in Colombia's medical schools. In El Valle, what began as a university project had spread to the entire province. Nonetheless, poor rural provinces like Chocó and Guajira lacked health facilities prior to 1975 and still do. In terms of coverage, access, and basic education, a health system geared to the majority was still a long way off, but the diagnosis, at least, was correct. Well, almost correct.

Did physicians not recognize the connection between high infant mortality and a "real" problem like chronic unemployment? Of course they did. A child with dysentery, however, had a "real" problem for which there was a remedy, chronic unemployment notwithstanding. For physicians, the logical place to start was health. Access to health care affected people's lives directly, families had some control over the factors that determined risk, and community action in public health campaigns built self-respect.

• Bogotá

On a cool savanna 8,400 feet above sea level, Bogotá commands the reaches of the Eastern Range. Mountains tower over the city along its eastern edge. To the west, the savannas have accommodated the city's rapid growth: from under a million in 1955 to over four million thirty years later. Bogotá, however, has competitors in Medellín, Cali, and other large cities. Of the country's urban population, only about 25 percent lives in Bogotá, which yields a fairly balanced growth pattern overall. In the Dominican Republic, by contrast, over half of all urban dwellers claim Santo Domingo as their home; similarly, in Argentina, 45 percent of the country's urbanites reside in Greater Buenos Aires.[30]

Bogotá's colonial quarter holds out nobly against the automobile. The spacious Plaza de Bolívar recalls the city's former dignity. Modern Bogotá, however, is selfish with parks and mean-spirited toward pedestrians. *El Tiempo* called the architecture incoherent and accused developers of defrauding the public.[31] Often as not, city "planning" is a con game played at the public's expense—a simple fact a title search can verify, and not just in Bogotá.

May opens Bogotá's rainy season; most days bring downpours and then a chilling drizzle. A warm, sunny afternoon, however, occasioned a walk from my hotel to the city's colonial barrio, La Candelaria—well, at least a try. Against snarled traffic and bounty-hunting cabbies I have a distinguished combat record in the streets of São Paulo, Lima, and Buenos Aires. Bogotá was my waterloo. Along Caracas Avenue, four main thoroughfares converge to test the mettle. My evasive tactics, bluff, and speed got respect from excited motorists. But the intersection crossed, battle fatigue set in. The noise and exhaust was too much. I turned back. People have a right to at least one quiet street, I thought, a noncombat zone for civilians. A brownish-green sign swayed helplessly above the intersection: "Live in Harmony with Nature."

The next time I went to La Candelaria it was on a Sunday and by cab. On the Lord's Day, felonious assault with a motored vehicle was much reduced. The old quarter's ancient dwellings with their sturdy walls had endured, recalling an age less addicted to disposability. The streets were closed to traffic all the way out Seventh Street as far as my hotel. On Sunday, at least, the streets were for the people; they came in from the city's working-class barrios for a stroll, to stop at a café, or for a movie. Every theater had lines. *Gandhi* won the day's popularity contest, outdrawing such competitors as *Pure Blood*, *Operation Dragon*, *Mad Max*, and *The Sexy Stewardess*. I walked back to the hotel by way of the city park. In Bogotá, every day should be lived like Sunday.

Nutrition

In the United States, nutrition means fewer burgers and more leafy vegetables; avoid cholesterol and sugar, watch labels for artificial additives, stock up on yogurt, granola, and bean sprouts. The middle class undoes the sin of protein with an overdose of vegetables. Health advocates are like theologians: they have Thomistic debates over the meaning of "wellness" and get grants to identify the "health locus." In the United States, what constitutes good nutrition is as much a question of ideology as it is of evidence.

In Colombia, by contrast, only the affluent had time for health-food hype. Members of the clinic staff did not quibble over definitions of "good" nutrition in the American sense; they were mostly concerned with malnutrition, for which there was an acceptable definition: a child's expected weight relative to age and height. Level one malnutrition was 76 to 90 percent of normal weight, level two 61 to 75 percent, and level three 60 percent or less. For a child's death to enter the statistics coded as malnutrition, it had to be unmistakably blatant—level three. In Colombia, malnutrition per se was not the major cause of infant mortality. Nonetheless, it was an associated factor: weight deficiencies heightened the risks from intestinal infections and respiratory ailments. Alternatively, malnutrition was a symptom of dysentery and parasitic diseases that inhibited a child's normal growth and development.

Bogotá was subdivided into five health regions. The Maternal-Child Care

Program, directed by Javeriana University, concentrated its efforts in the four health centers and the local hospital located in the city's northeastern zone—Region 1. The University Hospital provided specialized care for referrals. I spent several days at the project, visiting clinics, collecting project data, and listening.

I had met the director, Dr. Francisco Pardo, at the Cartagena conference. He was a tall, thin, serious man in his late forties. I expected a bit of resistance. The typical project was understaffed and its personnel overworked. Arranging a visit was an imposition, although no one would ever admit it. Because requests were never turned down, I had to watch for the telltale signs of visitor weariness. But with Dr. Pardo, I had no doubts. Before I left Cartagena, he had confirmed a schedule, booked me in a small hotel by the university, and supplied me with background documents.

The project's main office was cramped into three small rooms of the university hospital. I arrived late in the afternoon, as my flight had been delayed several hours. As a result, Dr. Pardo had to scrap the day's schedule. "I'll come back and start with tomorrow's agenda," I suggested. "That's not necessary," he said. "The first rule of community work is flexibility. Magarita Archbold, who supervises the nutrition program, said she'd stop here after work."

Composed of 21 barrios, Region 1 had a population of 160,000; the average family size was 6. About a third of the residents either purchased health care in the private sector or were covered by the country's social security system. This left two-thirds, or about 106,000, as the project's target population. Between 1976, when Javeriana began its work, and 1982, the number of women enrolled in the prenatal program had increased by 188 percent: from 1,700 to 4,900—the latter figure exceeding 100 percent coverage, as women came from barrios outside the project area.[32] "When childbirth occurs at home," noted Dr. Pardo, "we try to make house visits within forty-eight hours after birth; subsequently, we encourage infant checkups at regular intervals—ten over a five-year period. Health education, accurate record keeping, and vaccinations accompany each step.

"In just four years infant mortality rates in the project area declined by 42 percent: from 57 per 1,000 in 1977 to 33 in 1981. Better access, systematic checkups for children and pregnant women, the training of auxiliaries, and health education to reduce health risks at home—all contributed."

It was dark by the time Magarita arrived. She was an Afro-Colombian in her twenties from the North Coast; her specialty was nutrition. This was Magarita's last month in Bogotá, as she had received a fellowship for advanced training in Holland. "So," she said, obviously in a hurry, "what do you want to know?" I opened with a barrage of questions. She looked at me in surprise, took off her coat, and rolled up her sleeves.

"Colombia can be mapped by the distribution of malnutrition," she said. "The plains and the Amazon Basin are the worst regions, followed by the Pacific Coast from the province of Nariño to Chocó. Conditions improve along the Atlantic Coast and in the central highlands. Overall, Bogotá has the best record. In the project's target area, however, 33 percent of the children under five are at risk from serious malnutrition."

The project stressed nutrition as part of the clinic's ongoing work. How to treat dysentery, recognize the signs of malnutrition, and maintain infant health were discussed when mothers came in for prenatal exams and got reinforced at subsequent visits. Contaminated water and food aggravate malnutrition. Precautions taken at home—washing hands before preparing food, boiling drinking water, and disposing of garbage safely—help reduce the incidence of disease-related malnutrition, and limit its effects when symptoms develop.

The project also encouraged women to breast-feed their children. Lactation reduces susceptibility to disease and is associated with significantly lower infant mortality rates.[33] A moment's reflection will show that bottle-feeding is risky in an environment notorious for low public health standards. Bottles and nipples had to be sterilized, and many households lacked refrigeration, not to mention safe water.

Children faced two difficult nutritional adjustments: at weaning, between six months and a year old, and between the ages of two and three. Because special baby foods were expensive, mothers shifted their children to a regular diet as soon as possible. When they did, malnutrition jumped noticeably.

"The project can't increase a family's income," Magarita noted. "We have to accept this and work within the limitations household conditions impose. When a child's weight falls below normal guidelines, we outline steps that parents can take; we have to involve them in the problem. Sheer lack of food is usually not the cause. It is the traditional diet that is deficient: coffee laced with a little milk for breakfast, and some combination of oatmeal, cornbread, rice, pasta, and brown-sugar cakes for dinner. Soup, which appears at most meals, is a watery mixture of rice, potatoes, and cassava. The preference for starch and sugar shortchanges vegetables and fruits—the banana excepted. We suggest alternatives that are more nutritious—adding vegetables, a few beans, or viscera to soup; eating more fresh fruits. Obviously, we don't recommend chicken and beef, or apples, which people can't afford; and we have to respect traditional eating habits. We can encourage mothers to add to the evening soup, but not to abandon what the family is used to for something else. Finally, we have to respect the parents' responsibility and right to choose.

"Colombia can't afford to staff each clinic with a nutritionist. Doctors, nurses, and promotoras have to promote nutrition systematically, strengthen motivation, and outline the measures families can take."

In the late 1970s, 30 percent of Bogotá's urban households did not earn enough for statisticians to code them above a minimal subsistence level. Because poor families allocate roughly 80 percent of whatever money they earn to food, any loss of income, or a rise in the cost of staples, is felt immediately; they have virtually no discretionary spending they can transfer to food.[34] "Neural development," Magarita said, "is particularly rapid during the first year. At birth, an infant's brain weighs 25 percent of the adult weight; within a year, it reaches 70 percent. Severe malnutrition retards the brain's normal growth. Food supplements are particularly important for pregnant women and small children. For the poorest families, Colombia's National Food Program provides twelve coupons for each child between six months and five years of age; pregnant women are also allotted twelve, which increases to twenty-four while breast-feeding. Coupons defray about 80 percent of the cost of food purchases. Inclusion, however, depends on family size, living conditions, and household income. Selection is poorly monitored; coupons arrive sporadically; political affiliation determines target neighborhoods every bit as much as need. Considering the program's spotty coverage, food racketeering that diverts supplies to illegal outlets, and administrative costs, it is at best partially effective."

Community Action

A national survey conducted in 1974 put the portion of urban households with sewers at 80 percent. In most of Bogotá's working-class barrios, a worst-case public health situation does not pertain. Sewers may not always be underground, but the flow of waste is reasonably controlled. Most households have piped water, although boiling is still advisable. In Bogotá, criticism focuses on whether an existing sewer system is "adequate." Nonetheless, the city's rapid growth constantly spawns new settlements with minimal services. Outside the country's four largest cities conditions deteriorate, especially for the poorest households whose earnings put them in the bottom 40 percent of the country's income distribution. In 1974, for example, about a third of such households living in intermediate-sized cities lacked sewers; in small towns (under 30,000 inhabitants), about half the poorest households had no sewers.[35]

In Colombia, the rapid population shift from the countryside to the cities placed an additional burden on municipal services, quite apart from that aspect of urban growth attributable to the birthrate. In 1960, about 7 million people lived in cities; twenty-five years later, 19 million did: an increase of 170 percent. The pace of Colombia's urban growth has now slowed, as has the rate of population growth: from over 3 percent a year in the 1960s to 1.8 percent in the 1980s.[36] Access to urban services has improved since 1974, especially since programs targeted the poorest neighborhoods.[37] The 1974 pattern, however, is still valid: access is best in the big cities; poor neighborhoods are likely to have marginal services.

Lucía Laverde, a social worker, directed the project's community action program. She was in her forties and hard to find. True, she had an office, but was there infrequently. Most of her time was spent in neighborhoods and at clinics. I caught her early one morning.

"Services at the clinic can only accomplish so much," she said. "For lasting results, the community itself has to take an interest, whether it's campaigns to collect garbage, boil water, or keep animals out of the house. Health is more than tabulating how many patients are treated at a clinic. It is also a matter of community action and public health. A strong project, in fact, ought to reduce parasitic infections and dysentery, and hence the number of clinic visits."

Most of the barrios had health committees. Leadership came from local organizations like the civic defense chapters, which had legal status. "The barrios in the project's area," Lucía pointed out, "are primarily working class; most families have relatively stable incomes. Nonetheless, they don't understand an abstraction like health promotion; they're not accustomed to it. The health committee's task is to work on neighborhood projects people consider important. Once people participate, the effect multiplies."

Rat control was a good example of an obvious problem where community action had a practical impact. "The rat poison," Lucía told me, "did not pose a danger to children or pets, but the project required neighborhood meetings to explain this and show how to use it to the greatest effect. That was the first step. Garbage was usually heaped in the streets and got collected haphazardly; needless to say, it attracted vermin. With the health committee's backing, neighborhoods put large bins in different locations, and families started keeping their refuse in adequate containers. Then the committee demanded that the authorities regularize collection. The barrio was also pockmarked with vacant lots where tall grass and garbage provided a haven for rats; such areas were cleared out and the grass cut and kept short. The project dealt with a recognized irritant, and it did so in a way that combined neighborhood action with public health education."

Action was not always related to public health. One committee set up a day-care center that was managed by women from the community. As part of the program, the center taught better health habits. But what it told children to do, parents routinely violated at home. The center ended up providing health education for adults.

"Few of the outlying barrios have an adequate sewer system," Lucía said. "Drainage ditches are old, while the number of families using the system keeps growing. When families are too far from the main line, or if there isn't one, they install a septic tank; it is a second-best solution given the rainy season. Once the ground is saturated, the sewage mixes with and contaminates the surface water, creating a serious health hazard. Although families can take defensive measures, the long-term solution requires additional investments in municipal services; that happens when communities pressure the authorities— as they did on garbage collection."

Why septic tanks pose a problem in urban areas may not be readily apparent. In Bogotá's poor neighborhoods, officials do not waste time on septic tank specifications. Families install their own, buying materials as they go along. The result is a storage tank that is too small, to say nothing of adequate drainage. Add to this large families and high-density neighborhoods and the result is a first-rate public health problem. "We now have volunteers from the engineering school working with the health committees," Lucía said. "I consider their contribution as important as that of any physician. The first thing most people want is a paved street or a septic tank that works. When doctors join a health committee, what they want to do is not necessarily the community's priority. When they impose their own schemes, the consequence is passive resistance. The president of the health committee should run meetings, not doctors from the clinic. The community has to make its own decisions."

Minuto de Dios

To live in a barrio is to be amidst people: kids in the street, neighbors lounging in doorways, arguments overheard. Houses are packed together, built in fits and starts by their occupants; rods sticking out from the top layer of cement blocks attest to second-story ambitions. Middle-class visitors note the smells, the garbage, and the mud. They overlook the barrio's capacity for neighborhood action. For fiestas the barrio pulls itself together, collecting funds, decorating the streets, and hiring a band. Barrios are also relatively stable. Once families settle in, they are likely to stay. Most cannot afford to move, so they improve what they have. Barrios usually have a core of good housing occupied by residents of long standing. Schools and clinics reinforce the neighborhood boundaries communities recognize. For the middle class the automobile propels people out of their neighborhoods. Barrio residents do not have such luxuries; they stay closer to home and to each other: a concentration of small shops, cantinas, and cafés attests to this. People know who is respected as a leader or who is a midwife. Despite its poverty, a barrio has a firm basis for neighborhood action if it can be tapped. A project with practical objectives people support attracts attention and participation; it breaks the drab cycle of oppression as a fiesta does. People do not have much, they do not count, and they know it. Community projects may be practical—rat control, garbage collection, improved drainage—but they also build solidarity and self-respect.

Lucía invited me to a health committee meeting scheduled for 9:00 A.M. on Saturday in the barrio of Minuto de Dios. She called at the last minute: "Go to

Fourteenth Street and take any bus that says Minuto de Dios; once you're there, anyone can tell you where the health committee meets." I went to Fourteenth Street where several buses passed marked "Minuto"; I decided this must mean "Minuto de Dios." I took the precaution of bringing a map of Bogotá. By the time we stopped at Minuto, half the bus was watching for my stop. The driver directed me to the health center several blocks away. From there, inquiries brought me to Minuto's Community Center.

A sunny Saturday after a spell of rainy days cut down on attendance, for it was a time to hang up wash and enjoy being outside. Besides the doctor from the clinic, Lucía, and two student nurses, the meeting drew only seven people from the community, including three men—health work is not simply consigned to women. It started off with a lively discussion about rabid animals and the responsibilities owners have to control their dogs and cats. The main business, however, was to organize a training course that covered first aid and common health problems like dysentery, fever, and nausea. Because the clinic was not open twenty-four hours a day, community members trained in health care were a valuable resource for their neighbors. They decided the course would run from 8:00 A.M. to 1:00 P.M. on four successive Saturdays. Procedures were arranged for publicity and enrollment. The limit was set at twenty participants, although thirty could sign up: "People say they will come and then never show up." They defined some enrollment prerequisites. Participants had to be well known in the community, the kind of people others could trust and turn to in an emergency. The course was restricted to adults over eighteen years of age. A literacy requirement was considered but then rejected; for as one woman noted, "people are respected for what they do, not whether they can read." Those interested had to sign up at the health center within two weeks.

We had convened in a small center equipped like a classroom with desks, a blackboard, and maps of Colombia. To the people of the barrio, a schoolroom commands respect. Proudly displayed in the corner stood the organizational chart for the local Civil Defense chapter: committees for youth, women, sanitation, and sports. Support for the health program came from the barrio's leadership network.

The meeting over, Lucía showed me around. Minuto had a well-kept plaza of shade trees and gardens. There were basketball courts, a soccer field, a community theater, and the health center. Altogether, the recreation area covered about two acres. Few barrios have the luxury of civic space; they are crowded, and space is at a premium. The unusual case of Minuto was the work of Padre Rafael, one of its founders. He insisted on public property and attractive surroundings, even for a barrio. There were trash cans about, and they were used.

Trucks called "supermarkets on wheels" crammed the main streets leading to the square. Some specialized in dairy products, others in meat, vegetables, or canned goods. Families waited patiently in line with their baskets. Licensed by the city, the mobile markets reduced food costs in the barrios: no advertising, frills, or costly overhead. The trucks were convenient and saved time, as few families had cars for shopping.

By the playground near the square was a busy café and bakery. It was a lively place where everyone came to meet their friends. "Did you expect community action to be more exciting?" Lucía asked me with a laugh, ordering a second cup of coffee. Before I could answer, a young man in his twenties stopped at our table with his family. "We missed you today, Ernesto," said Lucía. "It's too nice a day for a meeting," he said, "but honestly, I just forgot." Lucía mentioned plans for the first-aid course. "Esmeralda," she said, turning to his wife, "you ought to enroll; people respect you and your mother is a midwife." "Well," Esmeralda responded hesitantly, "on Saturdays the children aren't in school." "You mean, who will watch them?" asked Lucía. "No problem; you've got Ernesto. At our last meeting, Ernesto, didn't you say women should be more active in the health program? Well, now's the time to apply the principle. We need Esmeralda's help, and you know she'd be good at it." "I guess someone has to take the lead," Ernesto admitted, "but it's Esmeralda's decision." "In that case," Esmeralda said, "I'll enroll." "Community action, Jaime," Lucía said after they left, "begins with small steps."

• Medellín

I flew to Medellín, the capital of Antioquia Province and Colombia's industrial heartland. It was a beautiful day of clear skies, the land below stretched out in a spectacular panorama. From the savannas of Bogotá, the Eastern Range begins its sharp drop to the Magdalena Valley. The river is navigable only as far as Honda; one could see why. Above the city the Magdalena River turns into a bog of flats and sandbars; at Honda itself, rapids preclude further ascent. To the north, the river slowly snakes its way through the rainswept lowlands toward the Caribbean coast, where it spawns a vast marsh apart from the main channel. To the west, the Central Range soars skyward.

Medellín is squeezed into a narrow valley surrounded by high escarpments—as if scooped out by some galactic steam shovel. At 5,000 feet, the city's elevation is lower than Bogotá's, but the surrounding mountains are more abrupt and severe. Approaching by air, the pilot scraped over the peaks of the Central Range and then dropped down to the city.

Medellín paid a price for industrialization. Pollution hovered oppressively in the valley, trapped by the mountains. Were it not for fifty-five inches of rainfall, the situation would have been worse. Medellín had a population of almost 2 million. As the city already covered the valley, there was little room for expansion except up the mountainsides. It was the indigent newcomer who got consigned to these inhospitable barrios, which lacked both transportation and public services: no water supply, electricity, or sewerage. Downtown, Medellín was a vibrant, attractive city. The narrowest streets were converted to permanent walkways. And traffic seemed a bit more manageable than back in the capital. With parks, cafés, and sidewalk vendors, Plaza Bolívar was the city's crowded pedestrian hub. To those who prefer the calm of the suburbs, being "surrounded" may not be a plus. But I like a place close to the pulse of the planet.

Family Health

I first met Dr. Hernando Molina, a project supervisor, at the Cartagena conference. We had suffered through a lecture on "epistemology"—the necessity of redefining standard concepts like sickness, primary care, and patient. The explanation came with a complex diagram of diagnosis, ethics, institutional levels, and curricula. The man next to me shook my arm. "You're falling asleep, my friend. This is important. Colombia's health system may be underdeveloped, but not our analysis." I was not sure if he was kidding or not. He introduced himself after the session—Hernando Molina. "Did you like the presentation?" he asked me. "Not much," I admitted cautiously. "Well," he said, "it was all backwards. Change the practice and let the concepts catch up." He described some of his work in Medellín, and I managed to extract an invitation. He had brought project documents with him, which he passed on to me.

Hernando arranged my schedule at the project. I spent most of my time with him and with Francia, a nurse in her late twenties who helped organize the student health teams; she was an Afro-Colombian from the Chocó.

Medellín's Institute for the Health Sciences had three faculties: medicine, dentistry, and nursing. The medical program was six years; dentistry, five; and nursing, three. About 40 percent of the students enrolled in the medical school were women; the proportion was roughly similar in the dental school. The philosophy applied at the Institute was to supplement academic training with practical experience geared to the needs of the community. The Family Health Program, for example, emphasized community service, preventive medicine, and community action. Under the program, a team of three students (doctor, dentist, nurse) worked with six families for a year and a half. As of 1983, over eight hundred families had participated in the program. A key aspect of how the Institute organized health care was the special training it provided for women who volunteered to be family health collaborators. Over 230 women had taken the health education course, which covered first aid and the community's most common health problems: malnutrition, amoebic dysentery, malaria, and tuberculosis. In addition, the course stressed public health, family hygiene, and disease prevention. The training program consisted of twenty classes of two hours each. Students worked directly with community groups to organize and teach the course. The program involved students in health care based on the family as a unit rather than on the isolated treatment of individuals. During their first four semesters, whether specializing in medicine, nursing, or dentistry, students were primarily observers. Only later were they allowed to work directly with families and patients.

Sabaneta

The project area was in Sabaneta, a predominantly working-class town on the outskirts of Medellín. Located in a narrow valley, the municipality used to be a rural retreat for Medellín's wealthy families. As industries expanded in the 1960s and 1970s, however, it attracted urban migrants as an alternative to the overcrowded city. The rich pulled out, leaving behind their mansions, some converted now to schools, others in decay awaiting higher land prices. Coffee and banana groves still lined the hillsides, a vestige of the town's rural past. Approximately 45 percent of Sabaneta's population was under age fifteen; only 2 percent was over sixty-five. Low-income families, whether in Colombia or the United States, have more children than their affluent counterparts in the suburbs. Only half the households in Sabaneta had access to the town's sewer system. Inadequate waste disposal showed up in the health statistics: in 1978, diarrhea-enteritis and infectious hepatitis were the diseases recorded with greatest frequency at the clinics. Mumps and whooping cough were not far behind—ailments that vaccinations presumably had under control. Most dwellings had piped water, but it still had to be boiled prior to use. Garbage collection was frequent and dependable; when I was there in 1983, however, it was still dumped into the Medellín River.[38]

The Institute had its own health center in Sabaneta. "Since we work out of our own clinic with our own personnel," Hernando pointed out, "it's easier to promote health education at every step—from the classroom to the clinic and the community. Our strategy is intensive: the home visits made by student teams and the training of neighborhood collaborators strengthen health at the base, where it's needed most. Using the experience we gained at Sabaneta, we've helped train personnel and strengthen health promotion at the Health Department's clinics."

The Institute's health center combined the services of a clinic with those of a small hospital; it was an attractive, modern building set in appealing, well-kept surroundings. Its design, with a penchant for open spaces and airy, suspended ceilings, dispelled the gloom that so often characterizes the hospital. Physical appearance was no minor consideration: it suggested the attitude the Institute had toward its clientele. Not only was attention lavished on architecture, but also, once inside, patients did not face the indignity of long waiting lines.

Records could actually be found, and people were treated with respect—civilities all too often denied the indigent.

In the health center's dental wing, simplified equipment was arrayed in a circular format that bordered an attractive work center. From within the circle, where they were easily monitored by the staff, students performed identical procedures on several patients. This reduced costs without sacrificing quality. At the health center patients paid for services rendered, but the charges were nominal compared to the fees of the private sector. In fact, the Institute subsidized health care: what patients paid covered only a small part of actual costs.

"Families have come to respect the quality of the care they get," Francia emphasized. "We do more than treat illness—we provide an extension program in health. Getting recognition from the community was a real achievement. People assumed that treatment by students was second-rate. Even the poor were biased in favor of the big hospital and professional stature."

The Family Health Program directly linked the community to the Institute's health center. A student health team made weekly visits to participating families. The team worked with the same households throughout the internship period. Of course, students also had clinical experience at the Institute's health center. But the Family Health Program made them confront the health environment most families faced, and, consequently, helped them understand the importance of preventive medicine, public health, and the role played by the collaborator.

Assessing Risk

A key aspect of the Family Health Program was risk assessment. In the United States, "risk" is determined by a medical history, a physical, and a battery of tests. The home place is presumed to be relatively benign. In low-income barrios, by contrast, risk also depends on living conditions: factors not easily identified at a clinic. As students worked with families, they compiled a risk profile that included but went beyond the standard history and routine physical.[39] For housing, the risk index (0 = low risk, 1 = medium risk, 2 = high risk) included ventilation, access to direct sunlight, yard space, and construction materials—which could be cement blocks or cardboard braced by wooden slats. Assuming the structure was permanent, students next considered its state of repair—was plaster or thatch falling from the ceiling, were there holes in the walls?—and the dwelling's facilities: the type of waste disposal system in use—if any—and its cleanliness, whether the family had a place to wash up separate from the kitchen sink, how many persons per bedroom, and the source of the household's water supply. Finally, they rated environmental factors: were pets vaccinated and kept out of the kitchen, did the neighborhood have garbage bins available, did open sewers drain near dwellings or down the sidewalk, were dwellings rat-infested?

Beliefs and customary practices also figured in a family's risk profile. For example, the home remedies used to treat illness, or assumptions about what caused disease, alerted students to the family's definition of illness and its likely response. The composition of the household's typical food purchases allowed a rough assessment of whether nutrition was adequate. Finally, a family's socioeconomic characteristics—from literacy to job stability—had to be considered. The scale used made distinctions at the bottom of the income ladder. The highest category was "sufficient," followed by "average," "less than average," "minimal," and "indigent." An "average" household consisted of six to eight persons and was economically stable: that is, employed by a company with social security coverage. Furthermore, wage earners in the "average" category had completed high school or had at least some technical training; the family also usually owned its dwelling. A household whose resources were judged "minimal" had nine to eleven members; unskilled jobs of a semipermanent character made the family's income precarious. The "minimal" household's wage earner was just barely literate, and the family usually rented its dwelling.

The student team, of course, also ascertained the family's medical history: difficult pregnancies, past and current health problems, and dental care, if any. So although, on the surface, "risk assessment" seemed straightforward enough, in practice it required students to confront the diverse conditions that placed a family's health in jeopardy. Consequently, the strategy they applied at the household level reflected a diagnosis that was as much social as it was medical. The front line was the household itself, rather than the clinic, for health promotion had to take a family's circumstances into account. The recommendations made, whether on nutrition, hygiene, or sanitation, had to be realistic. Weekly visits gave students a chance to reinforce suggestions and verify the results.

Francia arranged for me to spend the morning with one of the health teams, which included a home visit. Hugo Fernando Trespalacios, a medical student in his early twenties, headed up the team; his manner was gentle and unassuming. The family we stopped to check on had eight members: the household's head was a woman in her late twenties with four children, two of them still too young to be in school. She also supported her parents and a younger sister. The house was of cement block, and the floors were earthen. There were two bedrooms in back; the small dining room in front had been converted into a bedroom for her parents. The family obviously liked Fernando, and it needed the attention of a weekly visit. The grandmother, an alert, outgoing woman, had swollen ulcers on her legs; walking was difficult and painful for her. The medical textbook recommends complete bed rest for open ulcers on the ankles. The best Fernando could do was adjust his advice to fit the circumstances. "Sit down when you are preparing food; when neighbors come don't stand in the doorway, pull up a chair." The grandfather suffered from emphysema—after a life of railroad work. His chest was distorted and bony. When we arrived at about 10:30 A.M., the old man was just dressing. He had a quick checkup, then came into the front room; the old woman, who was sitting, held his hand.

The younger sister was recovering from an eye operation: glaucoma had been diagnosed just in time. Fernando had a gentle way with the family. He went into Martha's room to examine her bandaged eyes; he sat down beside her and took her hand reassuringly; quietly he asked how she was. The young mother needed emotional support; Fernando's manner noticeably relaxed the anxious, worried look she had when he arrived.

The grandmother kept house and cooked; her daughter held a full-time job. The old woman's spirit kept her body going; she did not complain. "Knowing you are needed," Fernando remarked when we left, "is a powerful force. She will live to see her grandchildren in school. Then her daughter will be able to manage."

Community Health

In Colombia, training community members in health has been a long-standing strategy. In 1958, the medical faculty at the University of Antioquia (Medellín) began training rural promotoras in Santo Domingo County. Over the course of eight years, infant mortality dropped by half, vaccination campaigns produced a high level of coverage, and rural communities undertook a variety of sanitation projects. In 1964, Colombia's Ministry of Health signed an agreement with the university to train 15 teams, which returned to their home provinces and introduced the promotora program. The following year, 31 courses trained over 700 promotoras in 76 counties dispersed over 15 provinces. When Colombia reorganized health care in 1975, it recognized the promotora as an essential feature of the system. Promotoras now received a salary; the basic guideline was one promotora for every 200 families. The Institute's program for health collaborators complemented the promotora system. The objective was to strengthen health promotion at the neighborhood level by training one collaborator for every six families. The promotora had fixed responsibilities at the clinic such as prenatal examinations, infant vaccinations, and routine record keeping. The collaborator's role, by contrast, was first aid and neighborhood health; she was a resident expert on how to use Sabaneta's health system.[40]

In Bogotá, you will recall, Minuto's health committee wanted women from the community trained in health. In Sabaneta, the collaborator represented the same strategy organized in a slightly different fashion. The Family Health Program's intensive character had involved households directly in public health measures and disease prevention. The interest this generated provided ample recruits for the collaborator program—most volunteers were past participants in the Institute's Family Health project.

Fernando took me to visit one of the collaborators, an older woman in her late fifties. Señora Marina was a high-spirited, hefty woman with flashing eyes and a direct, forceful manner. "What did your training course cover?" I asked her. "Well," she said, "first aid for accidents and injuries, and of course, childbirth. Also vaccinations and nutrition, and common problems like dysentery, parasitic infections, and rashes. Finally, we studied public health, for example, safe water and waste disposal." "Do many people consult you, and what do they want to know?" I inquired, following one question a bit undiplomatically with another. "Mostly," she said, "people want to know if a problem is serious, if they need to see a doctor or not. And they want to know where they should go, just to the clinic or to a hospital? They don't understand procedures, so I explain what they should do. Of course, depending on the problem, like rashes or dysentery, I explain the measures they can take on their own. The clinics, you know, aren't opened on the weekends or at night; problems don't occur just when it's convenient. So parents get worried about a sick child and ask me to come; they want to be assured it's not an emergency. But there are emergencies, too. Last Sunday night I had to put a splint on a broken leg; I also went to the hospital—the parents were afraid to go alone."

On her living room wall, Señora Marina kept a picture of St. Christopher, the patron saint of travelers. He was depicted in traditional fashion: carrying the Christ Child across a stream's torrent. Below appeared an inscription, *llega quien camina*: "to arrive, you must get started."

Fernando later gave me a copy of the training manual for collaborators. I looked it over. "The truth is," I told him, "the collaborator knows more about health problems and treatment than I do." "If you lived in Sabaneta," he laughed, "you'd learn fast."

Antioquia's Health Department staffed most of Sabaneta's clinics. We stopped at one of the health posts where I talked with the vaccination promoter. He kept track of the families in his district, making sure both children and adults had the required inoculations. He had just canvassed the thirty neighborhoods in two sections of his district. In one neighborhood, sixty-eight families lived in fifty-two dwellings—a double occupancy rate of 30 percent. "Why," I asked him, "is the vaccination job left for the men?" "Going from house to house in neighborhoods where you are not well known is dangerous for women," he noted. "By contrast, when the promotora makes a house call, it's to a family she knows, and the collaborator works in her immediate neighborhood."

Table 2.1 Distribution of Medical Schools in Colombia, 1983

Province	Capital City	Number of Medical Schools
Cundinamarca	Bogotá	6
Antioquia	Medellín	3
Valle del Cauca	Cali	2
Atlántico	Barranquilla	3
Bolívar	Cartagena	1
Cauca	Popayán	1
Caldas	Manizales	1
Quindío	Armenia	1
Risaralda	Pereira	1
Santander	Bucaramanga	1

Priorities

Back at the Institute's campus, the bulletin board advertised an upcoming conference. It featured a cardiovascular surgeon from Georgetown University in Washington, D.C. He had sent along a photograph. With glasses in hand and a pin-striped suit, he had that studied, professional look. Research on heart disease is of obvious importance. But in Latin America, malaria, Chagas disease, and schistosomiasis afflict the impoverished and take a much greater toll than heart ailments. The prestige accorded U.S. medicine favors a transfer of technology that downplays parasitic diseases and basics like family medicine and community health.

Regional disparities within countries can distort priorities every bit as much. For example, Colombia's twenty medical schools were concentrated in only nine of the country's twenty-two provinces; the cities of Bogotá and Medellín alone accounted for almost half of them. (See Table 2.1.) This left an underserved belt of provinces that skirted Colombia's Pacific Coast (Nariño, Chocó), the Caribbean (Córdoba, Sucre, Magdalena, Guajira), and the Venezuelan border (Cesar, Norte de Santander).

The graduates of Colombia's medical and dental schools were obligated to provide a year of national service. In practice, however, regional loyalties were hard to overcome. "Students prefer their home provinces," Hernando said, "as close to the capital as possible. Rural areas, especially in the underdeveloped fringe that can't recruit from its own medical schools, get bypassed. The inequity shows up clearly in the way malnutrition and high infant mortality rates are concentrated in peripheral regions. Poor provinces like the Chocó have only a few poorly equipped clinics; the roads are impassable, and the amenities few, so it's hardly a young doctor's first choice."

Development rationed its benefits according to political clout: first the great cities, then the surrounding countryside. Colombia's lowland provinces, far removed from the citadels of power, got what was left, health care included.

Recession

Because Colombia was self-sufficient in petroleum, the price hikes of the 1970s did not create a trade deficit, as happened in the Dominican Republic and Brazil. Between 1975 and 1981, Colombia had a modest trade surplus and its GNP expanded at an average of 4 percent. When the debt crisis hit in 1982, Colombia was a model of solvency. Nonetheless, the banks stopped loaning to Colombia just as they did to less credit-worthy customers. So Colombia ended up short of cash in the 1980s, with its growth rate much reduced. In 1982 and 1983, its GNP expanded by only 1 percent. That was better than the -2.5 percent registered for Latin America as a whole, but it was still less than Colombia's population growth rate.[41]

Medellín, Hernando told me, was the country's second largest city, but first in problems. Although Colombia's chief industrial center, in 1983 it was hard hit by the recession. According to *El Colombiano*, the local newspaper, unemployment was 25 percent. Textile mills and cigarette factories had either closed down or laid off workers. The result was a 300 percent increase in street vendors in just two years. Because they added to the congestion downtown, the police harassed them: Medellín's City Council, complained the newspaper, refused to let the vendor make an honest living.[42]

I did not quit smoking in Medellín, but I did change brands. I arrived in the midst of a national boycott against Marlboro. Medellín was the home of the country's depressed tobacco industry. Adding insult to injury, an influx of contraband Marlboro cigarettes had undercut the domestic market. Beginning in the universities, the revolt spread to the general populace. To buy a pack of Marlboro bordered on treason. In support of "nationalistic fervor," *El Tiempo* cited the 1980 figures on contraband as estimated by the Planning Ministry: 27 percent of all household appliances and cigarettes, 20 percent of wines and liquors, and 10 percent of the textiles—for a tab that approached $500 million. The newspaper blamed the situation on the high taxes Colombian firms had to pay on production. By contrast, when foreign goods escaped the tariff, they had a price advantage that made domestic industries less competitive.[43]

In Colombia, one is surrounded by American products, contraband or not. To amuse myself between TV programs I kept track of the ads over a two-hour interval: Certs, Charms, Mounds, Aero Wax, Marlboro, Ponds, Alka-Seltzer, Johnson & Johnson, Alert, and Eveready Batteries. American corporations have instructed the world on headaches and bad breath, on waxed floors and flashlights.

The Bus

The new highway (*autopista*) to Bogotá goes directly east from Medellín to La Dorada, down in the Magdalena Valley on the other side of the Central Range. From there, it is a short trip to Honda, the gateway to Bogotá. The old road, by contrast, circles south from Medellín to take in a dozen towns; only then does it cross the Central Range. The old route to Bogotá was obviously more interesting, but it took an extra ten hours and I did not have the time.

I rose at 6:00 A.M. to a dreary day. The hotel's electricity was off, and it was raining. A bus trip through mountain fog is tedious, so I made a reservation with Avianca just in case. I sought advice from the bellhops. It had rained most of the night, they said; their unanimous forecast was for clearing. I paid the bill and left for the bus station.

Colombia's bus companies included Rápido Ochoa, Rápido Tolima, Flota Magdalena, and Expreso Bolivariano. Rápido Ochoa came highly recommended and had a bus scheduled to depart at 10:20 A.M. I arrived early and pointedly asked for a ticket on the 10:20, only to find 9:45 marked on my ticket as I was hurriedly ushered toward Rápido Tolima. The bus looked comfortable enough, was not crowded, and promised the autopista.

The bus had both a driver and an assistant whose job was to add passengers along the way. Not everyone, of course, was going to Bogotá. Some only wanted passage to La Dorada, or perhaps Honda. The bus had a tapedeck, so it was Cumbias, Salsas, and Roberto Carlos all the way to Honda. The autopista rarely passed through a town; it had been gouged out of the mountains, provoking erosion and landslides. Where the elements had tossed aside the pavement, we inched our way through the mud. Because Medellín is situated at 5,000 feet, crossing the Central Range did not pose a particularly steep ascent. Overall, it was an easy drive; we arrived at La Dorada in three hours.

It was Sunday, and the depot at La Dorada was packed. In theory, my bus offered "express" service to Bogotá. As it turned out, the claim was negotiable. "We want to go to Honda," a man told our driver, "you're going there, and you don't have enough passengers." "But it's an express," countered the driver. "Look," the man reasoned, "you've stopped here and you have to stop in Honda; taking us doesn't add stops, so it's still an express." Logic won out. Before the driver could object, the word got out and our bus ended up jam-packed. Kids, luggage, and basket lunches were squeezed into every available space, including the aisle and my lap. The more the bus filled up, the hotter it got; on the other hand, the crowding made people talkative, in fact, downright cheerful. It was the best part of the trip.

The ascent from Honda to Bogotá is a climb of over 8,000 feet. We spiraled up to majestic vistas of the Magdalena Valley below. We also entered a nerve-racking war of trucks, buses, and automobiles. No quarter is given on the Honda-Bogotá road, one of the busiest highways in Colombia. We temporarily left the fray with a flat tire. The passengers did not consider this unusual; families sat around and ate lunch, others helped out. Our replacement tire was so bald it resembled one of Plato's innate ideas, and it had a menacing crack down the center. "The next time," said the man across from me, "I'm changing buses." He did not have to wait long. Minutes later the truck in front slammed on its brakes. No one was hurt, but our bus lost its windshield and headlights. That was enough. I grabbed my bags and joined the exodus. We flagged down a replacement with enough room for everyone, but arguments about the fare continued all the way to Bogotá.

I found myself next to Señor Jorge, a heavyset man in a rumpled suit coat and a sweaty tie. "Why aren't you on the airplane?" he had asked me, having guessed my nationality. "Colombia spent a fortune on airports so the wealthy could be comfortable; then you come and take the bus." "Well," I said, "I thought I'd see more of Colombia this way." "If you want to see Colombia," he replied, "go to a rural school and watch the children in line for a bowl of rice. They are thin and listless, they are covered with sores, their uniforms are shabby. That is Colombia." Señor Jorge was a rural schoolteacher from Villeta County, not far from Bogotá. "Once people leave the countryside," he said, "they don't come back. Young women go to the city, get fooled, and end up prostitutes. Here in Colombia we kill our women little by little. I tell people we have no future unless women are treated equally, unless we raise our children with love and not with the stick.

"The difference, my friend, is this. You can choose between the plane and the bus. Most people can't."

• Cali

I arrived in Cali dog-tired and airsick. My flight from Cartagena had first backtracked to Barranquilla for more passengers. From there, once beyond the coastal flatlands, the pilot flew up the Cauca Valley to avoid the mountains as much as possible. We made three more stops: Medellín, Manizales, and Pereira. This particular flight, I learned later, was dubbed the "milk route." I settled unsteadily into a cab, glad to be back on solid ground. The cabbie had other ideas. He roared off to Cali at a race-track pace, treating me—and numerous pedestrians—to a chilling display. I wobbled from cab to hotel.

I based my hotel selection on a judicious study of city maps and guidebooks. The smaller "C" and "D" hotels are usually on side streets away from the traffic. Luxury hotels, on the other hand, must be displayed, which means placing them in the thicket of the worst possible intersection. For sleep, the best advice is to stay with the hotel class labeled "comodo"—comfortable. The hotel I chose flanked a narrow one-way street with no traffic in sight. The clerk looked me over: one bag, disheveled, and alone. He asked if I had a reservation—a traveler's most feared inquiry. My answer—"no." So he began a perfunctory check of rooms, which ended in "no hay." In the United States "no room" means just that. In Colombia, however, "no" was an opening gambit. So I lied spectacularly. I had not made a reservation personally, but surely someone else had done so on my behalf: someone from the university, from the Education Foundation, from—I enumerated all the institutions on my Cali agenda. While he checked the reservations, I chatted away, displaying an acquaintance with Spanish. We compromised on a fictitious "lost" reservation. He had a room for just one night; he might have to switch me to another one on Sunday. I apologized for the mixup, expressed appreciation in pesos, and never changed rooms.

Cali is Colombia's third largest city and capital of the province of El Valle. The town's old colonial squares have surrendered to the internal combustion engine. The popular class far outnumbers the motorists, but pedestrians have no rights. Their sidewalks cut back, they make their way bunched together for safety.

The Cauca River cuts through the province south to north, a distance of approximately 150 miles. The broad plain thus formed reaches its greatest width near Cali, a span of around 20 miles. At an elevation of some 3,000 feet, it avoids the extremes of both the hot country across the Coastal Range and the frigid altiplano bordering Ecuador. With deep, alluvial soils, the Cauca Valley claims a stretch of Colombia's best agricultural real estate. The valley's land-lords, however, did not bother with food crops; they exported sugar abroad and surplus labor to Cali.

Between the 1973 and 1985 census, the city's population increased from 990,000 to 1.7 million; Cali had half the province's inhabitants.[44] New migrants faced unemployment, makeshift housing, and crowded barrios that lacked piped water and adequate waste disposal. El Valle's health teams worked in these neighborhoods, even those built over the mud along the contaminated Cauca River. This account, however, describes the health strategy applied in the province as a whole. For conditions were diverse: in some of Cali's barrios, public health meant installing septic tanks properly; in others, it meant simply helping families survive. So the content of programs had to reflect situations that varied greatly, not only in Cali itself, but also in the province's rural areas. The El Valle project was important because its approach to training, research, and extension viewed a generic problem like child health within its particular social context. And the way the project worked in health was relevant to the community's overall development. Because the clinics I had visited elsewhere worked in urban neighborhoods, this time I went to the countryside.

Map 2.2   El Valle Province

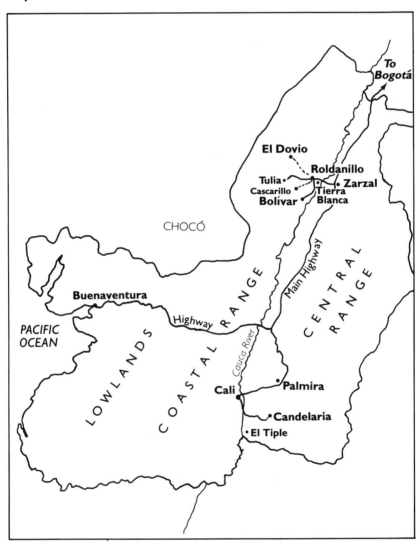

Health Care in El Valle

With support from the Rockefeller Foundation in 1950, the Colombian government established a model medical school in Cali. By strengthening the basic sciences and clinical training, the University of El Valle chartered a new course. It upgraded obsolete hospital facilities and introduced modern research practices. By the late 1950s, the School of Medicine had acquired a reputation for excellence. At the same time, a trend toward community action developed, spearheaded by the Department of Preventive Medicine and Public Health—the first such program at a Colombian medical school. The new department started a family health project in Cali's impoverished barrios. For the first time, infant mortality rates and debilitating diseases were tracked systematically. The result, as one participant told me, was devastating. "For most of us, it was our first real contact with the country's grim reality; we were shocked." Community health gained ground. A project in rural Candelaria County, for example, began training promotoras in 1961.

Gearing research and training to address what activists considered to be the country's health priorities had few precedents. Traditionalists resisted the threat such innovations posed to technical specialization. A period of confrontation followed. Critics demanded that social priorities become a central focus of the curriculum; they also rejected research funds from international sources as a covert form of control over programs. By the end of the 1960s, the trend toward technologically intensive medicine was countered; students received more training in community health. And to break the impasse on funding, a private Colombian Education Foundation was established to attract domestic support and to dispense international grants. The authorities acquiesced: "they had to accept initiatives on social issues or they wouldn't have a university or maybe not even a country."

Restructuring education so it reflected Colombia's health needs did not downgrade the university's reputation for excellence—at least not for long. The Division of Health Sciences, which included medicine, dentistry, nursing, public health, and health administration, devoted more of its research, teaching, and service to primary care and community health. By so doing, it applied the clinic model comprehensively, paving the way for the decisive change in national health policy effective since 1975. The University of El Valle, which had upgraded medical training in the 1950s, set the pace in community medicine during the 1970s.

It took me a while to appreciate the transformation that had occurred. I was accustomed to think of specific projects rather than a broad strategy applied throughout a province. After twenty years of field experience, research and action had advanced beyond the project stage. The advocates of community health controlled the bureaucracy: the university and the Health Department had been allies for over a decade. Administration, public health, and health

77

services were joint ventures. The province acquired a national reputation for the independent approach it took to health. It set its own agenda without interference from Bogotá, and its lottery transferred more funds to health than in any other province.[45] Characteristic of El Valle's eclectic style was the Education Foundation, which funded pilot projects.

Señor Alex Cobo, a hard-working, decisive man in his early sixties, was chairman of the board. Equally at home in English and Spanish, he sat behind a huge desk and took a dozen phone calls while we talked. "Over the past twenty years," he told me, "the Foundation has built up a permanent endowment of over $10 million, most of it from Colombia's private sector; it also manages bank deposits from the public that total around $42 million. The endowment supports programs in health and nutrition. In addition, for 1981, we contributed over $1 million to projects in rural education, urban development, and conservation.[46] The Foundation also administers restricted-purpose grants from international agencies, private foundations, and the Colombian government. Our work has shifted from a narrow definition of health to social development." For once, I thought, executive talent was applied to solving the country's social problems.

My brief stop at the Foundation began a hectic, two-day orientation. I was not scheduled for fieldwork, Dr. Alfredo Aguirre explained, until I understood the logic behind El Valle's approach to health. Alfredo was in his forties; he headed up the Center for Health Development, a subprogram at the Foundation that assisted health projects in several regions of Colombia. "What's the point of seeing a single piece in a puzzle," he asked me, "if you can't tell where it fits? We'll start at the top and work our way down. Next on the agenda is the Health Department."

Dr. Himbad Gartner—tall, graying, and thin—was a graduate of El Valle's medical school; he headed up program coordination for El Valle's Health Department. His office wall was covered with an enormous map that pinpointed every health post in the province.

"Between 1970 and 1980," he said, "infant mortality rates in Cali dropped from 60 per 1,000 to 37; in rural areas they fell from 98 to 49. The key is a community approach to health. We didn't draw up health districts in an air-conditioned office. Where a health post is located has to make sense in economic, cultural, and social terms; it can't simply be based on the convenience of planners. A health district's boundaries have to be defined from the community's perspective. In urban areas, we have to respect the neighborhood divisions people recognize. We used the same approach in the countryside. El Valle's population is about 25 percent rural. To maximize access, we surveyed each rural district to identify sites near markets or along transportation routes.

"Each rural nucleus—and there are several hundred in the province—has a promotora. From the local hospital, health teams rotate to the rural clinics. In terms of physical access, the province's health system reaches about 93 percent of the population—probably the best coverage in Colombia. But if coverage means inclusion in a systematically applied health program, the figure is more like 68 percent. In El Valle, medical attention is subdivided according to target groups: maternal-infant care, school children, adults, and the elderly. How do we decide which aspects of treatment and prevention we should stress? We have to identify which diseases and health hazards pose the greatest risks to each group in specific localities. Then we work surveillance, treatment, and prevention into the protocols followed at the clinics, all the way to the promotora. A health system that is strong at the base is more flexible. Vaccinations, for example, are well accepted and coverage is high. So we concentrate on problems like child malnutrition and high blood pressure.

"I've talked about health, but that is only a place to start. Health can't be isolated from other aspects of life." The Community Development Center was a case in point. Backed by the Health Department, the university, and the Education Foundation, the rural Centers promoted health education, family gardens, agricultural extension, and handicrafts. "What does it cost to build and equip a Center?" I asked Himbad. "At maximum, 10 million pesos [$100,000]," he replied, "and that's cheap. Basic development doesn't cost much—it's a bargain. With a hundred Centers we could transform rural development, and it would cost less than Cartagena's convention center, less than an airport or a luxury hotel."

I left Dr. Gartner's office with a packet of reports, manuals, and brochures. At each stop, the collection expanded. What follows is a summary of my interviews and project documents, along with observations of my own.

Getting Things Done

El Valle province was broken down into nine health regions—each with a general or intermediate hospital—and forty-eight districts—most with health centers. Finally, there were several hundred health posts managed by promotoras. Low-risk cases and primary care were handled at the health post, with referrals made for more specialized treatment. A health team rotated to the clinics and provided supervision. But it would be a mistake to view the health post as a terminal unit in a tidy system. For treatment was only one objective; prevention was equally important. The "system," in fact, opened out to a less tractable world of health committees, neighborhoods, and families. So a health post was only a first step. To reduce infant mortality and improve public health, the project had to upgrade skills, work with health committees, identify risks, target specific groups, and coordinate referrals. It was one thing to have an outline on paper (see Figure 2.2), quite another to get results. To make sure that programs had an impact on health conditions was first and foremost hard work.

The same rigor the university brought to medical specialization in the 1950s

Figure 2.2 Decentralized Health Care: El Valle

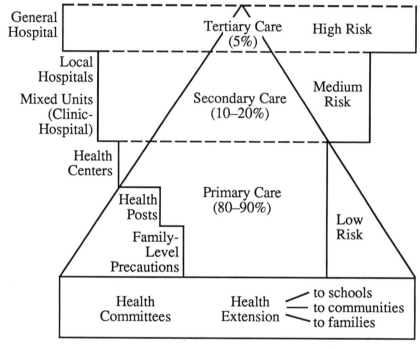

Source: Adapted from "Propuesta para el desarrollo de un programa de atención primaria en salud y Medicina Familiar," mimeographed (Facultad de Salud-Universidad del Valle, Cali, 1983), p. 22–b.

and 1960s resurfaced in community health. Training illustrates the point. Given the levels of medical attention—from health post to hospital—and the range of personnel involved—from nurse auxiliaries and dental technicians to public health agents and promotoras—the Health Department had to gear education to the specific group in question and the settings in which it worked. Nurse auxiliaries, for instance, had a secondary education and a year of special training. Some worked in hospitals, others in health centers; in rural areas they rotated to the health posts as part of a team. Consequently, no single scheme for ongoing education could be applied: a distinction had to be made between nurse auxiliaries in hospitals, those in urban clinics, and those assigned to rural health posts.

Programs had to be evaluated, changed, tested, and applied. This could not be done without good "administration." I use the word cautiously, as it usually implies a specialty taught from a six-pound textbook. The least relevant "school" for training is all too often the world of work. At the University of El Valle, by contrast, fieldwork at the clinics was a degree requirement for health administrators. Just as a physician's training had to reflect Colombia's circumstances, an administrator started with the requirements of community health. As was stressed on numerous occasions, the Health Department's personnel did not just stay in the office: "How can we implement something without fieldwork first?" To facilitate practical application, administrators held joint appointments at the university or they helped organize research projects.

Research at El Valle was action-oriented. Dr. Jaime Rodríguez, whose specialty was social medicine, outlined the research scheme. He was dressed in a suit and tie, and started out with a formal presentation. Once he concluded my interest was genuine, we adjourned to the nearest café.

"The strategy," he said, "is to focus teaching and research on local health problems. Application comes as new directives for health promotion are implemented at the clinics. Research on tuberculosis, for example, began at the health posts close to the community. We first tracked the incidence and distribution of the disease. Then we designed a program for surveillance and prevention that changed clinic protocols and was incorporated into continuing education cycles, special workshops, and manuals. Application occurs at all levels: from the medical school's curriculum to the measures families take to reduce risks. This also changes health administration, since you revise programs.

"Research is a joint venture between the university and the Health Department; work is done in teams, which always include members from relevant administrative units. The objective, after all, is not mere diagnosis but application and results. There are standing research teams for maternal-infant care, family nutrition, adult health, minor surgery, and administration. The adult research division recently completed studies on high blood pressure. To improve detection and patient education, the Health Department provided special training for thirty nurses and eighty nurse auxiliaries in Cali. Later, the work was extended to include rural promotoras in a neighboring county. Finally, with the support of the Health Department, the research team produced four short film strips and accompanying pamphlets. In maternal-child care, current research stresses infant icterus [jaundice] and premature births. A special program to promote breast-feeding is also under way."

The Promotora

How research could be combined with training, and even involve the community, is shown by the work of El Valle's Education Assessment Group. Its task was to evaluate the promotora's effectiveness.

The Assessment Group was an interdisciplinary research team composed of Dr. Alfredo Aguirre, two anthropologists, an artist, a photographer, and a pedagogical writer. I spent most of my time with Marta González and Diego Ceballos, anthropologists who had spent several years directing a rural theater troupe. They were both in their thirties and had five children; the oldest was ten. Diego was outspoken; he had a knack for pointed criticism illustrated by examples. He never missed the mark, but he was not offensive or abrasive. Marta had a way of listening that heard what was not said; she could read between the lines with infallible accuracy. In fact, she had been asked to visit Plan Sierra to assess the project's health program. Alfredo Aguirre, as noted before, was director of the Center for Health Development. I met Maria Cristina Jaramillo, a commercial artist, later—over a game of *Uno* at Marta and Diego's house. I never met the group's photographer or writer personally, but their work figured prominently in the group's activities. Both Diego and Alfredo had university appointments.

Previous research had concluded that the promotora's training was deficient; she failed to carry out her assigned functions and did not cooperate with the health team. El Valle's promotoras supervised over two hundred rural health posts. Although health teams rotated weekly to the posts, prevention and health education relied on the promotora's work. Given this key role, the Health Department asked the Assessment Group to design a new approach to training that could be applied to El Valle's rural districts. The group agreed to undertake the project, but it refused to base its work on studies skewed to the observations of physicians. "We accepted the health team's point of view as valid," Diego noted, "but an adequate assessment required data from the community itself and from the promotoras." The Health Department balked at funding another study, but the group persisted. For the skeptics involved in grant applications, I hasten to add that the group's budget barely covered direct expenses. Most of the time its members subsidized the project, not vice-versa.

"You have to recognize that Colombia is a mosaic of cultures and ecologies," Diego emphasized. "The North Coast, Guajira, the Cauca Valley, and the highlands are not just geographical expressions; they represent sociological divisions. Even a program as basic as maternal-child care has a cultural matrix; you can't apply the same strategy everywhere without modifications. The basic design might be the same, but, as with a tailor, you adjust each suit to fit the customer. In El Valle, we wanted to make sure our diagnosis reflected the province's economic and cultural differences, so we selected districts along the Pacific Coast, in the North, in the Cauca Valley, and in the South. In this fashion, we had districts that varied culturally—Afro-Colombians, Indian communities, and mestizo towns—and economically—districts of small crop farmers, the sugar zone, and the coffee region."

In each district, the Assessment Group members observed the promotora and the health team in situ; then they interviewed promotoras and community members: from the clinic's clientele to local leaders and traditional healers (*curanderos*). When they analyzed the results they identified common themes that crosscut districts, placing them under three separate headings: coordination with the health team, the promotora's training, and structural problems.[47] The group's critique is summarized below.

The health team, which usually included a physician, a nurse, and a dentist, was expected to coordinate its work with that of the promotora. In practice, "team" members carried out assigned tasks in isolation; they had scant sense of a group effort among themselves, much less with the promotora. Health promotion was part of the health team's mandate. When physicians did not reinforce the measures stressed by the promotora, health promotion was downgraded and the promotora along with it. Doctors viewed their main function as treatment; they did not bother with health education, which they relegated to the promotora. Then, when physicians discovered patients were not boiling water, the promotora was blamed.

The promotora was supposed to teach the community to use the health system appropriately, yet she did not clearly understand either its organization or procedures. She was expected to provide primary care to a disparate clientele (from prenatal exams for mothers to blood pressure tests for adults), to undertake home visits and patient education, and to handle vaccinations. Without direction and support from the health team, duties accumulated that were not worked into the promotora's scheduled routine. The health team wanted the promotora to stress prevention; the community, by contrast, wanted to expand the role she played in treatment. The promotora, for example, was not allowed to prescribe or dispense medications—a restriction the community opposed.

The tension between popular medicine and the formal health system posed a structural problem that reduced the promotora's effectiveness. The community usually designated its own candidate for training. People selected someone they trusted who was identified with traditional practices, like a midwife, a curandero (healer), or their kin. The promotora's training, however, downgraded folk remedies even though the community had faith in them. Popular medicine was flexible; the community saw it as a supplement rather than a substitute for the formal system. For its part, professional medicine rejected folk remedies out of hand, a prejudice that rubbed off on the promotora. She found herself divided between a world of medical folklore endorsed by the community and the "standards" imposed by the health system.

Based on the above critique, the Assessment Group set three objectives its educational strategy had to meet:

1. Strengthen both treatment and prevention at the clinic level.
2. Enlist the support of popular medicine on behalf of health promotion.
3. Improve health conditions through community action.

At this point, the assessment team was expanded to include representatives from the Health Department and from the Training Center in Cali, whose responsibilities also included the promotora.

It is always advisable to set ideal objectives, but then what? The Training Center already had a vision of the ideal promotora, complete with blueprints. To Marta and Diego, however, the task was not a better blueprint but a flexible strategy that could take into account the particular health teams, promotoras, and communities within specific districts.[48] Their view prevailed; the group designed an active approach that involved the parties to the problem in its definition and solution. Continuing education turned out to be a series of activities rather than a series of lectures.

"We can't recommend a strategy to El Valle's Health Department," Marta observed, "without testing it first—no matter how good it looks on paper." As the site for a pilot project, the Assessment Group chose the Health Region of Palmira, situated about thirty miles east of Cali; it included Candelaria, one of the communities studied previously. Palmira's thirty-two rural districts all had promotoras. Supervision was provided by five health teams that rotated to the posts from the region's health centers and local hospitals. Before the project started, Marta drove to every district in Palmira checking the distance and clocking the time—"the campesino," she laughed, "won't wait around if you're late."

The first priority—*to strengthen treatment and prevention*—depended on cooperation between the promotora and the health team. The group started with a joint session involving all the promotoras and health teams in Palmira, followed by district meetings at the health centers. Finally, the group held community meetings in each township, with the promotora and the health team in attendance. Meetings took place in the evening or on weekends.

"Our objective wasn't just to have discussions," Diego emphasized. "We had to find ways to strengthen joint efforts, to create a mutual awareness of what the problems were and the steps everyone had to take to promote their resolution. And we had to do this without creating a hostile situation in which people blamed each other. This was especially difficult given the social distance between a promotora and a doctor, and between the community and the health team. After some preliminary experimentation, we devised a series of games that prompted a spirited exchange. Once members of the health team started to participate in community meetings, they began to see their work and that of the promotora as a group effort.

"We created hypothetical situations; for example, a sick child who dies in the hospital after referral from the clinic by the promotora. The promotora has to take the doctor's role and analyze the case from his perspective. Usually, she will blame the promotora for the child's death: 'You didn't diagnose the case early enough; you're inefficient and careless.' The doctor, now playing the promotora, faults the hospital: 'They didn't take my referral seriously; they wasted time and lost the child'—a radical departure from the doctor's usual line. People knew each other's scripts so well, it was hilarious."

To help the health team, the promotoras, and the community think through the logic of a problem together, the Assessment Group designed a board game with a series of slots arranged in columns. For each row, a key word corresponded to a basic health procedure:

qué	*what* is the problem?
cómo	*how* should the problem be treated?
con qué	*with what* specific remedies?
con quién	*who* should apply the treatment?
para qué	*for what purpose* should the remedy be applied?
dónde	*where* should the treatment occur?
cuándo	*when* should the treatment be given?

"The game," Diego noted, "is a disguised version of the scientific method; it involves the same logic without the name. Once they get the knack, promotoras analyze problems better than students who hear the scientific method preached all the time." *Qué* was the hypothesis; *cómo*, the methodology; and the remaining steps, a kind of testing. The scheme could be applied to any number of health problems, whether treating dysentery or understanding the importance of safe water for household use. For example:

what is the problem?	dysentery
how should the problem be treated?	with a solution
with *what* specific remedies?	salt, sugar, and water
who should apply the treatment?	the mother
where should treatment occur?	at home
for *what purpose* should the remedy be applied?	to prevent dehydration

To help explain how the health system worked, the Assessment Group used a videotape put out by the Health Department. Although a bit general and sometimes difficult for people to follow, the tape presented an ideal version of the health system, precisely the reason why it evoked criticism. "That ambulance they showed, we called it and it never came." "How come that community has latrines and we don't?" The tape also posed questions to the community. "Do you follow the promotora's advice?" "Are you going to the local hospital for problems the health team and the promotora can resolve?"

The Assessment Group wanted to seek solutions democratically through the joint effort of the community, the promotoras, and the health team. Applying an active approach was part of the remedy, a point illustrated by the way the group pursued its second objective: *to enlist the support of popular medicine on behalf of health promotion.*

"We didn't realize how much people used the curandero," Marta told me, "or how much popular beliefs determined the community's response to promotoras and the health system. At first, we couldn't get people to talk, not even the promotora; everyone knew that educated people viewed popular beliefs with contempt. Discussing folk remedies with professionals was virtually taboo. We didn't want to stamp out popular medicine, but rather to work out an accommodation that promoted community health. People often feel more comfortable with traditional healers. When a child gets sick, they go to the curandero first; by the time they show up at the clinic, it's often too late."

The Assessment Group discussed the problem directly with the community, focusing on three topics: popular beliefs about the evil eye, local practices associated with childbirth, and the curandero's role in the community. At community meetings, people diagnosed the evil eye: its symptoms were vomiting, fevers, and dysentery; its victims were children; its cause was the evil malicious adults could inflict on families they did not like. Protection consisted of a small amulet obtained from a curandero and attached to the infant's arm. To discourage such blatant superstition, doctors routinely removed the bracelet, threw it away, and lectured the mother—a practice that drove people away from the clinic rather than encouraging its use.

To exchange views, the group devised a game called *alternagram.* It began by selecting a common health problem such as dysentery, tuberculosis, or parasitism. A series of steps were noted on the game board: consultation, suggested remedy, patient response, and final outcome. Suppose that a player chose dysentery for the game's health problem. The first step on the board was "consultation," so the player spun the wheel and turned over the card selected. This random card could read doctor, promotora, curandero, or neighbor. The next step was "remedy," so the wheel was spun again and a "remedy" card was chosen. This continued until the health sequence (consultation, suggested remedy, patient response, and final outcome) was filled in. Then the pattern was discussed and evaluated. Because there were several possible cards for each step, numerous variations were possible. For example, a child with dysentery was sent to the promotora; she made a referral to the hospital but medical treatment only made the condition worse—the child died. An alternative sequence might have led to consultation with a curandero, a folk remedy, and a recovery. Each card set led to a discussion of the two systems of medicine with their respective merits and deficiencies. The game helped players be more outspoken about what they believed—as opposed to what they knew the health team thought.

For the game called *intergram,* players assembled a large photographic puzzle. When pieced together it displayed contrasting pictures of the two health systems: a child being vaccinated versus a child wearing a charm bracelet, severe dysentery treated by a curandero versus treatment in a hospital, childbirth at home assisted by a midwife versus hospital delivery.

"The community had no objection to a preventive measure like vaccination," Marta pointed out. "Children can get injections and wear the amulet— double protection. The hospital, by contrast, provoked fear and resistance." The picture puzzle showed a two-year-old child hospitalized for dysentery— alone in its crib, hands and feet bound, and an IV attached. Restraint was a common practice because hospitals were understaffed: one nurse could easily be responsible for forty patients. "At community meetings mothers denounced such treatment as inhuman," Marta emphasized. "They'd rather have a curandero treat the child at home under their care—even if it meant the child would die—than abandoned in the hospital." This sentiment was so startling, and the rejection of the hospital so complete, that it shocked everyone on the staff.[49] As a result, the local hospital at Candelaria let mothers and curanderos attend to children, which allayed fears and made families more receptive to treatment.

"Women voiced an almost total preference for the midwife and childbirth at home," Marta continued. "They conceded that the hospital was sanitary, but they had little else to say in its favor. They considered it an alien place 'full of strangers.' The home place, by contrast, 'is filled with our smells, our things, my family, the food I am used to.' At home, women are never uncovered during childbirth; they have privacy. In the hospital, they said, 'we aren't treated with respect; they do things to suit the nurses and doctors, not the mothers.' They feared the delivery bed too, considering it more painful to give birth lying down. At home, women give birth in a squatting position on a chair—a procedure arranged for the mother's comfort, not the midwife's."

Popular belief categorized various physical states as either "hot" or "cold," a condition traditional remedies counteracted. During childbirth, for example, women were "cold" and needed warm fluids like chicken broth, soup, or hot chocolate both before and after delivery. Chewing on cinnamon stick was credited with speeding parturition. At the hospital, mothers complained, "they clean out your stomach [enema]; you get nothing to eat until after childbirth, and then it is food you don't like." Following the community's critique, local hospitals in Palmira provided traditional foods and cinnamon to chew on.

"Most promotoras have only about five years of grade school; for many people in the community, it's less. If you're not careful," Diego pointed out, "you end up with educational material that's too sophisticated. And with few exceptions, what's available on health is based on the city and its problems." Consequently, the Assessment Group produced its own material for use at community meetings. The first was a cassette tape that simulated the ever-popular radio soap opera; in this instance, the drama of a family confronted by the evil eye. The dialogue relied on colorful slang and popular characters: an outraged father who narrows his possible enemies down to a dozen, an anxious mother who does not want things stirred up, an officious doctor, and an aged, partially deaf curandero. The second was a beautiful videotape based on the life cycle: to plant (birth), to bloom (childhood), to ripen (adulthood), to return (old age). People vividly described their experiences, revealing their understanding of illness, childrearing, old age, and nature. The result was a gentle, loving portrayal created by the collaborative effort of the community, the promotoras, and the health team.

Although more happenstance than plan, the health system had set the promotora up as its advocate—a circumstance that made her an opponent of folk practices, if only by association. The Assessment Group's work altered the equation, releasing the promotora from her identification with the health system's intransigence. At the same time, the health team's participation at community meetings symbolized the beginning of a truce. Discussions focused on health promotion, but within a context that accepted popular medicine as a point of departure. Whether *alternagram*, *intergram*, or a soap opera, they all pointed to the importance the community assigned to traditional beliefs. To learn more about popular medicine, the Assessment Group, with the help of the promotoras, conducted a family survey in Palmira's districts.

Besides such basics as family size—an average of seven—they asked about the evil eye, about foods taken before and after childbirth, and about beliefs, prohibitions, and special behavior during pregnancy. Finally, they collected data on medicinal plants and herbs: those used during menstruation and pregnancy, or for specific ailments. The communities liked the attention: "If we skipped someone," Diego laughed, "they complained to the promotora." The study not only generated interest; it also helped build rapport: between the health teams, the promotoras, and the Assessment Group in designing the questionnaire, and between the promotoras and the community in its execution.

The Assessment Group had yet to tackle its third objective—*to improve health conditions through community action*—at least not formally. The steps already taken pulled communities into discussions about health care and folk medicine; the data collected in the survey would be presented in each district— and interest ran high. So in the process of pursuing its first two objectives, the group had laid the groundwork for active health committees and community-oriented projects.

El Tiple

I visited some of Palmira's districts with Marta and Diego; we stopped at El Tiple and dropped by the promotora's house, jumping over sewage ditches to get there. Mercedes lived in a cement-block house with brightly painted floors and walls: maroons, blues, and lavenders. The living room had plastic-covered aquamarine armchairs and a coffee table with a holy picture: Jesus driving the moneychangers from the temple. She brought in some stools from the kitchen and offered us "refrescos." Ignoring our polite no-thank you, she produced three orange-flavored beverages and one Coke. With impeccable logic, the Coke went to me.

Mercedes was in her late twenties, olive-skinned with long black hair, strong-willed, capable. Clinic hours were from 8:00 A.M. to noon and from 2:00 to 6:00 P.M. She put in about nine hours a day, which included an average of eight house calls. Time was set aside each day for routine diagnosis; she staggered targeted programs throughout the week—prenatal sessions, child care, and tuberculosis control. Based on risk, she scheduled appointments for patients with the health team; she administered the clinic and kept records; and she was trained in first aid and emergency childbirth. Mercedes listed the district's most prevalent health problems as parasitic diseases, dysentery, malnutrition, colds, and lung problems.

"The health post here is very busy," she told me. "That's not true everywhere. The important thing is to understand people and gain their respect. You need the community's confidence; it takes time and patience. There are a lot of frustrations; you make appointments and people come late or don't show up. Cooperation with the health team is very important, but it depends on the doctor's attitude. One year the doctor contributes a lot, and the next year he's not interested; the health team changes too much.

"The community accepts vaccinations, but they don't like physicals or tests for TB. They realize that if a curandero doesn't help they should come to the clinic. We used to feel we had to compete with the curanderos, but now there is more cooperation; the curandero can go into the hospital, which helps patients psychologically. You try to get the two systems to help each other. I let mothers mix a pinch of herbs in with the solution recommended for dysentery. If it doesn't hurt the treatment, a popular practice helps motivation. There are some things we can't do, like make injections directly into the vein; people want us to—they think it's more effective."

Mercedes was anxious to have the study on popular medicine discussed with the community. "People keep asking me; they don't want to miss it." The Assessment Group already had presented preliminary results at a two-day conference in Cali attended by health teams, administrators, and promotoras from surrounding areas. It provoked so much discussion that the group had to add on extra hours. El Tiple's promotora opened the conference—with a spirited didactic poem (*trova*) composed for the occasion.

Roldanillo

The Training Center held short courses that reinforced the promotora's skills. This was reasonable for Cali and surrounding areas like Palmira. Health regions in the North such as Roldanillo and Zarzal, however, were too far away to use the Training Center systematically. The rationale behind the promotora project was to gear continuing education to locales, which was difficult from a facility so tied to Cali. A different approach was required for the North where the rural population was more widely dispersed. In Palmira, for example, sugar plantations had pushed out the small proprietor; the rural work force lived in relatively concentrated settlements. Dispersed coffee farms, by contrast, were more characteristic of the northern highlands, even though agribusiness predominated down in the valley. Diego's recommendation was for a mobile training team that could rotate through the North, drawing promotoras together from adjacent health districts. The Health Department supported the plan; my visit provided the pretext for a brief field trip.

Situated in the narrow, northern neck of the Cauca Valley some 140 miles from Cali, Roldanillo was the headquarters for Health Region 8. Diego, Marta, and I left early, stopping for coffee along the way. To this we added *pan de uno*, a small biscuit-sized cheese bread with the texture of an English muffin. The day before, El Tiple's promotora had lectured me about smoking. I drank my coffee without lighting up in a futile attempt to apply health promotion to myself.

We met with Flavio Rangel, director of the Roldanillo Health Region and a graduate of El Valle's M.A. program in health administration. The local program's top priority was community education. Roldanillo's health teams, for example, worked directly with twenty-six health committees. Dressed in blue jeans and a short-sleeved shirt, Flavio was not exactly the stereotypic administrator. A more apt description would be community organizer.

"You have to take an active approach to health," Flavio stressed. "If you don't, you go backwards. In rural areas, communities are dispersed; you can't centralize basic development. That's why you have health posts, rotating teams, and promotoras. When it comes to community education, the nurse is the team leader. If doctors help, it's only for credibility; the nurses do the work.

"For training, supervision, and referrals, each promotora is linked to one of the region's local hospitals at Bolívar, El Dovio, or Roldanillo. For the promotora, the key is continuing education and support from the health team—which means doing a better job on the health team's orientation. In public health, priorities include more accessible health posts, a safe water supply, and the construction of latrines. The communities, through the health committees, have organized effective campaigns for better waste disposal. Granted, not all the committees are equally active, but there are some exceptional groups, especially in the coffee-producing areas. To create greater awareness about health, you have to begin with education—about sanitation at home, about how to treat dysentery, about nutrition during pregnancy. And it has to be done in terms people can understand."

Roldanillo had a special health program in the schools. Teachers were trained in primary care and nutrition; they worked with the health committees to draw up plans and set priorities. The strategy was to reach the children at school and the adults through the health committees. The dental program had mobile units that circulated to the schools and clinics. "There is only so much a dentist can do," Flavio said. "People live on carbohydrates and *panela* (brown-sugar cakes). You have to match treatment with prevention, which is why education in small groups is so important, especially for school children."

Tierra Blanca, a few miles from Roldanillo, was the site for one of El Valle's Community Development Centers. The health team supported joint programs with the Center: family gardens to improve nutrition, and campaigns to vaccinate farm animals against rabies. Local health committees and farmers' cooperatives provided a base for the Center's work. Nonetheless, the Center's impact was restricted to its immediate locale. Regional agencies had yet to design a systematic approach to extension that combined health, agriculture, and education. Specific groups had programs at the Center—for example, Roldanillo's technical high school offered extension classes. However, the only regional agency that had a unified strategy was the Health Department: from treatment to community education and public health.

Being keen on community action, Flavio arranged a meeting with Cascarillo's health committee that afternoon. Then he left on his rounds. Diego, Marta, and I went into town for lunch, passing several posters that announced a week-long health fair in nearby Tulia. I had a helping of rice and beans, which I mixed with cassava, cabbage, and carrots, and downed with beer; I lit up my first cigarette of the day. After coffee, we assembled in the courtyard of Roldanillo's hospital, awaiting a jeep. By now it was midafternoon; the sun had reached its punishing best, working havoc on my injudicious mixture of cabbage, beer, and cigarettes. I headed dizzily for the nearest shade tree. Propped up against the trunk, my dizziness was in retreat—and then in rout. I had blocked an anthill with my posterior; the ants were biting mad, and everywhere. I jumped up, reverting to my native language for some choice expletives. Diego and Marta ran over to help, brushing off ants between fits of laughter.

The jeep finally pulled in; mercifully, I ceased to be the center of attention. Because many of El Valle's mountain settlements lacked electricity, the jeep had a generator adapted for the health team's audiovisual material. Two nurses had decided to come with us; they worked at Cascarillo on weekends, but took advantage of an occasion like this to make an extra visit. While we waited for them, a young doctor recognized Diego; he had been sent to Roldanillo for his year of rural service and had signed up for another year; he had great praise for Flavio.

Cascarillo is only ten miles from Roldanillo, tucked back in the mountains that line the valley's western edge. The road started out in a flourish of paved hospitality, changed itself to gravel, then to dirt, and finally to muddy ruts: user-unfriendly to everyone but the mule. Even by jeep, it took us almost an hour to get there. Several thousand feet above the Cauca River, Cascarillo's cool breezes warded off the afternoon's heat. The hamlet's thirty-four houses were strung out amidst coffee trees shaded by guava and banana groves. Most of the families derived a living from their small coffee farms.

We met in Cascarillo's Community Center, an open-air veranda with a sandy floor and a thatched roof spread over wooden beams braced by posts. An afternoon meeting was unusual—community gatherings normally took place in the evening when the day's chores were finished. When the health team held community education sessions, or met with the local health committee, it was invariably at night or on a weekend.

About twenty people attended the Cascarillo meeting, held specifically for us. The head of the town council summarized various projects. Cascarillo had built the Community Center and a health post at its own expense. Its health committee had organized a vaccination campaign that covered all the town's families. Because Cascarillo did not have a pharmacy, the town council stocked the health post with medicines—sold to families at cost. The previous week, the community had finished vaccinating farm animals and pets against rabies.

Diego was asked to speak. He described the Training Center and the Assessment Group's work with Palmira's promotoras. Inadvertently, he touched on a sore point. Cascarillo did not have a promotora. The community had selected someone, but she refused to leave her family for training in Cali. People preferred the old system in which each hospital trained its promotoras. "Sending a young woman to Cali isn't sensible, and, besides, it's dangerous." "She's going to work here in Cascarillo—what does Cali have to do with it?" A general listing of Cali's faults ensued, which bore a generic resemblance to small-town views of New York City. Diego finally got things back on course, noting that the Health Department was considering a mobile training team. The town council agreed to write a letter of support if Diego would deliver it in person.

By the end of the meeting most of the town's residents had drifted down to the Community Center. They stepped from the road into the meeting place, acknowledging all assembled with a loud *buenas tardes*, a courtesy returned in unison. The etiquette of proper entrance took precedence over speaking rights: everything stopped for the greeting ritual.

The visiting American provoked considerable curiosity. After Diego got called on, I realized I was not to be spared. I was still a bit frantic when they asked "Señor Jaime" for his views on health. "Doctors and nurses," I said, "can't do everything; they need strong community support. A health post treats people, but prevention has to be a family and community effort. The people of Cascarillo already know this; the Community Center and the health post show what can be accomplished by working together. The United States has many poor people; we don't have promotoras or health teams that work with the community. Some people think development only means roads and airports, but it also means health committees and community action."

Cascarillo had electricity and technology's version of the evil eye—TV. Colombia imported programs from the United States, which meant a healthy dose of hospital melodrama. The people of Cascarillo caught the incongruous association of the United States with the word "poor," and a suggestion of less than ideal health care. It did not wash. "The United States," they pointed out, "is a rich country, isn't it; it has everything. Then how can some people be poor?" "You have lots of hospitals and doctors, so much equipment; why can't you take care of everybody?" Like they say, a little knowledge is a dangerous thing.

I will spare you my answers: inadequate then, inadequate now. The community's residents finally accepted the possibility of poor families in America—however temporary. After all, to be in a city without a job, and poorly educated, was part of the Colombian recipe for poverty, too. But they refused to accept the logic of private medicine as practiced in the United States.

They asked us to stay for a meeting of the School Committee that evening. It was already dusk and we still had to get back to Cali, so Diego declined on behalf of his five children back home. We compromised on a tour of the local schoolhouse. We followed a path through coffee and fruit trees that led to a spectacular bluff with vistas on three sides. It was a school to turn out poets. Flowers lined the entranceway, and children kept a garden in back; there were no broken windows, no graffiti. The panorama looked across the Cauca Valley to the Central Range beyond. On the plain below, we could see the lights of Roldanillo and Bolívar; above, the evening star.

• A Review

What the Colombian projects accomplished was based on a systematic approach to health care. For treatment, a health post network maximized access; projects defined risk assessment in terms that were both cultural and medical, they stressed treatment at the appropriate level, and they targeted programs by priority: prenatal care, nutrition control, tuberculosis. Prevention depended on education and public health measures applied both at home and in the community. Physicians and nurses provided supervision. To help people understand what health care meant in practical terms, projects relied on the promotora and community action. Much of the work was routine; rigidity and complacency were always a hazard. Training programs helped counter the tendency. There were internships, rotating health teams, continuing education programs, and collaboration with neighborhood health committees. Research identified which health problems should have priority, and it turned up gaps between theory and practice, as the Assessment Group's work with the promotora demonstrated.

The lesson the projects taught went beyond building health posts. Treatment, prevention, training, and research had to reach into neighborhoods and communities. Consequently, projects could not impose prefabricated solutions. They had to work in a flexible way that respected the differences between localities and fostered participation—a tall order by any standard.

Consider El Valle's Assessment Group. To apply its work elsewhere, it would have to take the characteristics of different health districts into account. The basic approach might be the same, but mere duplication would be insufficient. Even then, its impact would not be the same everywhere. Some districts would always lag behind with health committees that were fictitious, with promotoras who did not want their routines disturbed, with health teams that simply bided time. In the end, I think that Marta and Diego worked on faith. "For every door that closes," Marta told me, "another one opens."

• Trumpets

The mind wanders in airports. On Marta's advice, I had checked in early at Cali's terminal for an Avianca flight to Bogotá at four o'clock.

The words of preacher Robinson occurred to me: "Gabriel's trumpet called the earth's people to apocalypse. The Saved crowded self-selected by Heaven's Gate: self-assured, comparing notes, eager for salvation. The damned: knowing it in their hearts and silent in their shame, huddled in the distance. The earth shook in terror and judgment. Hell swallowed up the Saved. Heaven embraced the dispossessed."

Black preacher James Robinson, I recalled, had talked in sermons that hot New York City summer of 1969. By then, he had passed seventy and survived two heart attacks. Robinson had founded Operation Crossroads Africa in 1957; each year, groups of Crossroaders spent the summer in African countries. Along with their African counterparts, they worked on development projects. My destination in 1969 was the Gambia; I was a project leader. As was characteristic of Crossroads, the contingent sent to the Gambia was "interracial"—an adjective called upon so frequently the hyphen is omitted, as if mere language could substitute for practice. Crossroads dealt with race in action more than words. For his efforts, Robinson ended up on the FBI's list for un-American activities. Hoover was certainly right: the Melting Pot is for worship only.

Crossroads Africa subsidized the cost of participation, as few of us could pay for the program. Fund-raising covered the deficits, an endless and never quite successful struggle against red ink. Robinson once got a check for

$100,000, he told us, from Mafia boss Frank Costello. It came with a note attached: "for the competition." Robinson convened his board of directors; after much deliberation, it decided not to accept "laundered money." Robinson said he certainly agreed, which is why he had "already cashed the check."

The United States trusts there is no God to judge the world at Heaven's Gate. A $3.6 trillion gross national product anchors the earthly scale to its advantage—against a paltry $39 billion for a country like Colombia.[50] Despite its wealth, the United States bickers over food stamps—not even the crumbs from its table. The rich are supposed to find salvation as difficult as camels squeezing through the needle's eye; but in the United States, the self-proclaimed affinity for salvation rises with income. Religion is perverted to a shoddy Jesus slicked up by TV charlatans, to dial-a-Bible scriptures and bombed abortion clinics.

I come from a clever country, I thought, that practices but does not believe. No God, no trumpet, and no judgment. Lucky for us. "Flight 226 now boarding for Bogotá"—garbled unintelligibly in English, backed up, fortunately, in Spanish. I started for the gate. How presumptuous to stamp our coins in God's name, as if He were our private monopoly. Blasphemy. "Ye who count thyselves as two and thy neighbor as one believe not and are not saved," said Cotton Mather.

We boarded at 4:00 P.M., only to be deplaned without explanation. Like their airline counterparts in the United States, Avianca proved short on specifics. I came prepared with Loren Eiseley's *The Unexpected Universe*. Transistor radios appeared. Torrential rain, we learned, had knocked out the electrical system at "Eldorado," Bogotá's airport—a situation described as temporary.

Robinson's first and last advice had been "expect the unexpected." How often I recited that in 1969 and since. So I dreamed of Africa and Robinson's sermons—their dignity and strength, dipped into Eiseley, and chased rum with black coffee. My mind raced. Which universe is it that stalks us? I was once much given to religion. Scarce shelf space has long since consigned St. Augustine, Francis of Assisi, and assorted Papal Encyclicals to used bookstores. I kept Thomas Merton: *Seven Story Mountain, The Birds of Appetite,* and his translation of Chuang-Tsu. Eiseley, however, is about as close as I get to meditation now. I went back to the bar.

Training promotoras will not change anything. Plan Sierra is great, if you think an extra ton of cassava matters. They are either crazy or know something I do not. Why do they do it, can't they see it is hopeless? We are going to annihilate the planet, blow it away. Everyone knows that. We cannot build weapons of destruction indefinitely and not use them indefinitely. Only an idiot could believe that. "Flight 226 now boarding." I grabbed my passport and ran to the gate—Eldorado, opened at last.

I fastened my seat belt and tried to sleep. Apostates preach, those farthest from religion have the greatest faith. Colombia has guerrilla warfare and drug trafficking; half the country is destitute. How can Diego believe in promotoras? It is not logical, it is faulty analysis, it is. . . . The captain interrupted, ordered seat belts fastened, and beat a hasty retreat to Cali's airport—another blackout in Bogotá.

Avianca had only one attendant to find hotels and taxis for two hundred irate passengers. It was a matter of principle—it was also 1:00 A.M. I got my own taxi and headed for town. We live in a world of canceled flights, of Eldorados with faulty wiring: a universe run down, a red dwarf star. To sift the burning embers is a great and noble act, to draw out hope against the odds—an unexpected universe.

3
SMALL FARMS

In the 1950s, most Latin American countries had equated development with industrialization. The emphasis was hardly surprising, given the region's past experience. Dependence on commodities like coffee and sugar had fostered a boom-to-bust syndrome. Rising demand and high prices engendered overproduction and hard times. The Great Depression proved the point. Demand for primary products in the industrial world collapsed, and so did commodity prices. The conditions the depression created, however, provided a rationale for manufacturing. Unable to afford the imports their economies needed, countries fostered domestic production as a substitute. Consequently, the advocates of export agriculture lost the influence they had once exerted over economic policy; the state promoted manufacturing and cast its lot with industrialists.

Even though commodities still dominated Latin America's exports, industry became the most dynamic sector. During the 1950s, for example, manufacturing in Colombia and Brazil expanded by over 8 percent annually.[1] Granted that the regional trend did not apply everywhere, and that when it did the timing of events varied, most countries ended up with a modernized urban economy and a backward rural one.

The assumption that domestic industries held the key to development depended on a rapidly growing market. In the early years, when domestic firms started to replace imported textiles, footwear, paper products, and consumer durables, they could hardly do so fast enough. Eventually, however, they saturated the market and growth rates slowed to replacement levels. The culprit once again was agriculture.

• Trends in Agriculture

In the 1960s, almost half the region's population still lived in rural areas.[2] But agriculture was slow to adopt modern techniques. Yields were low, large estates had vast holdings they left unused, and the sector's sharecroppers and small farmers were impoverished. Modernizing agriculture was expected to boost productivity and income, turning the rural population into consumers. This was to be achieved by combining new production methods—from improved seeds to soil additives and tractors—with land reform. Because rural families would not be reliable consumers without a dependable income, dividing up unproductive estates had to be the first step. To displace powerful landowners for the benefit of sharecroppers, however, was not the brand of politics most countries could implement. So they had to skip the first step. The result has been a technical success and a social failure. By ignoring the social inequities that already existed, the state's intervention only reinforced them. Considering the policies adopted, this is hardly surprising.[3]

Export agriculture had long been the most privileged. It had access to financing, to marketing services, and to transportation. To modernize other sectors of agriculture, the state expanded subsidized credit, promoted mechanization, improved storage facilities, and created an efficient distribution system. The overall results were impressive. Between 1970 and 1980, the area devoted to crops increased by 18 percent and the harvested volume by over 30 percent. Poultry production almost doubled, and the egg supply grew by half. Beef and pork output jumped by an average of 30 percent, and milk registered an increase of 37 percent.[4] Agriculture kept ahead of the region's population growth. So did the sector's inputs. If progress is tallied by the number of tractors used (up 42 percent), the quantity of fertilizer consumed (up 88 percent), and the volume of pesticides applied (up 75 percent), then progress there was.[5] On the other hand, if who benefited is considered, a few qualifications are in order.

Credit went primarily to those who had the collateral and the know-how to use it profitably. The backward hacienda of the past became the successful agribusiness enterprise of the present. Given their education, their wealth, and their connections, the old landlords were in the best position to understand what market access, cheap credit, and mechanization meant. As they adopted new technology, they undercut one rationale for land reform. For mechanization reduced reliance on sharecroppers and tenants, the very clientele land distribution was supposed to assist. Reduced to the status of migrant labor without the right to even a subsistence plot, rural families headed for the cities.[6] Between 1960 and 1980, the portion of the region's population that was rural declined from a majority to 35 percent.[7]

Small farmers, even if they held title to their land, rarely benefited from the state's incentive program. Lacking sufficient assets, unable to fill out forms, and caught in the clutches of assorted middlemen, they were the kind of high-risk, time-consuming clients the banks avoided.

Big producers gained the most, small holders profited little, and share-croppers lost out. That being the case, it is not surprising that income distribution in agriculture ended up even more inequitable.[8] Despite modernization, most rural families were still poor. In 1981, 60 percent lived in conditions of poverty, over half of them indigent.[9] Nor did their ranks decline. Between 1960 and 1980, the rural population increased by 15 million, even though the cities gained in relative terms.[10] The vision planners had of prosperous rural families lined up for transistor radios and refrigerators was still a long way off. Development under the aegis of state-supported agribusiness simply generated a different version of the old social structure.

Was the cost modernization imposed compensated for by increased production? The statistics lose much of their luster when scrutinized. Crop production is a good example. Export commodities like soybeans, sugarcane, and cocoa did the best. The output of staples like potatoes, corn, and beans lagged far behind.[11] The reason was that big producers either favored exports or concentrated on the supermarkets, fast-food chains, and salad bars so popular with the middle class. Food processing in all its frozen and reconstituted forms became a vertically integrated growth industry. The result was a system prejudicial to the crops the majority depended on.[12] By the late 1970s, the region's food imports were increasing twice as fast as during the previous decade.[13]

Agribusiness cornered the export and specialty markets. For dietary staples, by contrast, the region still relied on small farmers. At the beginning of the 1980s, they accounted for 80 percent of all holdings but only 20 percent of the available land. On this, they grew half the region's corn, 60 percent of its potatoes, and 75 percent of its beans. Overall, small farmers produced 40 percent of the food destined for domestic markets, and they did so without the credit subsidies and expensive technology agribusiness depended on.[14]

There were good reasons then for governments to reassess developments in agriculture. Mechanization had driven migrants to the city faster than the urban economy could employ them. Those who stayed behind were still too poor to be consumers for the city's industries. Having invested in the infrastructure that made large-scale production profitable, countries ended up with food deficits they had to cover with imports. Given the rapid population growth in the cities, self-sufficiency in food crops had become a matter of considerable urgency.[15] A new strategy took shape, this time geared specifically to small farmers. Colombia's "integrated" approach to rural development is a case in point.

How did events in Colombia differ from the regional trends sketched above? In the 1960s, the government went a bit further with land reform than was true elsewhere. It allotted some 88,000 parcels comprising 2.8 million hectares: this represented about 6 percent of the country's farm families and 10 percent of its agricultural land. Most of this "distribution," however, involved squatters already settled on public land; only 200,000 hectares were actually expropriated.[16] Still, legal title meant security for thousands of family farms.

During the 1970s, even the cautious definition of land reform lost favor. Agrarian policy stressed modernization. The result followed the regional pattern: consolidation of estates, migration to the cities, and neglect of food crops. In the fertile Cauca Valley, for instance, the sugar industry expanded at the expense of small holders. Along the Atlantic coast, credit helped the region's landlords convert to cotton and ranching.[17]

Although the Agrarian Bank also helped small farmers, it was mostly in the coffee zone that extension and credit reached them on a regular basis. This reflected the sector's atypical characteristics. Colombia relied on coffee as its chief export, and small holders had dominated production since the 1930s. Well-organized and relatively prosperous, they were too important to simply be displaced.[18]

The allegation that agribusiness was a social failure also has to be qualified. Consider Colombia's rice. The introduction of a high-yielding irrigated variety made the country self-sufficient, and at a much higher level of consumption. Between 1966 and 1982, output tripled. As a result, prices fell and rice became Colombia's main staple. So although the large producers took advantage of new technology, credit, and irrigation, it was the urban poor, who were disproportionately the country's rice consumers, who gained the most.[19]

Regardless of how Colombia's agribusiness is assessed, the lot of the rural poor stayed much the same. Like other countries, Colombia had a stake in rural development. Poverty was antithetical to consumption, and small farmers still played a major role in food production. If that was insufficient, guerrilla movements in the countryside provided a justification based on national security.

Colombia's integrated approach to rural development began in the late 1970s. Both liberal and conservative administrations have supported it. So has the World Bank. The strategy's weak point is coordination.[20] Field-workers understood this perfectly well. They focused on project management, and so does this report.

The account begins in Bogotá at the Colombian branch of the Inter-American Institute for Cooperation on Agriculture—hereafter referred to as "the Institute." Just as the Pan American Health Organization plays a regional role in health programs, the Institute provides technical assistance to member countries, only in this case, for agriculture. Both are affiliated with the Organization of American States. The Institute's headquarters is in San José, Costa Rica, which I visited in 1982. In addition, each member country has a national Institute office.

The question posed by the Colombian project is how the work of different agencies can be reorganized to benefit small farmers. Most countries, Colombia included, already have extension programs, agrarian banks, and marketing organizations. But they were designed with commercial agriculture in mind. Big producers have entrepreneurial experience and can afford to take risks. The small farmer, by contrast, has much less room for maneuver. To be successful, each step in technical assistance has to be carefully coordinated, from training sessions to marketing arrangements. And with small farmers, it is hard to get the kind of quick results that occurred with rice. Reshaping agencies and their services takes time.

This report is about getting things done. People explain how an integrated project is organized and the steps involved.

• Rural Development

At the Institute's Bogotá office I met Alfonso Bejarano, a program director. A Colombian in his late forties, he quickly established how little I knew about the Institute's work in Colombia. With a mixture of enthusiasm and resignation, he forged ahead with a basic orientation. "The Institute emphasizes practical research, rural development geared to small farmers, and training programs that strengthen national agencies active in the rural sector. There is no single Institute—there are twenty-seven; each country's office develops its own agenda in collaboration with national programs. The Institute is a technical assistance organization; we do not have funds for projects of our own. If a country wants to help small farmers, it is likely to draw on the Institute's staff.

"Colombia has half a million farms with less than 20 hectares [1 hectare = 2.47 acres]; they produce almost 40 percent of the country's food. To increase food production, raise farm incomes, and reduce urban migration, Colombia started a rural development program in 1976 called DRI: Desarrollo Rural Integrado; it included seventeen rural districts in eight provinces. The program's key agency was Colombia's Extension Service whose responsibilities included food production and technical assistance. During the early 1970s, the Extension Service had advocated an integrated approach to rural development. It helped set up several pilot projects. The program increased budgets for rural agencies active in DRI districts such as the Extension Service and the Agrarian Bank. Similarly, additional funds went to training [SENA], cooperative marketing [CECORA], and natural resources [INDERENA]. The problem was that each agency had its own program and a separate budget. There was some cooperation, but not a combined strategy for each district.

"Before the DRI program expanded further, the Institute was asked to conduct an evaluation, with special attention to project management. Rural development requires joint planning, local participation, and skillful direction—three parts work for each part money. I don't mean to downplay funding,

Figure 3.1 DRI Organization for Rural Development in Colombia

Production

Technical Assistance: Extension Service
Farm Credit: Agrarian Bank
Training: SENA
Marketing CECORA
Natural Resources: INDERENA

Social Services

Water Supply
Health Clinics
School Construction
Teaching

Public Works

Roads
Electrification

but a project comes with more than just a price tag. It is a way to accomplish things. A project isn't something to buy, it's something to do. To do it right requires a good approach to management.

"We conducted the evaluation with the Extension Service; it cited poorly defined interagency objectives, unsatisfactory coordination, and overcentralized decision making.[21] We proposed lateral management, a strategy we called PROPLAN, which pushes back planning and coordination as close to the farmer as possible. The agencies responsible for *production*—from extension to credit and marketing—draw up a common strategy, executed jointly and supported by a single budget. Similarly, *social services* and *public works* are part of a district's overall plan of action. (See Figure 3.1.) In 1979, we started out in Pamplona, a pilot district located in the province of Norte de Santander; we presented results to DRI district directors in 1980. As of 1983, eighteen districts had adopted PROPLAN. By then DRI had entered its second phase, adding fourteen new districts in eight provinces."[22]

"Why," I asked Alfonso, "don't you dismantle agencies, wipe the slate clean, and start over?"

"A better plan could be devised," he agreed, "but there isn't time to reinvent a new scheme for each country. You have to work with the agencies already there. PROPLAN decentralizes administration; agencies have a common agenda based on each district's situation, and results can be assessed consistently. To change procedures is possible, to eliminate agencies is impossible."

My four hours of sleep was starting to show. I did not have the stamina to ask Alfonso to be more precise about the wonders of PROPLAN. And I doubt he relished going over them. So I asked for background material. He returned with about fifty pounds of pamphlets. We chatted about Plan Sierra and my prior visit to the Institute's headquarters in San José. What I really wanted was to visit Pamplona but I could not just impose myself. I mentioned my fleeting exposure to planning documents in San José. "What did you think?" he asked. "Totally unintelligible," I replied honestly. He was sipping coffee and practically dropped his cup laughing. He mentioned that Enrique Polo, one of the Institute's consultants, had to go to Pamplona the day after tomorrow. I jumped at the chance to go along. We arranged plane tickets to Cúcuta, capital of Norte de Santander and headquarters for the province's DRI districts. In the meantime, I resigned myself to PROPLAN pamphlets and pineapple pizzas, a Bogotá specialty.

Why take a good idea like rural development and hog-tie it in management flow charts? I met Enrique Polo at the airport, a bit on the skeptical side.

Cúcuta

The morning drew forth a spectacular blue, the view marred only by the eroded mountainsides below. Located about 390 miles north of Bogotá and east of the mountains, Cúcuta shares a lowland plain with neighboring Venezuela. It is a pleasant city with many trees; its spacious central square is a marvel of shade and flowers, a welcome relief from tropical heat. Cúcuta is a border town of over 400,000. Its hotels, restaurants, and shops used to draw a steady clientele from Venezuela, because their oil-rich currency, the bolivar, outclassed the cheaper Colombian peso.

Cúcuta's businessmen kept their savings in bolivars as a hedge against inflation and a weak peso. Venezuela, however, unexpectedly devalued against the dollar early in 1983. In a single day, the value of bolivar-stashed savings dropped by half—from 16 pesos to 8 pesos. By the time I got to Cúcuta, the bolivar had recuperated to 10 pesos, but not the tourist trade. Compared to the year before, Cúcuta was now almost twice as expensive. So was Miami; 1983 was a great year to buy a condominium in south Florida from bankrupt Venezuelans. In Cúcuta there were unfinished hotels and vacant

Map 3.1 Norte de Santander Province

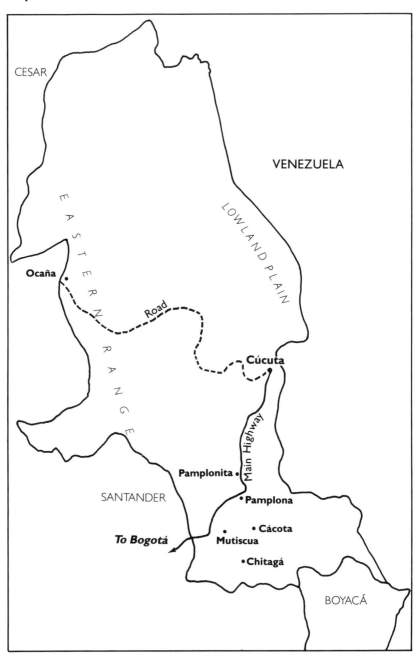

office buildings everywhere. The world's volatile money markets had left the Cúcuta rich insolvent and 20 percent of the poor unemployed. Protecting cash assets fed a rampant speculation in U.S. dollars that began on the streets of Bogotá and reached up to the country's wealthy entrepreneurs. It was safer to buy dollars than invest in Colombia. Capital flight transferred Colombia's savings to U.S. banks at a hefty clip.[23] By then, "recovery" from the 1982 recession in the United States was the big story in *Business Week*—a fact that had not registered in Cúcuta. The first meeting of Latin America's indebted nations took place the next summer at Cartagena: the port that shipped South America's silver to Spain.

District Selection

Hernando Linero, project director for the province of Norte de Santander, met us at the airport. He came in a muddy jeep, khaki pants, and a short-sleeved shirt. He told Enrique: "I threw some mud on my jeep; you fellows from the Institute like to think directors are always in the field." "We know your tricks," laughed Enrique, "I'm not impressed." "And you," said Hernando, turning in my direction, "if you're a gringo, where's your suit and tie?" "If you're Colombian," I answered, "why don't you have sunglasses?"

We spent the afternoon at Hernando's office in Cúcuta, going over maps and production schedules. I kept up the questions, goaded on by Hernando's enthusiasm. "DRI's work," he told me, "is geared to small producers with 20 hectares or less who derive at least 70 percent of their income from agriculture. Increasing farm incomes and food production is the top priority; nationally, DRI's credit goes mostly to food crops, fruit trees, and dairy farming.

"The first step is to determine which counties should be included in a DRI district. We considered how much land small farms had in each county, whether enough credit was already available, how good production was, access to social services, and farm incomes." In 1979, twenty-one of the province's thirty-five counties were selected for eventual inclusion, almost all of them in the highlands. The project had a modest start in five contiguous counties (Chitagá, Pamplona, Mutiscua, Pamplonita, and Cácota) clustered in the south-central part of the province around the market town of Pamplona. For each county chosen, DRI had to survey rural townships, using the same criterion as for counties. A total of twenty-nine townships received priority rankings, and fifteen were selected for the project's first year.[24] Next came a microdiagnosis followed by an action plan. "Sounds like a lot of work, doesn't it," laughed Hernando. "In this business, you've got to be precise. When you cut corners, the campesino loses."

The diagnosis covered social services, public works, and agricultural production. It cast problems in local terms and depended on the collaboration of community leaders. Hernando gave me two mimeographed volumes on Pamplona. I found the work impressive. It illustrated the principle that good projects begin with an eye to specifics. The strong point was agricultural production, and that is what the account emphasizes.

Diagnosis: Services

At 94 per 1,000, the district's infant mortality rate was double the figure for Colombia as a whole: gastrointestinal infections, respiratory diseases, and malnutrition headed the list of causes. Only 44 percent of school-age children in rural townships attended classes, and the adult illiteracy rate was 33 percent. Half the households lacked potable water, and the vast majority had no access to electricity. Of the district's seventy-five miles of roads, 40 percent were impassable during the rainy season. Add to this a land tenure pattern of small plots, which yielded little income, and one sees why young workers migrated to Colombia's cities.[25]

Diagnosis: Land Distribution

In 1980, the five counties that composed the Pamplona district had a population of approximately 100,000, of which only 36 percent was rural. This was because Pamplona County's municipal seat had 60,000 residents. In adjoining counties, rural families accounted for between 78 percent (Mutiscua) and 84 percent (Chitagá) of their respective populations. Classified by size, the Pamplona district's five counties had 4,664 farms covering approximately 120,000 hectares; overall, 77 percent were farms of less than 20 hectares. Of these, two thirds had at least 3 hectares; the remaining third had less. Although the majority of small farmers owned the land they worked, a quarter were tenants. Jointly, small farms held 17 percent of the land. Large holdings of 20 hectares or more accounted for 23 percent of the district's farms and covered 83 percent of the land, their average size being 93 hectares.[26] (See Table 3.1.)

The diagnosis did not further disaggregate large properties. The majority were probably middle-sized farms of between 20 and 50 hectares, with a small number of big estates at the top.[27] How unequal distribution was, however, depended on the quality of the land held. In the Pamplona district, for example, small farmers held 48 percent of the land devoted to food crops and 22 percent of the land in pasture.[28]

Scaled down to the townships selected for 1981, DRI started with 1,055 families. For 1983, the figure had increased to 2,519—reaching somewhere between 60 to 70 percent of the district's small farmers.[29] Multiplying the number of families that year by the average family size of 6 gives a total of about 15,000 beneficiaries.

"Isn't land reform an obvious priority?" I asked Hernando. "Sure, but the

Table 3.1 Landholdings in the Pamplona District, by Size of Farm and Area Occupied*

Size of Farm (in hectares)	Number of Farms	%	Total Area (in hectares)	%
Less than 3	1,240	26.6	1,711	1.4
3–9.9	1,594	34.2	8,603	7.2
10–19.9	765	16.4	10,095	8.4
Over 20	1,065	22.8	99,953	83.0
Total	4,664	100.0	120,362	100.0

Source: Compiled from "Diagnóstico microregional en el Distrito de Pamplona—Norte de Santander," 2 vols., mimeographed (Programa de Desarrollo Rural Integrado/Instituto Interamericano de Cooperación para la Agricultura [DRI/IICA], Pamplona, 1981), 2:22.

*Includes the counties of Chitagá, Pamplona, Mutiscua, Pamplonita, and Cácota.

first question is what the land is good for, and that depends on each locality's elevation, soil quality, and rainfall. Steep hillsides, for example, can be suitable for grazing, but they are unsuited to most crops. For potatoes, if the soil is good and the land relatively level, 10 hectares makes for a middle-sized farm. On the other hand, a dairy farm with 50 hectares of rocky pasture is too small. Land reform is a practical problem. What a farm produces has to be specified, and the land's characteristics determined. Otherwise, the definition for "small" or "large" is bound to be arbitrary. And even when a holding is large, you should consider how productive it is. By extending wet rice production, for instance, Colombia became self-sufficient; yields per hectare are over four metric tons, which is surpassed only in Uruguay.[30] The story in rice is the work of relatively large producers. In the Cauca Valley, by contrast, sugar plantations took over some of Colombia's best crop land for the sake of an export of little value to the country overall. What's left behind is a landless rural work force that health teams can worry about." I had, of course, mentioned my recent visit in Cali.

"DRI," Hernando continued, "is not a land reform project—one of its limitations. Nonetheless, its emphasis on credit, marketing, and training constitutes the basis for practical land reform. DRI is not an employment program either. In 1980, the five counties scheduled for inclusion had about 10,000 *jornaleros*; they constituted the region's rural work force, paid a daily wage when employed.[31] Whatever land they owned, it was not sufficient for commercial production. To the extent we can increase productivity, strengthen cooperative marketing, and foster food processing, the landless may get higher wages and more regular employment. But our program does not deal with land reform or rural unemployment directly. In each township involved, some families benefit indirectly, at best, from the project. Our diagnosis looked at overall conditions, but our plan of action is more restricted. We cannot do everything; we start where we can have the greatest impact quickly, for as many families as possible, and at a sustainable cost."

Diagnosis: Production

About 90 percent of the district's arable land was at elevations above 6,000 feet, which made for a cool climate suited to temperate vegetables. The potato was the region's chief food crop, favored by a third of the district's small farmers. Following in importance came wheat, and then a mix of carrots, beets, onions, and cabbage. For each crop, DRI mapped production, traced the marketing chain, calculated productivity, and charted prices. Fieldwork on potato production, for example, showed that Chitagá County produced half the region's 43,800 tons, and that 40 percent of the region's potatoes were sold in Cúcuta. Farmers rotated crops or interspersed potatoes with beans. Still, at 9 tons per hectare, yields were low even by Colombian standards, which averaged 14. The main reason was the poor quality of the potatoes held to seed the next crop. In addition, soil preparation did not adequately deter erosion, even though such losses were moderate. Although most farmers applied fertilizer, the quantity added averaged 30 percent below optimal levels. Pamplona's small farmers earned a mere 20 percent of the per capita income that characterized the rest of Colombia. After subtracting production costs, potato farmers made only a 5 percent profit in 1979. Intermediaries, by contrast, marked up the price to shopkeepers by 21 percent. As to credit, loans from the Agrarian Bank covered only 24 percent of production costs. Nonetheless, farmers had an excellent repayment record. As of 1980, only 2.7 percent of the bank's crop loans were in default.[32]

Besides potatoes, DRI analyzed production, marketing, prices, and credit policies for wheat, vegetables (carrots, cabbage, beets, onions), and milk production. Based on this information, DRI outlined priorities for small-scale farming as a whole: better production methods, higher yields, expanded credit coverage, cooperative marketing, and stronger community organization.[33]

The problem was how to convert priorities into a coherent plan of action. For six months, DRI's technicians had nosed around in the district's townships, squeezed data from agencies, and made flow charts for potatoes. The result of its fabled diagnosis was a list of catchall priorities anyone could have cribbed from a high school textbook on agronomy. This is, of course, precisely the point. Everyone knows that marketing has to be part of a production strategy. The problem is not marketing in general, but in particular: specific crops, produced with a locality's characteristic technology, and distributed by a network whose ad hoc structure textbooks do not reveal. Because DRI planned to market potatoes through a cooperative, it had to know what percentage small farmers produced, and it needed a purchase system that competed with Cúcuta's truckers. The diagnosis spelled out the situation in terms of which priorities had to be implemented. Without this detailed handbook as a guide, a plan of action was just fancy charts with arrows.

The Action Plan

The diagnosis was only one step. DRI's work depended on the coordinated efforts of several agencies. For each priority—such as improving production methods or expanding credit coverage—an Action Plan specified the agencies involved and their responsibilities. This was done crop by crop for a five-year period. The Action Plan reversed the usual chain of command: budget estimates and the work outlined for each year came from the field. The training agency (SENA), for example, did not apply for funds on its own behalf; its allocation depended on the work assigned to it. To illustrate what each agency did, consider the exemplary potato.

For the Extension Service, the main task was technical assistance to farmers. Based on its study of current farming practices, it estimated the return to farmers who adopted new techniques as 1.5 pesos for each peso invested. Extension work included better seeds, the introduction of improved varieties, fields prepared to minimize erosion, adequate fertilization, and more careful disease control. Over the course of five years (1981–85), the Extension Service expected to increase yields from 9 to 17 tons per hectare. In 1983, its agronomists worked with a third of the region's potato farmers; it conducted extension work on both an individual and a collective basis. It had also completed 900 farm surveys for potato production and held over 60 workshops in the region's townships. Loans made by the Agrarian Bank covered the cost of new techniques, and the amount per hectare was adjusted for inflation.

The project's approach to rural development was community-oriented. SENA, the training agency, worked with local groups and agricultural cooperatives. Because seed potatoes were so important, SENA held eighteen short courses in 1983 on production methods, selection, and storage.

To strengthen the small farmers' bargaining power, the project sponsored cooperatives. In the Pamplona district, the potato cooperative, Agropapa, began storage and marketing operations in 1982. Keeping track of prices, outlets, and issuing local bulletins fell to the marketing agency, CECORA. Educating members about how cooperatives worked, the importance of product quality, and budget management was a joint effort shared with SENA. In 1982, for example, CECORA-SENA held community meetings and organized short courses for 120 members. Overall, the potato cooperative was expected to increase the price paid to farmers by 25 percent. For 1985, the goal was to sell at least 4,700 tons through Agropapa.[34]

How large a staff did the project require to implement its production component? In 1981, the Extension Service had twenty agronomists, the Agrarian Bank had eight inspectors, SENA had ten instructors, and CECORA had two cooperative promoters and a price analyst.[35] Including supervisors and secretaries, the production staff came to fifty-six—hardly a padded payroll.

The production budget for the period 1981–85 allocated $4.4 million to the credit program, a revolving capital fund DRI expected would finance loans worth twice that amount over the course of five years.[36] Consider a group of ten potato farmers who borrow $1,000 apiece at 10 percent for the 1981 crop. At harvest time, they pay back the loan ($10,000) plus interest ($1,000). So the Agrarian Bank starts 1982 with $11,000 and is able to extend a total of eleven $1,000-loans. Over the two-year period, the initial loan fund of $10,000 provides $21,000 in credit. Only a portion of DRI's loans, however, cleared on an annual basis. To increase milk production, for instance, farmers had to purchase stock, plant better pastures, and improve animal sanitation. Such loans were retired over several years.

Table 3.2 indicates the number of loans scheduled for 1981–85 by type of production, the number of farms covered, the total loans made, and the credit required. For crops, of course, the loans made exceeded the number of credit recipients, because farmers took out a new loan each year. Potato farmers who had their first loan in 1981 would be in their fifth credit cycle by 1985.

"Why bother with tables for loans, potato production, cost estimates, and market flows?" asked Hernando rhetorically, getting up from his desk for a final comment. "To manage a project well, we need to know our position each year. Otherwise, we can't evaluate what has been accomplished, and there is no accountability. Any agency can make projections, with or without data. What counts is what stands behind the figures. In DRI's case, it has an Action Plan for implementation based on a diagnosis of local conditions.

"We started with a year of field research first. For potatoes, we analyzed production, from seed quality to how farmers spaced plants and applied fertilizer. Then we estimated the cost of each new technique and calculated the benefits to farmers: in both potatoes and pesos. And we had to be right. The campesino will not participate in schemes that don't pay off.

"Planning is not just a paper exercise. Each year, the agencies that work on production formulate a joint strategy. They assess where the project stands and update the Action Plan. Agencies have to set joint goals, which provide a basis for each year's budget. I don't determine how much goes to the training agency or the Extension Service; that has to be worked out in the field. Of course, this gets tedious. Well, so what? Rural development is 80 percent drudgery and 20 percent results; it's a long-term commitment."

How did the Pamplona district fare in 1983? The budget for that year surpassed original projections. By then, the project had expanded to 7 counties and 47 townships; the number of farm families covered had doubled. Agropapa's membership and scheduled potato loans exceeded original targets. The

Table 3.2 DRI Loans to Small Farmers in the Pamplona District, 1981–1985

Type of Production	Number of Loans 1981–1985	Farms Covered by 1985	Credit Allocated 1981–1985 (in millions of dollars)
Potatoes	2,000	600	5.3
Carrots, cabbage, beets, and onions	1,705	300	1.7
Wheat	570	145	0.4
Milk	919	919	1.3
Total	5,194	1,964	8.7

Source: Compiled from "Componente de producción: Programación 1981–1985," mimeographed (Programa de Desarrollo Rural Integrado/Instituto Interamericano de Cooperación para la Agricultura [DRI/IICA], Pamplona, 1981), pp. 11, 16, 34, 43, 69, 92, 127.

milk production program, on the other hand, had moved more slowly than anticipated. In the province's northwest, a new DRI district at Ocaña covered 91 townships in 8 counties. For Colombia as a whole, DRI's budget increased from $57 million in 1982 to $95 million for 1983, even though the number of districts remained unchanged. By then DRI reached 90,000 farm families in 435 counties—about 20 percent of the country's small producers.[37]

• The Potato

Today's authors include statements about their politics. So I admit to a bias in favor of the potato, and rally to its defense.

The potato has fallen victim to the opinions held by weight watchers. Eating potatoes, they say, makes you fat—an allegation both vicious and erroneous. The plain truth: a potato is no more fattening than a pear; you can eat 7 pounds a day and still weigh in under the recommended dosage of 2,500 calories.[38]

Spuds yield second-rate nutrition—another lie. If you add a bit of milk, you can live on potatoes exclusively—a claim neither wheat nor rice can make. The quality of potato protein is higher than that of soybeans; a single spud provides half the daily vitamin C requirement for an adult. Rice, people think, is the world's most productive crop. Wrong again. An acre of potatoes gives back twice as much food as one planted to rice.

Disrespect has undermined the potato's reputation. At restaurants, it is desecrated by sour cream and melted cheese. The result is not a potato but a concoction injurious to health. North America has reduced a tuber once famous for its shapes and colors to strains fit only for the french-fry cutter—an unsupervised carnage of five billion pounds a year.

The potato likes a cool climate. Its native habitat is the Andean altiplano near Lake Titicaca. The Incas domesticated the wild strains that thrived in the region. Today, Andean farmers cultivate over three thousand varieties. In sheer weight, however, the potato balance has shifted decisively to the Soviets. They account for a third of the world's harvest; add Poland, and half the planet's potato crop is behind the Iron Curtain. The United States, with only 5 percent of world production, is small potatoes—perhaps irrevocably so. When it comes to the space race or the arms race, the Defense Department is all ears; unfortunately, it has no head for potatoes.

My four-day sojourn at Pamplona did not suffice to cover every aspect of the project, so I specialized in spuds. True, potato production is a key aspect of DRI's work in Pamplona. But my avoidance of carrots and beets reflected a long-standing loyalty to the potato.

• Pamplona

Enrique and I set off for Pamplona early the next morning; Hernando came up from Cúcuta the following day. I left behind about five pounds of sweat—mostly in my hotel room where I had to choose between a noisy air conditioner or an occasional breeze laced with mosquitoes. I opted for the humidity and generous applications of *OFF*. The ascent to Pamplona provided welcome relief. At an elevation of 7,800 feet, the town is in the *páramo*, a cool zone that favors temperate crops. Pamplona is only 60 miles southeast of Cúcuta; the road is paved, as it is the main highway to Bogotá. Nonetheless, it is a challenging trek of hairpin spirals that takes over two hours.

An agronomist in his late forties, Enrique had worked on Peru's land reform program before joining the Institute's staff in Bogotá. He directed the conversation away from potatoes to a book I had written on Spanish and English colonization. He asked for a concise summary of the main differences between the two. For every generalization I offered, Enrique came up with an exception. I turned to novels: Gabriel García Márquez, a Colombian, had just won the Nobel Prize for literature. Enrique patiently heard out my comments on *A Hundred Years of Solitude*. "True enough, but aren't all his novels alike?" he countered. "Take the Peruvian, Vargas Llosa; each of his novels is different: *Time of the Hero*, *Captain Pantoja*, *Aunt Julia*, they're all fresh and original." On novels, too, I was outclassed.

Our hotel in Pamplona was almost empty; unfavorable exchange rates kept its usual Venezuelan patrons away. I checked out my quarters. The bed came equipped with two thick woolen blankets—a place for serious sleeping.

Table 3.3 Distribution of Potato Farms in the Pamplona District, by Size and Area Occupied*

Size of Farm (in hectares)	% of Total Farms (1,440)	% of Total Hectares (3,566)
Less than 3	26	25
3–9.9	30	29
10–19.9	17	17
20–49.9	16	16
Over 50	11	13
Total	100	100

Source: Compiled from "Proyecto para la producción de semilla mejorada de papa en el Distrito DRI de Pamplona," mimeographed (Programa de Desarrollo Rural Integrado/Instituto Interamericano de Cooperación para la Agricultura [DRI/IICA], Bogotá, 1981), p. 29.

*Includes only the district's potato-producing counties: Chitagá, Pamplona, Mutiscua, and Cácota.

Production

We met at the DRI office in Pamplona. Representatives from each agency explained their work. In the afternoon, César Villamizar, an Extension Service agronomist, took me by jeep to visit potato plots. He was in his twenties, had studied at the International Potato Center in Lima, and had worked with DRI in Pamplona since the project started. We set off in a light drizzle. Clouds had collected in the valleys, setting off the brilliant green of pastures and potato fields. When we reached a pass that opened onto meadows below—with mountains towering behind us—César pulled off to the side. "I always stop here," he said. "Once I crossed the pass without noticing. I turned around and came back."

Potato production concentrates in four counties: Chitagá, Pamplona, Mutiscua, and Cácota. Neighboring Pamplonita, whose valleys lie mostly below 6,000 feet, favors dairy farming. The potato is comparatively egalitarian. Of the district's 1,440 potato farms, small holdings of under 20 hectares comprised 73 percent of the total and covered 71 percent of the acreage devoted to spuds. (See Table 3.3.)

"Sharecropping," observed César, "makes extension and credit management difficult; fortunately, 80 percent of the district's potato farmers own their land. Our work is to transfer better production techniques to farmers. For potatoes this includes control of insect predators and plant diseases, the use of better seeds and heartier varieties, soil preparation, the spacing of plants, and crop management after germination."

We stopped at DRI's experimental plots where seeds and new potato variet-ies were under production. Workers trained by DRI were retrenching furrows between potato rows and spreading excess soil around the plants. On another plot, a worker sprayed plants with a motorized applicator. It was carried on the back and the insecticide was applied by hose. The hand model used by farmers was cheaper, and easier to use and repair.

At a farm nearby, a campesino was testing soil additives to see how much they improved wheat yields. He had carefully set off treated and untreated parcels, which alternated from level ground up the hillside—thus controlling for variations attributable to placement. "We didn't teach him to do this," said César. "He saw how we experimented with potatoes and decided to apply the same test to his wheat crop."

The timing of the spring rains differs for each county, almost for each valley. Potatoes are planted over a four-month period that starts in mid-March, and the harvest takes place five to six months later. Between September and November, during the fall rains, farmers plant a second, although smaller, crop.

We stopped at a potato patch, where a farmer was applying a dose of granular insecticide with a smooth, short stick hollowed out at the end to measure one gram precisely—a rustic tool supplied by DRI. I asked César about pest control.

"The *gusano blanco*, a white worm, is the region's worst potato predator. About a centimeter in length, it bores into tubers, eating and tunneling away for forty to fifty days. The eating cycle complete, the worm begins a twenty-day metamorphosis, ending up as a tiny, coffee-brown bug (*cucarrón*). The cucarrón does not fly, but it is fast-moving, hard to spot, and a menace to crops. It feeds on the tender leaves of the potato plant and lays about five hundred eggs. Twenty to thirty days later a new worm generation begins boring into the tubers. Losses to the gusano can be staggering—half the crop; some-times, everything. The insecticide FURADAN is 90 percent effective against the gusano blanco—if applications are made correctly. Three treatments are necessary. At planting time, a gram is spread around the seed potatoes. After germination, a liquid application is sprayed around the plant's base, where the cucarrón is found. Then, after weeding, a final one gram gets sprinkled at the base. Correct dosage, proper application, and timing are all required for good results. Dry rot fungus also poses problems, particularly at low altitudes. So we urge farmers to use their highest plots.

"FURADAN controls insects effectively; the prime obstacle to productivity now is the poor-quality tubers set aside for the next crop. For seed, farmers should select well-rounded potatoes of medium size. They should be healthy and selected from the best plants. In practice, farmers maximize profits by selling off the best potatoes first, holding over the smallest, or unsightly large ones, which are sometimes partly rotten and worm-ridden. If farmers buy seed tubers, they tend to cut corners, ending up with a cheap consignment of poor quality for the next crop.

"We encourage farmers to allot a small parcel specifically to seed production. For best results, the seed crop needs repeated weeding and tilling, more fertilizer, and careful applications of FURADAN and fungicides. Once harvested, seed tubers require storage facilities that keep the potatoes cool and dry. Counting greater labor costs and more inputs, a seed field is much more expensive than the regular DRI-financed crop. To farmers, higher costs mean greater risks, and it takes two seasons to translate seed spuds into pesos. To speed up the process, we provided special training and credit to local farmers who agreed to specialize in seed production. In addition, we produce seed tubers for sale and distribution on our own experimental plots. Agencies like SENA constantly preach the merits of high-quality seeds. The long-run strategy is to distribute seeds through the potato cooperative, which will obtain its stocks both from DRI and local producers.

"Extension work isn't piecemeal—the gusano blanco one year, and seed selection the next. When farmers take out DRI-sponsored loans, they apply our methods to the plots financed. The local farmer does not borrow money just because it is available. Our methods are more expensive and more work: farmers have to use better seeds, apply 60 percent more fertilizer, and add lime; there's extra tilling, more disease control, and different spacing for each potato variety. The direct costs for a hectare so planted come to 82,000 pesos [$1,300]—all of which a DRI loan covers. Nonetheless, that's 40 percent more than it takes to grow potatoes the old way, and farmers have to pay interest charges on a larger sum. By and large, farmers don't convert wholesale to DRI's production techniques. What happens in practice is that some farmers apply the new scheme on a limited basis. In 1981, for example, 140 farmers planted an average of 1.2 hectares on DRI-oriented plots. They had their choice—smaller loans for the old methods or larger sums using DRI rules. Most of them combined the two, planting small parcels under our direction but using the traditional way for the rest of their crop.

"Once farmers agree to a trial run, the staff must provide adequate supervision. Agronomists are assigned to specific townships and live in the districts where they work. It's their job to assess each farmer's credit needs, explain DRI's production methods, and provide on-the-spot advice. In the meantime, farmers attend training sessions on credit, improved seeds, and cooperative marketing. When the Agrarian Bank's inspectors come around, technicians have to certify that farmers implemented the DRI scheme—an important consideration for campesinos. If the crop fails, they don't have to repay—as long as they applied our recommendations conscientiously.

"If we can't demonstrate a new technology's worth in pesos, the campesino won't buy it. We spend a lot of time on cost estimates and the methods that apply to each crop. We have to know beforehand that our production norms fit the conditions; we want cautious profit projections, not best-case assumptions. A new fungus-resistant potato strain, for instance, has to be pretested in Pamplona's microclimate, soils, and social context. A potato variety that deviates from the size, shape, and texture preferred locally faces marketing problems; if it requires three times the fertilizer, or complex alterations in the soil's chemical composition, it faces cost-benefit problems. Unless an innovation undergoes local testing first, it is likely to fail."

In 1981, yields on DRI plots surpassed the district's average by 60 percent. After subtracting loan repayments, farmers netted twice as much as under the old system. The repayment rate was 98 percent. The tally on potato loans for 1983 stood at over four hundred in May: by year's end, DRI expected to be far ahead of original projections.

"Helping small farmers to use credit and new technology is a net gain to the community," noted César. "As they gain experience they can apply our production plan to additional plots and with less supervision. They tend to find their neighbor's accomplishment more impressive than our experimental plots. Those already initiated in seed selection and erosion control provide a pool of resident experts other farmers can consult. The key is to begin modestly and build. To start with a lot of speeches, and then have to cut back, creates distrust that is hard to overcome."

The Agrarian Bank made as many loans as the staff could handle. Farmers with more than 20 hectares were eligible too, but not at the reduced rates reserved for small producers. César criticized this standard as arbitrary and unfair. "One farmer has 25 hectares, most of it rocks, and someone else has 18, all good land. And for dairy farming, even 50 hectares is small. The Agrarian Bank won't give DRI rates to a farmer over the limit, even by half a hectare. Many potato farms have between 20 and 50 hectares; that isn't excessive, but they don't qualify for the special rate."

Marketing

The towns of Pamplona and Cúcuta were the local potato's principal markets, taking, respectively, 26 percent and 41 percent of total production. Hernando described the distribution system. "Farmers close enough to Pamplona cart their potatoes there by oxen. For outlying areas, truckers schedule pickups at the county seat; farmers cart their potatoes to the town square, load up a truck, and then head with their families for Pamplona. Once there, they negotiate a price directly with wholesalers. From there most of the potatoes go to retail outlets in the city—Pamplona has 60,000 people—or to outlying towns. With Cúcuta it's a different story. Farmers bring their crop to the roadside and wait for a merchant-trucker who sets a tentative price, gives the farmer a small cash advance, and then takes off for Cúcuta. Once there, the trucker either finds a wholesaler or sublets the cargo to a vendor—who shops around for an outlet at a commission of 80 pesos per 50-pound bag. Cúcuta is short on warehouse space, and truckers can't afford to holdout for a good price. The push is always to sell, and as the day slips by—at any price. Farmers get the short end of the deal, and it's often less than the price originally promised.[39]

"Because they show up unsorted as to size, appearance, and quality, the potatoes produced around Pamplona are far from the first choice of Cúcuta's shopkeepers. Mesh sacks display attractive specimens on the surface, while rotten ones are concealed within—a stratagem for which the Pamplona farmer is notorious. And Cúcuta can afford to be choosy: potatoes from Pamplona make up only 10 percent of the city's supply. For potatoes, Cúcuta draws from highland provinces farther south like Cundinamarca, or neighboring Boyacá.

"To the extent the potato cooperative can penetrate the region's marketing chain, it can appropriate a larger share of the shelf price on the farmer's behalf. Agropapa's current priority is to build backward linkages to improved seed and production methods, and forward linkages to quality control and market outlets in Cúcuta. With a reputation for a superior product, the cooperative's 220 members can get better prices. Agropapa also helps reduce the cost of DRI technology, since it buys seed tubers, fertilizer, and pesticides in bulk. As higher yields spread to more farms and fields, gluts loom as a potential threat to the project's continued success. Solving one problem creates another."

Fostering entrepreneurship was part and parcel of the project's overall agenda. The Agrarian Bank provided credit both to individuals and to community associations, the cooperative being the prototype. The guidelines required that small farmers constitute half the membership. Under this rubric, Agropapa could borrow to finance its marketing activities, purchase machinery, build storage facilities, and mount agroindustrial enterprises.[40] When I discussed the potato's future, project agronomists stressed the role food processing played as an outlet for production. Specifically, they hoped the cooperative would eventually lead to local industries of the instant, mashed variety, which would stabilize prices and create employment.

"Too often rural development is promises without action," Hernando said. "Before DRI came along, Ocaña had a cooperative, but it fell apart. Now everyone is skeptical. In this work, we have to be optimistic. If we accomplished everything in our Action Plan we'd qualify for the Nobel Prize."

Natural Resources

The task of the conservation agency (INDERENA) was to restore the region's forests and watersheds. The government did not consider its work a priority. The argument was that acid rain, erosion, and toxic waste were the price of development. Imposing environmental controls increased production costs and undermined competitiveness.

While I was in Bogotá, *El Tiempo* featured a story on Los Nevados, a national park located in the Central Range. Indiscriminate lumbering had so reduced forests that flash floods and landslides had devastated the park. The dumping of human waste and garbage had polluted streams and rivers; the uncontrolled extraction of sand and rock had undermined embankments.[41] The conservation agency, it noted, was the country's most neglected, starved for funds and personnel. So, too, in Pamplona.

DRI officials complained that INDERENA lacked the staff necessary even to map the region's ecological zones and identify priority watersheds, much less define a viable conservation strategy. Although the agency maintained nurseries in the district, reforestation was at the farmer's expense. Only large landowners could afford a long-term investment in pines and eucalyptus. INDERENA's main task locally was to plant a narrow strip of trees along watersheds and streams—the agency's legal prerogative whether owners wanted it or not.

In Pamplona, the agency's most successful project was fish-tank aquaculture. Families obtained credit from the Agrarian Bank, and INDERENA provided technical assistance. A well-maintained tank supplied a source of protein on a regular basis. While traveling in Chitagá County one afternoon, Hernando decided to prove to me just how good trout was when fresh from the fish tank. We stopped at a village whose restaurant specialized in trout. It was lunchtime, and we were lucky to find one of its five tables empty. We did not have to order: to stop here was to stop for trout. When I imagined the finned product that awaited me, I thought up a fat ten-incher. Instead, what passed from the tank outside to the frying pan and to my plate looked more like big sardines. Because the bone structure was soft, I followed Hernando's lead and ate my trout whole—minus head and tail fins, of course. As everyone agreed, it was delicious.

Health and Education

The agencies that worked on production had the countryside as their vocation. Once they worked out a joint plan, cooperation was a manageable venture. Although I did not visit clinics—I suffered from an overdose of health acquired in Cali the week before—the district's health program paled in comparison to the legions assembled on the potato's behalf. The training agency held sessions on family gardens, but it was not part of a nutrition program backed by the clinics. As to primary education, project records spelled out the problem in sufficient detail, but no remedy was in sight. Despite the charts, health and education continued on as separate spheres controlled by provincial bureaucracies. Rural districts got what was left over: doctors and teachers ill-prepared for rural life who did not have enough merit, or connections, to get the appointments they wanted.

Hernando mentioned that Pamplona had an agricultural school. I told him I would like to stop there, but promptly forgot about it. Late one afternoon, after an exhausting day of field trips and discussions, Hernando pulled up in front of the Rural Institute. "Here we are," he said. "It's all arranged." As we advanced on the director's office, I tried to think of some questions. Hernán Correa Otero, a short but powerfully built man in his late forties, ushered us in. Mercifully, I was not the center of attention; his main interest was in the contingent from DRI.

The Rural Institute was an intermediate school; it provided the final two years of high school, with a specialization in the agricultural sciences. In addition, it offered a two-year advanced concentration in agronomy, community development, and teaching, which led to a technical degree. Most of the students came from rural areas; about 80 percent of those who completed high school at the institute continued into its advanced programs. "We have 15 hectares for demonstration plots and 45 head of cattle on 28 hectares of pasture," Hernán said. "Our students learn by putting new techniques into practice; they want the kind of education that provides skills they can use. Unfortunately, many employers, including those in the public sector, don't distinguish between a high school diploma and a degree from an intermediate school—both get the same starting salary.

"The school has dormitory facilities and a cafeteria, which the students manage. Most of the food produced on experimental plots ends up in the cafeteria. Our students aren't from wealthy families. By running the cafeteria, they keep costs down to $25 [2,000 pesos] a month. Some days are without meat, but that's a decision the students make. In the universities, students are always on strike over food, but not here.

"Norte de Santander has over three hundred teachers in rural areas who don't have even a high school diploma. A typical teacher thinks a rural assignment is a demotion, a sign of failure. Why build rural schools and then staff them with people who lack motivation and don't want to be there? Rural schools need excellence. It takes a skilled teacher to confront the rural conviction that education is meant for somebody else. The country people are right, too. We use books drawn from the reality of the urban child. We need materials geared to rural children that show respect for their way of life.

"A rural teacher has to be dedicated to the farmer and community development. We train only a few teachers each year, but they are the best. We require them to have a background in agronomy. Our method is to help children learn by involving them in practical tasks like planting a school garden. I've seen kids that can't add or subtract on the blackboard get the knack when they use carrots and potatoes. If the schools did things right, they could teach agriculture and basic skills at the same time.

"Each student teacher has to complete a four-month internship in a rural school located at least an hour's journey from Pamplona. The fact is, our students are better prepared than most of the teachers they assist. The province's Ministry of Education should appoint our graduates to the district's rural schools. Instead, they have to take jobs in other provinces. Of course, they do excellent work; but they ought to stay in Norte de Santander, the province that trained them."

Hernán was suggesting indirectly, and diplomatically, that DRI should recognize the special qualifications of institute graduates. And he wanted DRI to put some pressure on the Ministry of Education—neither point missed by Hernando. Hernán had his own agenda, my presence notwithstanding.

"We encourage our students to work out practical internships as part of their training," Hernán continued. "They could work with DRI's staff on agricultural extension or help promote cooperatives. It could be easily arranged if DRI provided transportation." He also suggested a continuing education program for rural teachers, organized by the institute and financed by DRI. Hernando obviously liked the idea of internships; he promised transportation and agreed to iron out the details. As to continuing education, he was all caution. "That depends on the ministry, and I don't control their budget. You're right about the teachers. The standards are appalling, and it's a shame. When it comes to appointments we all know what's involved. Still, it's worth a try."

Mutiscua

The field trips I took with Enrique, Hernando, and César touched bases in almost all the district's counties. Hernando felt that "cooperation comes from friendship and respect, not a paper mandate. A director has to keep in touch with everyone; rural development can't be managed from a desk." My visit, obviously, had not interrupted his routine.

As we jeeped our way between towns, Hernando pointed out electrification projects and new roads completed under DRI. We passed beautiful stretches where forested land still remained; plots of potatoes dotted the mountainsides. During a downpour, we picked up two women on their way to town. Hernando asked them about DRI. "There's a community meeting on cooperatives next week," they said with evident enthusiasm. "What's the most important work DRI does?" asked César. "I couldn't say," said the younger of the two. "Our gardens, the community, we have loans too: there isn't just one thing, señor." After dropping them off, we went on to a seed distribution center. A farmer had just finished loading sacks with seed tubers; his two mules waited impatiently nearby. Hernando could not resist an inspection. "Some of these potatoes are too large, my friend, and that one—it's rotten. Take only the best seeds." "I can't do that, señor, what will be left? I take some good ones and some bad ones like everyone else." Hernando helped load the mules. Later, a bit miffed, he said to César, "Everyone works hard, and I know it, but seed distribution has to be watched carefully; we can't afford to pass out bad seed— not a single one."

Late one afternoon, we dropped by the town of Mutiscua, a county seat. Hernando wanted to check on potato loans with Jorge, a DRI agronomist stationed in town. Mutiscua had been an important pre-Colombian settlement, noted for its workmanship in gold and marble. As we descended into the valley, the town appeared like a jewel set in the emeralded mountains. It was a peaceful place with its square arrayed in flowers of crimson and gold. The enemy of small-town sociability, the automobile, had yet to strike; Mutiscua got along with a well-used hitching post for mules. Jorge, it turned out, was making his rounds to some nearby farms, so Hernando set off to find him. In the meantime, César took us to the house of a local craftsman who chiseled delicate figurines from marble. His workshop was out back, with the main room in front reserved for display. The sculptures he sold were realistic— animals of forest and farm carved to the smallest detail. For himself, he preferred the abstract. "I can always sell an elephant," he laughed, pointing to a case lined with graceful creatures, some tiny, others a foot tall. "But something like this"—he showed us a four-inch column from which square knobs jutted out irregularly—"is from inside of me." "What does it represent?" I blurted out, witless when it comes to art. "The column," he said, "is life, to which all creatures cling, great or small."

Back outside César noted the requirements for a respectable town square: a church, a branch of the Agrarian Bank, a telephone office, a town hall, a grade school, and, last but not least, a general store—where we withdrew for a rum laced with anise. By then, Hernando had returned with Jorge. A battered pickup truck, piled high with burlap bags of corn and rice, ground to a halt in front. Hernando began questioning the driver on the rates charged for hauling potatoes; in the meantime, the rest of us unloaded the truck. Usually a stop for rum means one shot. The driver, however, purchased two menacing bottles. I felt obligated to consume my share and quickly lost count. Fortunately, my stomach was braced by mashed potatoes consumed at lunch. So I was not the one who got sick, although my taste for rum declined considerably.

On the way out of town, Hernando and César stopped at a roadside stand to bargain for carrots and prime cuts of liver. A young engineer, who worked on road construction for a mining company, came over to chat. In provinces like Norte de Santander, Colombia has great coal reserves. "Do you think mining threatens the environment?" I asked him. "Where are you from?" he replied. "The United States," I said. "Well, you can worry about the environment there," he observed heatedly. I had obviously touched a sore point. "Here in Colombia, the main thing mining threatens is the miner. I've seen young kids hunched over in three-foot tunnels, digging away with pick axes. What did they have for protection?—nothing: shorts and a T-shirt, that's all. If this is how we're going to mine coal, I say leave it in the ground. And the multinationals, the rules they follow abroad don't apply here. . . . " Enrique spared me an attack on corporate America, deftly diverting the conversation to Peru's copper industry.

That evening, over dinner, Enrique recalled our meeting with the engineer. "To most of us, the United States is a contradiction. It provides a disproportionate share of the Inter-American Institute's budget and supports development projects. On the other hand, so many of its policies run counter to basic social objectives. Adjusting debt payments to what a country can afford to pay would do more for Peru's development than any other measure, and it would create tremendous goodwill. Yet, the United States procrastinates. How can Peru create a stable democracy if the government has to impose austerity to pay the debt? The cost is too high politically. You can't tell workers to sacrifice so Peru can export its capital to foreign banks. They won't support it, they can't see how it benefits either themselves or Peru. When you travel in Latin America, you're going to find hostility toward the United States—like the engineer."

The feast of Corpus Christi is a national holiday in Colombia. Hernando came up from Cúcuta for the occasion. Along the roads, families made their way to town, carrying roses and wild flowers, carrots and potatoes; they placed their offerings of garden and field on the simple altars that set off each town's square. The Holy Eucharist passed in procession amidst song and fireworks, the innocence of childhood, and the heartbreak of adulthood. In Colombia's mountains the gods still work their magic, far from the evil unleashed below. I remembered my own childhood in St. Joseph's parish, the great May procession, the crowning of the Virgin Mary. In youth and innocence, the gods still stir within. They are banished now, to a corner of the heart, the edge of earth. What power can bring them forth in love instead of retribution?

Application

César always had his handbook with him in the field: *Potato Diseases, Nematodes, and Insects.* It was tattered and stuck out of his back pocket. He let me page through it. The potato's enemies were legion, it was a wonder they survived to be french fries.

"The problem with agricultural research," I instructed him, "is that industrial countries monopolize it; in the Third World, research favors agribusiness and exports, not food crops." My training was strong on dependency theory, although a bit thin on the facts.

Since the 1970s, a network of research centers located in developing countries have worked on behalf of the world's food crops. The International Potato Center in Lima is a case in point. It has developed heartier, more disease-resistant varieties, it distributes germplasm, and it researches seed production,

pest management, storage, and processing. Testing occurs under diverse ecological conditions and with the constraints small farmers face in mind. Regional training programs, such as the one César had attended, help transfer the
results. And the potato was not alone. In Cali, Colombia, the International
Center for Tropical Agriculture specialized in rice, beans, and cassava.[42]

"The problem," César pointed out, "is not so much research as how to apply
it to small farms." As DRI's work demonstrated, "application" involved more
than bulletins on seed storage and pesticides. To have an impact, it had to
convert production strategies into family income. To do that meant concerted
action on several fronts: from credit and extension to training and marketing.
And DRI had to reshape an agency's plan of action to fit local situations. It was
hard work and did not bring dramatic results overnight. Big producers could
hire agronomists and pay accountants to fill out their credit forms. Small
farmers could not afford to be so enterprising.

• Back to Bogotá

Enrique and I returned to Cúcuta on a Saturday morning. I spent the rest of
the day on my field notes. On Sunday, Hernando took us to the airport. I was
anxious to get back to Bogotá. Monday afternoon I had to catch a flight to
Cartagena, where I had arranged to meet Sharon. I was cutting it close as
always, ignoring all prior experience. Because Cúcuta is a border town, we
had to go through passport control before boarding.

"What is this, señor?" the guard demanded. "Your visa is stamped for
fifteen days and you've been here five weeks—that's illegal." My heart sank.
"I thought I had fifty days, not fifteen," I blurted out. "Can you read or can't
you," he countered, much annoyed. "You can't leave here until this is renewed—that's the law. Immigration is closed today; you'll have to go to the
police station and get a temporary permit." Enrique tried to intervene, men-
tioning that he was a consultant from the Inter-American Institute. "Where are
you from?" the guard asked. The minute Enrique said "Peru," he was automatically discounted. The guard turned back to me. "What are you doing here?" I
mentioned the Cartagena conference, Bogotá, Medellín, Cali—he was not
impressed. So I rapidly went on to DRI, dropping every name I could think of:
Hernando, César, Hernán at the Rural Institute. "The one for teachers?" he
interrupted. "My nephew went there; he's now in Meta." "Yes," I agreed,
"that's what Hernán said; they train teachers, but the ministry won't appoint
them here. They have to go somewhere else." Having found a weakness,
Enrique pressed our advantage, turning me into a consultant.

"Look," said the guard, "if you go to Bogotá today, you have to get this
renewed Monday. Otherwise, you're in for a lot of trouble." He picked up a

pink slip, stamped it, and stuck it in my passport. Enrique did his best to calm me. "I'll get a letter for you from the office tomorrow morning. The Institute gets courtesy visas from Immigration all the time; it's routine." Still, my heart pounded all the way to Bogotá. Once the unexpected hits, you start expecting it.

PART III
BRAZIL

4

NEWS

"**Y**ou can't go to Lapa, senhor," said the cab driver with a note of reproach. "What you want is Copacabana: the beach, comfortable hotels, beautiful girls; downtown is no place for a tourist."

I had spent the last twenty-four hours on the bus, arriving in Rio from Salvador, a journey of over a thousand miles. I was on a tight budget, restricted to hotels in the category *simples*, one grade above *de emergência*. I could not afford Copacabana. "I prefer the old part of the city," I protested. "I like the architecture and I want to visit the museums." "If you want my advice," he countered, "go to the beach now and take a look at the girls; if you still want a museum take the bus." "No," I said firmly, "I want downtown." "Well, where?" he asked with resignation. So I named a hotel on Mem de Sá Street. "I don't believe it," he said. "You're here ten minutes and want a place that rents by the hour." He veered off Gomes Freire Street just below Mem de Sá and headed for a small, comfortable hotel set off on a side street.

I shortchanged Rio that year: 1975. I did not make that mistake again. I have spent more time in Brazil than in any other Latin American country, and more time in Rio than in any other place in Brazil. My home there has always been the hotel the cab driver selected. Except on one occasion. Instead of staying near Lapa, the picturesque, seedy section that was my haunt, I moved to Flamengo—a step closer to fabled Copacabana. I found myself surrounded by opinions offered ex cathedra, if not ad nauseam. "There's garbage everywhere," noted one woman as she worked on her latest stack of postcards, "it's heaped in the street." "It's garbage day," I observed, "and most of the piles are neatly stacked." "Yes, but it smells," she said. "Rio is beautiful but it's dirty." One fellow insisted on sandals and white bathing trunks splotched with black flowers—even in the lobby. His fantasy had to contend with the facts, for July

Map 4.1 Brazil

is winter in Rio and the temperature registered a stubborn sixty degrees. And from all quarters came the usual recital of stolen cameras, towels, and pocketbooks. The explanation was revealed to me in conspiratorial terms: "It's a nice country, but it has too many Negroes, too much carnival, and not enough work." The opinions of tourists and generals can be remarkably similar. I went back to Lapa.

How does a baby duck recognize its mother? Evidently, it is a result of "imprinting." The chick attaches itself to the first thing it sees after hatching. That is what happened to me in Lapa: loneliness fended off by the familiar. I eat at the same restaurants, stalk the same streets, even go to the same barber. He has no diploma, and offers no shampoo or layered styles. Out of respect for traditional craftsmanship, I take the oily kid stuff and a cloud of talcum powder. On a winter day damp with rain, the corner café is packed and warm with patrons. Behind the counter are great kettles of steaming coffee stirred with wooden spoons. The Bar Brasil adds extra potatoes to my plate, and the candy store weighs the jelly beans in my favor. I stick to Lapa: for the people, and for the neighborhood.

The hotel's switchboard operator, who used to panic at the sound of my voice, has finally mastered my Portuguese; the clerks have explained the bus routes to Ipanema, the soccer stadium, and the zoo. They have educated me, even about laundry. My first months in Brazil I spent huge sums at the cleaners: even my undershirts came back on hangers. I could not find the equivalent of a Laundromat. I asked Dona Teresa, the cleaning lady, where I should send my wash. "Do you have a suit?" she asked dubiously. "No, just underwear, socks, and jeans." "Well," she replied, "what do you want a cleaners for?" "Because," I said, "they're dirty." "So what?" she demanded. "Just leave them on the bed like everyone else and I'll take care of it." The next day a tidy bundle appeared with a handwritten note listing each article washed and the cost. The cleaning staff ran the laundry concession; I paid Dona Teresa directly.

"You wouldn't have so much wash," she observed one morning, "if you didn't wear a T-shirt under your short-sleeved shirt. Why do you need both? It doesn't look right and it's too hot." Having thus weaned me from a custom she considered unhealthy, Dona Teresa waited a couple of weeks before calling my attention to another. "You fasten all the buttons on your shirt; nobody does that. One or two at the bottom is all you need." We compromised on three, counted from the belt up. My wardrobe never really got her approval, however, until I acquired some lightweight shirts with the *TABOM* label, and switched from boots to Brazilian-made shoes. "That's better," she told me. "No one will know you're not from around here, if you keep your mouth shut."

Loyalty. In 1979, I stayed in Rio for six weeks and then left for São Paulo. I returned in the vacation month of July, the peak of the Argentine tourist season. At the time, the Argentine peso was riding high on Chicago School economics: cheap imports flooded into the country and Argentines poured out, thanks to an overvalued currency. I got to the hotel just as the clerk, with a hopeless shrug, sent off a contingent of would-be clients. I started to leave but noticed that the bellboy had eased my duffel bag under the counter. He whispered something to me that ended in the word *jeito*, which means the impossible is about to be done. When the lobby cleared, I asked Sérgio if there was still a room available. "No," he said nonchalantly, "but, of course, there will be."

On occasion, the clerks conspired together on my behalf. In 1980, I arrived with Sharon. Every time we appeared at the desk, they praised my past record for good behavior: "Senhora, he was an angel," said Sérgio, making his arms into wings and flapping them to everyone's delight. "And he never stayed out late; certainly he was always back by ten o'clock—isn't that right?" he called over to João for confirmation. "That's true, senhora," admitted João. "Well, almost always," he added with a wink. They did, as Shakespeare says, protest too much. Fortunately, Dona Teresa upheld my reputation with more conviction.

The hotel has no television, no refrigerator, no cellophane-wrapped plastic glasses, and no shag carpet. The lights are too dim for reading, the mattress is flimsy, showers can be lukewarm to cold. The low wattage bulb I replace with a brighter one from the supermarket, I time my showers for the hot water, and I glue the wobbly writing tables. The best spot is one of the front rooms, which face the sidewalk. On weekends, when the city's traffic has fled, kids, soccer, and kick ball fill the street. Saturday night, musicians gather on the corner. Here, I sleep with the windows open.

I have twice been reprimanded by Senhor Afonso at the neighborhood newsstand. The first time was for carrying a wallet in my pocket. "You can't do that, senhor, it's too easy to steal. You're not from around here—where are you from?" "The United States," I replied. "If you were in New York, would you walk around with a wallet in your pocket?" "No," I admitted honestly. "I don't know what's worse," he said, "foreigners being robbed or kids getting caught. Buy one of these." He grabbed a leather satchel with a long strap from his chair and hung it crosswise over his shoulder. "Carry your money in something like this, and take only as much money as you need. Leave the rest in the hotel's safe." Another day, I reached into my satchel—carried in the prescribed manner—and pulled out a clump of bills to pay for the paper. He shook his head disapprovingly. "If you do that, everyone knows how much money you're carrying." He took the bills, spread them out on the counter, and stacked them with the largest denominations on the bottom and the smallest on top. Then he folded them in half so that only ten-cruzeiro notes were visible on the outside. "When you buy a paper or cigarettes, you pull back the top corner until you find the note you want; no one can tell if you have a five-thousand note underneath."

The fat years of Argentine tourism gave way to recession and austerity. The hotel put up a brave front. The fresh paint of 1975 faded, and a much needed overhaul was indefinitely postponed. Small improvements had to suffice. Air conditioners reached the fifth floor in 1982; carpeting took over the lobby in 1984. Patrons are mostly truck drivers, an occasional family on holiday, and businessmen on a small per diem. The tourist hotels can peg their rates to the dollar; a local hotel must consider what its patrons can afford. In 1975 I paid $18 for a single in Lapa; the charge had dropped until it reached $12 in 1984: a 44 percent decline roughly equivalent to the dollar's gain against the cruzeiro. "It's cheap for you this year," noted the proprietor. "I can't keep up with the dollar; I hardly keep up with inflation here in Brazil." In fact, the customary 10 percent tip that patrons used to leave was now included in the posted room charges. "People just weren't leaving 10 percent; it wasn't fair to the clerks. So for now, it comes off the top of gross receipts. If things get better, we'll go back to tips."

The signs of bad times also showed up at the neighborhood supermarket. Past experience had taught me to avoid it between 4:00 and 6:00 P.M.: shoppers crowded in on the way home from work; piled rice, beans, stew meat, and produce into baskets; and lined up at the checkout. I mostly bought bottled water, razor blades, fruit, and potato chips, so I waited for the slack periods. In 1984, austerity had tamed the frantic rush-hour surge: short lines, half-empty baskets, rice without beans or meat, cash register totals awaited anxiously, food put back. A young woman at the front of the line, three kids in tow, produced every cruzeiro she had and still came up short: for a bag of rice, two cartons of milk, and bananas. As she searched her pockets a second time, the older woman behind her deftly placed a crumpled bill on the counter, which the checkout girl quietly slid under the rest. "I think you've got enough," she said. The bill paid, the kids scampered out, released from a vaguely perceived calamity. "Yesterday," said the girl, "this happened and I started crying; imagine, a crying checkout girl." "I know, dear," said the older woman, shaking her head and patting the girl's arm, "Brazil is a disgrace."

• *Jornal*

In the morning, the first thing I do is buy a copy of the *Jornal do Brasil*, Rio's leading newspaper. I spend at least an hour deciphering its pages over coffee. I no longer bother with the international edition of *Time* magazine. The *Jornal* follows U.S. affairs. Anyway, when I get back to the States, I can catch up with Doonesbury clippings and back issues of *People* magazine. Brazil, of course, is not my own country so I fancy its politics to be of monumental significance.

Since 1975 I have followed two presidents: Ernesto Geisel (1974–79) and

João Figueiredo (1979–85). As generals go, Geisel was an intellectual, identified with the "Sorbonne" faction in the military. In 1975, what passed for political commentary in the *Jornal* had degenerated to a form of augury: it picked through the bones left over after Geisel's dinner. It was as good a method as any. Geisel held his cards close to his chest; one never knew which he would play next or even how many cards he had. Consider *distensão*, a "process" Geisel initiated to reduce political tensions. What it meant in practice was impossible to predict, regardless of what Geisel ate. He permitted elections on a trial basis in 1976. Others would follow, he promised, if the opposition did not win. Such machinations held sway throughout Geisel's reign. Political analysis was reduced to military science; the elections that mattered most were the ones held at the Military Club.

I spent most of June 1975 in Salvador, except for side trips to neighboring towns of historic interest like Cachoeira; I was preparing a book on colonial Brazil at the time. The buses were packed in violation of transit codes. As we approached checkpoints along the highway, passengers without seats had to crouch down in the aisles. We ran a gauntlet of hostile inspectors and sullen-faced soldiers with automatic rifles. Invariably, they waved us through, but I always had a lump in my stomach from the slowing down and the uncertainty.

Geisel, I think, perceived this in the silence that so characterized him. Brazil slipped by unnoticed, had retreated to a secret place beyond reach. Fear could divert but never stem the exodus.

The path that brought Brazil to Geisel was forged in deception. The 1964 coup had depended on strong civilian backing, especially from politicians who opposed the populist policies of President João Goulart. The Brazilian Congress declared the presidency vacant and designated the revolt's commander, General Castello Branco, as Goulart's successor.

I heard the story in Belo Horizonte. The day of the coup troops surrounded the newspaper office. The sergeant in charge thought his mission was to protect the paper's distribution, not prevent its publication. Most of Brazil was like the sergeant. Because Goulart's opponents controlled Congress, they thought Castello Branco would govern only until the 1966 presidential elections. But once the military had intervened, they could not be so easily displaced.

The regime purged Congress, decreed Institutional Acts that curtailed civil liberties, censored the press, and converted a third of the country's senators into executive appointees. Even politicians who had supported the coup found their political rights suspended. The popular side of the 1964 coup disintegrated. The military consolidated its control over every aspect of the state from its politics to economic development. Brazil became a "model" that technocrats used to test their theories.

When the High Command designated Castello Branco's successor in 1966, it dispensed with the formality of consulting politicians; the military annexed the presidency. Cabinet positions, the directorships of state companies, and ministerial portfolios became adjuncts to military careers, as did the patronage they conferred. In the end, the regime's tenacity had as much to do with the spoils system as it did with ideology. By the time Geisel became president, direct from his cushy job at Petrobrás, the state oil company, the leftist phantoms of 1964 had long since vanished. Why, then, were there checkpoints on the road to Cachoeira? Why were machine guns aimed at buses? What were they afraid of?

It happened in Salvador. Chico Buarque, a popular song writer, had released a new recording entitled *In Spite of You*. Its ascent to the top of Brazil's hit parade caught the censors off guard. In the lyrics, an ill-tempered lover plots release:

•

Today you're the one who says what to do
You give an order and it's done
There's no discussion.

My friends, today my people walk around talking in asides
Their eyes to the ground.
But you're going to have to witness
The morning in rebirth
Scattering its poetry.

How will you explain it
When the sky clears suddenly
And with impunity?

How will you choke off
The chorus of our song
Thrown up against you?

In spite of you
Tomorrow has to be another day.

(translated and adapted by the author)

•

Anyone with a lick of sense got the message, and so too, eventually, did the military. *In Spite of You* was removed from record shops, radio stations were afraid to play it, and Chico Buarque, under threat of arrest and imprisonment, did not sing it.

Not long afterward, Chico gave a concert in Salvador to a packed house. He stuck to popular, if apolitical, subjects, like *Feijoada Completa*, whose lyrics feature the ingredients in Brazil's characteristic Saturday repast. When the show ended, the audience demanded an encore; they wanted *In Spite of You*. Chico cast a glance at the MPs stationed at each corner of the stage; he shook his head, he did not dare. And then it started, only a few voices at first but growing in strength. The band struck up the tune; *In Spite of You* burst forth. A thousand strong, they sang on his behalf: "When the sky clears suddenly, and with impunity, how will you choke off the chorus of our song?"

As the *Jornal* expressed it, "Brazil walked on only one leg." A regime that called forth technological wonders searched for subversion in every samba tune. When the military tried to dignify senators it appointed for life, it found them ridiculed as "bionic." With an eye to the double entendre, graffiti artists likewise challenged the regime's penchant for eradication. I rarely saw anything so unimaginative as "death to the military"—too obvious and lacking in linguistic resourcefulness.

My favorite slogan, in red acrylic that bled through a hundred coats of whitewash, was on Resende Street: "Viva o gordo e abaixo o regime." On the surface, it was publicity for a comedy show. *Gordo* means "fat" and *regime* means "diet." So it was just the show's humorous caption: "Long Live the Fat and Down with the Diet." But the slogan had a barbed edge that was unmistakable. Everyone knew that *regime* meant the military and that *gordo* referred to good times. To most Brazilians, the caption read "Long Live Good Times and Down with the Regime." This was confirmed each week on the popular TV show *O Gordo*. It featured corpulent Jô Soares. For the skit, "Captain Gay," he dressed up in shocking pink. He deftly wrapped each punch line in slang and double meaning. For astute political analysis, Brazilians preferred Captain Gay to the network news.

The death squads could not be mocked. Unchecked by superiors in Brasília, they terrorized the opposition. This was especially true in the state of São Paulo, where the army commander sheltered their operations. Defying the regime's moderate turn, the security forces tortured and killed one of São Paulo's leading journalists, Vladimir Herzog. The public outrage created by the atrocity gave Geisel a pretext to act. He placed his own man in command of São Paulo, dismantling the ring that kept the security forces beyond Brasília's control. Only later did Pinochet's Chile and Videla's Argentina compile a death count that overshadowed Brazil's evil hour.

Geisel brought a stone-faced dignity and personal honesty to the presidency. He tried to give the regime a "second leg," some vestige of popular support. *Distensão*, apparently, was the long-awaited crutch. But for every step Geisel took in the direction of a political opening, there followed two steps sideways and one step backwards. As tensions eased, the opposition became more outspoken. Geisel became more heavy-handed; he liked to keep affairs of state under his thumb. The critics he disliked the most he kicked out of Congress. By the time Geisel named his successor, General João Figueiredo, head of the detested National Intelligence Service, *distensão* was still more symbol than substance.

When I returned to Brazil in 1979, Figueiredo had lost fifteen pounds—a rigorous program of jogging and weight lifting reported faithfully in the *Jornal*. He had dropped his middle name, Batista, in preference to plain old João, and appeared frequently without sunglasses. When Brasília released his official portrait, it revealed a smiling, downright friendly looking president. A greater contrast to his dour predecessor can hardly be imagined. Geisel jogging?

What had been cautiously referred to as *distensão* under Geisel became a full-fledged "opening"—the famed *abertura*—under Figueiredo. In 1979, amnesty was the catchword. Politicians, songwriters, and scientists now found it safe to return from abroad. Those who had lost their political rights were restored to full citizenship. The *Jornal* took a self-righteous position. "Amnesty," it pointed out, "is for criminals." Those who had denounced the regime's assault on democracy had not committed "crimes" for which "amnesty" was required. Still, regardless of the rubric, Brazil was coming home.

In exchange for amnesty, Congress had to postpone the 1980 elections until November 1982, but everything would be up for grabs on the same day: county offices, state legislatures, every governorship, the Chamber of Deputies, and the Senate, except for its bionic members. Until the election, however, Figueiredo's government was in charge. New "packages" designed to strengthen the regime's election prospects kept descending on Congress. The most famous disbanded the obligatory two-party system for a free-market approach to political parties. Enough signatures in enough states brought official recognition. The assumption was that small opposition parties would proliferate on the left, leaving the regime with a majority at the center. Despite divergent views, the opposition held together and kept the same name as before: the Brazilian Democratic Movement. The regime's supporters also stood together. But given the disrepute that followed a decade of groveling, they thought it best to call the party "Social Democratic," precisely what they had not been. Except for small labor parties, the reorganization failed to split the opposition. Everyone knew that if the elections were held the government was in for a beating.

Whenever I got bogged down in the obliqueness of the *Jornal*'s editorial page, I took the bus to Copacabana and got Simón Schwartzman's interpretation. "The elections won't take place," he told me categorically, more skeptical than usual. "At best, the regime will devise another 'package' to its advantage; at worst, the elections will be canceled outright." His fears were not unfounded. The press had pointedly asked the president what guarantee Brazil had that the elections would occur. "Because I said so," he replied. And then there was an attempted bombing of an opposition rally in Rio. The bomb exploded prematurely in a military vehicle. What sinister forces had turned to terrorism: the army's High Command? the president himself? "They're a bunch of cowards," said Figueiredo contemptuously. "If they want to stop *abertura*, they can try killing me." When angry, Figueiredo said what he meant. The plot was not investigated, but the president, at least, was not involved.

The election did occur. The government won in theory but lost in practice. It controlled the Senate, but not with its accustomed grip. In the Chamber of Deputies, it mustered only a fragile majority that it could not trust. And although it won a majority of state governments, it lost the states of São Paulo, Rio de Janeiro, and Minas Gerais: the core of the nation's industry, finance, and media. The regime held the kingdom without the keys. Congress found new self-respect, the press found a new voice, and political analysis became a TV feature. Brazil came back, its passengers no longer crouched on buses. The country now walked on many legs, but the regime had only one.

In 1983, Brazil plunged into the worst depression of the postwar period, its $95 billion debt pushing the country toward disaster. Yet, economic policy was set by the president's inner circle, beyond congressional scrutiny. The regime did not consult its supporters in Congress any more than it did the opposition. Whatever the significance of *abertura*, it did not affect real policy. The old guard hung on as tenaciously as ever, jealous of power held at gunpoint. Would it let the state's patronage fall to others it could not control? It was the ultimate question.

The regime, however, still had a trump card to play. It held a majority in the electoral college, which would select the next president. Apparently, Figueiredo could designate his own successor. It turned out otherwise. The rebellion surfaced first in the regime's own party. Paulo Maluf, the former governor of São Paulo, announced his candidacy and began campaigning publically. Where Maluf led, others followed.

I liked Figueiredo. In 1983 he came to cut the ribbon on Rio's new subway system. In the spirit of good sportsmanship, the politicians declared a cease-fire; the event was nonpartisan. Figueiredo, his voice cracking with emotion, reminisced about his childhood in Rio. Was it so bad, I thought, reading the *Jornal*, to have a teary-eyed general as president? Brazil is not a logical place, thank God. Despite the contempt people had for how the regime dictated economic policy, they still had sympathy for Figueiredo. When he underwent bypass surgery in August, the health slogan on bumper stickers in Rio took on a new significance: *bate coração*—keep your heart beating!

They say of Figueiredo that he preferred friends to making enemies, that he was indecisive and overly emotional. He muddled through most of 1984, more spectator than participant. In March, for example, Brazil rallied to the cause of direct presidential elections. In São Paulo and Rio, marches drew unprecedented crowds of a million. Simón, with uncharacteristic enthusiasm, called it the most spectacular event he had ever seen.

Through it all Figueiredo remained painfully ambiguous. He said no to Maluf, but did little to stop him. He opposed direct elections, but allowed demonstrations to take place without incident. Figueiredo's very indecisiveness created the flexibility the opposition needed to negotiate its way to power. By the time I got back to the *Jornal* in June 1984, Brazil did not seem to have a government. Argentina had been filled with rumors about debtors' clubs and moratoriums. Brazil, however, had shelved the debt to concentrate on politics. In the end, it was the government's party that split. The turncoats formed a coalition with the opposition. Together, they had enough votes to control the electoral college. Their candidate was Tancredo Neves, an opposition governor from Minas Gerais.

In the United States, newspapers tried to explain Brazil's return to democracy. They focused on the skills of Tancredo Neves who had "delivered" Brazil to a new democratic era. That Tancredo knew his moment had come, recognized it, and seized it, no one can deny. But he took the path prepared by those who had filled the country's great squares on behalf of direct elections. They proved that Brazil was ungovernable at the hands of anyone tied to the old regime, and that included its candidate Paulo Maluf. The "campaign" underscored the point. Tancredo pretended it was a popular election and went on the stump. And Brazil rallied to the cause, turning out in jubilant, expectant crowds. Paulo Maluf, by contrast, could not appear in public without an armed escort, and even then he was pelted with tomatoes.

Figueiredo recognized the regime's slow death, but he would not prescribe emergency treatment. His regime died but the patient lived. The media interviewed Figueiredo during his last days as president. He was asked, at the end, for a final message to Brazil. "Forget about me," he said, bringing his arms together in the "up-your's" position. As they said, he was "too emotional." Geisel one respected or feared. Figueiredo one could actually like: a tragic flaw for the regime, a happy fault for Brazil.

President-elect Tancredo addressed the National Press Club while visiting Washington in January 1985. He responded to questions with an astonishing clarity and command of the facts; it was hard to imagine he was seventy-five. "I've been following you around three days," said one reporter. "I'm thirty years younger and exhausted. How do you do it?" "At my age," quipped Tancredo, "I don't have time to waste." He did not. Two months later he was dead. He had stolen fire from the gods, enough to ask of anyone. The mantle passed quietly to José Sarney, Tancredo's vice-president.

The news magazine *Veja* ran a feature on Sarney's "style" in office. It opened with a photograph of the president receiving heads of state. In the background, his granddaughter romped playfully with her friends.

• Play and Work

Popular culture in Brazil is inclusive and has remarkable staying power. The lyrics to each carnival's hit samba tune penetrate all social ranks. Anyone can see this at the Sala Funarte in downtown Rio. The late afternoon show costs a dollar and packs in a heterogeneous audience from sixteen to sixty. The Funarte's fame is its ingenious combination of discordant styles. A typical example was the show that featured the old-style recording artist, Nana Caymmi, backed up by the new-wave Bossa Nova band, Free Speech (*Boca Livre*).* The samba finale brought everyone to their feet. And they knew the lyrics too, whether the Boca Livre fans in the front or the fashionable Caymmi devotees farther back. In this, Brazil is singular, a nation in transition held together precariously by the power of musicians.

A reasonably good version of the samba lasts a lifetime—good for carnival, good for feastdays. Brazil used to revel in the frequent holidays the calendar declared. The military, embarrassed by displays of the country's backwardness, purged Santo Antônio and São João. Nonetheless, old loyalties die hard. They had to concede a local holiday option to the Northeast where Santo Antônio still finds things for people and São João sends the rain. In every hamlet and shantytown (*favela*), the country's patron saints are still remembered.

North Americans cast a reproachful eye upon the festivities common to the world farther south. "No wonder people are poor, they waste so much on fiestas." Brazil is particularly open to such criticism, for the calendar creates an excuse for *feijoada* every Saturday. Chico Buarque paid his respects to Brazil's popular dish in *Feijoada Completa*:

•

Friends are coming
With insatiable appetites
And a thirst unquenched since yesterday.

Let's get out the beer
Make sure it's cold as ice
Let's fill up the bean pot
And fatten up our friends.

This won't be much work
Don't set the table or bother with chairs
Just put out the plates, and that's it.

---

*Livre means "free"; *boca* means "mouth"—and, by extension, "speech." In slang, however, a *boca* is also the locale of a pot party.

Throw in some sausage, dried meat, and pork
Fry up the cracklings
Boil up the rice.

Times are hard
But for our brother, there's no bill
Just fill the pot with beans
Throw in the meat
Cover with water.

(translated and adapted by the author)

•

One can detect this spirit in the United States on Thanksgiving. People define family in extended terms, pulling in stray friends and neighbors on the flimsiest of pretexts. For a day, Americans forget to distinguish between worthy and unworthy poor, serving turkey dinners to bag ladies and bums. Even Congress, which relegated most holidays to the anonymity of Mondays, dared not tamper with the pumpkin pie.

"People may be poor, but at least they have their fiestas" is nearer the mark. In point of fact, a few extra Thanksgivings would do the Yankee soul a world of good.

The new president of City Bank, John Reed, dropped by Brazil to check up on his favorite debtor. He advised the country to "work harder." Consider, however, the women who prepare *cafezinho* in the hundreds of cafés within ten blocks of my hotel, or the thousands of workers at snack bars and restaurants, the people who collect Rio's garbage, the cashiers at supermarkets, or the bus drivers. If they want to hum and chatter while making coffee, pushing mops, and squeezing orange juice, that is their business. They certainly worked hard enough. The boys at the snack bar top the list for sheer speed and agility. In a cramped space of four square feet they manage hamburgers, grilled cheese sandwiches, five different kinds of sausages, assorted fish balls, and seventeen different choices of freshly squeezed fruit juice. So I was not sure to whom Mr. Reed referred. From what I could tell, it was not the local garbage man. And he could not have meant most middle-class Brazilians either, so many of whom moonlight at second jobs to make up for the inadequacy of the first. He probably meant the denizens of the Planning Ministry—the only fragment of Brazil he could possibly know firsthand.

• Cinelândia

Cinelândia is downtown Rio's movie district and the city's most popular gathering place. I kept track of the regime's shifting fortunes by the political debates and the number of rallies that filled the plaza. Cinelândia looks out to the rocky heights of Sugar Loaf Mountain across Guananbara Bay. To one side are busy sidewalk cafés, the stately columns of the old Legislative Assembly, and the Baroque Municipal Theater, sandblasted back to its old pretentious splendor. Across the way, is the stolid Victorianism of the Fine Arts Museum and the Greek Revival of the National Library. Despite the clash in architecture, Cinelândia pulls together in some secret way. Like Brazil, I have often thought, opposites balanced by some inner miracle, a greatness unperceived.

I read about the episode at my hotel in 1979. A Third World Festival in West Berlin featured Gilberto Gil, a black musician and songwriter from Salvador. He was supposed to exemplify the African character of Brazilian music. His performance did not. He mixed the samba with rock and experimental jazz, at times with English lyrics. The critics denounced him for "foreign models" and "imperialist" language. The reporter who covered the festival in the *Jornal* was indignant. "They expected something 'primitive' because Gilberto is black and from Brazil. He does not have to prove anything; he spent two years in exile, he can sing anything he wants."

On Friday, when the tour reached Bonn, Gilberto had dropped to last place on the program. When he came on stage, close to midnight, most of the audience had left—"so they could get up early," noted the *Jornal*'s reporter scornfully. Brazilians had come for the performance. They were only a few, but they gave Gilberto an uproarious welcome. The show over, they descended on a Greek restaurant—"the only kind still open after midnight," added the reporter in disbelief. They stayed until sunrise. Gilberto and his troupe played the music; exiled Brazilians and embassy officials did the singing.

Gilberto Gil was born into Salvador's Afro-Brazilian traditions, yet is prone to modernism in his music. And our reporter, irate at the Germans who thought Gilberto was too modern, caroused all night, disdainful of the locals who "slept away in the orderliness of their capital city." What is Brazil? Is it São Paulo's skyscrapers, the Alcohol Program, and the computer industry, or is it best portrayed by carnival, mulattoes, and São João? It is all of these, held together incongruously like Cinelândia.

The generals banned the film *Black Orpheus*: too many Negroes, too much carnival, not enough work. During Brazil's evil hour, carnival became a political act, one of the few forms of expression beyond the regime's control. Carnival draws its life from the Samba Schools, neighborhood organizations that plan the festival and define its themes. Not even the National Intelligence Service could infiltrate their ranks. Where a frontal attack could not succeed, however, starvation by development did. For twenty years, the regime's technocrats mortgaged the country's future unopposed. For jet aircraft and petrochemicals, Brazil has no peer south of the Rio Grande. But beneath the surface is a nation no better off than Peru. The regime's pursuit of greatness passed by those who filled the streets of Rio and Salvador in the fantasies of carnival.

The price of this neglect is now unmistakable, exacted in robberies and assaults, sacked supermarkets, and abandoned street children. Once you are seated comfortably at one of Cinelândia's cafés, children come with their sad eyes, hawking peanuts, newspapers, flowers, and shoe shines. When Tancredo spoke at the National Press Club, he was asked if Brazil would pay on its $100 billion debt. "Of course," he said, "and we have gotten something for it too. Brazil is the largest steel and automotive producer in Latin America, our alcohol industry leads the world in fuel technology, we have developed our hydroelectric potential, and our exports netted a surplus last year of almost $13 billion. I'm not concerned about the debt we owe the banks; my main concern is Brazil's social debt, what we owe to the majority of the country, the people whose lives, so far, development has not touched."

On its social debt, Brazil is much in arrears. Of the children who enter the first grade, 40 percent never make it to the second. In the country's favelas infant mortality is anywhere from 160 to 300 per 1,000. Half the labor force scrapes by on a mere 14 percent of the national income. The mutiny of the majority can no longer be indefinitely postponed by the magic of song, by carnival, feijoada, or São João. The forces that bind have found their match in a frantic worship of progress computed by additions to capital stock, but without the simple arithmetic of human welfare. The saints and spirits of carnival, shunned and displaced, have fled. This time, promises will not bring them back. The social debt must now be paid, not just the interest. To whom, in the end, does Brazil stand most in debt, to City Bank or to São João?

That is a bit melodramatic. Big development has left some assets behind. Paved highways stretch thousands of miles from Rio to distant targets such as Belém in the North (2,000 miles), Cuiabá in the West (1,300 miles), and Pôrto Velho (2,100 miles) in Rondônia, a state that borders Bolivia. From there, you can continue on to Manaus (1,500 miles), the capital of Amazonas. Whether you are a truck driver, a motorist, or a mere bus passenger, it is the kind of development you notice. And when Brazil stops paying City Bank, it will still have the highways.

To build Rio's metro, demolition squads assaulted the city's neighborhoods, turning them into quagmires when it rained and dust bowls when it did not. For well nigh a decade, Rio staggered under the blows of jack hammers and dynamite. When completed, however, the metro had cleared spaces above ground that were converted into playgrounds and pedestrian malls. From the subway stop at Cinelândia, a great walkway stretches almost a mile to the stop at Uruguaiana Street. The district so formed is downtown Rio's largest non-combat zone, a haven for weary pedestrians and vendors. In other areas of Rio, neighborhoods campaigned for parks, defeating plans for buildings and parking lots. Big development is a reasonable proposition, presuming you pay some attention to those whose needs are the greatest.

Marxism muddles its analysis of Brazil with the categorical approach bequeathed by its founder: ruling class, haute and petite bourgeoisie, lumpen and regular proletariat, and peasants with land and those without. To appreciate the great truth about Brazil, go down to the Municipal Theater and try crossing Rio Branco Avenue. Brazil has only two kinds of people, those with cars and those without.

I have considered arming pedestrians with hammers: one well-placed bash to a fender might bring the arrogant motorist to his senses. Cars whizz around the corner, scattering pedestrians like chickens. At its worst, development is hit and run. Until now, Brazil has fretted more over the welfare of its automobiles than the future of its children. When OPEC threatened the gas tank, the regime decreed alcohol substitution. A decade later, encouraged by subsidies and credits, production exceeded the ten billion liter target. But what of those without cars?

"Thief!" shouted a distressed woman, giving awkward chase in high heels. The culprit knocked against my table, sending beer bottles flying; he stumbled into a cop's iron grip. The woman, indignant, came over to retrieve her purse. The thief, a ten-year-old clad in ragged shorts, struggled hopelessly. He grabbed the woman's arm in desperation, sobbing. She stood there a moment, now almost as troubled as the child. "This isn't necessary," she insisted, "nothing is missing." "Look," retorted the cop, "he stole the purse and he got caught; if I hadn't grabbed him, everything would be gone." A crowd had gathered, adding partisans to the woman's cause. "The point is, it's her purse, she's got it back; if she doesn't want the boy arrested, that's her right." This went on until public opinion prevailed. The child stood motionless, released by forces beyond comprehension, and then darted out into the night, into the future that awaits us all.

5
BIG DEVELOPMENTS

A line drawn due south of Miami ends up in the Pacific Ocean, bypassing the South American continent, which lies to the east. The great bulge of Brazil lunges out into the South Atlantic reaching halfway to Africa. From Miami, Rio de Janeiro is almost as far east (2,500 miles) as it is south (3,300 miles).

• Brazil

Population

Occupying an area of 3.2 million square miles, Brazil is the world's fifth largest country: it is three times the size of Argentina, four times as large as Mexico, and surpasses the United States minus Alaska. With 135 million inhabitants (1985), Brazil is Latin America's most populous country, far ahead of Mexico's 78 million. Within South America almost half the continent's inhabitants are Brazilians. Overall, Brazil ranks as the world's sixth most populous country. When the military took over in 1964, Brazil's population was approximately 79 million; by the time the country's future once again fell to civilians, a growth rate of 2.9 percent during the 1960s, 2.5 percent in the 1970s, and 2.3 percent in the 1980s had added 56 million inhabitants to the total. In 1985, 36 percent of Brazil's population was under fifteen years of age and only 4 percent was over sixty-five.[1]

The southeastern states of São Paulo, Minas Gerais, Rio de Janeiro, and Espírito Santo had 44 percent of all Brazil's inhabitants in 1985; the Northeast, which embraces nine states, followed with approximately 29 percent. Adding in the Southern Region composed of Paraná, Santa Catarina, and Rio Grande do Sul, with a combined 15 percent, accounts for 88 percent of Brazil's population, but for only 36 percent of its territory. (See Table 5.1.) Despite a slight shift to the Center West, which followed the construction of Brasília, and toward the Amazon Basin in the North, the population balance between regions has remained relatively stable over the past quarter century. The main exception is the Northeast, Brazil's poorest region, which exported a disproportionate share of its surplus inhabitants to São Paulo and to boom states on the frontier like Rondônia. Overall, however, migration in Brazil has occurred primarily within regions: an exodus from the countryside to neighboring cities.

Factories

In 1960, Brazil had already acquired a strong industrial base. The contribution that manufacturing made to the gross national product (GNP) was over 25 percent, and the industrial sector's growth, at an annual rate of 9.8 percent (1955–62), had outpaced that of services or agriculture.[2] Brazil, for example, produced over 130,000 motored vehicles in 1960, which had a national content in excess of 90 percent.[3] Expansion continued at a rapid clip. Between 1968 and 1973, industry grew at a spectacular 13.2 percent annually, before dropping to the modest but still substantial 7.7 percent that prevailed until 1980. The rise in Brazil's GNP followed suit, averaging 11.5 percent (1968–73) and 7.1 percent (1974–80).[4] It was an impressive achievement. In 1980, Brazil's $196 billion GNP surpassed that of Mexico and Argentina combined. With vehicle production at over a million units and steel at 15 million metric tons, Brazil accounted for over half of Latin America's output of both.[5] From shoes, textiles, and consumer durables to petrochemicals, electrical equipment, and computers, Brazil's industrial capacity was sophisticated and diverse.

Brazil's transformation from a rural to an urban society occurred in fifteen years. In 1965, half the country still lived in rural areas; in 1980, only 32 percent did. Brazil began the 1970s with only four cities above the million mark but ended it with eleven cities in that category. Metropolitan São Paulo, already the country's largest urban area, continued its rapid growth from 8.1 million in 1970 to 12.6 million in 1980.[6] By comparison, the U.S. population, which struck a balance between the city and the countryside in 1920, took forty years to become as urban as Brazil.[7] In the United States, although industrialization was relatively advanced in 1920, large-scale mechanization in agriculture lagged behind. Agribusiness, for example, did not begin a frontal attack on the family farm until the late 1950s. When the South's sharecroppers and the Midwest's small farmers gradually transferred their labor to Birmingham's

145

Table 5.1 Population Distribution in Brazil by Region

Region*	% of Total Land Area	% of Total Population (1960)	% of Total Population (1985)	Change (1960–1985)
North	42	3.6	5.4	+1.8
Northeast	18	31.7	28.9	−2.8
Southeast	11	43.7	43.8	+0.1
South	7	16.8	15.2	−1.6
Center West	22	4.2	6.7	+2.5
Total	100	100.0	100.0	

Source: Anuário Estatístico do Brasil—1982 (Rio de Janeiro: Fundação Instituto Brasileiro de Geografia e Estatística, 1983), pp. 28, 77–78. The 1985 figures are estimates.

*STATES WITHIN REGIONS

North	Northeast	Southeast	Center West	South
Rondônia	Maranhão	Minas Gerais	Mato Grosso	Paraná
Acre	Piauí	Espírito Santo	do Sul	Santa Catarina
Amazonas	Ceará	Rio de Janeiro	Mato Grosso	Rio Grande do Sul
Roraima	Rio Grande do Norte	São Paulo	Goiás	
Pará	Paraíba		Federal District	
Amapá	Pernambuco		(Brasília)	
	Alagoas			
	Sergipe			
	Bahia			

steel mills or Detroit's automobile factories, they traded marginal employment in agriculture for more productive jobs in industry. The situation was drastically different in Brazil.

Between 1970 and 1980, Brazil's economy created over 5.6 million new jobs in industry, commerce, and services. Nonetheless, the additions to full-time employment fell far short of the country's needs.[8] Just to keep pace with population growth, Brazil's stock of jobs had to multiply by 2.3 percent each year.[9] To make matters worse, the way the regime promoted mechanization and land consolidation in rural areas pushed workers out of agriculture, increasing job applicants in the cities.

Farms

Between 1966 and 1979, output for export crops such as soybeans, cocoa, and sugarcane grew at an annual rate of 19 percent. On the other hand, food crops such as potatoes, rice, and corn barely kept pace with population growth; in the case of manioc and black beans, popular Brazilian staples, production actually declined.[10] The distortion reflected both a perverse distribution of land and the way the regime orchestrated agricultural credit.

Small farms proliferated, middle-sized farms declined, and large estates increased their share of the land available. Between 1960 and 1980, holdings with less than 10 hectares increased from 45 to 50 percent of all farms, although their share of the land stayed constant at about 2 percent. Holdings of between 10 and 99 hectares dropped from 45 to 39 percent of all farms. By contrast, large estates with over 1,000 hectares accounted for 1 percent of Brazil's farms yet controlled 46 percent of the disposable land—up from 44 percent in 1960. (See Table 5.2.) The credit system only reinforced the trend. Consider how the regime dispensed agricultural loans in the state of São Paulo. In 1977 only 6 percent of the credit went to small producers with between 10 and 20 hectares, even though they accounted for 21 percent of all the farms in the state. On the other hand, holdings of 100 hectares or more made up only 15 percent of the state's farms, but they got over half the credit.[11] For Brazil overall, credit subsidies went disproportionately to export crops. Between 1975 and 1979, for example, soybean production claimed 20 percent of all the crop loans made in Brazil. During the same period, cassava and black beans received a miserly 1 and 3 percent respectively.[12] Because food crops are the mainstay of small farmers, Brazil's lackluster performance on staples is not surprising.

Brazil's credit program disguised a net transfer of resources on a massive scale. Loans carried a fixed interest rate of 14 percent, whereas inflation averaged a hefty 40 percent from 1976 to 1978 and reached almost 80 percent in 1979. Under such circumstances, the $7 billion shelled out to finance production and mechanization in 1979 was paid back at year's end with cruzeiros worth half as much, and from harvests whose value had kept pace with inflation.[13] The more land one had the more one could borrow, and the more borrowed, the greater the profits.

Marcos Cintra Cavalcanti, a rural economist with the Getúlio Vargas Foundation, summed up the situation at a conference I attended in 1983. He presented his facts and figures in a methodical, cautious manner.

"Landowners," he emphasized, "used credit to directly finance production. They relied less on sharecroppers who they now saw as expendable. It paid the big producer and agribusiness to go into debt as a hedge against inflation. They covered operating expenses with subsidized credit, keeping their own capital in financial instruments that yielded a high rate of return. Able to draw on profits from such investments, they purchased additional land and consolidated their holdings. Throughout Brazil, sharecroppers were turned into a rural proletariat, housed in slums set apart from the estate, and denied even a small parcel of land for subsistence crops. Mechanization continued apace as cheap credit produced lopsided investments in sophisticated machinery, tractors, and trucks. Using 1969 as a base year [100], agriculture's industrial consumption index had risen to 500 in 1980. The sector's gains in output reflected increased acreage much more than they did higher productivity.

**Table 5.2 Land Distribution in Brazil, by Farm Size and Area
(1 hectare = 2.4 acres)**

	% of Farms		% of Area	
Size of Farm (in hectares)	1960	1980	1960	1980
Less than 10	45	50	2	2
10–99	45	39	19	17
100–999	9	10	35	35
Over 1,000	1	1	44	46
Total	100	100	100	100

Source: Anuário Estatístico do Brasil—1982 (Rio de Janeiro: Fundação Instituto Brasileiro de Geografia e Estatística, 1983), p. 302. Figures do not include farms without a declaration—less than 1 percent for each census year.

"Agriculture," he noted, "had a credit account without limit. This is how the government promoted soybean exports and the Alcohol Program. When they ran out of money, they printed it. By 1980, agricultural subsidies had become the single largest source of inflation."

It was a terrible irony. Inflation reduced the earning power of urban workers, and at the same time it put sharecroppers out of work. Between 1970 and 1980, the amount of land allocated to tenant farming, for example, shrank by over half; agriculture's share of the labor force dropped from 44 to 30 percent.[14] The dispossessed headed for the cities. Brazil's urban economy had not only to employ those already there, or entering the ranks of adulthood, but those swarming in from the hinterland. The regime's great miracle, padded by statistics on GNP, was as much fraud as fact, as much tragedy as development. Brazil's displaced migrants traded marginal productivity in the countryside for meager subsistence in urban slums.

Jobs

When the United States began its transfer out of agriculture, industry was more labor-intensive; it soaked up rural America and millions of European immigrants as well. For Brazil, the additions to employment suggested by statistics on growth were by no means a one-to-one match. In the case of transport equipment, production increased by 22 percent a year between 1967 and 1973, but the employment increment trailed behind at an average of 8.5 percent. For chemical products, an annual growth rate of 7.6 percent (1973–80) added an average of 1 percent to the industry's labor force. Considering the 1967–80 period overall, the most dynamic industries (electrical and transport equipment, machinery, metallurgy, and chemical products), whose output jumped an average of 12.5 percent a year, hired only 7 percent more workers.

In contrast, traditional manufacturing such as textiles, apparel, and food processing showed a slower 7 percent rise in output, but increased its labor force by 6.4 percent annually.[15] Nonetheless, the trend was away from labor-intensive manufacturing toward high-tech industries that required fewer workers. And those they hired needed more skills than was characteristic of the labor force as a whole.

And what happened to members of the unskilled labor force who were relegated to the country's shantytowns? If they could not find jobs in industry they tried for employment in "services," a heterogeneous sector that included everything from parking lot attendants and cleaning ladies to mechanics and transport workers. Or they joined the ranks of the unemployed. Although 1980 was a boom year for Brazil's economy, urban unemployment for men was still around 10 percent.[16] To be without a job in Brazil was to face starvation: there was no safety net to catch those rejected by the economy's hidden hand.

The simple fact of employment does not necessarily confer a living wage. For 1970, the World Bank defined as "modern" any job that yielded a monthly income equal to at least the minimum wage. By that calculation, only 45 percent of Brazil's work force was so employed. It further estimated that new jobs in the modern sector opened up at the rate of 3.7 percent annually, whereas the total labor force expanded by 2.7 percent. At that rate, it would take seventy-eight years for the modern sector to absorb the low-wage work force.[17]

Wages

The World Bank's definition hit rock bottom, for Brazil's minimum wage scarcely provided bare subsistence. Remember the woman back in Lapa's supermarket? If her husband earned Rio's prevailing minimum wage, which averaged 1,000 cruzeiros a week in 1980, could she afford to feed a typical family of five? Drawing from a list of food staples, and using the average retail prices for Rio in 1980, I have filled her weekly shopping basket with an eye to economy, both as to the items selected and the quantity allotted.[18] (See Table 5.3.)

I did not bother with beef (fresh or salted), cheese, pork, olive oil, or codfish; they may be popular for the middle class but they are not minimum-wage items. Absent too are luxuries such as frozen orange juice, boxed cereals, or soft drinks. And of course, toothpaste, aspirin, or cleansing agents are not included. Nonetheless, my motley selection totals to 1,200 cruzeiros— 200 more than the weekly minimum wage: there is nothing left for bus fares, clothing, or rent. Even though Brazil's low-income households spend about half their income on food, most of my purchases still have to go back on the shelf. What could be bought for 500 cruzeiros: half the 1980 minimum weekly wage? Not much beyond sugar, eggs, and starch.

Table 5.3 Average Weekly Food Expenditures for a Family of Five in Rio de Janeiro, 1980

Item	Cost (in cruzeiros)
5 lbs. sugar	48
2 lbs. coffee	147
2 doz. eggs	78
4 lbs. beans	150
4 lbs. rice	66
4 qts. milk	64
1 lb. margarine	74
1 qt. cooking oil	80
2 lbs. tomatoes	66
10 lbs. potatoes	75
3 lbs. chicken	102
3 lbs. salt pork	110
2 doz. bananas	50
1 doz. oranges	28
2 lbs. onions	62
Total Cost	Cr $ 1,200

Source: Anuário Estatístico do Brasil—1982 (Rio de Janeiro: Fundação Instituto Brasileiro de Geografia e Estatística, 1983), p. 647.

Distributions

In 1980, about 30 percent of Brazil's workers earned less than the minimum wage—down from 55 percent in 1970.[19] Yet the portion of national income that trickled into the shopping baskets of humbler citizenry was still a pittance. Taking into account that Brazil's GNP quadrupled between 1960 and 1980, where did the windfall go?[20] It went to those who had the skills and assets to profit from the modern sector's expansion, and most of the country was ill-equipped to grab its share. Whatever the merits of development, the recipe followed in Brazil did not include distribution. The richest 5 percent pocketed 28 percent of Brazil's income in 1960 and 38 percent in 1980. For the poorest 40 percent, their share had dropped to under 10 percent. (See Table 5.4.) In the United States, the wealthiest 5 percent in 1981 managed well enough on 15 percent of the national income. Although nothing to brag about, the bottom 40 percent took home 16 percent of the income.[21] Such details aside, economists certified Brazil's GNP growth as "miraculous."

In sheer size, Brazil's GNP makes its neighbors look second-rate. Viewed on a per capita basis however, Venezuela, Argentina, and Mexico did better

Table 5.4 Income Distribution in Brazil

Income Groups (Percentile: Lowest Income Group to Highest)	Relative Income Levels[1] (% of Total Income)		
	1960	1970	1980
1–10	1.9	1.2	1.1
11–20	2.0	2.0	2.0
21–30	3.0	3.0	3.0
31–40	4.4	3.8	3.5
41–50	6.1	5.0	4.5
51–60	7.5	6.2	5.5
61–70	9.0	7.2	7.2
71–80	11.3	10.0	9.6
81–90	15.2	15.1	15.3
91–100	39.6	46.5	48.3
	100.0	100.0	100.0
Bottom 50 percent[2]	17.4	15.0	14.1
Top 5 percent	28.3	34.1	37.9
Top 1 percent	11.9	14.7	16.9

Sources: 1. The 1960 decile distribution is from Sylvia Ann Hewlett and Richard S. Weinert, eds., *Brazil and Mexico: Patterns in Late Development* (Philadelphia: Institute for the Study of Human Issues, 1982), p. 320; for 1970 and 1980, see Carlos Mauro Benevides Filho, "Income Distribution in Brazil: 1970–1980 Compared" (Ph.D. diss., Vanderbilt University, 1985), p. 81.

2. For 1960, see Luiz Bresser Pereira, *Development and Crisis in Brazil, 1930–1983* (Boulder, Colo.: Westview Press, 1984), p. 184. The figures for the bottom 50 percent (1970 and 1980) are compiled from the deciles presented above; for the top 5 and 1 percent, see ibid., p. 184. All the data presented are based on individual income for the economically active population.

than Brazil in 1980.[22] The size of the pie is one thing, who eats it is quite another. Brazil's National Family Nutrition Survey, conducted during 1974–75, concluded that, from birth to age seventeen, only 42 percent of Brazilian children reached the weights considered normal for their ages. Overall, 20 percent suffered from second-degree malnutrition—61 to 75 percent of normal weight. The study further noted that even a minimal diet for a family of five exceeded a minimum-wage income.[23] If the hypothetical shopping spree previously calculated for Rio is any indication, the situation in 1980 was roughly similar. For the decade as a whole (1970–80), the real buying power of the minimum wage rose by only 3 percent.[24]

Using data from the 1970s, and taking into account urban-rural differentials within countries, the World Bank constructed a poverty index for each of several Latin American countries: it considered the costs of a basic diet, access to housing that could be considered "minimally adequate," and the provision of public services, such as health care, potable water, and primary education. For Brazil, 49 percent of the country's families were below the poverty line, 25 percent of them "destitute." For Argentina, the figures were 8 and 1 percent, for Mexico, 34 and 12 percent. GNP, superhighways, and petrochemicals aside, Brazil most closely resembled Peru: half the country poor, a quarter destitute.[25] Guesstimates, just because they are run through computers, do not necessarily inspire confidence. Nonetheless, applying the rule of thumb Brazilians use to define a survival income—from one and a half to two minimum wages—50 percent of the labor force still fell below the mark in 1980.[26] Some households, of course, have more than one wage earner, and families double up to save on housing costs. But one cannot mistake the grim facts that show up so blatantly in Brazil's health statistics.

In 1984, Brazil's infant mortality rate was 68 per 1,000, down substantially since 1965 (104), but still considerably above the figures for Colombia (48) or Mexico (51). Parasitic and infectious diseases, respiratory tract ailments, and malnutrition accounted for almost half the deaths among children under five. In the state capitals of Brazil's Northeast, 41 percent of those who died were children. Such stark realities were underscored by substandard housing and inadequate urban services. In the Northeast, the dwellings of the poor were without safe water and frequently lacked sewage disposal of any kind. For Brazil overall, 70 percent of the housing without waste facilities went to the families earning less than two minimum wages.[27]

The regime propped up GNP with massive development projects: alcohol substitution for petroleum, export promotion for industries, subsidies for agriculture's big producers, nuclear energy, and the world's largest hydroelectric complex—Itaipú. The benefits, however, had a perverse tendency to bunch at the top. Had Brazil continued to borrow and grow at the spectacular rates of the 1960s and 1970s, would the majority have eventually found healthy children, full shopping carts, and flush toilets? Apparently not. Big development is a trickster that lures in the thirsty and spits them out. Bewitched by a greatness measured in steel and cement, the regime borrowed from the banks and paid out in malnutrition and child mortality.

By 1980, even the regime recognized the distorted character of Brazil's development. Under Figueiredo, it was possible to denounce malnutrition without being considered a subversive. The necessity of building from the bottom took hold, however tenuously. The minimum wage, for example, was adjusted twice a year, covering inflation for the previous six months plus 10 percent. Allocations for low-cost housing, school lunches, and education all increased in real terms. Compensation for the sins of the past could not be achieved by a marginal shift in priorities, however well intentioned. Choices had been made; they could not be reversed overnight.

The regime invested billions to create a network of federal universities. In 1980, the system included thirty-four institutions in twenty-three states. Brazil occasionally runs out of black beans and onions, but it will never run out of technocrats. For Itaipú, the Alcohol Program, or nuclear energy, Brazil already had the requisite expertise. University enrollments, including federal, state, and private institutions, increased from about 300,000 in 1964 to 1.3 million in 1980.[28] While higher education supplied Brazil with engineers and physicians, primary education "produced illiteracy." Such was the assessment of Hector de Souza, vice-president of Brazil's Council of Education. A Figuereido appointee, he presented the facts candidly at a conference I attended in São Paulo.

"Compare the expansion of each educational level between 1968 and 1980: facilities for grades 1 through 8 (primary school) barely kept pace with population growth. (See Table 5.5.) Tracing the history of 1,000 typical students who had entered first grade in 1972, only half made it to the second grade and only about 25 percent remained by fifth grade.[29] (See Table 5.6.) Defining functional literacy as at least four years of primary school, most of our children are deficient. If Brazil's literacy rates are going up, it's because we attribute literacy to anyone who takes up a seat in the first grade. And in the Northeast, they are lucky to get that far: in some states only half of the children who are eligible for first grade are actually in school. Even in a wealthy state like São Paulo, where over half the kids make it to the fourth grade, the schools are overcrowded, running separate shifts."

Education, health care, and housing do not automatically find their way down to the lower social ranks. For Brazil to pay the arrears on its social debt will require a sustained commitment on a long-term basis. The strategy for payment designed under Figuereido was rapid growth with greater transfers to the less privileged sectors of society: but the government lost both will and way. After 1980, the economy took a disastrous tailspin that wiped out the marginal wage gains of the previous decade. GNP fell by −1.6 percent in 1981, squeezed out a pitiful +1 percent growth in 1982, and then tumbled again by −3.2 percent in 1983. The only increase of note was for inflation, which soared from 80 percent in 1980 to 142 percent in 1983.[30] Caught simultaneously in the clutches of the world's largest foreign debt, Brazil found itself handed over to the International Monetary Fund (IMF) and lectured on austerity. Unemployment in the cities had jumped from about 10 percent in 1980 to 20 percent in 1983. Nonetheless, the IMF's recipe for recovery was to curb wages. The lowest income groups lost the extra 10 percent added in 1980; for the rest, the correction in wages was held to 80 percent of inflation.

Passing On

Such was the inheritance passed on in 1985 to José Sarney, Brazil's first civilian president in twenty years. The economy had registered a modest 4 percent recovery in GNP the year before, but the debt was over $100 billion

Table 5.5 Educational Expansion in Brazil by Level

Level of Education	1968	1980
Higher Education	100	496
Secondary	100	351
Primary	100	154
Population Growth	100	130

Source: Presentation by Hector Gurgulino de Souza, Vice-President, Brazilian Council of Education, São Paulo, 18 July 1983.

with interest payments of $12 billion due. In the 1970s, Brazil had financed growth by borrowing abroad; during the 1980s, the world's capital headed for the safe haven the U.S. economy apparently provided. For the moment, only the United States presumes to buy prosperity with debt. So it comes starkly to this: Brazil must choose between its obligations to City Bank and its debt to the country's citizenry.

Addressing the United Nations in September 1985, Sarney promised that Brazil "will not pay its foreign debt with recession, not with unemployment, not with hunger." May it be so. Brazil today is no longer so credulous, so easily deceived by fraudulent miracles.

• Robin Hood

"The problem with our social debt," observed my Brazilian friend Paulo Calmon, half serious and half joking, "is that we're so out of practice, we've forgotten how to make payments." There is some truth in that. For twenty years the regime ignored the country's desperate need for social technology. No state in Brazil had a health system equivalent to Colombia's El Valle, or a rural development project as intensive as Plan Sierra. Nonetheless, Brazilians have implemented similar strategies, if on a more limited basis. And they have done so on shoestring budgets and with scant political support. The groundwork is already there, awaiting application.

"Why doesn't that rich 10 percent of Brazil reach into its pockets and cough up some cash?" demanded a friend of mine, opposed to wealth in principle but not in practice. In fact, the average income for Brazil's fabled 10 percent in 1980 came to only $1,097 a month. If you lived in Rio, that sufficed for a lower middle-class neighborhood like Flamengo or Tijuca, but not for Ipanema.

When "distribution" is defined as reaching into one person's pocket to fill someone else's, it is either robbery or social revolution. In the United States,

Table 5.6 Educational Attainment in Brazil for a Cohort Entering the First Grade in 1972

Year	Grade	Number
	Primary School (Grades 1–8)	
1972	1	1,000
1973	2	513
1974	3	448
1975	4	375
1976	5	264
1977	6	212
1978	7	180
1979	8	161
	Secondary School (Grades 9–11)	
1980	9	168
1981	10	132
1982	11	114
	Higher Education (Grade 12)	
1983	12	106

Source: Presentation by Hector Gurgulino de Souza, Vice-President, Brazilian Council of Education, São Paulo, 18 July 1983.

to a family with a household income of $20,000, those across town with $50,000 are rich—among the top 10 percent. But how wealthy are they in their own eyes? They will complain about a $150,000 mortgage, the payments on $30,000 worth of automobiles, and the high cost of entertainment. So they are not rich after all. Perhaps we could agree that a million-dollar income buys entrance to the coveted benefits of the truly wealthy. And maybe my friend is right—they all belong in jail for theft. But however desirable Robin Hood economics may appear theoretically, it is difficult to implement except at gunpoint. All things considered, I do not want social debts in the United States collected so uncivilly, and I cannot recommend it to Brazil.

What Brazil needs from its upper 10 percent is more ingenuity, an approach to health, education, and employment that yields tangible results to the majority. To pay the social debt, what has to be transferred is functional literacy, reasonable public health standards, and labor-intensive strategies for development.

• São Paulo

The Serra do Mar, a rugged mountain escarpment that lunges up from the sea near Rio, originates in the state of Espírito Santo and stretches over 1,000 miles south before giving way to the rolling grasslands of Rio Grande do Sul. The range is steep and stingy, allowing for only a narrow coastal strip between the mountains and the sea. The city of São Paulo is only 250 miles from Rio, but it is on the edge of a plateau across the coastal range. In colonial times, the mountains isolated São Paulo both from Rio and the Atlantic Coast. To reach the port of Santos from São Paulo is like jumping off a cliff: a breathtaking drop of 2,500 feet covered in a few short miles. Only after the railroad linked the plateau to Santos in 1868 did São Paulo become Brazil's foremost coffee exporter.

Compared to Brazil's statistical profile, São Paulo is a different country; it is the gateway to a more prosperous nation that extends south to Rio Grande do Sul. The size of Oregon, São Paulo is Brazil's most populous state. In 1985, it had almost 30 million inhabitants and was home to 22 percent of the country.[31] Over half of Brazil's industrial production in 1980 concentrated in the state of São Paulo; 80 percent of the work force earned more than the region's minimum wage.[32] A center for manufacturing and technology, São Paulo is also a leader in agriculture. In 1985 it accounted for 27 percent of Brazil's coffee harvest, over half the sugar crop, and was a major soybean producer.[33] During the heyday of subsidized credit, São Paulo benefited more than any other state.[34]

Compared to the Northeast, infant mortality rates drop by a third in São Paulo. Cancer and heart ailments take precedence over childhood diseases as the leading causes of death.[35] Most of the children who should be in the first grade are actually there, and 65 percent stay at least through the fourth grade.[36]

The Last Train

São Paulo is a city of unrelieved density that is always tearing itself down and building itself up; there is no old quarter charmed by previous destinies. Garbed in winter's dreariness, São Paulo turns to gray and frigid rain. The cheap hotels crowd into narrow streets below the Plaza República. Past the four-lane splendor of Ipiranga Avenue is a maze of small shops, cafés, and bookstores. There one can be alone, unseen and unknown. I think of São Paulo as a shipyard: luxury liners in steel and tempered glass with their prows turned skyward, the classy yachts of fashionable Jardim Paulista, the old tugs, and the rusty hulks that hang on, sodden and unseaworthy. Mostly I slip between the abandoned hulks. Had someone lived there once, thinking my thoughts and dreaming my dreams? Are we not all made from the same stars, as much each other as we are ourselves? Time and place betray us with false illusions. The atoms we share are the true miracle.

In São Paulo, cheese and cold cuts show up for breakfast. *Cafezinho* comes with the option of cream—a concession to the city's ethnic diversity. And recently, a Dunkin' Donuts opened on the Plaza República. What I got looked like a doughnut, but it weighed twice as much and came filled with condiments like guava jelly. If only Brazil's development were like the doughnut, a recipe altered to taste.

Like Argentina and the United States, Brazil attracted a great influx of immigrants. Between 1890 and 1920, over 2.6 million crowded into Brazil, destined primarily for São Paulo or states farther south; 40 percent came from Italy.[37] In the city of São Paulo they found employment in the textile mills, or headed west to the coffee frontier as sharecroppers. To judge from my walks, the Italians opened restaurants at an astounding rate. My favorite is on Sete de Abril Street. Downstairs is for pastries, snacks, and cafezinho. The custom at snack bars is that patrons start at the cash register. They state the desired items and the quantity of each. The cashier rings up the total, they pay, and then take the receipt to the counter. Simple enough—if one knows the names for a thousand different pastries and croquettes. For years I was faithful to a *mixto* of ham and melted cheese, one of the few delicacies whose pronunciation I trusted. In Rio, it is true, I did add the fish ball. But here, at last, opportunity struck: each tray was marked by name and price. It took a week to sample through the variety of downstairs; only then did I bother with upstairs and the formality of dinner.

From Sete de Abril Street, it is a short walk to the Municipal Theater. In 1980 *Grupo Corpo* staged a series of interpretive dances about life's track and Brazil's last train. The songs of Milton Nascimento sang of birth, youth, and love, of wisdom and old age. And so the last train reached its destination, the passengers gripped in anxious expectation. They tumbled out to a future packed in trunks and suitcases. They undid the latches: all open, all empty.

Cotia

Dr. Lourdes de Freitas Carvalho, dean of São Paulo's School of Public Health, knew where she was headed. She was a formidable, impatient administrator in her late fifties, and my Portuguese just barely edged me into her good graces. I stopped by her office as previously arranged to catch a ride to Cotia, a county seat twenty miles west of São Paulo and the site of a health project.

"I bought a summer house in Cotia," she laughed, "thinking I'd have a place to rest. Hah! The community had virtually no health facilities; in emergencies they had to go to São Paulo. In Brazil you have to fight for a medical system that is responsive to the majority. I don't know how many raffles, dinners, and dances people held to raise money, but without the community's leadership Cotia would still be without clinics and it certainly wouldn't have a hospital.

"Brazil's National Health Service is hopelessly bureaucratic and insensitive to the country's diverse conditions. Its solution for Brazil's health problems is to build hospitals; what a disaster! Go to any public hospital, it's overcrowded and understaffed. Patients come in from outlying districts, have to wait three to four hours, and then see a doctor for ten minutes. To talk about health education under such conditions is a travesty."

At the hospital in Cotia, I joined Dr. Nelson Ibanês, the project's director. In his early forties, slim, and soft-spoken, he provided a quick orientation followed by visits to health posts in surrounding hamlets: Tijuco Preto, Portão Vermelho, and Vargem Grande.

"Cotia has gained population rapidly since 1970; it's becoming a shanty suburb of São Paulo. That's not true everywhere in the county. Tijuco Preto, for example, is still agricultural, and most people in the district are long-term residents. But overall, 70 percent of the county's population has been here less than five years. Most came from the Northeast or from rural areas of São Paulo, pushed out of agriculture by mechanization. They are migrant workers with few skills and uncertain prospects. The vast majority are functionally illiterate; a temporary job is about the best they can get. Even when employed, 80 percent earn the equivalent of two minimum wages or less.

"The towns, including Cotia, don't have waste disposal or safe water; houses are rat-infested. Malnutrition is serious, both among infants and school children. It's ironic: Brazil is a great exporter of soybeans and coffee, but we don't produce enough rice, beans, and eggs at prices the poor can afford. For many Brazilians, the main consequence of development is deteriorating health conditions.

"It's easy to blame everything on the regime, and it's about time they took the criticism seriously. Nonetheless, many problems are at the family level, and that is where they must be resolved. To me, poverty is filled with contradictions. I see families with malnourished children, yet they make payments on television sets. People want to have things, they don't want to be left behind. To have an impact, we need a community-based approach that confronts the social context within which poor health and malnutrition are perpetuated."

The Cotia project was a strategy for community health and for advanced training. In Brazil, college applicants are admitted directly to a Faculty of Medicine for six years of general study—much as in Colombia. When finished, doctors acquire additional specialization in postgraduate residencies. Those in residence at Cotia lived in a dormitory near the hospital. The specialization offered was in social medicine, which emphasized general practice within the framework of community-oriented health care. Residents worked at all facets of community health, from hospital administration to public health campaigns and neighborhood meetings. They rotated through hospital internships in pediatrics, obstetrics, surgery, and clinical practice, rather than concentrating exclusively in a single area. When not on call at the hospital, they made rounds to the health posts.

"Brazil's medical system is like an inverted pyramid," Nelson said. "We depend too much on specialists and hospitals bunched at the top. We need a different approach that is less technological, that confronts the health problems of poor families directly. In Brazil, this implies community action focused on prevention, and health posts located so that primary care is accessible on a regular basis. It's the neighborhood health post and not the hospital that ought to be the basis of the system—the opposite of current policies. That's not to downgrade the hospital, but it has to be viewed as part of an overall approach to health and less as an end in itself.

"The hospital at Cotia, for example, doesn't provide specialized care for cancer or heart disease. It's a reference hospital for the health posts; we can handle minor surgery, complications that develop during pregnancy and childbirth, and we're equipped for diagnostic tests and emergency treatment. But for heart surgery, patients are sent to the University Hospital in São Paulo. The logic of the system is simple: let each level of the health system do what it does best, but make sure they work together and not at cross-purposes. The Cotia hospital provides training and supervision for the health posts; the work of small hospitals should, in turn, be coordinated with highly specialized ones in São Paulo. In practice, all the hospitals get swamped with routine cases that should have been resolved farther on down the line. What we need to do is push minor surgery back to the small hospital, bloody noses back to the health post, and prevention back to the people. Unfortunately, the whole system is in disarray because we've ignored its most basic unit: the simple health post."

Health care involved the community. The Cotia hospital provided training for promotoras,* reinforced by continuing education sessions. The promotoras were responsible for primary care: basic diagnosis, vaccinations, pregnancy tests, and prenatal sessions. They scheduled appointments with the doctors who made rounds to the health post. Unlike Colombia, the promotora in Brazil dispensed generic drugs supplied by Brazil's National Medications Center. Each of Cotia's health posts was backed by a Community Association, which sponsored public health campaigns and raised funds. "The contribution they make to the budget isn't much," said Nelson, "but it fosters participation, strengthens self-respect, and builds self-reliance. We can't sit around waiting for people to show up at the health post; we have to be aggressive and we have to look for allies. Parents bring their children to the clinic only when they

---

*The Brazilian term is *auxiliar*; for consistency, however, I have retained the Spanish term, *promotora*.

become seriously ill. So we have to look for ways to diagnose symptoms earlier and initiate preventive measures."

At Cotia, the county's primary schools were part of the project. All the teachers had attended a general course in basic diagnosis. In addition, each school had a health coordinator: a teacher who lived in the community and had more intensive training. The health coordinator attended to children referred by her colleagues. If there was not a health post nearby, she scheduled appointments for the doctor's weekly visit. Each school had a supply of medications, which the health coordinator could dispense.

With Nelson as my guide, we stopped at Vargem Grande's primary school. The crowded classrooms seemed ripe for mischief. I asked Marli, an energetic, high-spirited woman in her forties, who was also the school's health coordinator, about discipline problems. As she hesitated, I congratulated myself for a grasp of fundamentals. Put poverty and public schools together anywhere and you get guerrilla warfare. "I don't understand the question," she responded, a bit confused. "Are you asking if poor kids are difficult?" "That's right," I said, "compared to middle-class children." "The first four years," she observed, "aren't so difficult. Truancy starts later, when kids are old enough to assume responsibilities at home; they care for the younger ones so both parents can work. It's not unusual for a ten-year-old to take some kind of job; the families need the money. Overall, the schools aren't adapted to the special needs of poor children." I had asked the wrong question, but got the right answer.

I went with Nelson, interrupting classes. If good behavior alone conferred literacy, you could believe the claims made by Brazil's *Statistical Yearbook*. Even doubled up at desks, the children seemed so fragile, so eager to be good, so desperate to understand.

Nelson asked for names and ages, what they ate last night, where they lived. He had brought a novelty, he told them, someone who spoke a language different from their own. I was pressed into a demonstration that produced "the pen is on the table" and "where is the American Embassy?" They stared back blankly. Encouraged by this success, I asked them to point at anything they wanted and I would magically change it into English. Thus did *livro* transform itself to book, *lápis* to pencil, *caderno* to notebook, *cabeça* to head. "That proves it," I told them. "I'm not so different, I see out of the same eye that you do."

By this time Marli had made her rounds, collecting several children for Nelson's special attention. I asked her what she considered the main health problems. "Intestinal parasites, ringworm, lice, and fleas," she said, "and, of course, malnutrition. Most of the children have a very short attention span; they come to school hungry and they are in poor health. They faint from lack of food, that's common enough. When a child has learning difficulties it's hard to know if it's actual disability, malnutrition, or a parasitic infection. I try to involve the parents in health precautions they can take at home. The important thing is to be consistent, reinforcing the work done at the clinics and in the community." Since meeting Marli, I have been to a dozen schools, crowded with kids and teenagers. Why, I asked myself, did they not break the windows, carve up the desks, and disfigure the walls? Are poor Brazilian kids simply nicer than the delinquents that pass for children back home? Poor kids in the United States seem to know the table is set, but not for them. To that great feast of consumption that is America, they are not invited, have never been, will never be. What will happen when Brazil's children learn the truth?

When the Cotia project began in 1976, the county's infant mortality rate was approximately 150 per 1,000; it had dropped to 50 when I visited there in 1982. Nelson said that coverage on infant vaccinations came close to 100 percent. The incidence of tuberculosis and schistosomiasis had also declined substantially. About 85 percent of all childbirths occurred without surgical intervention. In many of São Paulo's hospitals, Nelson said, the cesarean rate was between 65 and 75 percent. The World Bank, whose advisers visited Cotia in 1979, recommended the project as a model for health care reform in Brazil.

Brazil's health system divided treatment and prevention between agencies. All salaried workers, whether in the private or public sector, paid into Brazil's National Health Service (INAMPS) managed by the Ministry of Social Security. It was a high-cost, urban-centered "service" system focused on hospital treatment. How to fund, staff, and supervise agencies responsible both for people who had coverage and those who did not was unresolved. The responsibility for public health and disease control fell to the Ministry of Health. Throughout the 1970s, the budget for the Health Service expanded enormously, while that for public health and prevention dropped sharply.[38]

The middle class, although subject to the payroll tax, purchased health care privately, and at additional cost. The public service was considered substandard, overcrowded, and understaffed. Although the National Health Service managed its own network of hospitals—at least one per state—it had only a fraction of the beds needed to handle the demand. Consequently, it contracted out treatment to private hospitals and reimbursed expenses. It did not have the capacity to verify actual costs; audits always created a scandal.

"The Health Service," observed Nelson, "ought to provide much better service than it does. But the regime diverted its funds to finance projects like the Itaipú dam. The state of São Paulo, which contributes 57 percent of the payroll taxes the National Health Service collects, gets back only 10 percent. And the difference does not go to clinics in the Northeast, I can tell you that."

Cotia's hospital, although a nonprofit community-managed venture, was a private institution. To help defray expenses, it had a contract with the National Health Service. "Nonetheless," Nelson pointed out, "20 percent of our patients come from families that don't have coverage. It's even worse this year, given the recession. So we run a large deficit. Faced with rising costs and indigent

161

patients, hospitals have devised all kinds of stratagems. They perform unnec-essary surgery—that's why the cesarean rate is so tragically high—or they routinely charge for treatments never provided. Sometimes it's simply graft; in other cases, hospitals are just trying to get by. I refuse to do this. It's not because I'm a saint, but I don't think I could just cheat a little. Once you start, you can't control the practice."

Cotia's hospital did get a reward for its good behavior: a global contract to cover its routine expenses. Even the National Health Service likes a place it can actually trust.

Uno

Cotia's main streets were paved—except for that leading up to the hospital. Running the local concession in health is usually part of the mayor's patronage system. In the case of Cotia, the community had circumvented the mayor, bringing in outsiders. So now he stubbornly refused diplomatic recognition. Why did Cotia not turn out its recalcitrant public servant? Because the regime had put the country's municipalities into deep freeze a decade before. The same mayors continued on, without any formal check on their petty tyranny or petty larceny. Such were the small delights of a "moderately authoritarian" regime.

Nelson arranged for accommodations in the dormitory. At the hospital cafeteria, I met some of the residents over dinner. We gathered later for a game of *Uno*. I asked Dr. Antônia about the road and the local election scheduled, at last, for November 1982. She looked out from between her cards. "Well, the mayor has built three soccer fields this year, but, on the other hand, there are no sewers or clean water." "So it's soccer versus sewers," I said. "Well, more or less. What do you think people will vote for, Jaime?" she asked with a sly grin. "Probably soccer," I replied. "Don't be stupid," she laughed, playing her *Draw Four* card with a flourish, "they've already got the soccer fields."

• Petroleum

Brazil's record on health care and education stood in sharp contrast to the decisive way the regime tackled the energy crisis. When OPEC's price hikes threatened Brazil's oil-dependent development with near collapse, the regime displayed imagination, even courage. The facts were stark enough, and for once the Planning Ministry got the arithmetic straight.

Between 1970 and 1974, Brazil's industrial production increased by almost 40 percent. For example, the country's automobile fleet grew from 1.5 to over 3 million vehicles: almost exclusively a consequence of domestic output. Petroleum consumption, of course, kept pace. In 1974 Brazil used over

800,000 barrels per day—up 40 percent from 1970. The regime was hooked on gas-guzzling development, but, then, so was everybody else. And the habit was affordable. In 1972, a barrel of oil cost less than $3. Even though Brazil imported 80 percent of the petroleum it consumed, the tab came to only $376 million: an unbelievable bargain in retrospect.[39]

By the end of 1974, OPEC had revised the cheap-energy formula beyond recognition. The price of petroleum had jumped to $11 a barrel, and Brazil's oil bill was a staggering $2.8 billion. The country's trade balance, which had been relatively stable, ended up the year with a $4.7 billion deficit. To cover the disparity and keep up the pace of development, Brazil borrowed heavily from the banks. In 1972, the country's foreign debt was a manageable $9.5 billion; two years later, it topped $17 billion—an increase of almost 80 percent. (See Table 5.7.)

The crisis Brazil now confronted undermined the very premise upon which its development rested. Industrial output was energy-intensive; if growth required a commensurate escalation of oil imports, then growth itself was not sustainable. To abandon rapid growth was to surrender the main claim to legitimacy that sustained the regime. To forge ahead meant borrowing unprecedented sums. As to the choice, the regime did not flinch. It continued four square on the big development track.

Brazil was not the only country caught in the energy crunch. The United States, usually tolerant of monopolies, denounced OPEC's profiteering and demanded a free-market price. The energy crisis proved a painful affair injurious to the national ego. Highways built for a casual cruising speed of 75 miles per hour were demoted to a snail's-paced 55 miles per hour. There were depressing lines at the gas pump and quarrels with fellow motorists. President Nixon even lowered the White House thermostat to a frigid 65 degrees. Imitating their chief, American households followed suit.

The United States talked defiantly about energy independence, but the measures taken depended mainly on petroleum conservation. Congress legislated a more fuel-efficient vehicle, the Energy Tax Credit showed up on Form 1040, and motorists organized car pools. Schemes to replace petroleum with solar energy, organic waste methane, or biomass alcohol were treated with pragmatic disdain.

The Alcohol Program

In Brazil, the regime also invoked the slogans of energy independence, but it did not waste time on bluster. Foreign nations already had a corner on the world's capital and advanced technology. Petroleum had simply been added to the list. Brazil attacked the problem at its source. It was the only country bold enough to adopt alcohol substitution on a massive scale. Only a small fraction of Brazil's petroleum went to residential heating. Automobiles, trucks, and

Table 5.7 Balance of Trade, Cost of Petroleum Imports, and External Debt in Brazil, 1971–1980

Year	Exports*	Imports*	Trade Balance*	Oil Prices**	Cost of Oil Imports*	External Debt*	Cost of Oil Imports as % of Total Exports
1971	2,891	3,256	− 365	1.93	280	6,622	09
1972	3,941	4,193	− 252	2.13	376	9,521	10
1973	6,093	6,154	− 61	3.39	718	12,572	12
1974	7,814	12,562	− 4,748	11.29	2,812	17,166	36
1975	8,492	12,041	− 3,549	11.02	2,747	21,171	32
1976	9,961	12,346	− 2,385	11.77	3,460	25,985	35
1977	11,923	12,022	− 99	12.88	3,664	32,037	31
1978	12,472	13,628	− 1,158	12.93	4,089	43,511	33
1979	15,244	17,961	− 2,717	30.87	6,189	49,904	41
1980	20,132	22,955	− 2,823	34.50	10,300	53,847	51

Sources: For exports, imports, the balance of trade, and oil prices from 1973 through 1980, see James W. Wilkie and Adam Perkal, eds., *Statistical Abstract of Latin America* (Los Angeles: UCLA Latin American Center Publications, University of California, 1984), 23:513, 504 (hereafter cited as *SALA*). For 1971 and 1972, oil prices averaged Saudi Arabian and Venezuelan crude; see *SALA* (1980), 20:342. For the cost of Brazil's oil imports, see José Goldemberg, "Energy Issues and Policies in Brazil," mimeographed (Institute of Physics, University of São Paulo, 1981), p. 48. For debt figures, see Luiz Bresser Pereira, *Development and Crisis in Brazil, 1930–1983* (Boulder, Colo.: Westview Press, 1984), p. 171. Oil imports as a percentage of total exports are compiled from the table.

*In millions of U.S. dollars.
**Prevailing dollar price per barrel.

industry accounted for almost 90 percent of the demand. The strategy was to hold petroleum imports constant without sacrificing rapid economic growth. To accomplish this, alcohol substitution first concentrated on gasoline. The petroleum savings thus realized could be diverted to diesel fuel and industrial consumption.[40]

Brazil's Alcohol Program was inaugurated in 1975. Four years later, virtually all the automobile fuel sold was gasohol— gasoline mixed with 20 percent ethanol alcohol.[41] The regime, of course, set pricing policies and made gasohol pumps mandatory at filling stations. The key to the Alcohol Program, however, was not government decrees; it was production. And Brazil had the agricultural base, the technical skills, and the determination to convert rapidly to gasohol.

Ethanol alcohol can be produced from sugars such as sweet sorghum, sugar beets, and sugarcane; from starches, notably corn and cassava; and from wood cellulose. The advantage of the sugar group is that the extracted juice is already in fermentable, glucose form. By contrast, the liquid crushed from starches must be broken down into sugars by enzyme conversion prior to fermentation, an additional step that imposes higher capital and operating costs. For cellulose, which has a more complex molecular structure, the reduction to fermentable sugars requires acid hydrolysis, a technology still in the experimental stage. Brazil opted for alcohol distillation from sugarcane, an obvious choice given the advantages it had over alternatives like cassava.[42]

Brazil was the world's largest sugar producer. In 1975, before the Alcohol Program was in place, total output came to 91 million metric tons, far ahead of Cuba's 56 million.[43] A well-organized sector accustomed to large-scale production, the sugar industry also benefited from established research and extension programs. In addition, sugar refining had processing components conducive to alcohol production. For example, crushing out the cane stalk's juice is the first step in both sugar and alcohol production. And the by-product of sugar refining, molasses, can be fermented directly and then distilled into ethanol alcohol. Before 1975, molasses was distilled into alcoholic beverages, or it was discarded as a waste, polluting the rivers near the sugar refineries. Some conversion to ethanol alcohol also took place, mostly for industrial use as a solvent. The Alcohol Program's initial phase simply added a distillation unit to existing sugar refineries, either to process molasses or to produce ethanol directly from cane juice.[44]

To produce ethanol alcohol, the extracted cane juice undergoes batch fermentation with yeast in large vats. The yeast is then removed from the fermented mash, treated, and recycled back to the fermentation step. Ethanol alcohol has two variants: hydrous and anhydrous. If the end product is to be hydrous alcohol with a 94 percent ethanol concentration, the fermented mash is distilled by steam in two boiler columns. Hydrous alcohol is used in vehicles fueled exclusively by ethanol. For anhydrous alcohol, which is mixed with gasoline to produce gasohol, the excess water is removed in a third distillation column; the result is ethanol that is 99.8 percent pure.

From a production standpoint, the advantage of hydrous alcohol is its higher water content. Thus, the same amount of fermented cane juice yields more hydrous alcohol by volume than the anhydrous variant. In addition, hydrous alcohol does not require the extra distillation column, so it is cheaper to produce.

Almost 70 percent of the energy required in alcohol production is consumed in the distillation process. With sugarcane, the woody stalk (bagasse) left over from juice extraction is burned to fuel the crushers and distillation boilers, thus supplying the installation's main energy needs. For alternatives like cassava roots and corncobs, the starch component is separated from stalks in the field. The extra cost required to collect and dry the discarded stalks is virtually prohibitive. With the exception of sweet sorghum, which yields bagasse in juice extraction, alcohol derived from other sugars, or from starches, has to rely on external energy sources, a factor that adds a hefty increment to production costs.

The Alcohol Program reduced molasses dumping, but it created another environmental hazard of equal proportion. For each gallon of ethanol distilled, twelve gallons of watery stillage were left behind. Given the high content of chemical solids, stillage dumping turned the rivers adjoining distilleries into brackish, smelly sewers. Fortunately, stillage has alternative uses. Because it contains fertilizer nutrients, it boosts yields when recycled to cane fields. In São Paulo, some distilleries used the surplus steam power bagasse provided to pump the stillage to nearby hillsides. From there it was gravity-fed into irrigation systems. For more distant sites, it was trucked to the fields and sprayed on the ground. Finally, stillage can be evaporated down to about 50 percent solid material and mixed with animal feed—an expensive option in use on an experimental basis.[45]

Critics charged that Brazil's Alcohol Program favored the sugar lobby to the detriment of small cassava farmers. The factors that favored sugarcane, however, were insurmountable, especially for a regime that desperately needed a quick fix. The sugar industry had the capacity for rapid conversion to alcohol production, and prior research on distillation technology had focused almost exclusively on sugarcane.

The way the regime financed the Alcohol Program merited the criticism it received. The regime channeled enormous subsidies to the sugar sector. The government financed 80 percent of the cost of distillery construction at only 4 percent interest. There was a three-year grace period, with repayment spread over twelve years. To add to the attractiveness of the loan package, the outstanding debt was corrected for only half of the prevailing inflation rate. The result was a direct subsidy whose value increased with inflation. As of 1980, the regime had committed a massive $5 billion to the Alcohol Program, most of it for distillery construction. From the profits owners made on production they paid back loans whose real burden decreased substantially each year.[46] The regime covered the risks, producers got the profits, and Brazil's taxpayers got the bill. It was a new twist to what Adam Smith once called the *Wealth of Nations*: socialism for the rich, pay-as-you-go for everyone else.

The regime wanted results; results it got. In 1975, Brazil produced about 150 million gallons of ethanol alcohol; in 1979, output came close to a billion gallons, over 75 percent of it the anhydrous variety targeted for gasohol.[47] During the same period, Brazil's economy had expanded at an average rate of 6.5 percent, but not at the cost of increased petroleum consumption. For the moment, the regime had managed to wring more growth out of the same number of oil barrels. As in the United States, improved gas mileage from greater engine efficiency was part of the story. The regime also closed gas stations on weekends and jacked up prices far above those that prevailed in Western Europe. To various conservation strategies, however, the regime had added direct substitution. In 1979, that saved Brazil 20 percent of the petroleum that would have gone to gasoline: an overall savings that represented 5 percent of the country's total petroleum consumption.[48]

My local gas station assures discriminating motorists they are getting the real thing—"no alcohol added." Actually, a gasohol mixture of up to 20 percent anhydrous ethanol does not reduce gas mileage. In fact, it boosts the octane rating, reducing the necessity for lead additives.[49] Of course, as I have been warned, "gasohol corrodes the engine." That was not true in Brazil, at least with respect to the engine proper. The main complaints were damage to the carburetor and the gradual deterioration of the fuel pump, fuel hoses, and gas tank—all of which the automobile industry quickly resolved with plastic coatings and resistant materials.[50]

Despite gasohol's merits, it did not provide a long-term solution for Brazil. The petroleum saved in 1979, for example, would cancel out as soon as the number of cars increased 20 percent. A vehicle that ran exclusively on ethanol (hydrous alcohol) was the only option that could cut gasoline consumption permanently. The regime had reached a turning point in its flirtation with substitution. To stop at gasohol put a damper on alcohol technology and reduced the initial gains to a passing shot. To plunge ahead implied a fundamental commitment to alcohol: by the sugar sector, motorists, the automobile industry, and the regime. Once the die was cast, it could not be easily retracted. For a while, Brazil tinkered. To take advantage of alcohol prices—half that of gasohol—motorists had their gasoline engines adapted to run on pure alcohol. The results were unsatisfactory, especially when roadside mechanics converted engines at cut-rate prices. The alcohol engine's bad reputation came from such early ad hoc adaptations.

In 1979, the Iran-Iraq war, coupled with the uncertainty created by the hostage crisis, put a squeeze on oil supplies, which within a year doubled prices. The regime hesitated no longer. The automobile industry likewise saw the handwriting on the wall: without cheap petroleum, the gasoline engine was dead in Brazil. In 1980, the first alcohol vehicles reached the showrooms; within a year, Brazilians had purchased 200,000 of them. The Alcohol Program had entered a new phase.

Gasohol stole the headlines in the 1970s; the alcohol engine took over in the 1980s. The regime earmarked another $5 billion to expand ethanol production, and this time around distilleries were not second-rate adjuncts to existing refineries. Now free-standing units with more efficient crushers, they had continuous fermentation technology that jacked up the alcoholic content of mash, and a distillation design that improved heat recovery. The new generation of distilleries had a peak capacity of anywhere between 25,000 and 75,000 gallons per day. Output shifted toward hydrous ethanol for Brazil's expanding alcohol fleet: half a million in 1982, a million strong at the end of 1984. By then, ethanol production had reached over 2.4 billion gallons, meeting a target every source I ever read discounted as "overly optimistic." Of that total, 70 percent was hydrous. Brazil had opted for the alcohol engine in no uncertain terms. In 1985, 90 percent of all the cars sold were alcohol vehicles. A gasoline model had to be special ordered.[51]

The regime, of course, promoted the transition. By financing new distillery projects at a rapid clip, it undercut the naysayers who predicted supply shortfalls at the filling station. Hydrous ethanol it set at only 65 percent of the price for gasohol, thus making up for what was initially a 20 percent loss in fuel economy for alcohol vehicles. That looks like a bargain. To cover production costs, however, the regime simply raised the price of gasohol and then jacked up hydrous ethanol to the specified 65 percent. In Brazil, what motorists shelled out for fuel reflected the cost of the Alcohol Program as much as it did OPEC's price hikes. Brazil ended up with expensive fuel any way you look at it. The question is, was it worth it?

Whether the Alcohol Program was actually cost-effective is much disputed. Who wins the debate depends on the factors considered and the importance attributed to each. Through 1982, price trends favored the Alcohol Program. The cost of petroleum kept going up, and sugar prices, though fluctuating, held to a long-run decline. The World Bank estimated in 1980 that an efficient cane producer like Brazil would still find ethanol substitution marginally profitable with sugar prices at $12 a ton and a barrel of oil at $24.[52] Although the sugar assumption still held, the cost of petroleum in 1985 was at the break-even point. Chances are Brazil was paying more for alcohol than for petroleum. On the other hand, the alcohol was Brazil's and the petroleum was not. It had cornered the market on alcohol technology, and even exported model distilleries abroad. If you add in the jobs created by the sugar sector (estimated at half a million), orders for crushers, fermentation vats, and distillation equipment (all filled by Brazilian companies), and spin-off industries like bagasse paper mills, the equation was to Brazil's advantage. In the final analysis, however, the Alcohol Program was not simply an economic exercise based on cost estimates. It was a matter of national security, of Brazil's dependence on external energy supplies. "National security," as we all know, covers a multitude of sins. The regime did not lose much sleep over cost-effectiveness, no more than the Pentagon does.

The Alcohol Program targeted gasoline substitution. Brazil, however, did not restrict its research to only one of petroleum's applications. Ethanol can also substitute directly for petroleum derivatives in numerous cleansing agents and solvents. When converted into a chemical feedstock such as ethylene, its range of applications expands to synthetic fibers, paints, and shoe soles: the domain of the petrochemical industry. Compared to the rapid growth of gasoline substitution, the gains on the chemical side were modest, but significant nonetheless. In 1982, Brazil produced 17 percent of its solvents from ethanol; Union Carbide and Salgema, a Brazilian company, had started ethylene production with a combined output of 100,000 tons annually. Additional ethanol-based installations were scheduled for completion by 1984.[53]

Research also focused on diesel fuel substitution. The options ranged from mixtures of diesel with ethanol or vegetable oils to wholesale substitution with biomass methane derived from eucalyptus. The advantage of methane is that it requires minimal engine modifications.[54]

If you did not venture beyond the Alcohol Program or the state of São Paulo, you would wonder why Brazil is considered part of the Third World. What Brazil is depends on the kind of statistics one prefers. If it is steel production, alcohol substitution, or automobile output, Brazil turns itself into Western Europe. But in terms of infant mortality, functional literacy, or gainful employment, it is more like Bolivia. Even Ronald Reagan got confused. In 1982, while in Brazil spreading goodwill, he displayed a rare bent for philosophy. "I'm glad to be in Bolivia," he told his hosts. "No, wait a minute. I was there yesterday; now I'm in Brazil." Actually, Reagan had been in Colombia the day before. But then, Brazil is a confusing place. The *Jornal do Brasil* admitted as much: "Both Brazil and Bolivia," it observed, "begin with B."

Piracicaba

The state of São Paulo is Brazil's industrial giant. It is also home to 3.6 million passenger cars, 40 percent of the country's automobile fleet.[55] Had the Alcohol Program developed outside São Paulo, it would have distributed a bit of the state's wealth. But São Paulo was also Brazil's foremost sugar producer. The state's sugar sector embraced the Alcohol Program early on and has maintained its preeminence. In 1984, it produced 57 percent of Brazil's sugar and had 41 percent of the distilleries.[56] São Paulo's lead also came from the head start it had on research. The state's Sugar Association (COPERSUCAR), headquartered at Piracicaba, had a Center for Applied Research that worked on soil analysis, genetics, and disease control. And at Piracicaba's state university, research emphasized alcohol technology. I went there in 1983 with my friend Carlos Gasparetto, an engineer from Campinas. We met with Senhor Urgel de Almeida Lima, associate dean and professor of biotechnology. Urgel was in his fifties, a direct, plain-speaking man I took to immediately.

"How did Brazil convert to alcohol so quickly?" I asked him. "Brazil never abandoned alcohol," he observed. "During the 1930s, we had a gasohol program, and we continued mixing at various percentages until the 1960s. Research never stopped. In 1975, when the Alcohol Program went into effect, we had the technology to expand alcohol production rapidly, both as a molasses derivative or directly from cane juice. At Piracicaba we had developed quality control techniques for distilleries that produced 20,000 gallons a day, and models for output in excess of 60,000 gallons. Research on engine performance at different alcohol levels was likewise ready for direct application. The result was that São Paulo headed up the Alcohol Program. And it made sense to concentrate the industry close to the source of demand. São Paulo was not only the leading sugar producer, but the largest gasoline consumer. To supply São Paulo from the Northeast would have added a hefty transportation cost to the final product."

The acreage Brazil devoted to sugarcane increased almost 85 percent between 1975 and 1984; São Paulo led the way.[57] To critics, Brazil fed its cars first and worried about people later. So I asked Urgel about the food-fuel controversy. "You have to consider whether the switch is actually from food staples," he said. "In São Paulo, sugar also gained at the expense of exports like coffee and soybeans. And production doesn't necessarily preclude staples; once the cane is cut you can plant a food crop between the rows before it resprouts. About a quarter of the land is rested each year, so you can rotate to other crops. Neither alternative, however, is practiced as much as it should be.

"The state's sugar zone extends north from Piracicaba to Ribeirão Preto, and southeast toward the city of São Paulo. In 1982, producers harvested enough cane to supply 65 percent of Brazil's alcohol and 43 percent of its sugar. To meet projected demand, São Paulo has the capacity to double cane production and increase alcohol output to over 2 billion gallons a year. The plan is to promote sugar production in the western part of the state, which is currently a ranching area, rather than to compete with food production.

"I'm not minimizing the problem; you have to strike a balance between staples and energy crops. In São Paulo, at least, the balance is a reasonable one. And some of the gains are due to higher yields and not simply additional acreage. São Paulo averages around 68 tons a hectare, while the Northeast gets about 50. You have to look at land utilization on a state-by-state basis. São Paulo has good soil and adequate rainfall. In northeastern states like Pernambuco and Paraíba, only a narrow coastal strip gets sufficient rainfall for cane production, but this is precisely the area best suited to food crops. The Northeast, consequently, faces a food-fuel tradeoff of greater proportions than São Paulo. The interior can't produce cane without an enormous investment in irrigation. Many of the projects under way along the São Francisco River, for example, are slated for cane production—a questionable use of expensive, irrigation technology."

I found myself out of questions momentarily, so Urgel offered to take me through the distillery, a small unit with a capacity of about 260 gallons a day, where students got hands-on experience. The school also had about a thousand hectares, both for research on sugarcane production and to supply the distillery.

"A key factor," Urgel noted, "is the efficiency of the crushing equipment. In new distilleries, juice recovery exceeds 90 percent. For smaller units, it's about 50 percent, but given their modest output, it's not worth purchasing new crushers. A distillery operates between 180 and 200 days a year—as long as it has a steady supply of sugarcane. While most of the distilleries also have land allocated to cane, the larger mills aren't self-sufficient; they draw additional supplies from cane growers in the surrounding area. To keep a big distillery furnished with a steady influx of cane poses a tremendous logistical problem, especially given a daily capacity of anywhere from 40,000 to 80,000 gallons. Sugarcane, for instance, has to be processed almost immediately after harvesting. This requires a careful scheduling of deliveries. With too much cane the stalks start to dry up, reducing juice extraction. Not enough cuts into productivity. The harvest is concentrated in a five- to six-month period, while demand is spread out over the entire year. Most of the refineries have storage facilities. When demand falls off, you face a storage crisis.

"About a third of the region's mills are small-scale enterprises that shift back and forth between sugar production and alcohol. When the sugar price is high, they restrict alcohol production to surplus molasses. When it's low, they divert cane juice directly to alcohol output. That's illegal, but their operations are so flexible they can easily adapt to market conditions."

We walked over to a nearby cane field, deep green against the dreariness of a gray winter day. "In Brazil," Urgel continued, "sugarcane is still harvested manually. An experienced cutter lops off the immature top of the cane stalk, which has minimal sugar content—a split-second judgment based on the stalk's size and thickness. Since the base contains the richest liquid content, he severs the stalk a bit below the ground's surface. Cutting low also reduces insect problems at resprouting. Only 25 percent of the acreage is replanted each year. The rest is left with the roots in the ground to resprout. Harvesting equipment is wasteful because it cuts all the cane to a uniform size. The machinery is heavy, compacts the soil, and is thus prejudicial to resprouting. If labor is cheap, as is true in Brazil, it doesn't make sense to mechanize the sugar harvest. Cutters are paid by tonnage. In São Paulo, the rate compares favorably to unskilled employment in the urban sector.

"The Alcohol Program has certainly generated employment. Subsidized credit, however, has benefited large farmers with the collateral and know-how to manage funds. For agriculture as a whole, the consequence has been land consolidation, greater mechanization, and the expulsion of sharecroppers. I sometimes think that for every job we add in the sugar sector, the regime's credit system subtracts two somewhere else. Still, when you concentrate on the ethanol technology Brazil has developed, as distinct from the policies behind agricultural production, the Alcohol Program is the boldest venture we've ever tried."

"I don't want to seem negative," I said hesitantly, "but hasn't the runoff from production polluted the rivers, especially in São Paulo?" "That was true at first," he acknowledged. "Producers didn't take the Alcohol Program seriously; it seemed more like a stopgap measure than a long-term strategy. Consequently, they didn't want to invest in stillage recycling or evaporation technology. Once they were convinced that alcohol production was a viable, permanent commitment, they started recycling, and São Paulo enacted strict laws to speed up the conversion. The quality of the water in the Piracicaba River improved dramatically, as anyone in town can verify. And if you consider automobile emissions, the alcohol engine produces much less pollution.

"Brazil's Alcohol Program is here to stay; its growth is independent of oil prices. We don't have dollars, and that's the only currency OPEC accepts. To reduce petroleum imports further, Brazil has to find a substitute for diesel fuel in trucks, buses, and farm equipment. We can, I'm confident, work out a solution. With only four years of experience behind mass-produced alcohol vehicles, engine efficiency has improved substantially and will soon overtake gas mileage. In São Paulo, we already produce special ethanol grades for industrial use. During my lifetime, Brazil has always imported its technology. This is the first time we've actually taken the lead, and now we export entire distilleries abroad. That's a gain for Brazil that goes beyond an accounting ledger."

• Hydroelectric Power

The regime's energy strategy did not stand on alcohol substitution alone; the other leg was hydroelectric power. In 1975, only 21 percent of Brazil's total energy consumption was accounted for by hydroelectricity—compared to roughly 43 percent for petroleum. For fuel alone, Brazil's industrial sector used roughly 30 percent of all the country's petroleum. Converting industrial consumers to electricity was an obvious alternative, but it could not be sustained without a massive boost of hydroelectric capacity. During the 1970s, electricity consumption had grown at an average rate of 13 percent a year. Demand was disproportionately concentrated in the states of São Paulo, Rio de Janeiro, and Minas Gerais, which took almost 70 percent of the country's total output in 1980. The case of São Paulo is illustrative. It accounted for about 40 percent of all consumption, with demand expanding at a rate that would soon outdistance the state's installed capacity.[58]

To speed up Brazil's conversion to electricity, the regime financed hydroelectric expansion under the aegis of Eletrobrás, the National Utility Company. Brazil had tremendous untapped capacity, of which it had harnessed less than 15 percent.[59] The showcase was Itaipú, the largest hydroelectric project in the world. Constructed on the Paraná River along the border with Paraguay, Itaipú was a joint country project, although most of the financing, construction, and supervision came from Brazil. The *New York Times* sent a reporter down in 1983 to get the story. By then, basic construction was complete, except for turbine installation and the transmission lines. "The peak work force," he reported, "had numbered 100,000." The workers had poured enough cement "to reconstruct all of New Orleans or the equivalent of 600 domed stadiums." The dam itself was 5 miles long and over 600 feet high. The 18 turbines were the largest ever assembled: "they were 130 feet long and 52 feet in diameter, each weighed 7,000 tons, and could generate 700 megawatts of capacity. The entire Potomac could fit through any of the 18 sluices that will feed the Paraná through the turbines." Itaipú, the reporter said, was even larger than Grand Coulee Dam in Washington State. The total cost his sources estimated at about $15 billion. "When it comes on-steam," they noted, "Itaipú alone will boost Brazil's hydroelectric capacity a staggering 60 percent."[60] For that event, however, São Paulo still waits: the city is over 600 miles from Itaipú, and the project's transmission lines and substations are still not in place.

"The priority now," noted José Goldemberg, president of São Paulo's Electric Power Company, "is to convince industry to convert from fossil fuels to electric power." The opposition had captured the state in the 1982 elections, and Goldemberg, a nuclear physicist, was appointed to head up the Electric Power Company. He was a brimful of energy, wit, and intelligence. "In the city, we're expanding the grid for electrical trolleys, and we have a reward system to concentrate industry's electrical consumption during slack periods. We can compete with fossil fuels, if industry can time its demand."

I had, of course, heard plenty of complaints against the regime's preference for development sized to extra large. So I asked Goldemberg for his opinion. "São Paulo," he observed, "followed a strategy of smaller dams. The system is about half the size of the TVA, with some twenty hydroelectric plants strung out along the state's rivers. The Tietê, for example, has a dam approximately every 100 miles. One of the advantages is flood control. Along the São Francisco the regime built two huge dams, but they don't have a flood-control capacity. In the far north in the state of Pará, Brazil has another enormous project underway on the Tocantins River at Tucuruí. The dam will flood almost 800 square miles. No one knows what the environmental impact will be. To defoliate the area, they used Agent Orange. In Brazil, we don't lose sleep over ecology.

"The point is, Tucuruí was built with a capacity all out of proportion to the region's energy demands. I'll admit that to exploit the mineral deposits at Carajás, we needed hydroelectric power. But we didn't need it on the scale of Tucuruí. Carajás is in the Amazon; most of Brazil isn't. To invest on such a scale to meet a theoretical demand most of us won't live to see, and then ignore the pressing human needs at our doorstep, is inexcusable. We have to develop our hydroelectric potential, but in a way we can afford. Anyway," he laughed, "we've run out of money. The regime had to shelve some of its Amazonian schemes, the only savings we've got from the debt crisis.

"Brazil is a rich nation the size of Belgium inside a poor one that threatens to overwhelm it. Compared to the 25 percent who live in a sophisticated urban context, the rest are impoverished. You might say that Brazil works to benefit São Paulo. Consider per capita energy consumption. São Paulo uses electricity at a rate four times that of the Northeast and almost double the national average. Consumption in the city's wealthy neighborhoods is comparable to that of France. At the same time, households in the city's favelas can't get lines installed. With inequalities of such magnitude, we have to have new strategies. In Brazil, the rich can take care of themselves. With support from the World Bank, between January and March of 1983, the Power Company provided electricity to 10,000 homes in São Paulo's favelas; the goal for the year is 100,000. That's the irony. For Itaipú, the regime found the money. For electric lines in a favela, we have to borrow from the World Bank."

Accounting

How successful was Brazil's energy strategy? Consider the case of gasoline. Between 1975 and 1979, the automobile fleet's size grew by 50 percent, but gasoline consumption went up by only 7 percent. For 1980–84, recession held down the fleet's expansion to 12 percent. Nonetheless, the amount of gasoline used had fallen 38 percent, and the gasoline produced went predominantly to gasohol.[61] The sharp drop also showed the impact that new cars fueled exclusively by alcohol had. Not only did Brazil use less gasoline, it used less petroleum as well. Between 1980 and 1984, the amount of energy the country used increased by 20 percent, but petroleum consumption fell. And Brazil's energy profile had shifted significantly too. Recall that in 1975, Brazil derived 43 percent of its energy needs from petroleum and 21 percent from hydroelectric power; in 1984, petroleum's share was down to 33 percent and hydroelectric power was up to 29 percent—with Itaipú still in the wings.[62] Finally, Brazil's petroleum production had increased significantly.

The National Oil Company, Petrobrás, had invested some $7 billion in offshore drilling, primarily in the Campos Basin north of Rio de Janeiro. In 1984, total domestic production by Petrobrás reached half a million barrels per day, almost 30 percent of it from the Campos Basin. That made Brazil the third largest oil producer in Latin America. Compared to 1975, when Brazil met only 20 percent of its petroleum needs, the share had reached almost half in 1984. Strikes at Campos in 1986, estimated at between 1 billion and 2 billion barrels, doubled the country's known reserves. Added to the Alcohol Program and hydroelectric development, the oil strikes provided the country with unprecedented energy flexibility. When Itaipú's transmission lines reach São Paulo, Brazil's energy crisis will be over.[63]

The energy ledger promised to balance in Brazil's favor; the debt ledger did not. The regime imputed a constancy to the world economy it did not have.

In the aftermath of OPEC's quadrupled price hikes of 1974, the oil sheiks took in dollars faster than they could spend them. The surplus ended up in the world's banking system. The likes of City Bank had such an excess of capital that executives begged countries to borrow. And the money was cheap; Brazil could take it in for a mere 7 percent.[64] Under such circumstances, the regime took the plunge. It wagered it could cover the oil bill and keep expansion hopping. As growth outpaced oil prices, the crisis would subside. All the regime had to do was borrow enough.

The regime played a great game from a position of growing desperation. The value of what Brazil sold abroad doubled between 1976 and 1980; despite such accomplishments, Brazil's trade balance showed a cumulative $8.5 billion deficit, largely accounted for by petroleum. After OPEC doubled prices in 1979, Brazil's oil bill increased to $10 billion, a disastrous jump from the $4 billion of 1978. (See Table 5.7 above.) To make ends meet, the regime borrowed for projects that bolstered Brazil's export capacity. From sales abroad, the regime wagered it could pay interest plus amortization and eventually realize a profit. No one could fault the regime for slack borrowing habits. The country's foreign debt doubled between 1976 and 1979, and doubled again by 1983. Brazil ended up the $100 billion debtor—a world record.

In the mad dash to keep ahead of its bills, the regime dumped money on any project that smacked of eventual export revenue. Agriculture got credit subsidies so Brazil could boost exports of soybeans, sugar, coffee, cacao, and orange juice. Likewise, industry got kickbacks and tax relief for everything from shoes to automobiles as long as the goods ended up in foreign markets. To keep Progress on its course, the regime scattered infrastructure's bric-a-brac everywhere, as if construction alone inevitably conferred development's benefits. São Paulo needed hydroelectric power, so it got Itaipú. The São Francisco Valley, short on rainfall, got irrigation projects. The Amazon Basin, once neglected by the Planning Ministry's developers, now found itself under attack. The 2,000 mile Trans-Amazon Highway was called forth and then abandoned as a maintenance fiasco. The bridges collapsed, the banks caved in, trucks were left to die in the mud.[65]

The regime had its failures, but successes too. In the Carajás highlands just south of the Amazon Basin and west of the Tocantins River, Brazil discovered iron ore reserves estimated at 15 billion tons—the largest in the world. To exploit the deposits, the regime spared no expense. Working through the Rio Doce Steel Corporation—56 percent of which was owned by the government—the regime got the requisite mining infrastructure, an airport, a 550-mile railroad to the port of São Luís, and expansion of the port's facilities: all for $3.6 billion—a billion less than originally projected. To this sum, however, one must add in the cost of the Tucuruí dam on the Tocantins north of Carajás—approximately $5 billion. When iron ore extraction began in 1986, Carajás operated with an initial export capacity of 15 million tons a year, with a peak output of 35 million tons.[66]

In adding up the price tags for Brazil's assorted development packages—

credit and export subsidies, the Alcohol Program, Itaipú, Carajás—it does not take long to accumulate the country's huge foreign debt. The fortune foretold by the regime's Planning Ministry was not the one the world economy delivered. During 1981, the prime rate set by U.S. banks reached an unprecedented 19 percent. Because the interest charged on Brazil's debt was not fixed, but varied according to prevailing rates, the cost required to service the debt mounted apace.[67] As long as the banks kept lending, the regime kept borrowing, hoping against hope that the ledger would yield the prospect of a balance. In 1982, Mexico's debt payments collapsed under the weight of accumulated interest. The banks panicked. The flow of fresh capital that had financed Brazil's big development schemes halted. The next year, Brazil went into IMF receivership. The regime had lost its wager with the banks, and, in 1985, it surrendered, bankrupt, to democracy.

When it came to paying the bill, the IMF lost no time identifying the culprit: it imposed austerity on Brazil's spendthrift work force. Brazil had Itaipú, an Alcohol Program, a Trans-Amazon Highway, and Carajás. But if that was the regime's dream, it was likewise the poor man's nightmare. Brazil was also like Bolivia, and, for this impoverished reality, the regime had not bothered to solicit funds. Big development was great for construction companies, assorted contractors, and Brazil's money managers. For the majority of the nation's children, it spelled a slipshod excuse for literacy that scarcely sufficed to read a bus ticket. Tancredo Neves acknowledged the regime's accomplishments. But its legacy likewise included the dispossessed, waiting still for some entries on their account.

Cubatão

"My child was born dead without a head," the woman whispered, stifling tears. I heard the Cubatão exposé on Brazilian television in 1979. I did not believe it.

Located on the coast just north of the port of Santos, Cubatão is along the road to São Paulo. The city's 100 factories specialize in steel production, cement, and petrochemicals. With a population of approximately 100,000, Cubatão is one of Brazil's largest industrial zones. Still, you will not find Cubatão listed in *Quatro Rodas*; evidently, Brazil's Automobile Club assumes no one is dumb enough to stop there, not even to catch a glimpse of Brazil's industrial hardware. Small wonder. Emissions with high concentrations of sulfur dioxide, phosphates, and iron particles hover over the city in ocher-gray layers. Of 16 pollutants monitored by São Paulo's Environmental Agency, "6 reached the highest levels so far recorded anywhere in the world. A hundred times a year Cubatão's pollution index exceeds 240 micrograms of chemical dust per cubic meter of air; an exposure level that produces long-term health damage." Acid rain in Cubatão is the most contaminated ever registered. It has so defoliated the surrounding mountains that factories need protective dikes against mud slides. Higher rates of cancer, tuberculosis, and birth defects prevail in Cubatão than in any other place in Brazil.[68]

When I read such claims, it is hard to forget that woman and her child.[69]

6

RURAL INTERNSHIPS

With almost 15 million inhabitants, landlocked Minas Gerais is Brazil's second most populous state.[1] Most of the U.S. Midwest—Ohio, Michigan, Indiana, and Illinois—could fit inside, with enough room left over for Kentucky. Minas skirts the coastal states of Rio de Janeiro and São Paulo, reaches up into the Northeast, and stretches west toward the vastness of Goiás and Mato Grosso. A rugged state carved up by steep escarpments, it lays claim to the headwaters of the legendary São Francisco River, whose tributaries rise outside the state capital, Belo Horizonte. The São Francisco flows north for over 300 miles through the mountains, rolling hills, and rich flatlands of Minas. Entering the state of Bahia, it continues its northern course 400 miles to Juazeiro, and then arches eastward 300 miles toward its confluence with the Atlantic Ocean.

• Minas Gerais

In colonial times, when the rivers of Minas were awash in alluvial gold, contentious prospectors from Brazil's Northeast—the famed *Nordestinos*—traced the São Francisco to its source. They founded a string of towns in what became colonial Brazil's first interior province. And from across the mountains, far to the south, gold likewise brought the *Paulistas*—the arrogant native sons of São Paulo. Two different versions of Brazil—Nordestino and Paulista—clashed in the backlands of colonial Minas. And for once São Paulo met its match, its intruders expelled by the Nordestinos.

Minas turned out to be an errant colony. The province's wealthy miners married slave women and passed on their estates to mulatto offspring. Slaves learned trades like metalwork and carpentry; they panned for gold, or worked for shopkeepers and merchants. So many eventually purchased their freedom that colonial Minas ended up with as many freedmen as slaves. Despite complaints from royal officials that in Minas diverse races mixed indiscriminately, the unruly province stuck impenitently to the practice.[2] Thus, there opened a middle ground between slave and freedman that altered the way Brazilians perceived race. Not that Brazil escaped slavery unscathed. But the legacy diverged sharply from the caste system slavery left to the United States, where race is either black or white. In Brazil, the mixture is neither black nor white, but simply *bem Brasileiro*—"very Brazilian." Some reservations must be noted. Hispanic neighborhoods in New York City can be as ambiguous on racial identity as any place in Brazil. And at the margins of the color spectrum, Brazilians see black and white every bit as much as Americans do. Nonetheless, the crux of the matter is what ordinary people do with the facts of race they encounter every day. In its public schools, urban neighborhoods, and factories, Brazil flaunts its penchant for miscegenation.

Colonial Minas defied the rules of race; its political economy likewise diverged from the standard pattern. The coastal colonies developed as docile exporters of sugar, tobacco, cotton, and hides. Minas, by contrast, insisted on a self-sufficiency that made it less dependent on trade with the mother country, Portugal. And it was Minas that first plotted independence. To the authorities, it was a cantankerous place, and it still is.

Minas once banished the Paulistas. They are back today as corporate executives consolidating land for agroindustry. The once proud Nordestinos have returned too, but this time as displaced field hands trekking south through Minas toward São Paulo. Likely as not, they end up in the favelas of Belo Horizonte, just short of the promised land.

Minas Gerais lives in Brazil's two worlds, mixing poverty with promise. Part of the Northeast and part of Brazil's industrial machine, it is also very much itself, an interior kingdom where Brazil's autonomy was first born.

Rio's fashions come from Paris, São Paulo's money from New York; but Minas takes its bearings from Brazil. When the state's politicians learn the lessons that Minas teaches, they juggle like masters. Juscelino Kubitschek, the last civilian president to complete his term (1956–61), came from Minas. Other than Getúlio Vargas, he is the only president of this century Brazilians bother to remember. Juscelino transferred the nation's capital from Rio to Brasília in the backlands of Goiás—a characteristically Mineiro vision of Brazil. Tancredo Neves was likewise from Minas. By his magic, Brasília slipped from the regime's grasp: the tablecloth vanished with the plates still in place. One hopes the old master has trained an apprentice. When Jânio Quadros, a Paulista, followed Juscelino to the presidency in 1961, he resigned in six months—a bungler, not a juggler.

What is the lesson of Minas? That Brazil cannot live by the industry of São

Map 6.1   Minas Gerais

Paulo alone. For this truth, one can consult the testimony of João Guimarães Rosa (1908–67), Brazil's greatest novelist and a Mineiro. He writes in *First Stories* of "cause and effects," of "honeymoons" and "treetops." In his masterpiece, *The Great Path through the Backlands*, Brazil lives without reference to São Paulo's wealth.[3] This Brazil, abandoned and living on its own wits, holds one key to the country's future; São Paulo holds the other. The great lock that bars the future cannot be opened without both. Other doors there are, fashioned in deception, in tricks and lies.

Belo Horizonte

"Beautiful Horizon" is the city's name. It is mostly a joke now: industry turned more powerful than nature. The population of the metropolitan area, the third largest in Brazil, increased by over 50 percent in ten years—from 1.6 million in 1970 to 2.5 million in 1980. During the same period, the state's rural labor force dropped by 20 percent. In 1980, two-thirds of the state's population lived in urban areas, and one out of every four of them within a sixty-mile radius of Belo Horizonte.[4] Within this circle, Minas concentrated its industries. Given the state's rich deposits of iron ore, bauxite, and nickel, it was Brazil's foremost producer of laminated steel and cast iron, and a leader in metal alloys and aluminum. Although far behind São Paulo in total manufacturing output, Minas vied with Rio de Janeiro for the distinction of second place.[5]

Industrial growth, however, took a disastrous plunge in 1981. Minas Gerais, where new industries had just taken hold, was hit hard. (See Table 6.1.) "Unemployment is over 20 percent. The government's figure, 12 percent, is ridiculous," noted Dr. Roberto Martins, an economist at Belo Horizonte's Federal University. "Negative growth of such magnitude is unprecedented. When you consider that the labor force expands by 3 percent a year, Brazil's economy needs rapid growth just to keep pace, much less absorb the unemployed. When you see negative figures in Brazil, it means disaster. Brazilian companies hold most of their debts in dollars. With the cruzeiro already devalued by 100 percent so far this year [1983], their debts have become twice as expensive.* Most of the industries in Minas sell in domestic markets; they're not exporters. How can they make enough cruzeiros when the economy is contracting so fast? They face bankruptcy."

Venda Nova

The signs of depression were everywhere. I was staying in Belo Horizonte with my friend Dr. João Magro; it was Sunday morning. Ragged children

---

*The final tally for 1983 reduced the cruzeiro's value by almost 300 percent in dollar terms, a consequence of rapid inflation.

Table 6.1 Annual Manufacturing Growth Rate in Minas Gerais,
1978–1983

Year	Growth Rate (%)
1978	+7.1
1979	+4.4
1980	+7.7
1981	−9.5
1982	+3.5
1983*	−7.8

Source: Presentation by Professor Roberto Martins, Belo Horizonte, Minas Gerais, 11 July
1983.

*First six months of 1983.

walked the streets, begging leftover scraps from house to house. "They're very organized," he pointed out. "I see the same kids every week. They've divided up the neighborhoods into separate territories. It's the right idea; it's just backwards. We ought to divide the favelas into territories and attack the problems block by block."

A physician in his thirties and a faculty member at the Federal University, João helped organize the Medical School's program in Venda Nova, an impoverished, makeshift city of 600,000 about fifteen miles from downtown Belo Horizonte. In the United States, the poor are relegated to the inner city; in Brazil, they are banished to the periphery. In either case, the jobs are somewhere else.

Venda Nova began as a squatter settlement. Those who arrived first benefited from Belo's new industries; today they make up the district's relatively prosperous working-class core. One can estimate length of residence from the type of housing. The square, cement-block structures belong to the privileged. They are typically one story, plastered, and painted in pastels. A step down, construction tends to wooden slats protected by a coating of mud. At the bottom of the heap are the latest invaders. They stake out claims in cardboard and straw mats, perhaps with an abandoned sheet of rusted, ribbed roofing balanced on top.

Brazil is riddled with Venda Novas, the illegal constructs of massive invasions that take place overnight. If not expelled immediately, the squatters cannot be displaced except by force and much bloodshed. The result is a standoff. They stay, but the city refuses diplomatic recognition; hence, no piped water, sewers, health clinics, or bus service. Squatters' rights eventually prevail, usually when the favela has expanded to such proportions that benign neglect becomes impossible. By then, the settlement has an awesome backlog of unmet needs from sanitation and paved streets to electric lines and schools.

How curious this should happen in Brazil, a country that dotes on its Planning Ministry.

Venda Nova pieced itself together in a no-man's-land lodged between Belo's outskirts and Sabará, a town of 25,000. It stayed there, misbegotten and unclaimed, until Belo reluctantly annexed it in 1981. João introduced me to Baptista, Venda Nova's recently elected councilman. A young man in his twenties, Baptista had contracted polio as a child; he hobbled around on crutches like the district he represented: disabled in body, but not in mind or spirit.

"Parts of Venda Nova are in good shape," he said. "The homes have electricity and basic services. Most of it, however, is still a favela, the water supply is inadequate, there's no sewage system, garbage collection, or paved streets. Families build their own septic tanks, but most of the time they aren't installed properly and only help spread infection. Children suffer from malnutrition, which makes them all the more susceptible to contagious diseases. We're in desperate need of nutrition programs and survival tactics—what the doctors call 'health education,' " he said, turning to João with a grin. "We have primary schools, but most kids drop out after first grade. There isn't a single public high school—and Venda Nova is a city of 600,000. Transportation services are a disgrace. To get to the center of Belo Horizonte takes an hour and a half on two different buses, and 80 percent of the district's workers hold jobs outside Venda Nova. To get to work by 7:00 A.M., you have to be up at 4:30 A.M., and when you're finished, and tired, you still face the long ride back. A worker's salary gets eaten away by the bus. It's an insult. That's why people burn buses when the fares go up—they're angry. They waste their lives on the bus, and have to pay for it too! And even then, they're lucky to have a job; 30 percent of the families here are unemployed.

"I sound like a complainer, don't I? Well, you asked about the problems. People here will work for their families and their neighborhoods if given a chance."

We stopped at Venda Nova's Community Center. The government built it and then staffed it with outsiders. "No one used it," said Antônio, secretary of Venda Nova's Community Association. "It was imposed from outside; people broke the windows and plastered the walls with obscene slogans. The authorities decided it was impossible to help ne'er-do-wells like us," he laughed, "so they abandoned the building. Later, when the associations got started, we realized the Center's potential. People stopped being so negative; they ended up repairing the same building they had mistreated. Since then, we've built a soccer field, a day-care center, and a kindergarten. The Center is managed by a council, whose representatives come from each of Venda Nova's seven associations. We support the Center by fund-raising in each neighborhood; they all contribute, even the poor favelas."

The Medical School at the Federal University in Belo rotated its staff and students to Venda Nova's ten clinics: a precarious base for meeting the health needs of half a million people. When I last saw João in 1984, he was frantically scrounging up funds—like the kids on his block—for a Community Development Foundation.[6]

"Government programs," said João, "write prescriptions without bothering to see the patients. The premise behind the Foundation is to see the patients first and respect their diagnosis. Development should be democratic; the community should help set the agenda. To people in Venda Nova, how things are done is important; they want to be involved at each step. For twenty years the regime ignored the favelas. The Venda Novas of Brazil will wait no longer."

In Venda Nova's case, the associations already had established an agenda. Their priorities included health posts, a safe water supply, sewage disposal, and home improvement loans. They were adamant, too, about schools, the bus service, and space for playgrounds.[7]

Polio, Chagas, and Schistosomiasis

Diseases tracked down Brazil's population in a way that shows how progress favored particular regions and social groups. Brazil's health system so doted on technology that malnutrition and parasitic diseases continued unchecked by "development."

On occasion the regime could rally itself to the cause of health. The campaign against polio is a case in point. A day each year was set aside for inoculations. Soccer players, TV stars, singers, and presidents combined together in a media blitz, pleading with parents to have their children vaccinated. Churches, schools, and town halls got converted into temporary health posts; thousands of people volunteered to set up facilities, keep people in line, and dispense injections. In a single day, Brazil managed to inoculate around 15 million children.

Less dramatic childhood afflictions, although preventable by vaccination, fell far short of the coverage rates registered in the fight against polio. In 1981, 25 percent of the children under six had not received even one dose of DPT (diphtheria, whooping cough, tetanus) vaccine; 29 percent still ran the risk of contracting measles, and 33 percent were not protected against tuberculosis.[8] Even when reduced to a one-shot deal, the system could not deliver, at least not without considerable fanfare. And in the end, Brazil's health problems had more in common with Chagas disease and schistosomiasis than with polio.

A parasitic affliction, Chagas disease is contracted from the barbeiro, an insect that is host to the parasite and whose bite, when infected, transmits the disease.[9] The barbeiro's natural habitat was the dense stub forest and underbrush of the cerrado, a region of sparse settlement that included much of Brazil's interior. The stimulus Brasília's construction gave to cattle ranching and large-scale agricultural production reduced the forests, depriving the barbeiro of the woody nooks and crannies it preferred. It found a substitute in the thatched, wattle and daub dwellings of the rural poor. A nocturnal insect, it strikes almost undetected at night, biting around the lips and eyes. The parasite that enters through the contaminated opening invades the bloodstream, lodging itself in tissue, especially that of the heart. In its initial phase, Chagas disease produces debilitating fevers; the chronic stage is characterized by arrhythmia, blockage of heart valves, and congestive heart failure. The disease is often prolonged, usually fatal, and without a known cure. In some counties of rural Minas and Goiás, Chagas has been detected in 30 percent of the population.[10]

The barbeiro hides in pockmarked mud walls and thatched roofs. In a solid dwelling, the risk is much reduced. To be on the safe side, however, one should exterminate regularly and sleep under a mosquito net. Controlling Chagas amidst the poverty of a favela is next to impossible; it requires house-by-house extermination, which cannot be done without community support and external funds. How mosquito nets can be worked into a minimum-wage budget is best left to the Planning Ministry. The barbeiro stalks its prey, following the path decreed by the country's income distribution: a kiss of death for the dispossessed.

The barbeiro is no longer confined exclusively to the countryside. Tracking Brazil's migrants and their shantytowns, it has slowly closed in upon the cities. If unleashed in Brazil's urban favelas, the barbeiro will exact a terrible toll.

For the Chagas parasite, infecting the human body is a kamikaze mission. Once the parasite is in, it cannot get out. Transmission from one person to another is rare. Schistosomiasis is very different in this respect: human beings are part and parcel of the parasite's life cycle.

Schistosomiasis (*S. mansoni*) is a waterborne disease.[11] The parasite's larvae develop in snails whose habitat is the water of lakes, ponds, drainage ditches, and irrigated fields. When one is bathing, washing clothes, or planting crops in an infected environment, a larva can readily penetrate the skin. Once in the bloodstream, it assumes its parasitic form, reproducing prolifically. The eggs are retained in the bladder and bowel, causing intestinal bleeding, severe dysentery, and kidney failure. Enlargement of the spleen and damage to the liver are also common. From the human host, eggs are passed in the urine and feces. If the eggs reach a suitable aquatic environment, they hatch. Stagnant water at a temperature of about eighty degrees is ideal. The larvae then have six hours to locate and penetrate a snail host. Between one and three months later, the new larvae reenter the water by the thousands; they have up to forty-eight hours in which to find a human host.

How serious the disease becomes depends on repeated infection and the consequent increase in the "worm burden." In most cases, schistosomiasis is debilitating rather than lethal, inducing periodic bouts of high fever, chills, abdominal pains, and dysentery. Over time, however, the damage inflicted on the liver, kidneys, and spleen has deadly side effects, which compound circulatory and intestinal ailments in later life.

Chemotherapy—a dose of oxamniquine—reduces the worm burden to acceptable levels and limits long-term damage. But the treatment's effects are only temporary if not combined with sanitation measures, a safe water supply, and health education. When children splash around in larval-infested water holes, or walk barefoot through exposed drainage ditches, they will contract schistosomiasis repeatedly. There is no simple way to break the cycle of excretion, water contact, and infection. Development, far from being a remedy, has created new habitats for the disease. In swiftly moving streams and rivers, the current's velocity reduces the chance for contact between snails and larvae. But the dams constructed to irrigate fields and generate electricity have created tranquil breeding grounds. Concentrating field hands in shantytowns, as opposed to the more dispersed sharecropping system, has likewise proved conducive to schistosomiasis. And migrants from the Northeast have increased the disease's incidence in states like São Paulo, although there the cycle breaks down in the winter when low water temperatures kill off the larvae and prevent the parasites' eggs from hatching.

Brazil's statistics on kilowatt-hours and agroindustry's contribution to gross national product (GNP) ought to carry figures on the incidence of Chagas and schistosomiasis. But there is no reliable estimate in Brazil's *Statistical Yearbook*. That is hardly surprising; Brazil's health system is so weak at the community level, it does not have the capacity for surveillance.

There is no quick fix for Chagas disease and schistosomiasis. The remedy lies deeper and points to the nature of things. Chagas disease follows the shacks, schistosomiasis the sewers. Both are fed by a system that counted value added in manufacturing with greater accuracy than infant mortality. To get to the root requires a radically different approach to basics, whether health, education, or employment.

Medical School

Guimarães Rosa, the novelist, was also a physician. As a young man, he practiced rural medicine in Janaúba, a small town in Northern Minas hundreds of miles from fashionable Belo Horizonte. There, he learned the lessons Minas teaches. His path has been retraced by doctors from Belo's Federal University.

In the 1960s, Brazil's medical schools took a textbook approach to the study of diseases. Training was insufficient and limited almost exclusively to hospitals. Even then, the student's role tended to be that of a passive observer; there were few opportunities for independent diagnosis. As a result, students finished medical school without much confidence in their skills. To make up for the deficiency, they had to arrange postgraduate apprenticeships. The consequence was that half the country's "doctors" never practiced.

Reform of Brazil's outmoded medical curriculum gained momentum during the 1970s, impelled in part by national legislation that encouraged a teaching-service approach to training. How seriously medical schools took such recommendations, however, depended on the support reformers could muster against those who followed the textbooks. At Belo's Medical School, an alliance of students and reform-minded faculty gradually pried concessions that in 1974 regrouped disciplines into four basic areas: pediatrics, gynecology and obstetrics, surgery, and clinical medicine. The new curriculum stressed general practice geared to prevention, basic diagnosis, community medicine, and treatment at small hospitals. To strengthen practical experience, students began rotations earlier, and they worked in a variety of settings from health clinics to the University Hospital. When social medicine became a basic area of study in 1977, community health received an additional boost.[12] Subsequently, it became an advanced program as well, geared to general practice, public health, disease control, and administration.

Belo's Medical School, of course, also offered specializations in cardiovascular surgery and oncology, which lacked neither advocates nor applicants. What distinguished Belo's program was the way it trained incoming medical students. When students graduated, they were prepared for actual practice, and their training reflected the social conditions that characterized the state. Students can still specialize, but in Belo's program they cannot escape the Brazil where malnutrition and parasitic diseases are facts of daily life.

The Rural Internship Program

The teaching-service approach is now standard at most of Brazil's medical schools. Belo's program, which began earlier, provided a model that other schools followed. Given its head start, the strategy's limitations became apparent earlier, too. The simple fact of rotating students to health posts did not create the kind of independence or in-depth experience a focus on community health implied. As Dr. Francisco Campos, one of the program's supervisors, pointed out, "a few hours a week in a clinic wasn't much. Students became too dependent on their supervisors and didn't develop sufficient confidence. In theory, they knew that social conditions perpetuated specific diseases, and they heard prevention stressed constantly. But rotating from clinics to hospitals didn't give students a chance to work with communities on a sustained basis. Medicine in a country like Brazil has to be more than simply treating illness. The state's high infant mortality rate is largely a result of dysentery, parasitic infections, and contagious diseases.[13] So you need an assertive strategy that combines prevention, community participation, and public health. How can you pass out pills and ignore nutrition or the community's water supply?—that's crazy."

Dr. Campos, known as "Chico," was in his early thirties and renown for his girth. And for every extra pound he carried around, he doled out ten of energy, intelligence, and humor. He was one of several faculty supervisors responsible for the Rural Internship Program. I had arrived in Belo from Rio on a Saturday, called Chico, and was immediately drawn into the vortex of the weekend's activities. We started at the Tavares restaurant, an old-fashioned place that still prepared Mineiro specialties in clay ovens and wood-burning stoves. It was famous for *feijão tropeiro*: red beans fried in crisp pork fat and cassava flour. I sat next to Chico and questioned him unmercifully until soccer came to the rescue.

The Internship Program was designed for students in the final year of medical school.[14] They spent three months at clinics in rural areas of Northern Minas. They could reenlist for an additional term, and about 15 percent did so. Pilot projects started in the 1970s with personnel from pediatrics and social medicine. "What could be accomplished in three months of intensive community service was vastly superior to fragmented rotations," noted Chico. "An internship is now mandatory," he laughed, "whether the students like it or not." "Why would anyone object?" I asked naively. "Students select Belo's program because the rotations give them practical experience," he observed, "not because they're necessarily dedicated to community health. They can hide from Brazil's health problems when they jump from clinic to clinic. But a three-month internship, when they're on their own in a town they never heard of, and where they face abysmal health conditions every day, that's different. It's a strong dose of general practice for those who think real medicine is cardiovascular surgery. And, of course, its scary. Most students know nothing about rural Brazil. On the other hand, the reluctant ones who think preventive medicine is second-rate sometimes finish the internship with a new respect for community health."

The Internship Program provided dependable staffing at over thirty rural clinics. To discuss special problems and on-site orientation, supervisors from the medical faculty stopped at each clinic at least twice a month. They also held joint meetings with the student team, the promotoras, and the community. Meanwhile, another group was being trained in Belo. Students who had completed internships prepared the upcoming group. Those who had worked in Jequitaí, for example, met with students assigned to the same locality. They outlined the work done so that the next group could provide continuity.

The internship sites in Northern Minas were located two to three hundred miles from Belo, many of them on dirt roads that were almost impassable during the rainy season. "Considering transportation problems alone," noted Chico, "an internship program in Northern Minas isn't very logical. But there were other considerations. In 1974, the Brazilian government had received funds from USAID [U.S. Agency for International Development] to construct clinics and train promotoras. The commitment this implied to adequate coverage and public health fit the internship's conception of medical practice oriented to the community. Having received funds to implement a model program, the government had at least a passing interest in making it work."

The Internship Program had financial support from several sources. The Minas Department of Health paid a monthly stipend to a maximum of eighty student interns. Funds also came from Brazil's National Health Service under the rubric of rural health. The participating municipalities provided food, lodging, and local transportation. Nonetheless, observed Chico, "without outside funds from foundations and international agencies, the project would have to be cut back. I doubt the Health Department would pay for it."

Keeping the program going required diplomatic skills of the highest caliber. Contracts had to be negotiated with an astounding number of agencies, including the mayors of each town. When the regime let something be done that bordered so dangerously on innovation, the authorities bound it in red tape. "We're constantly fighting petty battles at every turn," Chico said, "from the Department of Health to dissatisfied mayors. Health is political. A mayor pays maintenance one year, but then decides he doesn't want outsiders documenting malnutrition. So he refuses to have interns again. Then the community turns on the mayor and people pay maintenance out of their own pockets. That's Brazil, so valiant and so oppressive."

Soccer

"There's a soccer game today," Chico said enthusiastically. "We're playing Flamengo, or maybe you'd prefer Ouro Preto. Of course, if you want to rest. . . ." I had no desire to establish myself as a wimp—"rest" was out of the question. Ouro Preto had obvious attractions. The old capital of Minas and a national historic site, it is a breathtaking place of narrow streets twisted to fit a mountainous terrain. But I had been there before, and so had my companions. There were some advocates for Ouro Preto; if that was my choice, I apparently had support. To everyone's relief, including Ouro Preto's proponents, I endorsed soccer with convincing decisiveness.

The likelihood that the Belo team, Atlético, could defeat Rio's Flamengo was roundly discounted. After all, Flamengo had the notorious Zico, who considered himself Brazil's best player. We departed for the stadium in a flotilla of automobiles. I accompanied Dr. Luis, his wife, eldest son, and assorted relatives. Against the naysayers, Dr. Luis had staunchly defended a victory thesis. Fans carried banners and flags or proudly wore their sportshirts—all striped in black and white, Atlético's colors. We found our way to a parking space, ushered in by free-lance attendants. The ticket windows were surrounded by crowds. "The lines look awful," I lamented. "Oh, that," answered Luis absentmindedly, "just wait here." He disappeared into the throng. I braced myself for the wait. Children carrying huge thermos bottles and stacks of plastic cups sold *cafezinho*. I bought the first round, presweetened with a sugar to coffee ratio of 4 to 1. Luis was soon back with a fistful of tickets. "How did you manage that?" I asked incredulously. "Oh, it's never a problem. Hawkers buy up tickets in advance and then sell them off before the game. It's a service," he laughed, "so people can avoid the lines. For regular games the extra cost isn't much. Besides, it creates employment."

There is no fence-sitting in soccer. To purchase a ticket fans must declare an allegiance and enter the stadium through the gates assigned to the team the ticket designates. Within, the halls that led to rival sides were barricaded. Between factions in the stadium, the police maintained a defensible corridor of vacant benches at both ends. As the teams warmed up, the fans competed to display their support. They unfurled banners, waved flags, beat drums, and exploded firecrackers. It had rained off and on all day. Luis pronounced attendance "disappointing," a figure later announced at a mere 70,000. The hated Flamengo scored the first goal, its fans exploding in thunderous admiration. The Atlético side confined itself to a silence so complete it reduced the sting of predictable defeat. But Atlético recouped with a goal that brought us to our feet amidst a deafening racket of drums and cherry bombs. At halftime, there were cafezinhos and quart bottles of beer; for old time's sake, I added a face-full of cotton candy. The second half was less spirited, headed it seemed for an inconclusive tie. My friends started claiming this as a sort of victory for their underdog team. But at the last second, Atlético stole the ball and tore off toward Flamengo's net, a goal, and victory.

Outside the stadium, the celebration continued. Samba tunes took hold, attendants got extra big tips, and the predictable traffic jam was enjoyed in the good humor of victory.

Back in the United States, I am not much of a sport's fan. If I want to follow the big leagues, there is always the *Wall Street Journal*. As a kid, my gang spent its summers at Offerman's Stadium, home of the famed Buffalo Bisons. It housed a baseball diamond and up to 10,000 fans; 5,000 was a crowd. I can still recite the star-studded teams that brought us out for doubleheaders. In the 1950s, Casey Stengel claimed that baseball was a sport and not a business—and got away with it in front of congressional committees. Today, his tongue would rot. When I draw the *Trivia* card for sports, I do not know much since Casey left the Mets. Now, we have strikes, million-dollar executives disguised as players, and umpires who at $75,000 a head want overtime for the play-offs. Our wide world of sports is really corporate America at play, complete with network contracts, drug trafficking, and offshore banking. The "home" team?—you have to be kidding.

The American sports model has found its way to Brazil. For soccer there is now an international market that trades in players as in commodity futures. To Brazil's list of exports, one can put "soccer players" in the column with "growth industries." Thus does international capital find its way into the lives of Belo's soccer fans, stealing the home team on the basis of exchange rates.

At Chico's house we had a *churrasco* of charcoal-grilled beef, pork, and chicken. It was a high-spirited Saturday night, not only because of the victory, but also because Monday was the departure date for Montes Claros and a three-day internship evaluation session. Those who planned it had gathered for a well-deserved send-off. About midnight Chico decided to make for the dance hall. He soon convinced the undecided, and off we went. The moment of truth had arrived. I had survived soccer; could I take on who knows how many hours of dancing? Chico offered to take me home, but I decided to tough it out.

Brazil's dance halls attract all ages and social ranks, and draw across the racial spectrum. There is a band, and a dance floor that takes up half the place. The one in Belo had rickety tables, overhead fans, and veteran waiters to ward off dehydration with cold beer. The first and only rule was to dance. I was not allowed to plead ignorance of the samba. The ladies in our entourage valiantly kept me on my feet, bearing up under what I fancied was my tolerable facsimile. I was drenched in sweat by the end of each set, refilled with beer, and drenched again. We left about 3:00 A.M., just moments before my collapse.

On the way out, I congratulated myself for keeping step with a Brazilian Saturday night. We mulled around outside for a few minutes. Then I heard it: "Let's get a pizza." I could not believe it. Chico piled me into the car before I could mumble a protest. Cristina Fekete, having propped me up for the last dance, intervened from her place of influence in the front seat. "Jimmy, are you sure you want pizza?" "No problem," said Chico, "they've got hamburgers."

• Northern Minas: Health Care

When the wind clears off the haze, the sun sparkles in Belo Horizonte; the ancient mountains return majestic from their exile in the smog. On such a morning the dawn is full of promise.

Chico picked me up about 6:30 A.M.; we went to the courtyard of Belo's Medical School. At the end of each three-month internship, an evaluation took place in Montes Claros, headquarters for the region's health system. With a population of 215,000 (1985), it is the largest city in Northern Minas. Those making the 250-mile trip north included the supervisors in charge of sessions, a representative from the Pan American Health Organization, faculty members from other medical schools, and myself—altogether, about fifteen of us. We set out in two jeeps and three cars.

The São Francisco River, which flows through Northern Minas from south to north, gives the region great potential for irrigation. Comprised of forty-two counties, Northern Minas is approximately the size of New Mexico. It is like the Northeast in ecology and culture. Distinct rainy and dry seasons mark off the agricultural cycle. The region suffers from periodic droughts, although rarely as severe or prolonged as those of the Northeast. Much of Northern Minas is now converted to grassland, but it still retains the characteristics of the *caatinga*: a zone of scrub brush and short stocky trees adapted to dry spells.

Between 1970 and 1980, while the region's population increased from about 970,000 to 1.1 million, families left agriculture in both absolute and relative terms. The rural population dropped from 700,000 to 630,000; the region was 72 percent rural in 1970, but the figure had fallen to 56 percent in 1980.[15] Migrants either settled in towns nearby or left for distant cities like Belo Horizonte. In the favelas that clustered around the region's towns, families faced the high risks poor health conditions imposed. In 1975, almost 40 percent of the diseases treated at clinics in the counties of Mirabela, Januária, Rio Pardo, and Jequitaí were diagnosed as "water-transmitted." According to interviews conducted with physicians who practiced in Northern Minas, the principal causes of death in 1975 were gastrointestinal disorders, Chagas-induced heart ailments, malnutrition, and parasitic infections.[16] The sixty-five medical students on their three-month tour of duty were working against the odds.

Stops and Starts

Once beyond the range that encircles Belo Horizonte, the landscape becomes rolling hills and mesas. Then, in the central-west of Northern Minas, the flatness of Brazil's *cerrado* takes shape, reaching toward Brasília and the Amazon Basin. The sky stretches out as it does on America's Great Plains.

We stopped first in Morro da Garça, a tiny hamlet hidden between rocky hills: a few scattered houses, a church, and a small health post. We met the interns, Mauritânia and Marcos, a married couple with a small child. They had brought the program to Morro, no interns had preceded them, and the post did not yet have a promotora. The mayor was frail, but he had the dignity of a village elder rather than the slickness of a local politician. "They attend people day and night," he said solemnly, "whenever people come in from their farms. The little doctors are like us: they do not have a schedule." "Do you object when the doctors record bad health conditions?" someone asked. "Why should I object, my friend," he said, a bit puzzled. "People here don't have much." The cost of food and lodging for interns came out of the village budget. The community had fixed up an abandoned house, furnishing it with a propane gas stove and a refrigerator—luxuries they could not afford for themselves.

From Morro, we went on to Jequitaí, a hundred miles farther north. The county seat, it had a health center staffed by six promotoras, four student interns, and a supervising physician. The staff had packed the clinic's small waiting room for us with every spare chair and bench.

The students had prepared a data sheet on the county.[17] Between 1960 and 1980, the population had dropped from 13,500 to 8,400. The number of rural inhabitants had peaked at 11,800 in 1960, but only 5,000 remained twenty years later. In the meantime, Jequitaí, a mere village of 1,600 in 1960, had acquired the status of a town with 3,300 residents. It had the title, but not the amenities. About 40 percent of the dwellings had piped water; to serve the rest, there were only two public pumps. There was no sewage system, and only half the population had anything resembling a septic tank. Diseases transmitted by contaminated water and food were the most prevalent. The interns did not cite statistics on infant mortality or the leading causes of death, because available data "were too scanty and unsystematic to be reliable." Only half the county's children actually attended school. The main obstacles noted were that "families can't afford school supplies, children have work at home, and the material taught bears no relationship to the child's reality."

Employment, they pointed out, tended to be sporadic, with few opportunities for dependable, full-time jobs. The county still had pockets of small landowners and some prospecting, most of it panning for gold along streams and riverbeds. Employment as ranch hands, or seasonal work in agriculture, allowed most families to eke out a livelihood often supplemented by lumbering. By means of the traditional, slow-burning technique, most of the wood cut was converted to charcoal for use in Belo's iron foundries. Production was an important cottage industry, not only in Jequitaí but throughout much of the region as well.

Dr. Geraldo Cunha, a tall, enthusiastic man in his mid-twenties, had entered the postgraduate program in social medicine. Stationed at Jequitaí for his year of residency, he helped supervise the interns. "Given the frequency of rotations," someone asked, "how does the program maintain continuity?" "Of course," Geraldo agreed, "that's a basic limitation of a three-month internship. Students work hard on a specific problem, start getting results, and then it's time to leave. The strategy is to get the next group to follow through. The group that's here now, for example, has continued a tuberculosis control project initiated over a year ago. They knew medications were short in Jequitaí, so they obtained stocks in Belo and brought them out for free distribution."

The lack of generic drugs had, in fact, reached crisis proportions. Brazil's National Medications Center manufactured drugs for distribution to the country's clinics. The agency imported basic ingredients from the United States.

Whenever Brazil devalued its cruzeiro—part of the standard formula of the International Monetary Fund (IMF) for debtor countries—the buying power of the agency's budget fell immediately. The Medications Center was far behind production targets, and supplies trickled in months behind schedule if at all.

After the IMF was roundly condemned by all, the topic of continuity resurfaced. The interns emphasized the role the promotoras played in primary care and the importance of their support. Teresa, a dignified, serious woman in her fifties and Jequitaí's head promotora, acknowledged the compliment but immediately diverted attention to the accomplishments of the Internship Program.

"We keep much better records now than we used to," said Teresa. "Each file is marked in red (urban) or blue (rural), and the main problems treated are numbered from one to ten. We keep track of sanitation, too. For instance, we list whether the family's water is safe or not, and whether garbage or waste disposal pose health problems. So when someone comes in, you look at the folder and you can see what the problems were before."

"The promotoras," said one of the interns, "are the ones to thank. In the last five months, the health center saw over 1,300 patients; when you consider that most families have five or six members, we've seen at least one person from 70 percent of all the county's families. We couldn't handle this effectively if the promotoras hadn't kept track of prior visits. When new interns come, they find accurate family histories on file. The record system is a good one, but it wouldn't mean much if the promotoras weren't conscientious."

Teresa refused to accept what she considered unwarranted praise. "We all do our jobs," she observed, "that's what matters."

"At Jequitaí," Geraldo pointed out, "the midwives cooperate with the clinic. The last group of interns organized a training program, not so much because the midwives needed to improve their skills, but because we wanted their help. Holding the sessions at the clinic created mutual respect. Now, when they see that a pregnancy is difficult or note dehydration in infants with dysentery, they make referrals to the clinic. Before, they hesitated; they felt the doctors blamed them when complications set in. The point is, interns don't have to sponsor a new program for midwives every three months. One group laid the groundwork; what the next group has to do is continue the collaboration. The midwives deliver 90 percent of all the children in the county, and they encourage mothers to breast-feed; we recommend that too, but people pay more attention to the midwife."

Taking care of patients at the clinic constituted the project's service component. The community, for its part, regarded dependable treatment as an objective in its own right. The interns evaluated their own effectiveness differently. "No matter how many patients we see, the effect is temporary," complained one of the students. "Unless we can involve people actively so they take an interest in prevention, we're not changing anything." They had, in fact, initiated a child-care program, noteworthy for its emphasis on health education and group participation.

The Department of Pediatrics had successfully tested the approach in Belo's clinics, and the Internship Program had selectively introduced it to Northern Minas. The objective was to track a child's growth and development. Mothers received a folded card that marked an infant's progress on the "road to health." One side contained a chart for vaccinations, along with the number of doses required. Each block was filled in as the child received the necessary protection. Across from this was a list of motor skills a child should acquire, specified by age from the first month to five years old. When should a child start to grab, say its first words, walk on its own? Parents could consult the list for the approximate date, bearing in mind that the precise timing would vary from child to child. The back of the card contained a large table that kept tabs on a child's nutrition. The right hand column listed weights beginning at five pounds; the rows along the bottom specified age in months up to thirty-six. The area within the table was subdivided into three color ranges: red, yellow, and green. Take the example of a seven-month-old child who was weighed at the clinic. Less than thirteen pounds placed the child at risk (in the red zone), from thirteen to fifteen pounds suggested caution (yellow zone), and above fifteen put the child in the safe category (green zone). Below the table were small blocks to fill in the child's height and to note if the mother was breast-feeding. The card called a parent's attention to immunizations, child development, and possible malnutrition.[18]

At Jequitaí, the card was passed out routinely at the clinic, a procedure that did not permit adequate discussion of its use. Assisted by the promotoras, the interns canvassed the town block by block. They then visited each family with young children; they explained the card's significance and designated one afternoon a week as a special time for "child health and marking cards" at the clinic. Once they had established a satisfactory routine, they held additional sessions every two weeks at a time publicized in advance. At these meetings, which quickly became known as the "Card Club," they showed slides and films to illustrate aspects of child health: the diseases to which children are prone, vaccinations, the signs of malnutrition and how lactation reduces its incidence, and the measures working mothers can take to ensure their child's normal development. Club meetings, which were held in the afternoon, attracted up to seventy-six participants—a strong turnout for Jequitaí.[19]

One consequence of the project was a study that calculated the incidence of malnutrition. The cautious method used avoided absolute measurements that are prone to exaggeration. For Brazilian children, say age seven months, there is a known average weight. Any particular child, however, can fall below the "average" and still be within the normal range for his or her age group. To estimate how prevalent malnutrition was, the interns first determined how many children fell significantly below the average for their age group; they then adjusted for the expected variation in a normal population. Consider the distribution of one hundred children at age seven months. Assuming that the expected average for the group is seventeen pounds, just as many children should weigh under the average as above it. For those below the mark, only 3 percent, in the "normal" course of events, should fall into the red zone, and no more than 22 percent should fall into the yellow zone for caution. An additional 50 percent should cluster around the group average, with some a bit below or a bit above the normal weight: they are all considered safe—the green zone—and do not figure in the calculation for malnutrition. Finally, 25 percent should fall significantly above the group average, and are likewise in the green zone.

Suppose that ten of one hundred children ended up in the red zone. To decide how many had abnormally low weights, the interns would first subtract out the three children expected to be that much underweight in the first place. The same procedure was followed for children in the yellow zone. If thirty of our one hundred children fell into that weight range, the interns would have had to adjust the figure downward by the expected twenty-two naturally skinny children who would normally fall into that category. In this example, the rate of malnutrition sums to 15 percent: 10–3 percent (red zone) + 30–22 percent (yellow zone).[20] (See Figure 6.1.)

For Jequitaí, among children less than a year old, the interns calculated the malnutrition rate at roughly 8 percent. They compared this to an urban clinic in Ravena, a town on Belo's outskirts, where the rate exceeded 20 percent. The tolerable rate in Jequitaí they attributed to the prevalence of breast-feeding, a practice reinforced by the conservative bent of local midwives. After weaning, however, the incidence of child malnutrition increased dramatically. Of 300 children ages one to twelve, half fell into the "danger" or "caution" categories: 34 percent more than a normal distribution could possibly justify. To explain why so many children were at risk, the interns presented data on the monthly income of the 107 families enrolled in the Card Club: 80 percent earned two minimum wages or less, and the vast majority of households had 5 or more members.[21] "That's a good explanation," someone ventured. "Explanations we've got," said Geraldo, "but what does it change?"

"It changed something," noted Jequitaí's parish priest, who had kept a thoughtful silence throughout the proceedings, "at least from the mayor's point of view. Why do you think he stopped paying maintenance? He does not like meddling by outsiders. And don't you think it's significant that the town defied him, collected money on its own to keep the program?" "Well," Geraldo said, "you certainly helped with that, Father." "Yes, I gave my support, but I didn't collect funds. People could have refused to help, but they didn't." "Father," someone asked, "what do you stress most, the body or the soul?" "I stress the person," he replied without hesitation. "God's children aren't divided into pieces."

Figure 6.1 Weight Distribution and Malnutrition Rate
of Brazilian Children

Percentage Distribution of Children Whose Weights Are Expected to
Fall in the Red, Yellow, and Green Zones in a Normal Population

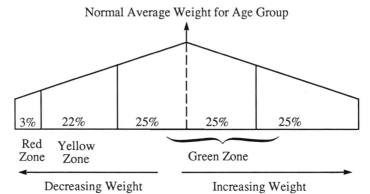

Percentage of Children Distributed
in the Red, Yellow, and Green Zones: Text Example

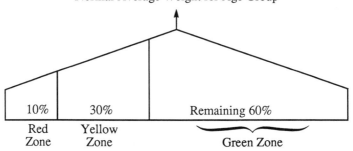

Malnutrition Rate Calculation: Normal Population
Compared to Text Example

	Red Zone	Yellow Zone		
Observed Rate	10	30		
Normal Rate	3	22		
Excess in Each Zone	7	+ 8	= 15	Estimated Rate of Malnutrition

Note: Red Zone = abnormally low weight—child at risk; yellow zone = child
underweight—suggests caution; green zone = slightly above or below normal
weight—child considered safe.

We had lunch in Jequitaí; it was already late afternoon. On the town's outskirts, a crystal clear river broke its way through boulders, rushing impatiently toward the São Francisco. We had set out for a walk, Geraldo in the lead; the sun's glare soon brought us down the bank. "Now, Jaime," said Geraldo, taking me aside, "let me show you how to prospect." He instructed me on the basics: rock formations, sedimentation, current. So I set off, jumping from rock to rock. When I had wandered out far enough, Geraldo shouted out gleefully: "Come here, everybody, Jaime's looking for gold." Not to be outdone, I grabbed a sample—as big a rock as I thought I could safely lift—and held it up in triumph. Well, momentary triumph. I slipped, dropped the rock, and ended up waist-deep in the water. "Enough prospecting for now," called out Geraldo. "More lessons tomorrow."

In town snacks awaited us, and a huge bowl of ice-cold *caipirinhas* made with mineral water, limes, and *cachaça*—a sugar-based alcohol distantly related to rum. By now I had built up an incautious thirst. The brew sampled, and deemed innocuous, I downed three tumblers full and boarded the jeep in high spirits. As we jolted and bumped back to the main highway, my head started pounding and the view out the window tottered unsteadily. Hélio, our driver, kept a bottle of mineral water up front. He passed it back. "Cachaça shouldn't be mixed," he observed. "Only take it straight and take a little at a time." "I'll remember that," I said. "For now, what I'll take is aspirin."

Our last stop was far enough from Jequitaí to permit sobriety to take hold. The Dolabela sugar mill dominated a drab company town, owned outright by a São Paulo corporation. It had its own police force, on guard even at the grade school. If you lived in Dolabela, you worked at the mill, which drew its sugarcane from the vast corporate estate that engulfed the town's hinterland. Housing was allocated on the basis of one's status at the mill. The unskilled workers had dilapidated row houses with broken windows, no doors in place, and no running water. Foremen and managers kept to policed, single-family dwellings with fresh paint and clipped lawns. The same rent was levied on workers and managers alike: 3,800 cruzeiros a month, equivalent to about one-third the minimum wage. "That's a pittance for a manager," noted Ricardo Ferreira, one of Dolabela's interns, "but it's a hardship for the workers, and an insult considering what the housing is like. The company owns everything: the housing, the supermarket, the drugstore; even the union is tied to the company. We kept track of prices—it's cheaper in Belo Horizonte."

Ricardo was in his early twenties, tall and powerfully built. Injustice made him angry, and it showed. The main clinic was in town; field hands, who earned 320 cruzeiros a day, were crowded into a slum about two miles away on the other side of the highway. To make treatment available there on a regular basis, the interns set up a makeshift health post. Ricardo drove me over and showed me around. "These people work twelve hours a day in the fields and what do they get for it? Look at that," he said, walking angrily toward a string of one-room hovels, "there's no ventilation, no water, no drainage, not even a place for a family to cook." We went around to the back. "See what they have, a couple of outdoor ovens; people cook in shifts, the same stoves for everybody." He pointed to some children who were bathing in a muddy pond. "The company has a sprinkling system for its precious sugarcane, but they won't bring a line up here, when it's people whose health depends on it. When you wash or bathe in that pond, you can't avoid parasites. Most of those kids aren't in school; at age eight or nine they're field hands. We outlawed slavery in Brazil a hundred years ago, but what's this if it isn't a slave quarters?"

The interns had presented data on malnutrition, using the approach previously outlined. For the 424 children studied, who ranged from one to ten years old, the malnutrition rate came to 35 percent.[22] "I don't trust the figure," Ricardo told me, on the way back to Dolabela. "Sixty percent of those kids were in the caution range or worse. The method corrects for predictable low weights, but it also says half the children should be at the average or better. You know how many children fall in that category, Jaime? Not one in five. The truth is that most children here suffer from chronic hunger; what they live on . . . it's pathetic."

I got back in the jeep, my head pounding. I did not bother with aspirin, either; I went for the cigarettes. I had puffed my way through three or four before I thought to offer one to Renato Assad, who had squeezed in next to me. Like Ricardo, he was stationed at Dolabela, but his bags were packed for Montes Claros, his internship now completed. He had been quiet and unassuming back at the Dolabela presentation; I had hardly noticed him. "You're smoking too much," he advised me. "In Brazil, I think people get addicted to fantasies, that's why they smoke. Anyone can buy cigarettes, but Brazil can't afford the fantasies that go with them. The reality is Dolabela." I asked Renato what he thought of the Internship Program. "I lived all my life in Belo Horizonte; I've never been in rural Minas before. At the Medical School they're always harping about the 'other Brazil'—I got tired of hearing it. To me, the Internship was just another requirement; a good one, because you had a chance to practice on your own, but still, a requirement nonetheless. And to be honest, my interest is surgery. But Dolabela, that's inexcusable. I don't know Brazil; I live only in a small piece of it. I see that clearly now. For most of the country, public health is more important than any specialization. I always respected the doctors in social medicine, but now it carries conviction."

"The first month, of course, is difficult," I ventured, "but once you get adjusted, isn't the work routine?" "I don't know what's worse," he countered, "the routine trauma you see every day, or the emergency. A man in his twenties, his leg bloody and smeared with mud, was rushed into the clinic; he got mauled by piranhas—the flesh was hanging out—and had lost so much blood we couldn't risk a transfer to the hospital in Montes Claros. We considered amputating. I thought, 'My God, this man has nothing; he can't lose his leg.' So we decided to try and save it, unless gangrene set in. We cleaned that wound I don't know how many times. That was the one thing we were sure of: clean it and bandage it so it couldn't get infected, no matter how contaminated the surroundings. We sewed it up, and thank God it worked."

Starry, Starry Night

Night cast its purple-black spell, banishing the sun's fiery crimson. The stars came forth and gathered strength. "Hélio," someone asked our driver, "can't we stop?" He pulled off the road. The Milky Way splashed its stars across the heavens; the Southern Cross shimmered silently on the horizon. "The Cross," observed Renato quietly, "you can't see it in the North." And then a great star shook loose, a talisman cast against the darkness. From the heart of Minas a thousand hopes and dreams took hold, carried to what destiny?

•

Sunsets and starry nights
   Tug at the heart
   And stir up life
   In gentle gusts.

Clarice Lispector, Pulsações
(translated and adapted by the author)

•

Evaluations

The sessions, which began Tuesday afternoon and continued until Thursday evening, took place at the Agricultural School, a branch campus of the Federal University on the outskirts of Montes Claros. The sixty-five interns, twenty-five of them women, converged on the campus from twenty-one counties; they subdivided into eight discussion groups, arranged so that different internship sites were represented in each. Their task was to define the principal health problems characteristic of each district, examine the causes, and evaluate the strategies applied: by the Internship Program, the local health team, the community, and public authorities. Group representatives reported their conclusions at general sessions.

The list was all too familiar: parasitic diseases, which included schistosomiasis and Chagas, skin and urinary track infections, and gastrointestinal disorders; for children, the inevitable infant dysentery and malnutrition, and for adults, hypertension. Causes included unsanitary living conditions, poor hygienic practices, family incomes that "don't deserve to be dignified with the word 'subsistence,' " and sheer ignorance.

"A woman came into our clinic," said Nilza. "She refused to see the interns and demanded the doctor." Nilza reported on her group's behalf. With steady, intense eyes she held back the quiver in her voice. "The promotora asked what she objected to. 'The interns,' the woman replied, 'tell me to do things I can't possibly put into practice. How can I, I have nothing? That hurts me. The doctors don't ask so much.'

"How can you expect that woman to worry about a secondary problem like hygiene," continued Nilza, "when she doesn't even have enough to feed her family? The truth is, people don't consider malnutrition or dysentery to be health problems until the condition becomes acute. Fevers, kids with distended bellies, dysentery—it's just part of life. Health education is important, but it's got to be practical. The Card Club I like; it's simple, something that's manageable. And later, you can add to it. But you can't start out with complex instructions on sanitation, or boiling all your water for twenty minutes. That takes motivation, and motivation takes time. Ignorance is one thing, but it's tied to hunger, to illiteracy, and want, that makes it something else." She sat down quietly—to applause from her classmates.

The next afternoon, I accompanied Dr. Vicente Silva, one of the Internship's supervisors. Perhaps thirty years old, wiry and bearded, he spoke the deep staccato Portuguese of the backlands. His manner conveyed a seriousness and presence of mind that commanded immediate respect. We stopped at one of the Montes Claros clinics in the barrio Delfino Magalhães.

While Vicente discussed the health card with the promotoras, I chatted with the dentist: a thin, phlegmatic man of around thirty-five. "At the public clinics," he observed drily, "there's no problem we can't solve by pulling teeth: that's the remedy for the poor, yank them out. Patients don't object much, they expect extraction. People's rights are violated so flagrantly every day, what's one less tooth? Perhaps it's not so bad for adults, but for young people, I just can't do it."

The local schools had no dental program; the clinic lacked supplies for even preventive measures like fluoridation. The dentist had equipped the clinic's office at his own expense; included were assorted drills for filling cavities—supplies he diverted from his private practice. "It costs me more to work here than I get paid," he said. "The regime lets you fight injustice if you pay for it yourself."

Vicente had one more stop—a rural health post he calculated to be thirty miles away. Over dusty, dirt roads on a hot afternoon, it seemed twice as far. Two promotoras ran the post; one of them already had a reputation as a midwife and healer. They earned the equivalent of 1.8 minimum wages a month—approximately $75. Vicente asked them about supervision and supplies. "We're lucky if a doctor comes once every two months; we don't have materials for health education; we've run out of medications." They considered the two nurse supervisors assigned to the post to be excellent, "but we rarely see them. It's not their fault: they're in charge of forty-five health posts." I asked the promotoras whether they attended continuing education sessions. "What sessions?" they asked. "When we were trained, continuing education was supposed to occur regularly. That was several years ago and it hasn't happened."

"Supervisors rarely stop there," Vicente confided to me later, over a beer back in Montes Claros. "They know they can rely on the promotoras, and, anyway, supervisors have pressing problems to tackle elsewhere." "Didn't the Internship Program opt for Northern Minas because the health system was so well organized?" I asked a bit hesitantly. "On paper, Jaime, it's the best system in Brazil." He took out pen and napkin, and instructed me on the distinction between theory and practice.

"The point is to organize health care so that it reaches people directly. The health post is the basic unit: it emphasizes primary care and public health. The promotoras, usually two, screen patients, work on targeted programs like prenatal care and child health, and are responsible for health education; the post should have an adequate supply of generic drugs on hand, which the promotora can prescribe. To reach a dispersed, rural population, health posts are located in small towns of approximately 500 to 2,000 inhabitants. Northern Minas, for example, has 186 health posts. To have a credible impact on disease control and prevention requires an assertive, district-level approach backed by the community.

"The health center is usually located in the county seat. From the centers, physicians should rotate to the health posts on a regular and predictable basis. The interns are lodged in the larger towns; they work at the health center and make rounds to the posts. Each health center should have a physician assigned to it; there are usually four promotoras. The health center should have a lab for routine diagnosis, including an X-ray machine; it should be equipped for setting broken bones and for performing minor surgery. Altogether, Northern Minas has fifty-seven health centers.

"The next step up is the local hospital, which receives patients from the surrounding counties. It is designed for routine treatment that requires longer periods of hospitalization. Northern Minas has the equivalent of a local hospital in a couple of the larger towns—as at Manga—but they double both as hospitals and health centers. Overall, the local hospital level has never been implemented systematically. Finally, the regional hospital at Montes Claros is equipped for sophisticated surgery and more specialized care. Viewed from a treatment perspective, this approach creates a sensible referral system: from the promotora to the visiting physician, to the health center for a more thorough diagnosis, and on up to the hospitals. In emergencies, the promotora can send patients directly to the health center; the posts near Montes Claros can make referrals directly to the regional hospital. The blueprint likewise suggests a strategy for distribution: the largest share of the budget should be allocated to primary care and health promotion projects at the posts.

"In 1975, Minas Gerais decentralized its health system, creating sixteen regions of which Northern Minas, with its headquarters in Montes Claros, is one. According to this scheme, each health region is supposed to be autonomous, developing a strategy appropriate to its needs. The region, in turn, should be subdivided into districts, which group together several counties. Special projects, continuing education for promotoras, supervision, and the distribution of materials and medications should be organized by district and implemented through the health centers. Regionalized health care has to be viewed as a strategy for making decisions. Each unit, including the health post, has to be allowed enough flexibility to adapt priorities to the situation it confronts."[23]

"In Northern Minas," continued Vicente, adding the logical directional arrow to his sketch (see Figure 6.2), "we have the physical structures: the posts and centers. But we don't have anything approaching a regionalized planning strategy. The Minas Health Department clings to its statewide patronage powers, controls budgets, and adheres to the fantasy of centralized planning. At Montes Claros, they can write some checks and it is a distribution point for medications; but in matters of substance, the Minas Health Department will not endorse a regional strategy that challenges its control. To this you have to add the division between treatment and prevention perpetuated by separate federal agencies—the National Health Service and the Ministry of Health, respectively—whose programs overlap and whose budgets, on the state level, are channeled according to the Health Department's priorities. The distribution of funds and personnel has more to do with politics than with health. At each level, from the planners in Belo Horizonte down to the promotora, health is held captive to payoffs and patronage. Despite the priorities regionalization implies, the funds that get allocated locally do not cover even minimal training and supervision. Initiative is all but stifled; we can't implement the kind of community-based program that people need.

"Over 150 promotoras received training in eight special sessions organized during 1976–77. Since then there has not been a single continuing education cycle, although they were planned on a regular basis. To make matters worse, construction of posts and health centers occurred more rapidly than the system's training capacity, so many of the promotoras haven't received the kind of orientation that emphasizes health promotion in the community. They see patients at the clinic and provide services, but they don't stress prevention. Part of the problem, of course, is lack of supervision and support. Except in a city like Montes Claros, you won't find a preventive health plan applied consistently to a cluster of centers, or follow-through at the health posts. Subregional strategies, designed and implemented in a self-sustaining fashion,

Figure 6.2 District Health System: Northern Minas

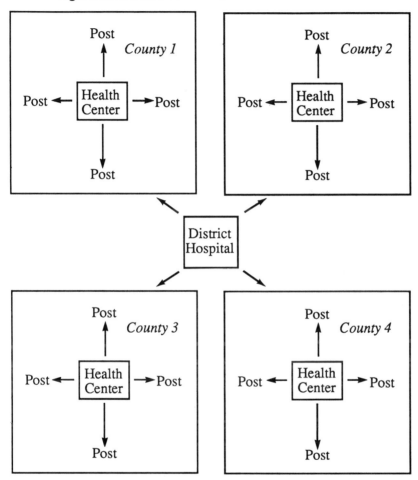

are largely fictitious. Funds are insufficient and the health centers are under-staffed. When doctors can circulate to the posts regularly, it's a major accomplishment, to say nothing of a rotating health team.

"And don't forget politics. The mayors select promotoras according to criteria that are as much personal as technical. Most of the time they compile a list of three, from which health officials select one, but the stamp of patronage is still there. Sometimes this doesn't matter. When the promotora is already respected, and the mayor supports her work, the obstacles to participation are less. Many rural communities, for example, have managed to install water pumps that provide safe water. But most of the mayors are simply indifferent, and a few are actually hostile, especially to community action they can't direct themselves.

"For students, the Internship Program is a mixture of promise and disappointment. As soon as they arrive, demand for treatment goes up, if only because of additional personnel. And, of course, people feel the interns treat them with respect, so they're encouraged to come. But the students don't want to confine their work exclusively to the clinic; they want to implement preventive strategies, and they want community support. That's almost impossible to accomplish in three months, especially when the region's health system lacks the staff and funds to sustain such initiatives on its own."

Greatness

That evening I looked for Chico. He had lugged a prodigious collection of camera equipment; when he was not capturing events on film for archival purposes, he kept an eye on a thousand details from general esprit de corps to scheduling and menus. Lunch and dinner featured huge pots of black beans and rice, a great tray of bread, an enormous bowl of salad, and, on occasion, pans of chicken. If there was method behind the madness of a meal, it escaped my attention. Just seconds before the kitchen struck with food, students covered the gym with tables and chairs in sixty nerve-racking seconds. Behind each pot, volunteers took up ladles and forks, divvying out the portions as plates and trays ran the gauntlet. A thirty-minute lull ensued, reinforced by coffee. Then, almost as suddenly, it ended. Plates were scraped and stacked, the silverware went into empty pots, tables got folded, brooms swept up.

My tray filled, heavy on the black beans as usual ("good for your complexion," Geraldo advised, heaping an extra generous portion on my plate), I spied Chico, in the thick of animated conversation. I caught the words "flood" and "São Francisco," and so entered the fray to reveal my celebrated knowledge of Brazil. "There's a dam at Três Marias, just below Pirapora, and one at Sobradinho, just above Juazeiro in Bahia." "And so what?" asked Chico, a bit nonplussed: "their sole purpose, my friend, is to generate electricity. The reservoirs are kept at near capacity levels; they can't absorb much runoff and are virtually useless for flood control."

In 1979, Chico was Internship supervisor for Januária, a river town of 21,000 about a hundred miles north of Montes Claros. "We got caught in the great flood," he told me, "it rained forty-two days. The São Francisco and its tributaries rose to record levels, inundating hundreds of square miles. The devastation left 3,200 families homeless in Januária County alone. Absolutely harrowing," said Chico, shaking his head. "Money meant nothing. Some families shared what little food they had, others hoarded. Ranchers worried more about saving cattle than about people." Chico and the interns helped with evacuation, but then refused to leave. "How could we?" said Chico. "For those left behind, the great threat was an outbreak of typhoid fever. We had the vaccine—it came in by helicopter. But the situation was so dangerous, I couldn't make the decision for anyone but myself. Still, all the interns stayed. We were responsible for public health, which included inoculating thousands of people. We didn't eat for two days at a time," he noted in a matter-of-fact tone. "Children and the elderly came first. The interns that year were phenomenal; if it hadn't been for them, I'm certain there would have been an epidemic."

The next year, Januária's mayor terminated the Internship Program. The funds to rebuild the city went into a luxury hotel instead of low-cost housing. The mayor did not want interns snooping around, questioning expenditures. "It's a shame," Chico said, looking around the room, "so much talent and energy. But what do they have to work with?—a system that can't keep a health post supplied with aspirin."

I do not know how they did it—Chico, Vicente, and the interns. The regime let them play at health, but never with a card higher than a ten. It named the trump suit and the wild cards. Still, my friends played. They watched for a false move so they could claim a hand on Brazil's behalf. They knew the game itself could not be won under the rules that prevailed.

The final session at Montes Claros arrived—an evaluation of strategies. The interns reiterated much of what Vicente had told me the day before. They dwelt at length on the system's deficiencies, until someone noted with finality, "We all have eyes, and we all were there." They endorsed preventive measures and community participation, noting that the treatment of individuals, "however important, is ultimately ineffective and illusory given public health conditions." Specialization was deemed important at the hospital level, but at the posts and centers "health education and extension have to be priorities." Finally, they stressed that "health cannot be isolated from education and employment."

The formalities over, guitars came out of duffel bags and music filled the night. I rarely caught the lyrics, but moods shifted unmistakably: from raucous ballads to mismatched lovers and lost causes. Eduardo, who I had not met before, sat down next to me. "Brazil," he said, "is not a serious country. You've seen it yourself. Kids half starving. We have to move mountains. And what do they give us—a pail and a shovel. That's pitiful." "True, it's hard to know where to start," I replied, reverting to platitude. "Do you think Brazil will ever achieve greatness?" he asked me. The word he used was *grandeza*, an invitation to controversy. The military talked up greatness constantly; it symbolized where Brazil was headed under the military's direction. I played it safe, pointing out the wisdom of Brazil's Alcohol Program. "No," he replied thoughtfully, "that's not greatness." I offered him a cigarette. He took it, dropped it, picked it up, and dropped it again. "I'm drunk," he explained, "so I looked for you. I wanted you to know about the pails." "What about them?" I asked. "It's filling them despite everything—that's greatness."

• Northern Minas: Agriculture

"To understand health conditions," Ricardo had noted at Dolabela, "requires a social analysis, not just a medical diagnosis." The Internship Program followed this sensible dictum. Logically enough, several years' experience in Northern Minas had taken the program beyond the confines of health to a critique of development strategies. In Northern Minas, schemes wrapped in the flag of progress had undercut the livelihood of the region's small farmers. Consequently, understanding how the regime's policies promoted the deterioration of rural life became part of the Internship's analysis of the region's health crisis.

Straying from the coordinates normally assigned to the physician's job description was not without its adversaries, whether local mayors or university officials. But as Vicente put it, "you can't have interns out here tracking the incidence of malnutrition and expect they'll never bother to ask why." With this in mind, two of the evaluation sessions at Montes Claros focused on the region's agriculture, backed up by a short documentary film the program had made on the region's reforestation program. The discussion below is based on the presentations made at the sessions. In addition, the Internship Program had prepared a fact sheet on Northern Minas with data for the period 1970 to 1975; I have updated this material with the results of the 1980 *Agricultural Census: Minas Gerais*, which was published in 1984. Finally, because the sessions occurred on the campus of the Montes Claros Agricultural College, Vicente arranged for me to meet some of the agronomists on the faculty.

Developments

In 1970, the rural population of Northern Minas numbered about 700,000 and accounted for over 70 percent of the region's inhabitants.[24] Had rural families stayed put, their ranks would have increased at least 28 percent by 1980, that is, as fast as the decade's population growth rate for Brazil as a whole.[25] The drive toward land consolidation and mechanization that the regime's credit subsidies (1970–82) accelerated did not bypass Northern Minas. When the decade ended, the rural population had actually fallen by 10 percent—a shift that pushed and pulled some 38 percent of the region's inhabitants out of farming. Where did they go? Most of them headed for surrounding towns: the population of the region's urban areas had increased 80 percent between 1970 and 1980. The rest left Northern Minas entirely, trying their luck in Belo Horizonte's favelas, or São Paulo's.[26] Why did they go? Because the agricultural sector no longer provided sufficient employment to absorb the region's population growth. For example, in a sample survey conducted with heads of families who had migrated to Montes Claros, 43 percent cited the lack of jobs as their primary motivation; in second place, 28 percent stressed the absence of schools for their children.[27] For Northern Minas at least, the exodus of the region's rural dwellers reflected a bleak lack of alternatives more than the city's attractions.

Prior to the 1970s, before subsidized credit became so profitable, landowners had to pay a respectable rate of interest on borrowed funds. Consequently, mechanization carried a reasonable risk and proceeded at a relatively slow pace. Without access to cheap credit, many fazenda owners preferred the sharecropping system, as it meant less risk to themselves. For the land that owners worked on their own behalf, whether for crops or for livestock, they kept a resident labor force, providing each family with a subsistence plot. For seasonal work, they could draw on squatters who lived without legal title on "unclaimed" land beyond the estate's boundaries. In the 1960s, Northern Minas was a patchwork of large estates that coexisted with subsistence farming and small-scale commercial production. Far removed from Brazil's great urban centers, producers sold their crops and livestock at local markets.

Otaviano de Souza, director of the Agricultural College, was in his early thirties. Thoughtful and deliberate, he did not state opinions without careful reflection first. "The old system," he said, "enforced a strict social hierarchy; sharecroppers had no recourse against a powerful landlord. It's a mistake to idealize sharecropping; at its worst, it was a form of bondage. Still, if sharecroppers had little to show for their effort, the system at least produced enough food and the food was cheap."

"The fact is," added Vicente, "when you consider what happened to the families forced off the land, the situation now is even worse."

After 1970, as the gap between inflation and the regime's subsidized interest rates widened, the risks associated with mechanization fell. Given their privileged access to cheap capital, big producers now had the cash required to consolidate their estates. Able to finance production directly, they substituted tractors for sharecroppers. To their field hands, landlords denied the traditional right to a subsistence plot and a residence. Families that worked in agriculture now had to fend for themselves off the estates' property. At the same time, paved highways drew Northern Minas into national markets, further accelerating the transformation in the countryside. Land now had a potential value for future exploitation and provided security for loans. Fazendas expanded, through purchase or outright expulsion. Corporations secured title to "unclaimed" land, undertaking subsidized projects that specialized in agricultural "development." The result was an even greater concentration of land ownership than formerly, and a brutal expatriation of families to rural favelas, where they had to sell their labor on a daily basis. Meanwhile, cattle ranching and reforestation projects had greatly expanded to the detriment of food production. Northern Minas, which used to be self-sufficient, became a net food importer.

"Why," I asked Vicente, "do small holders sell out in the first place?" "Much of the time they don't have a choice," he replied. "When the government designates a certain area for development, they're obligated to sell. And when big proprietors decide to buy land, they back up their offer with threats: the small producer is forced to sell. There is much deception, whether intended or not. Small holders often think the money offered is a fabulous sum. On their farms, however, housing is free, they produce much of their own food, and daily expenses are minimal. They have no conception of what it costs to live in town. They sell out, but are soon reduced to pitiful conditions. Some of them find employment locally as reforestation workers. But once a region is planted, the demand for labor falls drastically, so eventually many end up unemployed. They have little to start with, but come out with nothing. In the process, the big estates acquire even more."

In 1970, small producers with less than 50 hectares (1 hectare = 2.47 acres) held 9.2 percent of the land in Northern Minas—even though they composed 64 percent of the region's farmers. By 1980, although they still accounted for the same percentage of the farms, their land share had dropped to 7.6 percent. At the same time, the largest enterprises with holdings in excess of 2,000 hectares expanded their domains from 33 percent of the region's land to 40 percent. In 1980, 540 such establishments controlled over 3.6 million hectares.[28]

What the region produced also shifted dramatically. Compared to 1970, Northern Minas harvested 43 percent less cassava in 1980; bean production had fallen 20 percent, and corn had dropped 10 percent. The only staple that showed an increase was rice, up 9 percent, but the gain was less than the region's population growth. Compared to the dismal record on food crops, sugarcane production rose from 390,000 tons in 1970 to 630,000 in 1980—a 62 percent jump. The acreage devoted to pastures also increased: by over 1.4 million hectares. In 1980, the region's cattle herds had expanded by 20 percent and milk production was up by 60 percent.[29]

In Northern Minas, the rainy season begins in December and continues through March. Precipitation then tapers off; by May, the dry season is in full swing. "Improvements in beef and milk production," Otaviano explained, "came from crossing native stock with the zebu, a breed better adapted to the region's hot, dry climate. Ranchers didn't do much to improve their pastures because the region is prone to droughts, which can wipe out the investment. The expansion of ranching was as much a consequence of the zebu as it was the credit system."

Nonetheless, beef was mainly an export item destined for urban markets outside the region. And anyway, it was not a staple for low-income families, as they could not afford it in any quantity. Milk production, however, was oriented to the region's cities and towns. At Jequitaí, the interns noted that milk was cheaper locally than in Belo Horizonte, one of the reasons cited for the town's relatively low levels of infant malnutrition. To attract and foster local production, Montes Claros had become a significant processing center for powdered milk and sweets like caramel. Such qualifications aside, Northern Minas ended the decade with a food deficit and higher prices for most of the staples that composed a poor family's diet.

The Bigger the Better

Brazil's agroindustry is justified on the basis of production. To judge by the knowledgeable reporters of the *Jornal do Brasil*, when it comes to agriculture, the bigger the better. They have a knack for celebrating the marvels of a 40,000-hectare soybean conglomerate in Mato Grosso do Sul, wheat corporations in Goiás, and the orange juice trust in Bahia. What, then, are the noteworthy accomplishments of agribusiness in Northern Minas?

The *Agricultural Census* for Minas Gerais breaks down crop production by size of farm, but figures are for the entire state rather than for each region. So we will have to assume that the big estates in Northern Minas—enterprises that held 2,000 hectares or more—mirrored their counterparts in Minas Gerais as a whole. For the sake of comparison, I have put the big estates up against small farms with less than 50 hectares.

For Minas Gerais in 1980, the big estates controlled almost 10 million hectares or 21 percent of the state's land. Of the area in Minas devoted to annual crops, however, they accounted for only 7 percent of the total.[30] Small farms, although they scraped by on 12 percent of the land, accounted for 29 percent of the annual crop acreage; they produced two-thirds of the state's tomatoes, over half the potatoes, 46 percent of the cassava, 43 percent of the beans, and a third of the total corn crop.[31] By comparison, the big estates contributed virtually nothing to crop production and accounted for a mere 3 percent of the state's milk output. Their contribution to stock raising was greater, but not particularly impressive. In 1980, they kept 10 percent of the state's cattle on 16 percent of the total land area devoted to pastures.[32] By contrast, the state's small farms raised 15 percent of the cattle on 10 percent of the pasture land and accounted for 19 percent of milk production.[33]

To judge from the hype in the press, Brazil's corporate landowners were virtually public benefactors. Without denying the statistics on sugar and soybean production racked up by agroindustry, the facts in Minas Gerais show that the distribution of work and the overall contribution to production were rather different.

For most of the state's annual crops, for fruit production, and even for animal husbandry, the presumed contribution a unit's size made to total output was much overrated. To make the point, I have downsized the definition of bigness a notch, so as to include all holdings with at least 1,000 hectares. In 1980, Minas had 5,433 such units with 15 million hectares or nearly a third of the state's land.[34] If the aforesaid producers had folded in 1980, what kind of losses in output would Minas have sustained? It would have lost approximately 1 percent of its tomatoes and 3 percent of its potatoes; beans would have fallen by 6 percent, corn by 7, cassava by 8, and rice by 11; there would have been a coffee drainage of 6 percent, an orange squeeze of 12, and a banana slippage of 6; pork would have dropped 6 percent and milk production, 8 percent.[35] The only sizable losses incurred by striking out the big estate would have come in stock raising, soybeans, and sugarcane, which would have shown a deficit of 19, 26, and 45 percent respectively: precisely the areas of high-credit subsidies.[36] Nonetheless, using the yardstick of the land resources available to such enterprises—a third of the state's total—only in the case of sugarcane was the large estate's contribution to output disproportionate.

Productivity

I will admit I have been a bit unfair, but so too was the regime's credit program. The assumption that big enterprises ought to show output commensurate with the share of the state's land they have gobbled up is a bit simpleminded, despite a certain face-value validity. So what follows is more evenhanded. I judged the large estate not by its contribution to total output, but according to the amount of land it actually devoted to production in each instance. For example, if holdings of 1,000 hectares or more harvested 6 percent of the state's bean crop but did so on only 4 percent of the land that went to beans, then, presumably, they were a bit more efficient.

That Brazil's big farms should produce more on less land is not exactly an earthshaking assumption. The regime dumped cheap money into their coffers for well over a decade, so they had ample time and cash to invest in better seed varieties, fertilizer, chemical additives, and erosion control. The big producer could afford to take marginal land out of production and concentrate on higher yields from the best plots. The small farmer, by contrast, cultivated as much of his land as possible: good, bad, and indifferent. Any productivity test, therefore, favors large farms a priori. And it should. Why distribute credit disproportionately to large holders, paying them to expel sharecroppers, unless they can show results?

How the government allocated agricultural credit in Minas illustrates the big farm's advantage. For 1980, the total came to just under $700 million.[37] Of this, 70 percent went to farms of 100 hectares or more, only 30 percent to the state's smaller farms of less than 100 hectares. (See Table 6.2.) Every big

Table 6.2 Distribution of Credit, Land, and Farms in Minas Gerais, 1980 (by Size of Farm)

Size of Farm (in hectares)	% of Credit	% of Land	Number of Farms	% of Farms
Less than 20	6	4	217,538	45
20–49	11	8	109,539	23
50–99	13	10	63,080	13
100–999	52	47	83,357	18
Over 1,000	18	31	5,433	1
Total	100	100	478,947	100

Source: Compiled from *Censo Agropecuário: Minas Gerais* (Rio de Janeiro: Fundação Instituto Brasileiro de Geografia e Estatística, 1984), pp. 52, 26–27.

producer did not receive government-sponsored credit. Nevertheless, the trend is implicit for Brazil as a whole and documented for São Paulo—the larger the unit, the more likely it benefited.[38]

These reservations aside, how did smaller farms compare to their credit-heavy counterparts in productivity? Tables 6.3 and 6.4 present the results. The row labeled "cassava," for instance, shows the percentage of production that came from farms in each size category, and it notes the percentage of the state's total cassava acreage located on farms of that size. Table 6.3 subdivides farms of less than 100 hectares by size; Table 6.4 presents a summation for the category as a whole. Below, I refer to "smaller" farms as all units with less than 100 hectares.

For food staples, the state's smaller producers accounted for close to half the output in all cases, and for a hefty majority of the harvests in tomatoes, potatoes, and cassava. For sugar and soybeans, big enterprise dominated production. The larger farms likewise prevailed in coffee, milk production, and stock raising, but substantial output still came from farms with less than 100 hectares at their disposal. As for productivity—how much output from how much land—the big farm, given the funds at its command, is conspicuous for its lackluster performance. Take corn as an example. Farms with at least 100 but less than 1,000 hectares cultivated 40 percent of the land allocated to corn and harvested 43 percent of the crop. The smaller producers, by contrast, had 52 percent of the land in maize but managed only half the harvest. On the face of it, that was a bit of a productivity edge for the big farm—but not much. Given the incentives that fell so disproportionately to big enterprise, and the disadvantages that accrued to smaller farms, the overall results fall far short of an endorsement for the wonders of size. Big is not necessarily better, it is just more expensive.

Table 6.3 Agricultural Production in Minas Gerais: Small Farms, 1980 (Percentage of Production and Percentage of Land Devoted to Each Type of Production, by Size of Farm)

| | Small Farms (in hectares) | | | | | |
| | Less than 20 | | 20–49 | | 50–99 | |
Type of Production	% Pro	% Land	% Pro	% Land	% Pro	% Land
Tomatoes	43	41	25	23	14	13
Potatoes	33	35	23	24	16	16
Cassava	24	24	22	21	15	15
Beans	23	25	20	21	15	16
Corn	17	19	17	18	16	15
Rice	16	15	16	16	14	14
Coffee	11	13	16	17	17	17
Sugar	5	9	6	10	6	9
Soybeans	0	0	1	1	4	4
Milk*	6	3	13	7	17	10
Cattle	5	3	10	7	13	10

Source: Production by size of farm is compiled from *Censo Agropecuário: Minas Gerais* (Rio de Janeiro: Fundação Instituto Brasileiro de Geografia e Estatística, 1984), pp. 128, 116, 122, 120, 124, 114, 99, 118, 126, 95, 62. For land use by size of farm, see pp. 26–27.

*The figures refer to land in pasture. The census does not distinguish between land for cattle raising as opposed to dairy farming, so the percentages are identical in each case.

The Credit Bill

Whatever production the regime pried from its beneficiaries, the country paid for massively. Between 1970 and 1979, for example, credit to agriculture increased twice as fast as the value of output. The total credit allocation in 1979—for crop production, agricultural investments, and marketing—came to approximately $14 billion.[39]

Recall that borrowers paid back loans at nominal rates of interest pegged substantially below inflation. To illustrate, the highest charge in 1980 was 36 percent—a year in which inflation topped 100 percent. Consider the arithmetic. If the Bank of Brazil had loaned out 100 cruzeiros to finance the 1980 crop, and given the inflation rate of 100 percent, it had to get back 200 cruzeiros when accounts were settled—just to break even. But it did not; for each 100 cruzeiros loaned, it recouped a mere 136 cruzeiros: the principal—uncorrected for inflation—plus interest. That meant it started 1981 with its capital worth substantially less than the year before.

Table 6.4 Agricultural Production in Minas Gerais: All Farms, 1980 (Percentage of Production and Percentage of Land Devoted to Each Type of Production, by Size of Farm)

	All Farms (in hectares)							
	Less than 100		100–999		1,000 +		Total	
Type of Production	% Pro	% Land	% Pro	% Land	% Pro	% Land	% Pro	% Land
Tomatoes	82	77	17	22	1	1	100	100
Potatoes	72	75	22	20	6	5	100	100
Cassava	61	60	31	31	8	9	100	100
Beans	58	62	36	34	6	4	100	100
Corn	50	52	43	40	7	8	100	100
Rice	46	45	43	43	11	12	100	100
Coffee	44	47	50	48	6	5	100	100
Sugar	17	28	38	37	45	35	100	100
Soybeans	5	5	69	65	26	30	100	100
Milk*	36	20	56	52	8	28	100	100
Cattle	28	20	53	52	19	28	100	100

Source: Production by size of farm is compiled from *Censo Agropecuário: Minas Gerais* (Rio de Janeiro: Fundação Instituto Brasileiro de Geografia e Estatística, 1984), pp. 128, 116, 122, 120, 123, 114, 99, 118, 126, 95, 62. For land use by size of farm, see pp. 26–27.

*The figures refer to land in pasture. The census does not distinguish between land for cattle raising as opposed to dairy farming, so the percentages are identical in each case.

The difference between the interest on agricultural loans and the inflation rate had already reached 25 percent in 1976—and the breach kept growing on through 1982. The regime not only made up the shortfall each year, but over the course of the 1970s it also expanded the subsidized value of the credit available. For the period 1976–80, I have estimated the program's deficit using World Bank data. The difference between the value of the loans made and what the regime could hope to recover ends up in the red to the tune of $23 billion.[40] How did the regime cover deficits of such magnitude? It had recourse to what is called the "monetary budget," which is to say, it printed the money. In Brazil, the private sector lined up for the profits, and the public sector got stuck with the losses.

For those in a position to pick the country's money tree, Brazil's potential deserved the adjective "unlimited" that so frequently accompanied it. Such was Brasília's magic; it reached into the hamlets of Northern Minas, riding roughshod over the many and paving the way for a few.

Brazil's credit program did not go to all facets of agriculture equally. Livestock production got the single largest slice. For crops, 80 percent went to six specialties: corn, rice, wheat, soybeans, coffee, and sugarcane.[41] Referring back to Table 6.4, these are precisely the categories where larger estates (100 to 1,000+ hectares) contributed the most to total output—although without meriting any productivity awards. Moving on to the biggest enterprises (over 1,000 hectares), these had a proclivity for sugar, soybeans, and cattle. One citation is due for performance: the state's largest sugar producers managed 45 percent of the output on only 35 percent of the land so allocated.

Agribusiness may capture the imagination of the *Jornal do Brasil*, but if you ask who actually feeds Brazil, it is somebody else. Enterprises in Minas with over 1,000 hectares did contribute to production in Minas—when the regime paid them to do so. As to food crops, they avoided anything destined for the supermarket: low profit margins and not enough subsidies. The regime targeted credit to favor export crops like soybeans, geared as it was to the balance of payments. The Planning Ministry had to have its trade surplus; food deficits in Northern Minas did not register in the computer, and, anyway, who cared?

Eucalyptus

Returning to holdings that exceeded 2,000 hectares, recall that they controlled a fifth of the state's land, but contributed virtually nothing to food production. They held 16 percent of the state's pasture land, on which they raised only 10 percent of the cattle and accounted for a scant 3 percent of milk output. They had a surplus of over 4 million hectares they did not bother to use. What, then, did such conglomerates contribute to Minas Gerais? They raked in the profits from a subsidized reforestation program. In 1980, 85 percent of the state's 1.5 million hectares of reforested land was located on such estates.[42] Over a third of the acreage was in Northern Minas. To the interns gathered at Montes Claros, the eucalyptus tree symbolized the way the regime passed off highway robbery as development.

Minas Gerais is Brazil's largest iron producer. Concentrated around Belo Horizonte, the industry turned out over 7 million tons in 1980. The state's iron ore smelteries depend on charcoal, and Northern Minas is an important supplier, furnishing over half a million tons annually.[43] Although Brazil has substantial reserves in coal, a high ash content renders much of it unsuitable for smelting. So Brazil imports almost 5 million tons of coal annually, most of which goes to the steel industry.[44] For iron production, however, charcoal will suffice and it is considerably cheaper than imported coal. As Belo's iron industry expanded, it gradually exhausted surrounding forests, drawing charcoal supplies from farther away, which included Northern Minas. Trucks overloaded with bagged charcoal ply the main route between Montes Claros and Belo. They scorn the laws of gravity, so even the plucky jeep keeps its distance.

Lúcio Amaral, a short, energetic man in his forties, and an agronomist on the faculty at the Agricultural College, explained the local method for charcoal production. "Most of Northern Minas," he pointed out, "is a mixture of trees and thick underbrush. Since it's difficult to clear, landowners used to burn it to clear for pastures; now, at least, they harvest the land first for charcoal.

"To produce one cubic meter of charcoal requires two to three cubic meters of wood, depending on its quality. For eucalyptus and large trees generally, the ratio is about 1 to 2; with smaller, scrappy trees, it's usually 1 to 3. After cutting, workers season the wood for about a month. Then they pack it tightly in a kiln, which resembles an inverted bowl in shape. The kiln is then sealed off so it's airtight. Spontaneous combustion starts the wood smoldering. After about twenty-four hours the flammable part of the wood burns off, leaving charcoal with a high energy content. Timing is crucial; if the kiln is opened too early, the wood ignites and ends up in ashes.

"On occasion, kiln workers can draw an adequate wood supply from their own lands and make a tolerable living selling charcoal. But most are landless laborers who do the arduous tasks of logging and burning for the minimum wage. It's a dirty job that carries the health risks of coal mining. Inhaling so much dust and fumes, they have to drink milk constantly to detoxify."

As noted previously, the land devoted to pasture in Northern Minas expanded by 80 percent between 1970 and 1980, much faster than cattle production, which grew by only 20 percent. Evidently, creating pastures had as much to do with Belo's iron industry as it did with the zebu. Eventually, depletion of the region's vegetation had occurred on such a scale that the government required landowners to set aside 20 percent of any forested property as a reserve. And to reduce erosion, it promoted reforestation. Eucalyptus was the favored sapling; it thrives in a hot, dry climate, grows rapidly, and suited the iron industry's needs. The timber can be harvested after six years; a new tree then resprouts from the roots, making three additional harvests possible without replanting.

The interns at Montes Claros were certainly not opposed to reforestation. The region's eucalyptus boom, however, only took hold because the government made deposits to the right bank accounts.

"Government incentives," Otaviano pointed out, "turned reforestation into a lucrative venture. The expenses incurred could be used as a tax write-off. The iron foundries got into the business too, since they were required to plant eight trees for each cubic meter of charcoal consumed in production. And given their access to capital, São Paulo-based companies came in, building up eucalyptus estates. The result is absentee ownership, and whether the firms are from São Paulo or other parts of Minas, their interest in the region's welfare is minimal. Planting eucalyptus exclusively is not a balanced approach to reforestation. The tree's prodigious root system penetrates and depletes the water table, damaging an ecology subject to drought. In Northern Minas, one must look long and hard to find a pine or a cedar.

"Still, there are some benefits. Before, Northern Minas was even more exploited. The iron companies purchased the region's charcoal, but planted new trees closer to Belo Horizonte. Such predation is now mixed with reforestation. And some steady jobs have resulted, whether for planting seedlings or charcoal production."

The alleged benefits Northern Minas derived from reforestation were much disputed at the session organized by the interns. The region's soils, it was claimed, "are well suited to staples, but the companies withdrew land from production, creating food shortages. The program is supposed to target rocky soils and eroded hillsides; instead, the companies plant densely on good land. There's now more eucalyptus than the industry can possibly use, and it's not high-quality timber for charcoal either." Not everyone agreed. "The best soil, the rich bottom lands," one of the agronomists said, "becomes soggy during the rainy season. If companies plant eucalyptus there, it invites insect infestations, especially ants, that kill the seedlings."

That reforestation had been massive, rapid, and left behind greater land concentration and displaced farmers no one denied. In 1975, Northern Minas had 14,000 hectares in eucalyptus; five years later it had over 800,000 hectares—an enormous transformation, 95 percent of which occurred with government subsidies.[45] Who benefited?—enterprises holding 2,000 hectares or more. For Minas Gerais overall, as already mentioned, 85 percent of the state's reforested land was held by such estates. There is no reason to suppose the figure understates the case for Northern Minas. The way such holdings had expanded there—they controlled 32 percent of the land in 1970 and 40 percent in 1980—suggests that the regime's eucalyptus scam contributed substantially to consolidation. What did such enterprises contribute to the region's food supply? Virtually nothing. They were land trusts, speculating in eucalyptus at the country's expense.

That the poor should get poorer and the rich should get richer is a logical proposition, once you understand how profiteering slouches to the baptismal font—original sin forgiven by the magic of any trick that calls itself development.

• Irrigation

As the São Francisco continues north into Bahia, it enters the Northeast proper, where droughts are both more intense and more frequent than in Minas Gerais. Given the river's depth, and the dependable flows in its many tributaries, harnessing the region's water resources for irrigation had already commenced on a considerable scale. In some cases, landowners turned to irrigation at their own expense, and to suit their particular needs. During the 1970s, however, irrigating the Northeast became a cause célèbre in the Planning Ministry. Most of the irrigation works along the São Francisco Basin were constructed at government expense; supervision fell to the Development Company for the São Francisco Valley, CODEVASF, hereafter referred to as the Valley Authority.

I visited a total of five irrigation projects. They varied in size from only 840 hectares at Manducaru near Juazeiro in Bahia State to the massive works under construction at Massangano, fifty miles farther west and across the São Francisco River in neighboring Pernambuco. The project at Manducaru was planned in the early 1970s and benefited small farmers. Its design reflected the influence that Celso Furtado, a leading economist and social critic, had once exerted on the Northeast's Development Agency, SUDENE. By contrast, the Minas projects at Pirapora and Jaíba were planned later and escaped Furtado's influence. They were designed for production under corporate aegis.

Vicente had noted my interest in agriculture. When the Monte Claros sessions ended, he invited me to tag along on his rounds through Northern Minas. Besides scheduled meetings with interns, he was promoting the use of health cards for tracking child nutrition. One stop was at Jaíba, he pointed out, site of the state's largest irrigation project. I agreed to meet him in Belo Horizonte the next week.

Pirapora

While waiting for Vicente, there is time to talk about Pirapora, a project I visited in 1983 with Dr. João Magro, my guide through Venda Nova. About 200 miles north of Belo, Pirapora is a river port of approximately 32,000 inhabitants; it marks the São Francisco's farthest navigable point inland from the Atlantic.

According to the project's fact sheet, the Valley Authority completed work in 1978 after thirty months and at a cost of approximately $14 million.[46] The area irrigated was 1,500 hectares, subdivided into modules of 50 hectares each. Three intake pumps, which drew from the São Francisco, propelled the water through a fifteen-mile pipeline to a reservoir constructed at the project's perimeter. From there, the water was pumped through a network of feeder pipes to each module.

The Valley Authority's director at Pirapora, Senhor Marcos, was a short, frank man in his forties. We went to his office, a sparsely furnished room meant for work, and chatted over cafezinho. "The irrigation projects built by the Valley Authority fall into three categories," Marcos explained. "The smallest are geared to colonists; they are allotted plots that range in size from 5 to 10 hectares, and each settler is trained to use irrigation technology. The rest either work with companies or combine the two approaches. Pirapora was the first project designed for the small- to medium-sized company, in this case, Fruitrop and Cotia, both São Paulo-based enterprises. The land allocated to each—500 hectares to Fruitrop and 1,000 to Cotia—is broken down into modules managed by administrators who supervise the labor force. Each 50-hectare unit provides housing for between four to six workers.

"The project's irrigation system extends up to each module; distribution within the unit is the company's responsibility. User fees are based on the area cultivated—11,000 cruzeiros [$16] per hectare—and the amount of water consumed—6,000 cruzeiros [$9] per 1,000 cubic meters.[47] During the first five years, given the investments companies have to make to bring land into production, water is supplied on a subsidized basis: the fees don't cover the Valley Authority's costs. At the moment, the companies hold their land on lease. At the conclusion of the first five-year cycle, they'll have the option to renew, or to purchase at the price set when the project started—corrected, of course, for inflation."

The companies specialized in fruit production for the São Paulo market, timed for the off-season when prices were highest. The annual crops were primarily melons and pineapples. Orchards included papaya trees and mangoes. I saw Italian grapes, as well as cucumbers, processed for export abroad. For most production, the technology applied on the modules was irrigation by sprinkling. In the case of grapes, the companies used a dripping technique. A long hose was carefully braced over each row of vines. Smaller feeder lines, connected to and suspended from the main hose, branched out laterally so as to fall between three to five feet from the vine's base; so poised, dripping promoted the root system's expansion. Compared to irrigation by earthen canals, the sprinkling and drip technology was a high-priced alternative. From a water-use standpoint, it was many times more efficient.

We had come in July, during the dry season. The deep greens of irrigated orchards and fields seemed a triumph, no matter what the price. Still, the government had installed the basic system with the country's money: an up-front investment that averaged out to $50,000 per module. When it came to collecting benefits, I did not see why Fruitrop should be first in line. So I asked Marcos why the project had not targeted small producers. "In Brasília," he began, a bit hesitant, "they claim that projects with colonists haven't been successful. The rural poor are too ignorant to use irrigation technology. In the end, small-scale projects didn't create sufficient employment. In Pirapora's case, the companies generated about a thousand steady jobs. They pay only the minimum wage, but it's an improvement over seasonal work."

"Do you agree with that?" I asked as diplomatically as I could. "Beware the opinions that come from Brasília," he laughed. "If the objective is table grapes for São Paulo and production with a drip system, yes. For crops like beans, onions, and carrots, small producers get crops year-round and make a decent living on 5 to 8 hectares. The technology is simplified, and they do reasonably well. It depends on what you want an irrigation system to do, both socially and as regards production. The companies here have done their part; the project already has an enviable record, both for the quantity harvested and the yields registered. But if you don't think papaya for São Paulo is the kind of specialization that irrigation in Minas should promote, you'll never find the initial expense justified."

Marcos had me pegged. The fact sheet claimed that the value of output for 1979–80 had already "paid for the project." This meant that what the companies had made on sales equaled the government's initial $14 million investment—and the government still subsidized their water bill.[48] For Fruitrop's melons, the regime had a reservoir against thirst. For Brazil's poor families patiently queued up for drinkable water, the regime had banished them to line's end—after São Paulo's melons.

The São Francisco becomes a muddy torrent during the rainy season. By July it settles back; sandy beaches banished in March reappear, the water clears. João and I wandered along the banks, just beyond town. In the distance, a boy maneuvered his fragile skiff, darting between rocks and boulders against the current. João stood there, throwing stones absentmindedly, his eye on the boy. "Something wrong?" I asked. "That's Brazil," he said, "caught in the rapids."

At Pirapora, the companies produced something Brazil could eat. That was not the fate projected for the 42,000 hectares the Valley Authority planned to irrigate along the Jequitaí River. According to the *Jornal do Brasil*, the region was slated for sugarcane production and eight distilleries with a capacity of 120,000 liters each per day—"one of the greatest alcohol enterprises in Brazil."[49]

Jaíba

I met Vicente Silva in Belo Horizonte as arranged; we left that afternoon, with Montes Claros our objective by nightfall. Dr. Cristina Fekete, one of the Internship's coordinators, had worked in Jaíba. She knew all the promotoras in the region, and came to assist on the Health Card Project. She was not much over five feet tall, and weighed not more than ninety pounds: ninety pounds of sheer energy set off by gentle eyes of intelligence and hope. It was Cristina who had intervened against Chico's 3:00 A.M. pizza. Our driver, Hélio—graybearded and sandaled—kept his wits under any circumstance. Dr. Ayrton Lacerda took advantage of our jaunt too, as he had friends to visit in Jaíba. He had the ascetic quality of a mendicant, but without the vow of silence.

Tall and lanky, Ayrton brought enthusiasm to absolutely any topic. Once we had settled in for the long haul to Montes Claros, he began a harangue on classical music, which ended in a diatribe against the quality of Bach and

Beethoven recordings. Summoning up what little erudition I could muster, I threw in Jean Pierre Rampal, the renowned French flutist I once heard in Baltimore. "He's good, I'll admit," said Ayrton, "a bit of a stuffed shirt though. Take James Galway, just as good technically but much more versatile, don't you think?" I was on thin ice now, having ignored the danger Alexander Pope so rightly attributed to pretense. So I confessed my total ignorance of Galway's alleged virtuosity. Ayrton was gleeful. He reached into a bulging duffel bag, triumphantly extracting a cassette recorder and, believe it or not, a Galway tape. We had flute music for the next fifty miles until Hélio stopped for gas, the tank still half full. When we piled back in, Hélio had his transistor locked on a Samba channel, the volume at ghetto-blaster decibels. Cristina, between fits of laughter, negotiated a cease-fire that held all the way to Jaíba.

We arrived in Montes Claros after dark, crashing the dormitory where a few interns still lingered on clean-up detail from the week before. During the sessions, I had stayed at the hotel in town along with other observers. Now I could sample the quarters of the interns: three army surplus bunk beds squeezed into cement-block cubicles. Among the complaints interns had registered at the sessions, lodging had been conspicuously absent.

My experience in Belo had acquainted me with the rules that govern Brazilian hospitality. Whether at restaurants, the soccer stadium, or the dance hall, I could not, under any circumstances, pay for myself. The Belo pattern had followed me to Montes Claros, despite stops for lunch and cafezinhos. All attempts to part with a single cruzeiro failed, as did my speech in defense of the Dutch treat. At dinner that night, when time came for the check, I discreetly left the table, cornered the waiter, and paid the tab. I made it back with no one the wiser. When the waiter brought the receipt, Vicente, despite protests, had to accept a fait accompli. This maneuver put me on solid footing with Hélio. He judged Americans a dull lot, but I had done something clever, which suggested I was not a total loss. Thereafter, I was allowed to pay an occasional bill, although by no means my fair share.

The next morning we headed for Jaíba. It was March; the rainy season, drawing to a close, gathered clouds for a last torrential display. Jaíba is about 120 miles north of Montes Claros. The highway was paved a bit more than halfway, as far as Janaúba, where the railroad and express bus service to Belo likewise terminated. We passed a huge section of pipe, part of the irrigation system for the Gurutuba Valley. Vicente described it as a mixed project: for colonists, 750 hectares divided into plots of 8 to 12 hectares; for corporations, 4,500 hectares in modules of 50 to 200 hectares—a distribution that reflected the regime's appraisal of an appropriate "development mix."

Guimarães Rosa had once practiced medicine in Janaúba, which led to a discussion of Brazilian literature, a subject I preferred to flutes. Ayrton quizzed me on Machado de Assis, and awarded me an "A." On Jorge Amado I scored a "B"—Ayrton subtracted points for my not knowing Amado's early work. I did well enough on Clarice Lispector, and then got an unexpected "A + " on Márcio Souza, merited, as Ayrton explained, for being au courant. My knowledge, however, rested almost exclusively on readings in translation, so I stumbled badly on Guimarães Rosa. "His brilliance," lectured Ayrton, "is linguistic invention, which you can't appreciate in translation: a 'B − ,' Jaime, is the best I can do." I accepted this without complaint, as I could not imagine a Portuguese edition of *Electric Kool-Aid Acid Test*.

Beyond Janaúba the rains hit, turning the road into a muddy morass. We kept the windows open a crack, as our jeep had long since surrendered such vital organs as its defroster and automatic squirts. In front, Vicente, rag in hand, kept the steamed up windshield as clear as possible. Hélio concentrated on avoiding ruts and the mud splashed by oncoming trucks. They took turns at the wheel.

Back in Belo I had read a newspaper account of UFO sightings in Northern Minas. A campesino, in fact, had seen one land, got badly burned, and recited his tale in the kind of detail readers love—it was front-page stuff in *Estado de Minas*, complete with pictures of charred foliage. Ayrton pressed me for details with his usual rigor and, in this case, with unexpected, poker-faced sobriety. "There are a lot of sightings in Northern Minas," he noted gravely, as he reached for his shoulder bag. "Now you've done it," Cristina warned me. Unperturbed, Ayrton produced two "scholarly" books by "experts" of impeccable reputation who attested to UFOs with "undeniable authority." "For every expert you produce," I told him, "I can name an apostate equally authoritative. Carl Sagan, the great American physicist, for example, he's never seen one." "And so what?" countered Ayrton. "Sagan hasn't been in Brazil, yet Brazil exists. A very poor argument, Jaime, decidedly illogical. Most of what we think exists does so only by virtue of report. Your position restricts that which exists to things present to the observer at a particular point in time; ergo, most of what we conventionally term 'the world' doesn't exist at all."

There followed a discourse on the conditions under which something may be said to exist, ending with Kant's *Critique of Pure Reason*, which I had never read, and whose precise relevance escaped me. The gist of his argument, however, was clear enough. To deny the reality of UFOs on the flimsy pretext that neither I nor Carl Sagan had seen one, I had to accept a series of logical consequences, which, by comparison, made flying saucers not only plausible but absolutely essential to make the world itself tenable. Having demonstrated this to everyone's satisfaction, Ayrton described a recent case in which extra-terrestrials kidnapped a Brazilian businessman and dropped him off, weeks later, in Argentina. "You'd think they'd have maps by now," goaded Cristina. "To our greatness," laughed Vicente, "we have to add the UFO's marked preference for Brazil." "That's right," concluded Cristina, "Brazil's potential, visible from a flying saucer, invisible from a favela."

The rain poured down in sheets, trucks lay splayed across the road, jackknifed and mired in the mud. Wheels spinning, we maneuvered around, coming perilously close to the drainage ditch, which had turned into a brackish, swirling torrent. The sky relented just outside Jaíba, but one last disabled truck blocked the way. Vicente passed the wheel to Hélio, a veteran of long-distance trucking. "These kids today have no respect for rain and mud," Hélio observed with disapproval. "If the driver had any sense, he would've stayed in Jaíba." Fortunately, the road widened near town, but the trajectory to the right—our only hope—seemed knee-deep in mud. Hélio got out to make an appraisal, which included a check of the jeep. "We can get through," he decided. "But if the mud's as deep as it looks, it'll cost us the muffler." "It needs repair anyway," said Vicente. Hélio backed up, got a running start, and plunged in. We bogged down in the middle, the muffler clinging to the mud. "Sorry," said Hélio, rocking the jeep with frantic concentration. An ominous clank pronounced the muffler dead, the wheels caught, and we lurched forward.

A small settlement stretched along a ribbon of deep-red earth. Jaíba's right to a place on the map came from supply stores, cantinas, and Rural Minas— the state government's agency for rural development. We stayed with the interns at a lodge on the town's outskirts, which accommodated all visitors, from engineers to truck drivers.

By lunchtime the sun had dispersed the clouds, its intensity soaking up the rain's excess. Roads that seemed impassable a few hours before—at least to my uninstructed eye—gave no one the slightest concern now. Hélio returned from town with a muffler so quiet I only then realized at what small sacrifice we had braved the mud. We set out for one of the health posts near the São Francisco River, inspecting irrigation canals along the way.

Project Jaíba, according to the *Jornal do Brasil*, was one of the largest irrigation efforts in the world; the overall plan encompassed 230,000 hectares of which 100,000 would benefit from irrigation.[50] The project lay between the São Francisco and one of its tributaries, the Big Verde. An immense, twenty-mile concrete canal—already completed—linked up to a dense feeder network. We stopped to get a view of the reservoir, then under construction. The São Francisco, which rivals the Ohio in size and volume, is a dependable water source, but the yearly variations in its level make reservoirs a necessity, and they must be commensurate with a project's size. The one at Jaíba was massive enough to command anyone's respect.

The Valley Authority had suffered from considerable vacillation in Brasília, and work was several years behind schedule. As of 1982, Jaíba had absorbed around $95 million, with an additional $15 million allocated for its completion.[51] Responsibility for land allocation—as opposed to furnishing water—in this case fell to Rural Minas. "How did the agency ever manage to get its hands on 230,000 hectares?" I asked Vicente. "They confiscated most of it," he told me, "and without compensation. The regime recognizes squatters' rights, but does not enforce the law. The campesinos did not have land titles, and if they refused to leave peacefully, Rural Minas expelled them by force. For a while, Jaíba was virtually a war zone. Some, of course, had titles and sold out. But it is as I said before: the smaller holder is in no position to bargain, and what little he does get can't make up for the livelihood he's lost. Northern Minas isn't like São Paulo or Rio Grande do Sul. In the South, farmers are literate, they're organized, and they understand commercial agriculture. When they sell out, they know the price they want and what a cruzeiro is worth."

We continued on to the health post, which served a colonization settlement supervised by Rural Minas. Plots were neatly set off and well tended. The post, Cristina noted, had excellent promotoras and active community support. "See where they put the health post," she said, pointing to a mango grove in the distance. It was no small consideration, either. The benches in the court-yard took advantage of the shade. When people waited their turn at the clinic, they sat in the coolness of the mango grove.

For Cristina, there were warm embraces and playful scolding from the promotoras: "You've been away too long"; "look at that, you're too thin"; "what, not married yet?—you work too much, my child." Vicente and Cristina explained the health card—green, yellow, and red zones. The lesson finished, Cristina went over to the scale. One of the promotoras, a hefty woman in her fifties, came over to take a look. "See this, everyone," she called out, "just like I thought—the red zone."

Rural Minas

Having kicked the locals out, Rural Minas introduced a colonization scheme. As of 1982, it had settled roughly eight hundred families in the Jaíba region. Vicente arranged a meeting for me with one of the project's subdirec-tors. Several of the interns came too. Senhor Paulo, an agronomist in his early forties, soon had his desk covered with project maps.

As a development agency, Rural Minas's sphere of influence covered most of the state's northern zone and not simply the Jaíba irrigation project. During phase one (1971–78), Rural Minas invested over $171 million. It had to its credit over 700 miles of electrical transmission wires, 13 power substations, and 16 urban electrification grids; it had constructed over 1,400 miles of roads for "penetration," 600 miles worth for "local use," and various "internal systems" within colonized regions. I trust Senhor Paulo had other impressive statistics for me, but I interrupted, a bit abruptly, to focus on the agency's affinity for the small farmer. "How does Rural Minas organize colonization?" I asked him. "Tenants fall into two categories," he told me. "The 'free holders' have up to 30 hectares each, most of it in the segments not slated for irrigation. They can produce what they want, have land titles, and can sell their property as a single unit, but they can't make subdivisions. Those settled on 'directed' land have the right to farm 10 hectares apiece, to which they gain title after twenty years of continuous occupation. In addition, they owe labor services on communal lands, where they must plant the crops Rural Minas designates." "Which tenure system do applicants prefer?" I asked. "I suppose the freehold arrangement, but the project's design has to be considered before individual preferences."

I felt a bit uncomfortable asking pointed questions while Vicente appeared conspicuously uninquisitive. The Internship Program at Jaíba depended on agreements with Rural Minas, which was also responsible for the region's health system. I did not want to compromise the interns. On the other hand, when Senhor Paulo found my Portuguese unintelligible, Vicente translated with succinct bluntness. Thus encouraged, I asked for the total acreage to be irrigated, and, of this, the percentage allotted to colonization as opposed to corporate development. "Of 100,000 hectares, up to 30 percent for settlement," Senhor Paulo calculated, "and perhaps 70 percent for companies." As to the corporations in question and how much land was ceded to each, only Vicente's knack for translation prodded some rough estimates. "Each company, prior to authorization, has to submit a development plan. The Ometto Corporation has applied for and received 43,000 hectares, much of it for stock raising in confinement." Satisfied now that I got the message, Vicente intervened, expressing his thanks to Senhor Paulo and confessing bafflement as to my preoccupation with figures. We then sallied forth to the nearest cantina.

"There's nothing wrong with roads or electrification," said Ignácio, an intern in his early twenties. "If it weren't for the project's roads, we couldn't have the Internship here in the first place. But after all they've spent, the health center doesn't have the proper lab equipment or a decent X-ray machine. And when you point this out, they treat you like a subversive." "We're not opposed to development," Vicente added, "we're opposed to the way the regime distorts it. Whether it's the credit system or irrigation, the small farmer gets treated like the enemy, as if development required his elimination. The result is a tragedy in our cities that the government can't handle."

Faith

When the Inter-American Development Bank dispatched a technical mission to Jaíba in 1982, Rural Minas decked itself out as the small farmers' benefactor. After visits to colonization sites, the bank's technicians paid tribute "to one of the most successful projects of its type in Latin America."[52] The *Jornal do Brasil* had its own reporter in the region five months later. Evidently, Project Jaíba had experienced a remarkable transformation. Now its claim to fame rested on an alcohol production target of half a billion liters by 1986. The Agrivale Corporation, reported the *Jornal*, had 21,000 hectares of which 15,000 would benefit from irrigation. The company had two modules of 56 hectares each already in production, with five more planned, "subject to financing by the Bank of Brazil." Among the heroes opening up what the reporter declared to be "a vast demographic emptiness of unutilized land," was a South African responsible for implementing Agrivale's "high-technology development." He was, as the *Jornal* put it, "just one of the many foreigners in Northern Minas who labored with a rare patriotism—a belief in Brazil's limitless possibilities."[53]

The proofs the regime offered in exchange for Agrivale's faith were incontestable. They built the roads, put in the electrical grid, ceded the company 21,000 hectares, agreed to bring water to Agrivale's doorstep, and, if that was not enough, the Bank of Brazil stuffed a development loan in its pocket. To the likes of Agrivale, Ometto, and Fruitrop, the state's religion inspired credulity: a dollar's worth of faith for every thousand the regime invested. Only the United States presumes to purchase corporate confidence at a comparable rate of exchange.

Enterprise paid homage in Brasília and departed with the country's destiny. To the regime, development meant wiping the slate clean, starting over without facing Brazil as it was. If the illiterate and ignorant got in the way, developers removed them like trash.

When the U.S. State Department worked out the balance sheet on the "moderately authoritarian regime," it factored out such troublesome details. But then, it is devoted to mysteries proclaimed by great powers. Brazil will need its own revelations and faith in itself.

Common Sense

I returned to Rio a staunch advocate of land reform. I was with Eduardo King Carr, an agronomist with Electrobrás, the National Utility Company. Eduardo was in his fifties, tall, slim, and graying. "Don't make the opposite mistake," he warned me. "You can't replace companies with 50 million farmers on 20 hectares. That's plain stupid. Agribusiness can deliver in both quantity and productivity, as the Alcohol Program demonstrates. Brazil doesn't need a revolution, just some common sense.

"Size alone isn't the issue; it's production and who pays for it. To vilify the big producer, Jaime, is poetic license rather than a viable strategy. Companies have their place in irrigation projects. How much of the available acreage they get, how much of their own capital they ante up, and what they produce, of course, are open to question. After all, the infrastructure is built at Brazil's expense.

"Brazil has a stake in agribusiness, which is not surprising or particularly objectionable. That the regime pays its way at everyone else's expense certainly is. Small farmers have to cover the real costs of production; big enterprises don't. Despite such handicaps, the small farmer produces half our food

227

crops. What we need in Brazil is rural development that targets credit to the small producer and protects his right to the land. That's the first step, and it has to be organized state by state and county by county.

"I'm not opposed to land distribution. But in Brazil, if you hold rural development hostage to land reform, you court disaster. If we started with technical assistance, we'd get to land reform soon enough; even then, reform has to recognize legitimate interests, and that includes agribusiness.

"Land distribution is a matter of justice, but it's also a technical question. In Brazil, land use has to consider export crops and food staples, industrial products like alcohol and cotton textiles, animal production, and forestry. Given the diverse demands on agriculture, it's absurd to think there's some limit on a holding's size you can apply across the board. The balance on land use in São Paulo will always be different from Minas Gerais or Ceará. With respect to rainfall, soil quality, and good crop land, they're virtually different countries. And my guess is that land speculation varies enormously in each. In São Paulo, for example, land is simply too expensive to take it out of production. There can't possibly be a general rule for land reform in Brazil—the country is just too diverse. Anyway, the issue is dangerous politically. For distribution, the place to start is with the acreage that state companies control. And if Brazil taxed unused land at anywhere near its value, the conglomerates would have to sell off the surplus. Let big enterprise in Brazil be free to pay its own bills."

In 1983, insolvency forced the regime to reduce credit subsidies to 85 percent of inflation plus 3 percent. For 1985, the Bank of Brazil required its farm customers to pay a real, if modest, interest rate of 3 percent after inflation. For the first time in over fifteen years, even agribusiness had to pay something that approached the actual cost of production. This alone ought to check the scramble for machinery and land acquisition. Meanwhile, José Sarney's planners drew up a land reform bill that was as controversial as it was comprehensive. The Brazilian Congress, which had sixty-two members who allegedly owned 32 million hectares, revised the bill eleven times before passing it.[54] The final legislation set no limit on an estate's size as long as it was productive. For distribution that still left 100 million hectares of state-owned land and unutilized private holdings. Between 1986 and 1989, 1.4 million rural families are supposed to benefit from the reform.[55] Distribution, however, is only one step; making small farms productive is the next. On credit and technical assistance, Sarney's bill was rather vague.

How to improve the small farm's productivity was of more than passing interest. Between 1980 and 1985, Brazil's population increased by 14 percent. Food crops lagged far behind. Compared to 1980, rice was down by 8 percent, cassava fell by 2 percent, and potatoes registered a meager 3 percent increment. Only black bean production exceeded population growth. By contrast, the sugarcane harvest was up by 66 percent, soybeans by 20 percent, and the orange export crop by 30 percent.[56] Apparently, agribusiness could take care of itself, even without the old subsidies. The smaller farms, which produced the country's food, could not. Brazil finally had land reform on the agenda, but not rural development.

7
CHILDBIRTH
AND RURAL
EXTENSION

For statistical presentation, Brazil's states are grouped into regions. The rationale is more geographical than historical, except for the Northeast. With its own heroes, saints, and poets, the Northeast is a nation in its own right, held together by devotion to legends and lost causes: to Antônio Conselheiro whose Holy City of Canudos federal troops annihilated, to Padre Cícero whose miracles Rome never recognized, to the bandit king Lampião betrayed to the police. Despite opposition from bishops, the people canonized Padre Cícero and keep his picture even now. And in picture stories suspended from strings, the poor still defend their Holy City, and Lampião still taxes the landlords.[1]

• The Northeast

Today, paved roads lead to the hideouts of old heroes. Textile sweatshops have displaced traditional craftsmanship, historical research documents the region's folklore as much as current practice. True, ordinary people still depend on São João for the rain and turn to healers with uncommon fidelity. But considering what development has brought the majority, the preference is justified. Notwithstanding an occasional lapse on São João's part, he has proved a greater friend to the Northeast than any president in memory, military or civilian. And when rural women have the choice, they go to a midwife rather than a public hospital.

Summary statistics on Brazil's economic growth often overlook its regional concentration. Of Brazil's industrial production in 1980, for example, the southeastern states of São Paulo, Rio de Janeiro, and Minas Gerais accounted for 76 percent; the nine states of the Northeast, with 30 percent of the country's population, managed a trifling 7 percent.[2] Although the Northeast's industrial output almost doubled between 1970 and 1980, it still employed only half a million workers.[3] Overall, the region's share of Brazil's gross national product (GNP) in 1980 was only 13 percent.[4] Meanwhile, the Northeast's urban population had doubled from 12 to 18 million, and the region's rural population had declined from 58 percent of the total to 49 percent.[5] Although the Northeast was still home to half the country's rural labor force, the region accounted for only 20 percent of Brazil's agricultural production.[6]

The opportunities available to ordinary people, whether urban dwellers or part of the rural work force, showed up in what passed for gainful employment. In 1980, the earnings for half the Northeast's labor force fell below the minimum wage—compared to a third for Brazil overall. On a per capita basis, income was half that for the rest of the country. And of Brazil's poorest families, the bottom 10 percent who scraped by on 1 percent of the national income, 60 percent lived in the Northeast.[7]

The region's record on health and education was equally dismal. Infant mortality rates in 1984 came to 107 per 1,000, much above the country's average of 70. A nutrition survey conducted in São Luís (1979), capital of Maranhão State, found that 70 percent of the children under five were at risk from malnutrition—compared to 30 percent in the city of São Paulo. In 1985, the National Council of Catholic Bishops estimated that 4 million people in the region had schistosomiasis and 3 million had Chagas disease. In 1980, 35 percent of the deaths registered in the Northeast were for infants less than a year old. Of the school children enrolled in the first grade in 1979, only 38 percent were in the second grade in 1980, and only 22 percent had advanced to the fourth grade and functional literacy in 1982. In the state of São Paulo, by contrast, the percentages were 82 and 65 respectively.[8]

The Northeast is a region defined as much by its poverty as by its poetry. Brazil's poor showing on infant mortality, literacy, and wages is partly explained by the influence the Northeast has on such figures. Take the region out of the calculation and Brazil is almost a different country. This was, in fact, close to the regime's approach. It based greatness on the good news from São Paulo. Whatever the Northeast got, it got less and got it last. Credit for crops was no exception: in 1977 and 1979, the Northeast's share averaged 12 percent—compared to 21 percent for the state of São Paulo.[9] Throughout the 1970s, the Southeast profited most from the fiscal incentives Brazil's Development Council provided for industrial projects: 76 percent of the benefits ended up in the Southeast, 10 percent in the Northeast.[10] In 1979, when the regime endorsed the alcohol vehicle, the Northeast had only 10 percent of the country's passenger cars.[11] Eventually, of course, the region cashed in on the regime's penchant for infrastructure: hydroelectric projects on the São Francisco River, roads to Brasília, and loans to sugar producers. Such accomplishments notwithstanding, the regime spent more on its Amazonian fantasies than it ever did on the grim realities of the Northeast. In 1984, only 18 percent of federal health funds went to the Northeast, and only 15 percent of the outlays for education.[12]

Ceará's industrial confederation claimed that the Northeast's future depended on a $10 billion irrigation project.[13] To replace São João's rain was a question of feasibility studies, hydraulics, and construction loans. For health care, education, and safe water, there is no comparable solution. Social strategies depend on more than checks from Brasília.

• Childbirth in Fortaleza

Capital of the state of Ceará, Fortaleza is the Northeast's third largest metropolitan area with a population of over 1.8 million (1985).[14] Downtown, the city is a labyrinth of old squares and narrow streets. To the north and south, it offers beaches famous for their majestic coconut palms. Compared to the frantic pace of a big-league place like Rio, Fortaleza is less hurried and less addicted to high-rise symbols of progress.

I had been to Fortaleza before, mostly for the beach. This time, rural health was first on the agenda. For once, I had avoided the bus. Fortaleza was over 1,700 miles from Rio, a two-day trip by express. Even the *Jornal do Brasil* arrived a day late, if at all. Dr. Antero Coelho, coordinator of the district's Primary Health Care Program, met me at the airport. "Which hotel?" he asked. "The Continental," I replied, remembering its location on a street barred to traffic. "The best place in town," he laughed, "in 1920."

A tall, distinguished man in his fifties, Antero had studied medicine in the United States and had practiced in Boston; his specialty was kidney disease. "When I returned to Fortaleza," he told me, "I set up a private practice, but eventually gave it up for community health. People thought I would regret it, that I was throwing away years of training. Frankly, Fortaleza had plenty of specialists; one more or one less hardly mattered. For me, the majority had to come first; I have never looked back, and I have never regretted it."

When Antero questioned me on the region's history, I mentioned Padre Cícero and cited figures on income distribution. "When São Paulo's reporters come to the Northeast," he said, "they file stories on infant mortality and malnutrition. You know the statistics too, but what do they mean? Just because people are poor doesn't imply they lack ingenuity or ability. Poverty doesn't make a midwife incompetent, and it hasn't prevented communities from organizing their own clinics."

I spent a week discussing the project's work with physicians, midwives, and community health workers. Dr. José Galba, an obstetrician from Ceará's Federal University, started the project in the mid–1970s. He began at Paca-

Map 7.1 Fortaleza Project

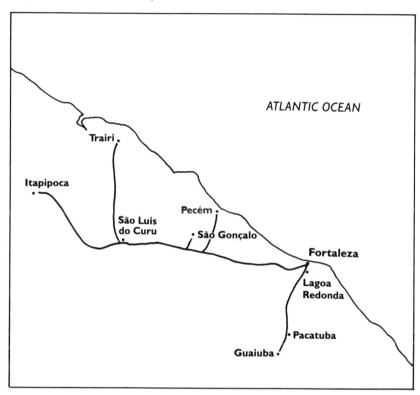

ATLANTIC OCEAN

Trairi .

Itapipoca
.

Pecém .

São Luis
do Curu
.

. São Gonçalo

Fortaleza
.

Lagoa
Redonda

. Pacatuba

Guaiuba .

tuba, a small town twenty miles from Fortaleza.[15] "From the start," Antero emphasized, "Galba had the good sense to ask not only what communities did not have, but what they did have. Rural areas lacked clinics and doctors, but they had their own midwives."

The project became a collaborative effort that allied itself with the community's traditional practices. Galba's group provided midwives with basic supplies, trained them to identify high-risk births, and set up a twenty-four-hour ambulance service. Because the sterilization techniques of hospital obstetrics could not be duplicated in the field, the group simply stressed cleanliness. To facilitate the midwife's work, the community converted an abandoned building into a childbirth clinic. The midwives provided staffing, the health team organized rotations for on-going supervision, and the community's association managed and supported the clinic. The Federal University's Center for Health Sciences backed the project. Emergency referrals, for example, went to the maternity ward at the University Hospital.

"Galba's work provoked tremendous controversy," Antero said. "Most doctors thought the midwife's practices were unsanitary and promoted infection. They felt she was ignorant and superstitious, that her work jeopardized the life of both mother and child. The Health Department's policy was to replace the midwives with physicians and centralize childbirth in clinics. Not only was this beyond the Health Department's budget, but it ignored all previous experience. The rural population was dispersed, communities distrusted the clinics, and women had a strong aversion to childbirth outside the home. In fact, the Health Department had closed many clinics because the communities refused to use them. To reduce infant mortality and maternal deaths, the Health Department had mostly empty schemes."

Based on the experience at Pacatuba, Galba's work expanded to other towns, and new components were added: primary care for children, adolescents, and adults; and nutrition programs that included food supplements, family gardens, and public health. The project's unique feature, however, was its successful work with midwives. By 1980, Galba had documented the project's results in such detail that even the Health Department had to acknowledge its achievements. After more than 2,000 births in the project's community clinics, not a single mother had died, there was no case of external infection, and only one infant who weighed above five and a half pounds at birth had died.[16]

When I visited the project in 1984, it included two of the state's thirteen health regions—rural Fortaleza and Itapipoca—for a total of sixteen municipalities and half a million people. Both regions were within seventy-five miles of Fortaleza, which permitted a round trip in a day.[17] The project managed training and supervision at health facilities whose support came not only from community groups but also from Ceará's Health Department and the National Health Service. As was true at other projects in Brazil, a health region was subdivided into districts so as to constitute a referral network.

"What has happened," Antero said, "is that the authorities had to accept the validity of our approach. So they have subcontracted the supervision to us. We're responsible for coordinating the work of over forty facilities, and each has its own history. What begins as a community health post, especially in a large town, signs contracts with the Health Department, adds to its staff, and expands. It ends up somewhere between the status of a health center and a small reference hospital, what we call a 'mixed unit.' Consequently, the distribution of facilities doesn't correspond to the blueprints administrators like to design. We have to accept the limitations reality places on theory. The project's objective is to strengthen the work done in education, preventive medicine, and public health. And we have to reorganize supervision so that the work of health posts, centers, and reference hospitals is reasonably coordinated. Granted the results aren't uniform across each district, but by and large the midwives have dependable backing."

Midwives

Dr. Marília Pereira, a soft-spoken woman in her late twenties, worked with the midwife program. We visited several clinics, some on the outskirts of Fortaleza, others in rural areas.

In 1984, the project had the help of over 350 midwives, all of whom had attended training sessions. About 300 had regular contact with project personnel. The remaining 50, although they had received training, lived in remote areas; they came to special sessions twice a year. Most midwives assisted at childbirth in the home, and about 70 worked in the clinics.

"A training program can't confer acceptance as a midwife," Marília said. "Only the community can. To designate our own midwives, or decide that literacy is a prerequisite for training, would be disruptive and counterproductive. In Ceará, the midwife's skills are not passed on by apprenticeship. Becoming a midwife is usually accidental—someone who had to 'catch' a baby in the midwife's absence. Of course, some women have experience helping the midwife and get called on in emergencies. Nonetheless, becoming a midwife just happens; it is not an inherited role.

"People call the midwife a 'catcher' because she waits for the fetus to be expelled naturally. She then places the infant at the mother's breast with the cord still attached. The midwife never puts her hands into the uterus, a custom that greatly reduces the risk of infection. The most she does is insert her middle finger a couple of inches to see if birth is imminent. At delivery, the mother sits on a birthing chair, stool, or hammock. From behind, an assistant, often the husband, presses gently at the base of the uterus. The entire procedure is calm and dignified. Women remain dressed; there's no shaving of pubic hair as in most hospitals. The midwife views childbirth as an unexceptional event, but one that brings great satisfaction. She conveys this in a practical, reassuring way. What characterizes childbirth with a midwife is its tranquility, the love and trust that prevail. Our rule is to avoid unnecessary interference. We want to enhance the midwife's capabilities, but we are not trying to teach them obstetrics."

For training, the first step was to meet with the community's midwives. The number involved depended on the community's size: as few as eight to ten or as many as twenty to thirty. Training occurred over five sessions and covered fetal development, parturition, and breast-feeding. This had to be done in a straightforward fashion with simple illustrations and by using popular terms rather than medical jargon. "Midwives have valuable skills and experience," Marília noted, "but many are illiterate or have minimal reading skills. While we add to basic knowledge, the main point is to prepare midwives for new responsibilities, to enlist their support on behalf of family health."

Midwives were trained to keep track of prenatal exams, the character of each woman's delivery, and the height, weight, and sex of the newborn infant.

Midwives who could not read filled out a simple pictogram by marking an "X" in the appropriate box. To assess risk, the midwives considered the mother's age, birth interval, and the difficulty of previous pregnancies. They referred high-risk cases to the clinic's physician. At childbirth, premature hemorrhaging or obstructed labor usually led to a hospital referral. The sessions also emphasized vaccinations and the role breast-feeding plays in infant nutrition.

"We can't accomplish everything during the first round of training," Marília said. "Follow-up sessions that reinforce skills and add new material are scheduled periodically. Some of the groups, for example, are in their fourth training cycle."

The midwives who ran the clinics had to have at least basic reading skills, as more detailed record keeping was an important aspect of their work. A midwife was available at the clinic at all times, everyday. Selection of the clinic midwife, sometimes two or three depending on the community's size, had to respect prevailing opinion. "We need someone the community holds in high regard, who is trusted and sought out," Marília said. "The midwife has duties similar to those of a promotora. The advantage the midwife has is that her role is of such obvious importance. When she stresses sanitation, she's listened to; when she plants her own garden, she's copied. Her skill in childbirth commands respect, even from physicians. In fact, the University Hospital has followed the midwife's example; it discourages obstetric intervention in normal childbirth, and is equipped with specially designed birthing chairs.[18] For all these reasons, the midwife doesn't have the problem of acceptance by the community or by the doctor that so often obstructs a promotora's work."

Midwives did not charge; they considered their work a community service. The project, however, insisted they receive a regular if minimal salary of between $25 and $50 a month. The project also supplied sterilized cotton, antiseptics, adhesive tape, a stethoscope, a blood pressure cuff, and a hand scale. Such rudimentary equipment was inexpensive. The hand scale, for instance, included a soft towel with loops on each corner. The infant was wrapped in the towel, which was then hooked onto the scale's balance. The midwife lifted child and scale together in one hand, steadied with the other, and the weight registered.

We made our way to São Luís do Curu County, some sixty miles from Fortaleza. The rains had returned, awakening the earth from its dormancy. A thousand shades of green glittered in the sun. An inland sea had once covered the coast; it has withdrawn now, leaving behind a broad plain flanked by mountains. When rain is abundant, marshes and shallow lakes appear everywhere. For a few precious weeks the coast revels in its prehistory.

"A midwife whose gentle but firm manner women trust is much in demand," Marília said. "As in any profession, word gets around and reputations are made. When we have unusual confidence in a midwife, and particularly when she works in a region beyond the reach of a clinic, we try to ease the burden by adding a birthing room to her house."

Dona Clarice was midwife for the Córrego Fundo district and had the kind of reputation that warranted a birthing room. She was a short, hefty woman in her sixties with deep-brown leathery skin. Energetic and expansive, she embraced Marília and, without the slightest hesitation, me. She took us in tow, one in each arm, to see her flowers and vegetables. The birthing room was freshly scrubbed, an observation verified by a slightly damp floor and rags drying outside. And it was simple: a bed with bathinette attached, a mosquito net, a birthing stool, a desk, and a cabinet for records and equipment. For our perusal she pulled out about fifty prenatal sheets, all filled out and active—"a busy year," she laughed. "Everyone knows I don't want to be surprised at the last minute, I'm getting too old. I want to see them first and hear the baby's heart." She kept her records in a neat, deliberate script; she tracked each child to make sure vaccinations were on schedule. In her spare time, she made follow-up visits.

"How many births have you assisted at?" I asked. "In the past three years since the addition," she said, "307 at the house, 44 away." It was the fourteenth of June; she had delivered seven that month. During her years as a midwife, she told us, "three infants were born dead." Marília asked if a mother had ever died in childbirth. "No, my daughter," she said, "God has blessed me; I've brought life forth, not sent it back."

Research

How well did a midwife do her job? Over a ten-month period in 1980–81, a research team tabulated the midwife's performance at four clinics.[19] Of 1,881 deliveries that began at the clinics, the midwives had referred 235 or 12.5 percent. For the childbirths completed at the clinics, there were no maternal deaths; less than one infant in a thousand was stillborn or died before discharge; 96 percent weighed at least five and a half pounds at birth, 99 percent had Apgar scores of between 7 and 10, indicating normal heart rate, respiration, muscle tone, and reflexes. Most of the women that midwives sent on to the hospital had obstructed labor, premature separation of the placenta, difficult positioning of the fetus, or fetal distress. The midwives had a slight tendency to overrefer, but, in childbirth, an error on the conservative side was considered preferable.

The project had made childbirth safe for thousands of rural women. For those who relied on the clinic system—including emergency referrals—the likelihood they brought their infants home was twice as high as in public hospitals: a remarkable achievement by any standard.

Healers

The project routinely immunized thousands of children. To the extent infant mortality was vaccine-preventable, coverage had significantly reduced the risk. During the rainy season, however, sewage runoff from saturated groundwater created contamination twenty times greater than normal.[20] The result was a predictable outbreak of enteritic infections. To improve public health, the project stressed the community's water supply: the use of inexpensive, household filters and better waste disposal. Nonetheless, the sources of contamination were many. The main cause of infant mortality was still the dehydration associated with dysentery.

"Mothers brought their children to the clinic as a kind of last resort," Antero said. "By then, dehydration was compounded by malnutrition. And if they lived some distance away, they often avoided the clinic altogether. Before we started keeping records, children came into the world and left it unnoticed by the statisticians. There are tiny graves marked by little white crosses all over rural Ceará. For much of Brazil, infant mortality estimates are guesswork."

A solution of salt and sugar dissolved in water inhibits dehydration. The clinics dispensed packets with the specified proportions free. To rural people, however, dysentery was not a medical problem; it was caused by malevolent forces as its name, the evil eye, suggests. Logically enough, they sought out a specialist—in this case, a traditional healer. Just as for childbirth, where women had trusted the midwife more than the clinic's doctors, for dysentery they trusted healers—in this case, the *rezadeira*.

The rezadeira dispelled illness with prayers, which she reinforced by prescribing herbs and roots. Most were women of advanced age. On occasion a rezadeira was also a midwife. "A rezadeira has great dignity," Antero said. "She never turns anyone away, and asks nothing in return. Her work is done in God's service. People respect her as a force for good. To reduce the incidence of dehydration, we wanted the rezadeira's backing. Treatment depends on an early diagnosis and mothers take their children to the rezadeira first. As with the midwives, we held community meetings and organized training sessions. They were receptive, I think, because our work in childbirth had created trust and goodwill. So far, over one hundred rezadeiras work with the project.

"What we emphasized at the sessions was our respect for the rezadeira's rituals. For example, she instructs people on how to strengthen a prayer's effectiveness: that they have to be contrite, procure various herbs, or hold a sacred object when they pray. We accepted the fact that prayer had the power to cure, so there was no reason to interfere with the rezadeira's recommendations. I can cite a typical case. I gave a woman some antibiotics for an infection. She returned a month later totally cured. 'Well,' I said, 'you followed my advice, didn't you?' 'I did,' she replied, 'but without mustard tea and a strong prayer from the rezadeira, those little things from you would be useless.' As far as I'm concerned, there's no reason to oppose a rezadeira's prayers, teas, and roots.

"At the sessions we filled a plastic bag with water to represent an infant's body. Then we punctured it and let the water run out. 'Prayer may plug up the hole,' we explained, 'but you still have to get the water back in. Prayer cures the disease, but it doesn't necessarily undo the damage the evil eye inflicts.' "

The project trained healers to diagnose the severity of infant dysentery and malnutrition. Serious cases they could refer to the clinics directly. For routine cases they dispensed dehydration packets and explained their use. The contents had to be mixed with a liter of boiled or filtered water; the solution was good for twenty-four hours and was not refrigerated. Given the importance of safe water in the treatment's efficacy, the rezadeira's recommendations reinforced the project's emphasis on sanitation. According to project documents, a leading source of household contamination, the shared water jug, had given way to ceramic sand filters with spouts, largely because of the rezadeira's endorsement.[21] She also played a key role in vaccination promotion, urging mothers to provide coverage for all family members.

"The work with rezadeiras," Antero noted, "had to build slowly. They had colloquial terms for different symptoms that we had to learn before a training program could be effective. If a rezadeira is younger, and literate, she can keep track of the children she sees, record their symptoms, and explain the rehydration packet's use. For elderly rezadeiras, this is asking too much. We rely on follow-up work by child health assistants from the clinics. They check with the rezadeiras daily, asking who got packets and how serious each case was. When warranted, they call on the family to make sure the packets were used properly and that the child is responding to treatment. Even an elderly rezadeira can at least tell the health assistants who came for prayers. And since the assistants live in the community, there's a good chance they already know the family, or at least recognize the locality, and can make a home visit."

Of all the project's endeavors, I found myself particularly fascinated by its work with rezadeiras. "That's predictable," Antero said, "it's the kind of novelty that appeals to outsiders. But don't ignore its practical side. There's a tremendous linguistic and social distance between a university-trained physician and the people of the countryside. Experience showed that the clinics intruded from a world people distrusted. So we had to find intermediaries. The midwife gave the clinics a legitimacy they never had before. But we soon reached an impasse. How could we treat infant dysentery when the symptoms weren't viewed medically? How could we promote a basic precaution like safe water if we didn't have a rationale that motivated people? The obvious ally on both counts was the rezadeira."

The day I accompanied Marília on her rounds Antero was meeting with rezadeiras, a scheduling complication I much regretted. To make up for the omission, we stopped at the house of a "holyman" (*espírito*) in the barrio of

Gonçalvez Dias in Fortaleza. I avoid the term "faith healer" given its legacy of fanfare and big tents. In common with their fellow believers, healers shared Brazil's poverty; they did not profit from faith. Like Estevão, most were elderly, even if they could not claim his ninety-six years. He received people in simple, somewhat austere, surroundings: the room's floor was concrete, the roof tiled, the walls wooden slats; there was a long table and benches. He was dressed in old clothes and a pair of sandals. "I can't read or write," Estevão said, "I only know my name. I cure through the power of prayer. This is not my power but God's strength working through me. I am an instrument of God's will. Why this has come about I don't understand; I only know it has happened and that it is a mystery. Illness is a problem of the soul and spirit, when we don't conform ourselves to God's path. I am a poor man, the people who come to me are poor; I don't charge them anything and I never turn anyone away, day or night." He described the goodness and kindness of man, the greatness of God, the power of prayer, the strength silence confers. "A truck driver had nightmares and couldn't sleep; he asked for my help. I gave him a prayer to say at dusk; but to hold the prayer's power, he had to keep silence till dawn. He slept."

In calling on God's power, he asked the intercession of St. Mary Magdalene and St. Francis of Assisi—intermediaries "who have time for the poor."

Estevão's warmth engaged those around him. His fifteen-year-old daughter, a late "child of love" he called her, interrupted when she thought her father omitted an important detail. The rapport between them was beautiful to watch. They joked and embraced, his spirit much alive in her. And if age weighed heavily, he drew strength from her vitality. His dignity owed nothing to props or technique. It came from within: a gift bestowed, a gift accepted, a gift strengthened with years. He told the story of St. Paul thrown from his horse by God's power. "I have suffered much. We are all like St. Paul. We have to be knocked down. But suffering makes us stronger, makes us see clearly. When we get up, we are reborn."

Community Education

The same gentle affection Estevão had for people in trouble Dr. Sílvia Bomfim brought to the project's extension program. She was a tall, slim woman in her thirties; her desk was piled high with papers and reports. "There's no vaccine against unsanitary conditions," she said. "Such risks can't be cured at a clinic, they have to be reduced by the community's effort.

"A clinic," Sílvia emphasized, "should also be a school that promotes health through the community's participation. The range of activities that can fall under health extension is broad, and the groups involved diverse. Over the past three years, for example, we've organized some sixty garden clubs:

family groups, housewives, even school children are planting fruit trees and growing vegetables. The clinics have become seed distribution centers."[22]

The project's extension team organized public health campaigns on weekends, holding sessions over a five-week period. When finished, the program rotated to another community. Sílvia had just completed work in Guaiuba, a rural community thirty miles south of Fortaleza. The extension team had consisted of a physician, nurse, and teacher. The first round was for the county's rural teachers followed by sessions for parents and adolescents. Although the sophistication and approach varied, the topics considered were similar: diarrheal infections and malnutrition, sanitation, first aid, and child development. The team stressed basic diagnosis with teachers, so they could monitor the health of students and make clinic referrals. With parents, they stressed prevention—sanitation, maternal lactation, family gardens. They also screened the material on child development scheduled for teenagers.

"Sex education couldn't be separated from child development," Sílvia said, "but we didn't want to inject unnecessary controversy. We went over the material with parents first so they could judge its suitability. If they objected, we could at least encourage them to discuss the topic at home. "So you had to exclude it?" I asked. "Not at all," she laughed. "Parents found it a peculiar idea, because, as they said, 'teenagers already know everything.' We could include the topic, that was fine with them, but they had no intention of 'discussing sex with their children.' They were skeptical, too; they didn't think health education had appeal for teenagers. In fact, they almost had us convinced. We had worked with community groups before, but never teenagers specifically. We publicized the program at Guaiuba's secondary school.

"To our astonishment, over ninety attended—that's almost more teenagers than the school had. They had invited dates and friends from neighboring towns. Even the youngest knew the 'facts'; that's not why they came. They wanted something more profound that stressed personal awareness along with health education. The session on 'sex,' for instance, began with the reproductive system, gestation, childbirth, and infant care; it ended with relationships and respect in marriage.

"We taught them how to identify health risks in the community, from contaminated water to accident hazards. Then they organized into teams, found examples, and made suggestions for improvements. They compiled the results in a resumé." Sílvia had the reports on her desk. The program's attendants had filed carefully written documents, some even with drawings, maps, and tables. "Teenagers have fewer inhibitions, more free time, and great enthusiasm. They quickly grasp that promotion and prevention are part of the same approach. Adults, by contrast, find it difficult to see health as anything beyond treating an illness."

At Guaiuba, the extension program had gradually worked its way through the community: from schoolteachers, to parents, and to students. The sessions improved the health skills people had with an approach they could understand and apply. The next step was to design specific community projects. Teenagers, for example, had already started a community garden; Sílvia had arranged for an agronomist to provide advice on weekends.

When sessions ended in one place, another round started somewhere else. In the meantime, follow-up work had to be maintained on a regular basis. When not scheduled for extension, the team evaluated results and revised material, including the audiovisual segments. "I don't see how you manage," I commented. "Do you ever get a weekend free?" "It's not just the hours, we're understaffed; the effort people make reflects what needs to be done, not what they're paid. Working for the project isn't just another job, it requires a commitment. On the supervisory level, the project is really a training school. We recruit most of our staff from the University's Center for Health Sciences. They sign up for internships, helping us design and apply new strategies. Many reenlist. Eventually they leave for better paying positions. Still, the project has helped train professionals who know how to reshape Ceará's approach to health."

"That's true," I replied, "but actually, I was asking about you." "Me?" she smiled. "Guaiuba was supposed to be my last project. Then I brought back the reports. If only those kids hadn't worked so hard, hadn't cared so much: 'Dr. Sílvia, the drainage system is a disgrace; Dr. Sílvia, we're ready for the garden.' They need so much, give so much. How could I quit?"

Lagoa Redonda

Located just beyond Fortaleza, Lagoa Redonda had become a working-class annex to the city; for outlying rural districts, it was still a market town. In the late 1970s, the clinic was almost exclusively for childbirth; in 1984, it also served as a district health center, which provided pediatrics and a general medical clinic for primary care. Lagoa Redonda's town council supported and administered the center. I stopped there with Marília. The staff consisted of a doctor, a nurse, and eight midwives; auxiliary personnel included two child health assistants, five nurses aides, and several midwife attendants.

Dr. Márcio, a young, soft-spoken man in his thirties, provided supervision. A member of the extension team and a pediatrician, he worked at the clinic four hours a day Monday through Friday for a total of twenty hours a week. In addition, two doctors came once a week for gynecology and general clinic. Referrals went to the University Hospital in Fortaleza. The town paid Dr. Márcio a salary of $84 a month—one and a half minimum wages. "That's not much," I sympathized. "Actually," he noted, "it's a bit more than the $77 dollars a month paid by Ceará's Health Department; the town does the best it can." "What about the National Health Service?" I asked. "Depending on whether it's part or full time, anywhere from $176 to $588 a month." "How do you get by?" I blurted out, incredulous. "Like everyone else," he laughed, "I have to keep up a private practice."

The clinic displayed its May totals in colored chalk on the blackboard:

births	66
prenatal exams	118
post-partum exams	164
hospital referrals	78

Dr. Márcio emphasized the excellent work the midwives did at the clinic. During the past eighteen months, his help was needed at only one childbirth; only three cases had required a transfer to the hospital. Because women close to town preferred birth at the clinic to the hospital, the number of deliveries had doubled from about 400 in 1977 to over 800 in 1983. Nonetheless, the district still hovered between modern and traditional attitudes. Of the 66 births at the clinic, 29 mothers had not made prior visits to the clinic for prenatal checkups. And most women in rural areas—half the district's total—arranged for childbirth at home. "The rural midwives tend to overrefer," Dr. Márcio said, "so we're scheduling another extension round." We glanced for a moment into the four-bed maternity room; infants rested in tiny baskets attached to the mother's bed, each carefully draped by mosquito netting. We did not enter, as a birth was taking place. Dr. Márcio pulled me aside so I could listen in: "Notice how quiet it is, hardly a sound." All I heard was the midwife's reassuring voice. "You can't imagine how different this is from a hospital ward," Dr. Márcio emphasized, "where women are scared and crying, it's noisy and impersonal. The University Hospital is an exception, but that's because we've applied the midwife's methods."

At prenatal exams and after childbirth, the midwives provided orientation on an individual basis. They discussed lactation, proper nutrition, how to prevent dehydration, and the sequence of required vaccinations. I asked Marília if the project also stressed family planning. She took me into the clinic's office and showed me the files. Women who lived in or near town were most likely to practice birth control; they usually had at least two children. The preferred method was the Pill, which the clinic dispensed. "A clinic that makes birth control its main objective," Marília warned, "won't be accepted; community life places too great an emphasis on children and families. By starting with childbirth and respect for the midwife, the project demonstrated its concern for the family's welfare. Within that context, we can promote family planning. Still, it has to be part of an overall approach to health, not an isolated program that leaves health conditions in the community untouched."

The center's two child health assistants, who worked with the rezadeiras, were both about eighteen. They wore neatly pressed cotton skirts and sandals—rather than jeans, T-shirts, and sneakers. Silvana was short and weighed scarcely a hundred pounds; Lea was a bit taller. They had both attended secondary school and a training session organized by the project's staff. They described their work with evident satisfaction.

"Some of the rezadeiras bring names to the clinic," Silvana explained, "so we have a short list to start with each morning; from the others, we find out who they gave packets to, and where they live. Then we go through the list house by house. We check the child's weight and make sure mothers understand how to prepare the rehydration solution. We also note if the child's vaccinations are on schedule. If the child is recovering as expected, we usually don't need to make another visit. But when the child is underweight and dehydrated we refer them to the clinic." "What happens if they don't go?" I asked. "We go back, that's obvious, isn't it? We don't just compile a list of sick children, we make sure they get treatment." "But how do you persuade them?" I persisted. "They're already worried before we visit," Lea added by way of clarification, "so when we add our warnings, that's usually sufficient. Sometimes, especially if a woman has never been to the clinic, she's scared, so we have to reassure her. And in an emergency, I ask the rezadeira to help, to go to the clinic with the mother."

A health assistant did not earn much, scarcely the minimum wage. "My brother complained I could earn more in a department store," said Silvana. "And it turned out to be his own son I referred to the clinic. He hasn't said a word since. And anyway, my father is proud of me."

Pecém

Antero took me by dirt roads to Pecém, a picturesque fishing village nestled among shady coconut palms. Pecém was approximately forty miles northwest of Fortaleza, still beyond the condominium's reach. The sea lay before us, high tide almost reaching the village square. White sand and palms stretched out to the horizon's east and west. For a change, children had a robust look, which, as Antero noted, reflected a diet rich in protein.

Like most of the health posts built by community associations, the clinic at Pecém had two rooms: one for physical examinations, the other for childbirth. The narrow hallway in between had a desk and a file for records. Midwives had responsibility for the clinic, which averaged about fifteen births a month. In outlying districts, childbirth occurred almost exclusively at home. The association had a contract with FUNRURAL, the rural division of the National Health Service; it provided a physician for two hours three days a week. The project's mobile health unit, which had simplified dental equipment for cleaning and filling teeth, stopped regularly in Pecém. When in town the unit's dentist conducted classes on oral hygiene at the village school.

Referrals from the Pecém clinic went to the small hospital in São Gonçalo, the county seat. In fact, Antero and I had come to Pecém from São Gonçalo accompanied by Dr. Cláudio, the regional supervisor. We had stopped to sit on a bench in the square, as much for the view as for a chat. Off in the distance, an old woman trudged resolutely toward us. "That must be Dona Eugênia, the midwife," said Cláudio. "There isn't a doctor in the region more highly regarded than her." "What an unexpected pleasure," she said, embracing Cláudio, "I couldn't miss a chance to see my little doctor."

Well into her seventies, Dona Eugênia had forty years' experience as a midwife, and she had equal renown as a rezadeira. For a healer, she had not the slightest trace of solemnity; quite the contrary, she had a jovial vitality. "After five years of marriage my wife and I didn't have children," said Cláudio, grabbing my arm for emphasis. "We went to specialists, had all the tests. Finally Dona Eugênia took over, talked to my wife, and gave her prayers. In a month she was pregnant with twins." "Perhaps I was a bit excessive in my choice of prayers," said Dona Eugênia, "or maybe I shouldn't have doubled the tea ration," she added with a laugh. "You got a late start little doctor, and one child alone isn't good. Anyway, you can afford a large family."

Trairi

The project's first phase had concentrated on towns within a thirty-five-mile radius of Fortaleza; from this base it expanded to fifty miles, and by 1984, to seventy-five miles. To the Northwest this brought the project as far as Trairi, which I visited with Antero. A small, unhurried place that bordered a marshy lake, Trairi was also the county seat. The town's small hospital was what the project called a "mixed unit." For clinics in outlying areas, Trairi's facility was a reference hospital; for people in town, it provided the services of a clinic. The unit's budget typified the ad hoc arrangements characteristic of Ceará's health system. Construction funds came from the State Department of Health, routine expenses were covered by a separate state bureaucracy that managed hospital budgets, the clinic got support from the National Health Service, and the Catholic church paid for administration.

Midwives handled childbirths at the clinic, about forty a month. The hospital itself was equipped for diagnostic tests, treating burns, setting broken bones, and minor surgery, including cesarean section. There was a pediatrics room with four beds, a ward for men with three beds, and one for women, also with three beds. The hospital's permanent staff included a nurse, four nurses' assistants, and three doctors.

The apppearance of the hospital, which was kept spotlessly clean, conveyed its efficiency; it was orderly yet unhurried, quiet but not gloomy, a consequence of the dedication two nuns brought to their work. "In Trairi," Antero pointed out, "the Church's lay associations have backed the project. Vaccination campaigns reach into every village in the county; in the town itself, extension workers know every house and family. The hospital is as much

245

a school for health as it is a treatment center. The staff rotates regularly to outlying clinics, which encourages referrals and makes supervision dependable."

Sister Cecília, who was making rounds, finally caught up with us and relieved Antero; the inspection continued—to the dispensary, kitchen, laundry, and sterilization area. A trained nurse, she kept to the blue habit of her religious order rather than to the medical profession's white. With a directness that caught me off guard, she inquired into my travels and into my background, drawing a straight line from my visit to the nuns back at my grade school. "Sister," I asked, "what do people value the most, that you're dedicated to God or that you work as a nurse?" "I think of it differently," she replied. "The soul and the body are nurtured together. Disease and death breed despair. In Traírí, it used to be that in a third of the childbirths, either the infant or the mother died. Such oppression created fatalism and a sense of abandonment. To me, changing such conditions is God's work because it changes people, makes them view their lives differently. Once they see children do not have to die, that health and disease do not just happen, and that their own actions are effective, then they understand themselves in a new way, then they understand they have the power to change things.

"The Catholic church used to be accused of preaching poverty's redemptive character. Now it is accused of favoring the oppressed. In the end, it's a question of social justice, that people find God's path in dignity, not through poverty and ignorance."

We had made our way to the pediatrics ward; Sister Cecília hesitated by the entrance. "The three children here suffer from third-degree malnutrition. Don't come in if it upsets you." I should have listened: there was a four-year-old girl whose large head protruded from a body not two feet high; the others were emaciated infants, hairless, covered with sores, their arms and legs dried-up sticks.

• Politics

I spent the weekend with Antero and his wife Aida; strong-willed, she organized artisan cooperatives in Fortaleza. She described her husband as "emotional," a quality she considered a compliment. We stayed in a village near the seashore, with walks timed to meet the fishing boats at dusk. "The catch," Antero pointed out, "is distributed according to need. The elderly, who can't work, get first pick." We helped roll in the boats, strung up some fish, and started back.

Antero's experience in community health included urban projects in Rio and Brasília, and consultant work for the Pan American Health Organization. He was also a poet whose work appeared in the local newspaper and in published collections.[23] In the course of walks, Antero gave me his estimate of Brazil's health system, weighing the sadness of opportunities lost against the hope of possibilities yet to come.

"You have to realize what we're up against. A former governor told me health reform wasn't practical. Why? Because he reserved 'second-rate' departments like health for patronage. In Ceará, the state government spends seven times more on its public relations budget than it does on its Health Department. Under the circumstances, we had to piece together support for the clinics—in some cases, with contracts from the National Health Service, in others, with contracts from the State Health Department. Most of the clinics have at least some regular funds. The project's role now is training, extension, and supervision. This is done so that each community has its own specialists like the midwives and health assistants. And the project's extension work has built support for community action and health promotion. Consequently, the communities could sustain the initiative, even if the project itself had to be dismantled. The objective, in the end, is the community's development, a strengthening of its capacity for independent action. Such an approach contradicts the policies so long entrenched in Brazil's National Health Service.

"The regime tried to centralize health care in hospitals. The cost proved so staggering that the strategy couldn't be sustained. The National Health Service went bankrupt long before even elementary services reached the majority. Colombia's system, by contrast, deemphasized the hospital in favor of community clinics. For basic health care, Colombia is twenty years ahead of Brazil. Colombia, for instance, has no overarching health bureaucracy comparable to Brazil's, which administers a separate budget for each of twenty-three states. Brazil's Health Service distributes funds according to political clout rather than infant mortality rates. The allocation for a rich state like Rio Grande do Sul surpasses the total for the Northeast. At the state and county level, overlapping agencies fragment what should be a joint effort. The result virtually defies coordination.

"Dr. Galba saw that increasing the budget for an approach that had failed only made the failure more expensive. To get $500 where it was needed, one had to start with $5,000 at the top. To be workable in a poor state like Ceará, the alternative had to be simplified and inexpensive; and to gain acceptance from professionals, it had to be demonstrably effective. To cite but one example, at most public hospitals cesarean section occurs in almost half the cases, a totally unnecessary proliferation of surgical intervention. For the project's clinic referral network the overall rate is only 2.5 percent. The community obstetric units cost about $200 a month to maintain, those at the larger health centers about $2,000. The project showed that childbirth could be safe, conducted with respect, and at minimal expense.

"To the experts that meant we had a 'cost-effective model' "—here, Antero invoked the precision English apparently conferred on abstractions. "The project," he added, "did so much more. I don't know if Galba foresaw the consequences, but the clinics created a demand for action, gave people a sense of their rights. Communities that didn't have the project demanded to be included. The project expanded not only because we wanted it to, but because communities pressured their mayors who in turn lobbied the Health Department.

"The regime cannot endorse community action. It prefers a passive approach like the hospital, where people go outside their neighborhoods for treatment. A community clinic is too active and decentralized; it represents the kind of democratic tendency the regime finds threatening. So we are caught in a contradiction. While the regime recognizes the health system's deficiencies, and in its own limited way acknowledges the success of various projects, it's incapable of applying the remedy comprehensively. In Ceará, the project's strategy is followed in two health regions; by now, it ought to be standard statewide.

"The work of a clinic is like a poem: a practice built up line by line and verse by verse, an expression that lies deep in the heart."

• Cocoa

Bahia is the largest state in Brazil's Northeast; it is bigger than France. With its 500 miles of coastline, only Pará in the far North claims more of Brazil's Atlantic real estate. Of the São Francisco's 1,000-mile course, 600 miles pass through Bahia. The river flanks the mesas and flatlands of Brazil's central plateau; near Juazeiro, where it bends east toward the Atlantic, it skirts the arid plains of Brazil's *sertão*. Along Bahia's southernmost coast, however, the prevailing winds drench the lowlands with over 60 inches of rain. To within 25 miles, the climate is that of a tropical rain forest: humidity in excess of 80 percent and little seasonal variation in precipitation.[24] Covering a coastal belt of 28 counties, the region produced over 350,000 metric tons of cacao beans in 1985—85 percent of Brazil's total output.[25] Brazil was Latin America's largest exporter, and second worldwide after Ghana.

The trend in Brazilian agriculture was to larger holdings and mechanized production. Export agriculture typified the transformation. Bahia's cacao zone was an exception. For the state as a whole, the portion of the population that resided in rural areas declined by 8 percent between 1970 and 1980. In the cacao zone, by contrast, the countryside actually increased its population share by 4 percent. Consistent with this trend was the persistence of the small cacao farm. In 1970, farms of less than 50 hectares held 28 percent of the land devoted to cacao and accounted for 30 percent of production. In 1980, their land share had increased to 31 percent and their production share to 33 percent.[26] The region's atypical character reflected the work of the Cacao Research Center near Itabuna.

When I took the bus to Itabuna in 1982, the city had a population of over 150,000: a fact that had not registered in Rio. "Where do I get the express bus?" I inquired nonchalantly at the Rio terminal. "To Itabuna?" was the incredulous reply. "Try the São Geraldo line, you'll get there sooner or later." All too true. Between Rio and Itabuna no town was too small for the São Geraldo. The 750 miles took 26 hours, 8 cheese sandwiches, and 6 bags of potato chips. Itabuna's boom-town reputation got confirmation at the bus depot: overcrowded and under construction. The only spot civic pride had spared was the riverfront park. So I lugged my baggage in that direction, hope reinforced by what seemed a small hotel. "A single?" I inquired. "No senhor, what's left is a big room with beds." There were six to be exact, and four overhead fans. I stayed three days.

Brazil has an excellent network of product-specific Research Centers and a National Extension Service. Each Center specializes in a particular staple, export crop, or animal product; the extension service transfers research results to farms. But technical assistance and credit rarely benefited the small producer. The result was that larger farms added trucks and tractors. The gains in output came from farming more land, not from higher productivity. The extension service had methods to improve the soil's quality, it had spacing and rotation recommendations, and it had more productive varieties; but it did not supervise how credit was applied. When it worked with small farmers, it had to battle with the banks over collateral and eligibility. This was not true in the cacao zone.

The assumption that small farms focused almost exclusively on food crops has to be qualified. True, the Pamplona project featured the potato, and Plan Sierra had gandul, cassava, and vegetable gardens on its agenda. Recall, however, that coffee was Plan Sierra's most important crop. Similarly, in Colombia and Costa Rica, coffee is still identified with the small farm. For Latin America overall, small farms accounted for a third of the region's agricultural exports in 1980. The work of Brazil's Cacao Center shows that research on export crops can benefit small farms and not just agribusiness.[27]

Extension

Situated on 1,500 acres just outside Itabuna, the Cacao Center conducted research on disease control, hybrids, soils, and processing; its findings reached farmers through a network of nine regional and forty-five local extension offices. "The Cacao Center," explained Waldeck Die Maia, "supports both research and extension from a single budget. Since cacao production is concentrated in a small, climatically distinct zone, combining both activities in one agency was a logical step." With a full beard, wire-rimmed glasses, and short-sleeved shirt, Waldeck had none of the formality I expected from a research administrator. He summarized the Center's work and then scheduled visits to nearby farms.

The region's cacao production had declined throughout the 1950s, a consequence of diseased trees and poor production methods. The farms were relatively small and producers were heavily in debt. The initial plan consisted of a minimum export price and credit concessions, but to little effect. Low-yielding trees had to be replaced by better varieties, and farmers had to adopt new techniques, both for effective disease control and for drying the beans. Otherwise, the region's decline could not be reversed. This implied a coordinated approach to research, credit, and extension. Since the mid-1960s, the revenue from a cacao export tax had been channeled directly to the Center. A secure budget made a tremendous difference in the project's extension work.[28]

"Cacao seedlings require seven years to reach maturity," Waldeck said. "To establish a new grove, cacao is planted in association with banana trees, which grow much faster and protect the seedlings. Shade trees have to be carefully spaced throughout; eventually, they overtake the banana trees and provide filtered sunlight for the cacao. To replace older trees with new cacao varieties is comparatively simple, as the shade trees are already established, but farmers still have to wait seven years. To restore the region's production, research alone wasn't sufficient. We had to convince farmers the investment would pay off; the approach had to be gradual but sustained. Farmers couldn't afford to replace all their old trees simultaneously. Instead, they planted a few hectares at a time, leaving enough acreage in old trees to provide a steady income. By applying fertilizer and adopting new disease control methods, they could increase the productivity of old trees while they waited for seedlings to mature."

The Bank of Brazil provided credit; the Center's extension division processed the loans and supervised how funds were used. When farmers renovated old groves or planted new ones, the loans carried a five-year grace period. Because farmers had to provide security for long-term credit, the Center provided collateral from a revolving fund, a strategy particularly beneficial to smaller producers. By the late 1970s, loans totaled $100 million, both short and long term; the average credit came to $10,000. The extension service worked directly with 9,500 cacao farmers, half the region's total.[29]

The gains in production began slowly during the 1960s, but mounted impressively thereafter. Compared to 1970, for example, cacao acreage had expanded 25 percent in 1980; total production was up 70 percent and yields per hectare had increased by 50 percent. During the interim, the proportion of new trees had risen from 12 to 42 percent of the total. The results coincided with an upturn in commodity prices; a ton of cacao in 1980 fetched three times as much as it had in 1970.[30]

"The cacao zone," Waldeck said, deftly downshifting a jeep he had rescued from retirement, "is reputed to be a region of small farmers. That's somewhat of an exaggeration." He veered onto a narrow dirt road flanked by shade trees. "To support a family of five adequately, a farmers needs about 30 hectares of cacao. Depending on how much of the land is actually suitable, it can take a holding of 40 to 50 hectares to net 30 in cacao. True, the region doesn't have corporate estates; 70 percent of the farmers have 50 hectares or less in cacao. Nonetheless, what we consider 'small' in terms of cacao is 'large' for black beans or manioc."

Waldeck slowed down in front of every planter cottage: frame dwellings with pitched roofs, cross ventilation, and porches. "We've saved a little piece of Brazil," he said. "Reviving the cacao farms prevented the incursion of cattle ranches and reversed the tendency toward deforestation. For the moment, it has also checked migration to the cities, not because the Center creates employment directly, but because cacao production is highly resistant to mechanization." He spent the rest of the day proving the point, step by step.

"When properly cared for," Waldeck said, "cacao trees maintain high yields for decades." The crux of the matter, of course, was the qualification. Cacao needed room to branch out, thriving amidst the forest's debris and irregularity. Consequently, "clearing out the accumulated underbrush twice a year" was high on the list of extension requirements. Then came the arsenal on behalf of plant nutrition and health: fertilizer, pesticides, and particularly, given the humidity, fungicides. Black rot, which attacked the fruit pods, was especially dreaded; effective control required two fungicide applications plus the destruction of infected pods. Without constant vigilance, black rot settled in, spreading from tree to tree. Motorized spray guns mounted on the back had to suffice, as vehicles could not fit between the trees.[31]

"On a mechanized coffee farm," Waldeck noted, "the trees are kept short, uniform in size, and precisely spaced. Even though not all the fruit is ripe at harvest time, the loss in quality is not great. By contrast, cacao's special habitat, its disease control problems, and its harvesting characteristics discourage mechanization. Harvesting has to be continuous; each tree puts out fruit constantly over an eight-month period. At any given time, some of the fruit is ripe, some not. Pickers rotate to each tree every fifteen days. When the fruit pods turn a uniform, golden brown, they're ripe. If farmers wait too long, they rot; if they pick them too green, the seeds have a high acid content, contain less sugar, and ferment poorly."

A cacao tree looks like a gigantic rhododendron. The fruit pods are oval and oblong in shape—six to eight inches in length, three to five inches in width. Once collected, the fruit is split and the seeds are removed. Each pod contains from twenty to fifty elliptical, sticky white seeds about an inch long. When crushed, they yield a clear, semisweet viscous liquid that has little in common with chocolate.

To end up with cocoa beans, the cacao seeds have to be fermented and dried. Pods split on the same day should be fermented together; mixed batches reduce quality and hence the product's grade classification. For fermentation, seeds are spread out in troughs to a depth of three feet and covered to retain heat; they are turned every twenty-four hours for four days. Fermentation confers the color, flavor, and aroma associated with cocoa, but the beans still retain too much moisture to be stored or processed. Drying is the final step, but it has to be gradual and uniform or the quality deteriorates. Cacao needs four or five days to cure in the sun; even exposure requires a turning over every half hour during the first two days. In a drying house, curing time drops to thirty hours, but quality control is more difficult. The beans have to be rotated constantly, and the temperature has to rise gradually without exceeding 130 degrees. The recommended method was to start in the sun and finish in the drying house.[32]

"A hectare of cacao can have several hundred trees," Waldeck noted. "Even a few hectares is too much for a family to manage. The production standards required for loans implied a qualified work force quite different from the unskilled, manual labor of the past. Since cacao farmers employed thousands of people, extension had to concentrate as much on the hired labor force as on landowners. During the 1970s, the extension division trained 15,000 to 20,000 people a year, many of them as specialists in disease control, fermentation methods, or drying techniques. By promoting exports, the Center created employment. Having borrowed to expand production, farmers wanted to avoid losses from a fungus like black rot; to do so, they had to hire qualified labor. Higher productivity covered the costs."

To back up its work in extension, the Center helped establish the Cacao Cooperative. It purchased fungicides, soil additives, and farm implements in bulk, and sold them at cost through the extension offices. In 1980, the Cacao Cooperative handled about 20 percent of the region's exports, up from 3 percent in 1970. In addition, it promoted local processing of bean cakes, cocoa butter, and liquor.[33] "We have to either export or process as quickly as possible," Waldeck said. "The climate here is too humid; beans can't be stockpiled without tremendous loss from mildew. With coffee, Brazil can buy up the surplus and store it almost indefinitely. With cacao, buyers in northern climates have the advantage; it's cool and dry enough to hold stocks for years.

"We can't stockpile, but we've helped producers manage their farms, passed on the results of our research, and trained thousands of people. To the regime, our success is counted in tons of cacao; to me, it's the vitality of rural life. Agriculture has to be more than production; people have a right to make a living where they are. To promote exports at the cost of displaced rural families is counterproductive, and, technically speaking, totally unnecessary. Cacao is a special case, but, if you think a moment, you'll see the general principle."

We made our way back to Itabuna, the evening sky a dark purple-blue. I thought as instructed—without discerning the apparent "principle" within.

"Well, what is it, Waldeck?" I asked, impatient with the Socratic method. "Don't you see," he said, "we've demonstrated Brazil can afford less mechanization and more employment in agriculture—the exact antithesis of the regime's policies. And it's been done with a sacrosanct export crop."

Schools

"Small farmers sell out because they can't make a decent living," Luiz dos Santos told me, "and young people leave because they don't think the region has a future. The school's objective is to show students how to manage a small farm, to equip them with the skills the region needs."

In his late twenties, Luiz was the principal of Uruçuca's Agro-Technical High School. His boots muddy, his dungarees and T-shirt grimy with sweat and dust, he held out his hand with apologies. "The school's motto is 'learn by doing.' I can't teach agronomy and stay clean at the same time."

It was one of four technical schools where room, board, and tuition were free; the teachers lived on campus. "The advantage the region's technical schools have," Luiz said, "is that they're financed and supervised by the Cacao Center. We can pay qualified teachers what they're worth, purchase modern equipment, and keep the curriculum flexible. The Center appoints the staff, not the Department of Education, so there's less turnover. In the rest of Bahia, teachers need a second job; they can't live on what they're paid. And every time the state has a new governor, he appoints a different secretary of education, who then switches principals in every school in the state. The Center's schools, by contrast, aren't part of the patronage system."

The school's curriculum provided concentrations in agronomy, food processing, farm management, and surveying. A majority of the students being sons of local farmers, agronomy was the most popular choice. Cacao production was of obvious interest, but students also planted model vegetable gardens. The projects in animal husbandry emphasized the needs of a small farm: poultry production, hogs, and rabbits. In addition, students learned to operate, maintain, and repair farm equipment. "The key to agronomy," Luiz noted, "is flexibility; we want students to be open to new methods and crops. Compared to agroindustry, which has a huge investment in crop-specific technology, the small farm can switch crops to suit market conditions. We stress food crops every bit as much as cacao; for a farm with only 20 hectares, cacao is a waste of time and land."

A course in extension was taught during the final year. The best students worked with training teams from the school, organizing short courses and on-site instruction for workers and farmers.

The program in food processing had equipment for juice concentrates, canning, cheese production, and milling. Farm management also attracted students, given the demand for administrators on the larger cacao estates.

253

Surveying was the latest addition to the curriculum, as highway construction, electrification, and drainage projects had created new opportunities. "We don't want students to simply fit into a job slot," Luiz emphasized. "We provide a solid base in general skills so they can adjust to a shifting economy. And we're not an elite school. Most of the students come with deficiencies in reading, writing, or basic math. So part of the curriculum is remedial: to bring students up to the school's standards. Reading and writing, for example, are taken every semester."

I had a lunch of beans, rice, sliced tomatoes, and fruit in the school's cafeteria. The atmosphere was lively without being noisy. Students stacked their trays and dishes on the way out. In its daily operation, the school instilled the kind of frugality that ought to characterize a family farm. The food produced in horticulture and husbandry went to the cafeteria, and scraps were recycled to the barnyard. Cassava processed at the school's mill ended up on the dinner table as *farofa*—flour lightly browned in olive oil. A student cooperative sold the surplus from special projects: vegetables, poultry, canned fruit juice, dairy products. The profits provided a rotating capital fund for new projects, and dividends to members. "The cooperative," Luiz noted, "teaches management, collective action, and participation—survival tactics for now, applications for the future."

CONCLUSIONS

"What Brazil has to do now," noted my friend Sam Morley, "is grow as fast as possible." The recommendation had all the authority of macroeconomics behind it. Having accepted the formula of the International Monetary Fund (IMF) for "stabilization," the regime imposed austerity and brought Brazil to the brink of disaster. It reduced domestic spending by half and restricted wage adjustments to only 80 percent of the inflation rate. As a result, consumer demand plummeted. In 1983, the worst year, industrial production fell 10 percent with a staggering 23 percent drop in the output of manufactured goods. Foreign journalists filed roughly similar stories: unprecedented unemployment in industries, tumbling per capita income, and sacked supermarkets.[1]

• Debts and Deficits

To keep Brazil's debt in the "performing" category, creditors organized "rescue packages" that converted the interest due into fresh debt. Brazil added to its debt but got nothing to show for it accept IMF certification as creditworthy. For their part, the banks ended up with new assets on their balance sheets.

Besides wage reductions and curtailed spending, the IMF required export promotion. To make its goods cheaper and hence more attractive abroad, a debtor nation had to devalue its currency and cut back sharply on imports. By selling more abroad and buying less, it could chalk up a trade surplus and thus cover interest payments. On its trade, Brazil turned out to be a model client. In 1984, it registered a $13 billion trade surplus, its largest ever. Compared to

1981, Brazil had cut expenditures on imported goods by almost 60 percent. For 1984, the economy expanded 4.8 percent, and Brazil dutifully met its interest obligations.[2]

The military regime followed the IMF prescription. The Sarney government, by contrast, broke with the IMF over wages. Austerity was a dangerous policy, because the regime's defeat had raised such great expectations. To consolidate democracy, Brazil had to recover the ground lost in income, output, and employment. For 1985, wages outpaced inflation by 12 percent and economic growth topped 8 percent, the best performance in a decade. Industrial production in São Paulo jumped by 13 percent, and the labor force expanded with 1.5 million new jobs. Brazil registered a hefty $12.5 billion trade surplus, it met more of its petroleum needs domestically, and it paid less for the oil it imported—$3 billion as opposed to $10 billion in 1980.[3] For the first time in nearly two decades, Brazil's debt declined; the country remitted over $10.5 billion to its creditors.[4] Even the banks were impressed. They reamortized $14 billion of the principal at lower rates of interest, and without IMF certification.[5]

Inflation held out against an otherwise rosy picture; in 1985, it increased a record-making 225 percent. José Sarney, backed by the Finance Ministry, went on the attack with measures so unorthodox they seemed more like magic than economics. Brazil got a new currency, the cruzado, which replaced the discredited cruzeiro at the rate of 1 to 1,000. The plan also froze prices and rents for a year; ended the automatic inflation-rate correction for wages, savings, and interest; and provided unemployment insurance for workers. To ordinary Brazilians, rent, food, and transit fares constituted the main household expenditures. Fixing prices had tremendous appeal. For the moment, Sarney had replaced Tancredo Neves on the list of popular heroes.[6]

Compared to the agony of the old regime's last days, Brazil seemed a different country. Sarney, on the stump, told a crowd: "The people rule; never again will something be done without their support."[7] Sarney hit the upswing, defied the IMF, and brought the growth rate back to its historic level. The significance of the achievement for Brazil's renewed sense of confidence has to be acknowledged. Nonetheless, Brazil has had miracle growth before, and with mixed results.

The lesson from Brazil is that growth alone has not, cannot, and will not retire the country's social debt fast enough. In the past, increments to the gross national product (GNP) were not matched by proportionate gains in functional literacy, health care, or adequate employment. For half the country, household income in 1985 was still below $150 a month; for the poorest 18 million families, it was less than $50.[8] This was true despite the fact that, in GNP terms, Brazil had rapid growth for over forty years. Between 1940 and 1981, it averaged 6.4 percent—the best record in Latin America.[9]

As emphasized before, Brazil acquired tangible assets for its debt. Between 1977 and 1982, investments in hydroelectric power, telecommunications, road construction, steel, and oil drilling accounted for 83 percent of Brazil's external debt.[10] The point is not to debunk big development with overbold adjectives, but to recall the unpleasant truth that modern industry replaces workers with technology. Petrochemical production added to Brazil's self-sufficiency; its contribution to employment, however, was modest, and its relevance for health care or education, negligible. There is no quarrel with growth as long as its limitations are recognized.

The recent experience of the United States illustrates the dilemma countries like Brazil, Mexico, and Colombia face. If they adopt the latest technology, the additions to employment will never be sufficient. Consider the new General Motors Saturn plant. A corporate investment of $3.5 billion was expected to create only 5,000 industrial jobs.[11] At $700,000 per job generated, it was an expensive recipe for employment.

For the U.S. automobile industry, labor still accounts for 25 percent of production costs, which is rather high compared to computer chips where it is only 12 percent.[12] For the U.S. manufacturing sector, while the value of output trebled between 1967 and 1983, the number of production workers declined by almost 2 million.[13] Knowledge industries like telecommunications, analytical instruments, and information processing are research-intensive—no place for blue-collar workers. As a result, the U.S. economy levels off at ever higher rates of unemployment. In the 1980s, 7 percent is accepted complacently; a decade ago, it signified a recession. For advanced economies, industrial output and industrial employment move in opposite directions.[14]

To the extent Brazil's growth is predicated on petrochemicals and computer chips, the returns in employment will be small. This is not to argue against technology. Brazil cannot produce steel, automobiles, or pharmaceuticals competitively by taking a backyard approach. Fortunately, basic wage goods —from processed foods and beverages to apparel, furniture, bicycles, and housing—are still labor-intensive.[15] And for many areas of the economy, mechanization provides no obvious advantage to anyone. Who cleans the streets in Teresina is a good example. In 1982, uniformed workers used brooms and shovels to collect the garbage and clean the streets. The City Council thought this was undignified for a state capital, so it decided to purchase a million dollars worth of equipment. Public opinion, backed by indignant editorials, reversed the decision. "Why import equipment to put Brazilians out of work?" aptly states the opposition's case.

To balance the low employment ratios in high-tech industries, Brazil has to target sectors comparable to Teresina's Public Works Department. In the past, credit and exchange rates subsidized the cost of imported technology. The incentives ought to be reversed. If umbrellas, beer, and shoes retain their labor-intensive character, it will not condemn Brazil to technological backwardness.

Basic health care, primary education, and rural development are likewise labor-intensive sectors. The unmet agenda is such that demand will exceed supply for years to come. If Sarney wants to put Brazil to work, it is a good place to start.

Evidently, that is the government's intention. Besides tentative steps on behalf of land reform, Brazil's First National Development Plan outlined steps to redress the country's "social deficit." The targets for 1989 included a 40 percent reduction in infant mortality, seven years of schooling for Brazil's children, and 800,000 dwellings for low-income families. For 1986, the budget doubled the number of school lunches, provided milk for 10 million children of poor and working-class families, and increased technical assistance to small farmers.[16]

"The only reason Brazil can pay on its social debt," I was told, "is because its economy is growing." That may be a necessary precondition, but certainly not a sufficient one. The military regime had growth too, but without the emphasis on social welfare proclaimed by Sarney. The difference between the two situations was political, not economic.

Argentine Economics

Brazil's success made it a popular newspaper feature in the United States. A country that paid promptly on its foreign debt seemed so reassuring. How long Brazil would cheerfully remit what amounted to 4.5 percent of its $250 billion GNP was less obvious.[17] If the United States had an external debt of equal proportions, that is, if it had to allocate 4.5 percent of its $4 trillion GNP to foreign interest payments, it would face a net loss of $180 billion annually.[18] Given the drain on resources a debt of such magnitude represents, Brazil's situation was still precarious. With a sharp drop in its trade surplus, debt payments could collapse.

Brazil, nonetheless, was the good news, the rest of Latin America the bad news. Excluding Brazil, the region's GNP in 1985 was still less than just before the debt crisis in 1981, and per capita income was down a depressing 11 percent.[19] To rescue its sinking Banana Republics, the banks swapped interest for fresh debt. In 1981, Latin America's external obligations came to approximately $277 billion; by the end of 1985, they had increased by over 32 percent to $368 billion.[20] Four years of bargaining left Latin America poorer and even more in debt.

Brazil, Mexico, and Argentina were the region's biggest debtors; in 1985, they owed $250 billion or approximately two-thirds of the total.[21] Brazil, as already discussed, borrowed to cover OPEC's price hikes and to keep big development projects afloat. Mexico went into debt in large part to finance

PEMEX, the state oil company. To tap the country's tremendous petroleum reserves, PEMEX borrowed over $40 billion between 1978 and 1982. Mexico thereby built up its drilling, refining, and production capacity. In 1982, total output averaged about 2.7 million barrels per day, up from 800,000 in 1975. Oil exports averaged 1.5 million barrels per day, and half went to the United States. The dependence on Arab oil that had so bedeviled the Carter years declined. After 1982, Mexico rather than Saudi Arabia was the principal foreign supplier for the United States.[22]

Borrowed money stood behind Mexico's petroleum output. As recently as 1981, experts at *Foreign Affairs* thought that up was the direction for oil prices.[23] To the banks, Mexico seemed a safe bet, just as oil-rich states like Texas did. The fortune-tellers, however, missed the mark. In 1981, Mexico's oil exports brought in $15 billion; in 1986, with oil prices around $12 a barrel, its petroleum was not worth half that much. And Mexico had counted on oil for 70 percent of its export revenues and 45 percent of its taxes.[24]

Against its debt, Mexico could at least point to PEMEX as an asset, just as Brazil could count its dams and highways. Argentina was not so lucky. When the military took over in 1976, Argentina's debt was a manageable $6.5 billion; by 1982, it had expanded over sixfold to $43 billion. The military financed routine budget expenditures by borrowing abroad rather than through taxation at home. With billions coming in, the country's overvalued currency cut the cost of imports. Between 1980 and 1982, Argentine consumers spent $5 billion more on foreign goods and travel than the country sold abroad. In the meantime, cheap competition ruined local industries.[25]

Latin America's day of reckoning came in 1982. Corrected for inflation, petroleum prices fell 8.5 percent that year.[26] Oil-dependent Mexico, caught short by the unexpected drop in prices, came close to default.[27] The rest of Latin America followed. Why? Money was cheap as long as oil exporters had surplus billions to recycle through the banks. When oil prices dropped and interest rates shot up, the combination spelled disaster. Most of Latin America's debt carried a fluctuating interest rate rather than a fixed one. So when the prevailing rate went up, so did the cost of servicing the debt. To make matters worse, the banks changed their tune.

Mexico seemed an isolated case at first. The IMF, after all, had successfully rescued debtor nations before. What turned out to be unprecedented was how quickly the crisis spread. After Mexico, the banks cut off credit everywhere, regardless of a country's past record. Between 1978 and 1981, for example, Latin America took in $50 billion more by way of corporate investments and bank loans than it paid out in profits and interest.[28] This is precisely what economic theory predicts. Rich nations whose banks and businesses have a surplus invest part of it abroad, with a reasonable sum ending up in developing countries. Between 1982 and 1985, however, the region's payments abroad exceeded new loans and investments by over $100 billion.[29] Latin America had turned into a net capital exporter. How was it that investors changed their minds to the detriment of economic theory? They had better fish to fry.

When the debt crisis hit, the United States could smugly reflect on its own apparent solvency. That was before the tally came in on Reaganomics. Congress cut taxes but ignored arithmetic. Propelled by defense spending, the U.S. budget deficit rose from a modest 1.6 percent of GNP in 1979 to 6.3 percent in 1983—a peacetime record. Between 1980 and 1986, the United States spent $1.2 trillion more than it took in as revenue; and the national debt more than doubled: from $914 billion to over $2 trillion.[30] Of course, the U.S. debt was different from Latin America's foreign debt. In the case of the United States, the government owed most of the interest to American citizens, banks, and institutions. So when it paid out interest, it was primarily an in-house distribution.[31] By contrast, Brazil's payments were a net loss; they went outside the country and did not come back. Nonetheless, the interest on the U.S. debt came to $153 billion in 1984, up substantially from the $60 billion paid in 1979.[32] And the comfortable notion that the United States owed the debt to itself was not the truism it used to be. In 1985, foreigners purchased U.S. Treasury securities at a record clip.[33]

Smart money had given up on Latin America and headed for a low-risk place like the USA. In 1981, foreign assets in the United States totaled $580 billion; by the end of 1985, they exceeded $1 trillion.[34] The United States became a debtor nation for the first time since World War I. Foreign ownership of U.S. Treasury securities, stocks and bonds, factories, and real estate exceeded the overseas holdings of American corporations, banks, and individuals.[35] In the meantime, Americans took advantage of an overvalued dollar to stock up on foreign goods. Between 1982 and 1986, the United States amassed a trade deficit of over $500 billion. How much is that? In manufacturing, it takes a million American workers a year to produce $42 billion worth of goods.[36]

Given the ratio of expenditures to tax receipts that prevailed from 1983 to 1985, the federal government collected only 76 cents for every dollar it spent.[37] Given a currency overvalued by 40 percent, Americans purchased a dollar's worth of imports for only 60 cents.[38] We have seen this combination before—it was called Argentine economics.

Catch 22

After 1982, the United States turned debt accumulation into a national monopoly. Latin America could hardly compete when the United States was up for sale. Between 1983 and 1985, capital flight from Mexico, Brazil, and Venezuela came to $30 billion; most of it went to the United States.[39] Latin America faced a contradictory situation that offered no apparent escape. Debt payments drained the region of the capital needed to restore growth, and retrenchment at home drove Latin America's domestic savings abroad. The one bright spot was the region's export surplus.

Like Brazil, other countries devalued their currency, promoted exports, and imposed import restrictions. What had been a small trade deficit for the region in 1981 turned into a $31 billion trade surplus for 1983 and stayed at roughly that level through 1985.[40] Success at last? Not quite. Debt payments claimed almost all of the surplus.[41] To make matters worse, export strategies had serious shortcomings for the 1980s.

The Carter administration's *Global 2000 Report* had predicted shortages in just about everything from raw materials to food and petroleum.[42] That will not happen, at least during the 1980s. Compared to smokestack manufacturing, new industries like microchips, plastics, and fiberglass require much less energy and raw materials for a given unit of output. Even in the automobile industry, plastic has replaced steel at half the cost.[43] The assumption that growth in the industrialized nations increases the demand for raw materials is still true, but the proportionate increment is much reduced.[44] For the 1980s, the trend in commodity prices is down, not only for Mexico's oil, Brazil's iron ore, and Chile's copper, but for most agricultural exports as well.[45] So while Latin America was urged to increase its exports, the value of what most countries had to sell was falling. How then did Latin America manage a surplus? Primarily because it cut imports so drastically. Between 1981 and 1985, Latin America's purchases abroad fell by 40 percent.[46] The region's success was at someone else's expense.

In 1981, U.S. exports to Latin America totaled $39 billion; in 1984, they came to $26 billion, a drop of 44 percent. What had been a $7 billion U.S. trade surplus with Latin America had turned into a $16 billion deficit.[47] Analyzing the fall in U.S. overseas trade, the *Wall Street Journal* noted that half the decline could be explained by the drop in Latin America's purchases. Furthermore, the Commerce Department estimated that every $1 billion lost in foreign trade cost the United States 25,000 jobs. For American workers, the IMF's rescue package subtracted 150,000 jobs from the U.S. economy.[48]

To undo the damage, Congress favored protection for U.S. industries. Applied in Latin America, that prescription would be primarily at Brazil's expense. Not only had Brazil reduced U.S. imports but it also dramatically increased its exports, most notably, manufactured goods. For 1984 and 1985, Brazil's surplus on its U.S. trade totaled $9.3 billion.[49] Consequently, it was on the protection lobby's hit list. But without a huge trade surplus, how could Brazil pay the interest on its debt?

Of the $235 billion Latin America owed to commercial banks in 1986, the largest share was held by U.S. banks: $82 billion or 35 percent of the total.[50] In 1981, for example, the nine largest U.S. banks had 44 percent of their capital in Mexico; its payments made up a third of their profits. In 1983, the interest due from Latin America's three biggest debtors made up 76 percent of the gross earnings for the five biggest U.S. banks.[51] In a pinch, the banks rescheduled interest payments, but they charged higher rates along with commissions and fees. Despite negotiations, the region's debt in 1986 was larger than ever, the banks were still overexposed, and interest payments were still too high.

To reduce the perils of default, banks built up reserves and swapped debt. In Brazil's case, such ploys did not change the balance sheet by much. In 1987, U.S. banks still held a third of Brazil's $67 billion commercial debt. The ten largest creditors had a third of their primary capital committed to Brazil. A default could cost them an estimated 25 percent of their profits.[52]

Latin American countries could not pay except at the risk of domestic strife. To cover interest payments, they had to lower wages, cut budgets, trim the work force, and live on less. The path to payment exacted a high political cost, and military regimes were the first casualties. Although the precise circumstances varied, paying creditors by imposing recession eroded what little support the military retained. Generals abdicated to civilians in Argentina, Brazil, and Uruguay. In democratic countries, IMF austerity discredited and divided governing parties. With few exceptions, the parties identified with recession, whether IMF-inspired or not, lost out in national elections held in Venezuela, Bolivia, Peru, Colombia, and the Dominican Republic.

For Mexico, not even elections provided relief. For half a century, the dominant Institutional Revolutionary Party (PRI) has kept an iron grip on every aspect of the country's life. It never lost an election of any significance. When the PRI applied the IMF's recessionary formula, its credibility disintegrated. To maintain victories at the ballot box required fraud of brutal dimensions. In Mexico, there was no alternative to the PRI.[53]

The Reagan administration finally noticed that bad times in Latin America showed up in U.S. trade statistics. The Treasury Department unveiled a bold plan in 1985: it asked the banks to increase their exposure and lend $20 billion of fresh money over three years. It was not a popular proposal. The banks wanted a way out—they already knew the way in. And south of the border, growth through debt had lost its appeal. As any number of commentators emphasized, plastic surgery would not suffice.[54]

What has to be done is no secret. The debt should be spread out so that payments on the principal fall evenly rather than bunching up, and interest rates have to drop significantly. Simply stated, each country has to remortgage its debt on realistic terms.[55] Brazil, for example, can afford $5 billion a year but not $10 billion; Mexico, $4 billion but not $8 billion. The solution, of course, has its catch. It reduces the book value of the debts due at the expense of the banks. They cannot risk that without guarantees from the U.S. Treasury, which in turn requires cooperation with foreign banks and international agencies. That is not likely compared to the appeal of muddling through.

Mexico at the brink of disaster strikes a bit too close for comfort. Perhaps, in the end, necessity will turn the United States to virtue. That the debt crises "strangles world economic growth," as *Foreign Affairs* put it, is no doubt true.[56] That growth should be restored where it is absent no sane entrepreneur would deny. Recession is unhealthy; no one is in favor of it. Latin America's future is better served by expanding economies, higher wages, and productive industries than by externally imposed austerity. Nonetheless, growth alone does not distribute health care or education, it does not create enough jobs, and it does not bring prosperity to rural families. When development mistakes the superstructure for the foundation, the building shakes with every tremor. For the middle class and industrial workers, opportunity expands along with the economy. For the many left behind, it does not. Both in good times and in bad, there is no substitute for projects that address the needs of people directly.

Brazil in 1986 was committed to social programs paid for with growth. Peru, by contrast, was just as determined, precisely because it had no other prospects. Between 1980 and 1985, per capita income dropped by 15 percent, the prices paid for Peru's commodity exports fell by a third, and its debt rose over 40 percent.[57] Peru had one of the worst income distributions in Latin America: the richest 3 percent had 60 percent of the wealth, the poorest 38 percent had to get by on 2 percent.[58] Half the population was either unemployed or had only part-time work.[59] In the 1985 election the discredited center lost to Alan García, candidate of Peru's Socialist party. Because the rich had already stashed their funds in the United States, García cast his lot with the country's poorer citizens. Peru broke with the IMF and limited debt payments to 10 percent of its export earnings. Because it could no longer borrow for big development projects, Peru retrenched to policies that favored the majority: rural development, self-help housing, community action programs, and public works.[60]

The point is that projects focused on basic development do not depend on growth for their justification. They are not luxuries to be dabbled in only when the world economy delivers prosperity. Solutions cannot wait for the best of times.

Local Knowledge

"The problem with your report," a reviewer warned me, "is that projects depend on local knowledge; you can't base policy on a reality so fragmented and unreliable." He was right; he just had his realities mixed up. Surely he did not mean to juxtapose the alleged fragmentation of a community against the unchangeable verities of the world economy. During the 1980s truth from that vantage point was noticeably difficult to ascertain. The world economy was the kind of place where oil prices dropped 50 percent in ten weeks, where the dollar was overvalued 40 percent one month and humbled before the yen six months later, a world of unpredictable interest rates and computer-driven stock markets, of capital allocated by currency speculation rather than productivity. For Latin America, such externalities had all the certainty of a casino. To find a stable policy-making environment, one had to look somewhere else.

Consider Brazil's case. To offset high oil prices, it invested in the Alcohol Program. If petroleum prices keep falling, the whole scheme could go down the drain. In 1986, Brazil's economy had another year of rapid growth, estimated at 7 percent. But the cruzado plan had failed and triple-digit inflation was back. Expansion had increased domestic demand so fast that Brazil's bill for imports mounted. By year's end, its trade surplus had dropped to $9.5 billion. For 1987, it was expected to fall to $8 billion and Brazil owed $12 billion in interest payments.[61] Brazil was back in the headlines, but it was all bad news. Write about the world economy before breakfast and revisions will be due after dinner.

Compared to the world economy's reliability, the certainties behind a health post have the ring of truth. For a dependable world whose needs were self-evident, Brazil had to look no farther than its own backyard. Brazil itself held the keys to decent health care, literacy, and justice in the countryside, not OPEC or protectionist lobbies in the United States. Clinics, schools, and extension posts are small things, but the problems they address are great and significant. The home place is where the promise of a country's future must first be secured.

• Taxonomy

"I'm pleased you never asked what the best project was," Dr. Mario Chaves remarked. "Projects are at different stages—that's the first thing you have to understand."

Mario had over thirty years' experience as a project evaluator, first for the Pan American and World Health organizations, and later for the Kellogg Foundation. Whenever I was in Rio, I went to his office. One room had project files, the other a desk and working table. Mario never talked from behind his desk; he always went to the work table, pad and pencil in hand. An unhurried, patient man, I had thought at first. But his voice conveyed an urgent sense of the possible and impatience for things undone. I was in his office twenty times, anxious to recount what I had learned; firmly but gently, he turned to things learned less than I had thought.

"We think in linear terms," Mario emphasized: "physician, diagnosis, treatment, and cure. From this standpoint, health care is a service that depends on facilities. As a diagnosis for the Third World, it is at best inadequate, and for the majority it is erroneous. Given public health conditions, the disease pattern is circular. To reduce risks is the hard part, and it requires a community-based approach. Centralization standardizes service, but it does not break the disease cycle. It applies the same strategy everywhere, even though it fits only a limited set of circumstances. The result is an expensive failure.[62]

"Community health projects do have basic features in common: primary care, training and participation, and research. Each component has to be geared to the neighborhoods and communities in question. The rationale is practical, not ideological."

Mario's remarks provide the basis for a project review.

Components

Primary care relied on community members, whether promotoras, midwives, or child health assistants. A health team provided supervision and attended to referrals. Community clinics made health care more accessible on a regular basis, they provided treatment appropriate to the needs of the majority, and they stressed prevention. Because the clinics were responsible for primary care, hospitals could concentrate on patients who required specialized treatment.

A project's first priority was to reduce infant mortality. Maternal-child care was the starting point. In young countries like Colombia and Brazil, women in their reproductive years plus children comprised at least two-thirds of the population. The initial emphasis on maternal-child health was less restrictive than it appeared. The next step was to extend coverage. The Fortaleza project provided an example. Many communities started with small maternity units built for the midwife's use. Later, they replaced these with clinics that made primary care available to the entire community.

"A project's strength," Mario said, "depends on training and community participation. Without it, many services a clinic provides have only a temporary impact. Families have to cope with water that is unsafe, inadequate waste disposal, and uncollected garbage, hazards that increase sharply during the rainy season. The risks can't be reduced unless families take precautions and the community takes appropriate action."

Each report highlighted a specific approach, but the overall objective was the same: to foster community action and self-reliance. All projects, for example, had a training component, whether continuing education for promotoras, first-aid courses for the community, or extension sessions on sanitation and nutrition. The precise tactics, of course, varied. El Valle used its research team to strengthen support for the promotora's work. In Bogotá, neighborhood committees took the lead in organizing public health campaigns. At Sabaneta, the Medellín project trained a collaborator for each block. In Brazil, projects also devised tactics appropriate to their circumstances. The Cotia project trained teachers to be health agents in the schools, whereas the interns in

Northern Minas established the Card Club. At Fortaleza, the project reached into the community by working through midwives and rezadeiras.

From a neighborhood standpoint, training programs made the community more self-reliant. Its own people, clubs, and associations took over responsibility for health promotion and disease prevention. As activities broadened, community members assumed positions as dental technicians, nurse's aides, and vaccination promoters. Expanding coverage was first and foremost a community enterprise based on the clinics.

Whenever Mario steered the conversation to the university I braced myself for a lecture on research. "With so much to be done," I once said, "research much be secondary." "Jaime," he replied, much annoyed, "stop thinking of research as an exercise without application. I'm talking about action research relevant to people and a project's implementation. Surely you can see that a project is also a research strategy, one that is geared to a community's characteristics."

I knew this well enough. The projects designed training manuals, pamphlets, and audiovisual material characterized by their local content. Mario's point, however, went deeper. Projects had to target the diseases and health problems prevalent in particular localities, and they had to evaluate the methods used and their impact. The medical school's role went beyond scheduling internships at health posts; it involved a practical approach to research that had a direct effect on how the project fared. At Fortaleza, Dr. José Galba had to carefully document the project's results before the Health Department provided support. In Northern Minas, medical students tracked health conditions in every town, down to the number of latrines and public water pumps. At Sabaneta, the risk index took into consideration income, housing conditions, and food purchases. The way El Valle strengthened cooperation between the promotora, the health team, and the community was a direct consequence of its innovative approach to research.

"Projects in Colombia and Brazil," Mario noted, "are not unique. For many years the World Health Organization has stressed community action, clinics, and neighborhood health workers.[63] Its objective of 'health for all by the year 2000' was based on successful projects in countries as diverse as Finland, Costa Rica, China, and Cuba.[64] In Latin America, the Pan American Health Organization backed community medicine during the 1970s, which helped counter the trend towards overspecialization. That projects were initiated later by medical schools is not accidental."

Stages

"When a project has worked out a successful approach in one location," Mario emphasized, "it should expand. Otherwise, the result is a small, paternalistic project that stagnates. That community clinics are essential to an effective health system is widely acknowledged, amply demonstrated, and fully documented. The next step has to be a broader application by region."

The special character of the Northern Minas project was how it applied student internships to the needs of an entire region. At Fortaleza, the project had trained midwives in seventeen rural counties. Geographic coverage, however, was only one aspect of a "regional" strategy. It also implied decentralization, that each region drew up and implemented an approach relevant to its circumstances. It suggested a further breakdown into districts, such that the health posts received support from the health centers, which in turn could draw on the specialized treatment available at a local hospital. And finally, it meant training, research, and action undertaken jointly by universities and health departments.

For Brazil, the Fortaleza project came closest to being a regional one. It had district-level referral and supervision, and applied its training programs and extension work comprehensively. Nonetheless, efforts rested on a patchwork of support contracts, some with the state's Health Department, others with the National Health Service. The project's regional character relied more on the staff's ingenuity than it did on the Health Department's commitment. Cotia, by contrast, was a district-level project; in Northern Minas, the Internship Program tried to salvage a regional blueprint the authorities disregarded.

For regional coordination, district-level planning, and research collaboration, the best example was El Valle, in Colombia. What started as a pilot project expanded to an entire province with a population larger than Costa Rica's. Administration was a joint effort that involved both the medical school and the Health Department. Colombian projects expanded in part because of the impact El Valle had on the rest of the country. But it was also a question of politics. In 1975, regionalized health care became national policy. In more democratic Colombia, rural development and community medicine received more support than in authoritarian Brazil, where containment was the regime's policy.

In densely populated urban areas, regions were defined as neighborhoods. The Bogotá project, for example, worked in only one of the city's health regions, but the clinics served a population of over 100,000. The Medellín project started first in Sabaneta, but in 1985 it also included neighboring townships with a combined population of 250,000.[65] In focus, however, they were like the Brazilian project at Cotia; that is, they concentrated on clinics, community action, and family health within a given referral district.

"Projects have to be organized more ambitiously," Mario said, "they have to learn from each other and build on past experience."

At Cartagena, for instance, projects shared results at a conference sponsored by Colombia's Medical Association. Colombia, in fact, has a national project network that El Valle's Center for Health Development helps coordinate. It provides research results, training seminars, and technical assistance that new Colombian projects can draw on. Recent projects at Bucaramanga and Barranquilla gained from El Valle's experience. From the start, they were planned jointly by the medical school and the health department, with regional application an explicit objective.[66]

Brazil did not have a national network in the Colombian sense. Given its size, eight times that of Colombia, a division of labor was more appropriate. When Brazilian projects held conferences, their impact was necessarily regional, but the principles involved were the same: a project's work should be subject to public scrutiny, and valid strategies should be applied to new districts. For application, it was no longer necessary to begin with maternal-child health in a couple of clinics. The basic approach was common knowledge, so a new project could plan broadly from the start. A recent example is the 1985 agreement between the Cotia hospital and the adjoining health district of Itapecerica da Serra. A district-wide clinic network was established with training courses for health workers, community extension, and rotations for physicians. What had taken Cotia ten years to accomplish could be transferred to Itapecerica in three.[67]

"Project expansion by district or region is important," Mario said, "but health is only one aspect of community development. We need alternatives in which health complements work in primary education, job training, and recreation. Given the importance of health, a project's justification can rest on that alone. Still, it leads to an oversimplification. Health is a starting point, but is insufficient by itself."

Some projects crosscut related fields. For rural Fortaleza, family gardens brought agriculture into what was ostensibly a health project. At El Valle, the Community Development Center included technical training. Nonetheless, dissatisfaction lingered. People wanted to get from symptoms to causes, and a health project, no matter how ingenious, was only the first step. That beginning, however, had a tremendous power to transform.

Community health projects had changed the way medical schools trained physicians. Students rotated to clinics and worked with health committees, promotoras, and midwives; they organized extension classes, tracked the incidence of malnutrition, and documented public health conditions. Their workshops consisted of neighborhoods and communities; they learned through action and application. They reconstructed medical practice on a cooperative basis. Health was not a product delivered at the doorstep. It depended more on community action than it did on prescription drugs. Health was something to be done, and the doing had to be a joint venture. Doctors could identify a community's health risks, but the remedy was as much social as medical. Consequently, projects viewed people as active participants rather than passive bystanders. Of necessity they delegated responsibilities, relying on community action to accomplish what good intentions alone could not. The community itself became the means to a partnership strengthened by training programs, health committees, and sanitation campaigns. The common effort a project required gave people a new sense of their own capacities. A project did not just change the statistics, it changed people. And what looked like a health strategy on the surface went much deeper. The way health projects organized their work was precisely the kind of approach needed in education, housing, and job training, and precisely the kind of approach followed in agriculture.

Rural Development

An agricultural project's priority was the small farmer's productivity. Research, training, and community action backed up the work in extension. At Pamplona, agronomists first studied the crops, production techniques, credit, and marketing arrangements that characterized each township; only later did they specify objectives. Local research on soil conditions or on a village's farming practices had to be the starting point for extension. For training, Plan Sierra had its center at Los Montones and extension outposts. Similarly, the Pamplona project had its field-workers stationed in small towns, and the Cacao Center had a network of extension offices. Local groups and cooperatives fostered self-reliance. Plan Sierra, for instance, expected Juncalito's coffee association to pay for an agronomist. At Pamplona, the potato cooperative organized community meetings and training courses.

Projects in health and agriculture thus converged in obvious ways. Both took the differences between localities as a point of departure, they relied on training programs, and results depended on community participation. Joint projects were the logical consequence of such affinities. Plan Sierra was the prime example. The way it organized health extension paralleled the work done in agriculture. When coffee growers attended credit sessions at Los Montones, family health was on the agenda. When women attended health sessions, they also learned about the credit program.

A joint project had a reinforcing character. By itself, a health project had only a limited capacity to alter a community's circumstances. Allied to agriculture, however, nutrition could improve dramatically as families planted gardens, set up fish tanks, or kept chickens. Cheaper credit, higher crop yields, and cooperative marketing increased family incomes, making latrines and water filters basic purchases rather than luxury items. My report emphasized the work at Plan Sierra, but convergence took place elsewhere. In Minas Gerais, for example, the Rural Internship Program teamed up with the Montes Claros Agricultural School in 1985. Food production and technical assistance now complement community health.[68] In Colombia, a recent project in Caldas Province combined extension work in agriculture, public health, and primary education, as did two projects I visited in Northeast Brazil.

My report shortchanged the joint project. That extension could be tailored to a small farm seemed obvious. In the United States, land-grant universities have long operated on this principle. The report showed how extension worked in the Latin American context. Once clarified at Plan Sierra and Pamplona, the logic needed little elaboration. The Cacao Center provided a Brazilian example of comparable dimensions. Of course, the benefits to smaller producers had more to do with cacao's characteristics than the regime's. Nonetheless, I visited Brazilian projects similar to Plan Sierra although on a much smaller scale. What the reader missed was animal husbandry applied to goat herding, household cheese production, and small-scale irrigation.

If Brazil wants projects of the Plan Sierra type, it has examples of its own. And it could draw on experience elsewhere. The Inter-American Institute for Cooperation on Agriculture worked on projects throughout the continent, Pamplona's rural development program (DRI) being but one example. Latin America also had a network of international research centers. In Colombia, the Center for Tropical Agriculture specialized in cassava, beans, and rice. Peru had the International Potato Center. In Costa Rica, the Agricultural Center for Applied Research concentrated on cropping systems, reforestation, and milk production geared to small farms. Latin American countries could find examples of successful projects in their own backyard, and research to back it up.[69]

The appeal an agricultural project had was that it dealt with causes directly. For small farmers who lacked funds and technical support, credit and extension provided solutions. Well managed, a credit program even paid for itself. For marketing, Pamplona had a potato cooperative; at Plan Sierra, the gandul crop went to Monción's canning factory. In Bahia, the Cacao Center helped farmers replace old trees with better varieties, and it backed joint marketing. Whether Pamplona's fish tanks, Plan Sierra's family cow, or the Cacao Center's job training, the projects reached some of the poorest families.

Agricultural projects had results one could see. At Plan Sierra, reforestation with coffee trees reduced erosion and helped farmers at the same time. Likewise, the Cacao Center's work countered the conversion of shade forests to pasture land. The Pamplona project could measure success in potatoes, carrots, and onions. Of course, they had their limitations. None of them supervised land distribution, although they had sufficient experience in credit and extension to make land reform a productive proposition. Plan Sierra's health program was reasonably successful. At Pamplona, by contrast, the Health Department kept its prior autonomy, making few concessions to community action. It had clinics, but not a strategy for health promotion. The Cacao Center branched out into technical education, but its basic mission remained production.

Agricultural projects had a validity that was easy to understand. The Dominican Republic, Colombia, and Brazil needed increased food production for a growing population. Small farmers favored staple crops like beans, manioc, corn, and fresh vegetables. All three countries still had at least a third of their labor force in agriculture. Continued migration at rates comparable to the past spelled disaster, for the jobs available in the cities had fallen dangerously short of employment needs. Rural development promoted food crops, reduced urban migration, and increased a household's income. Small-scale production was also labor-intensive. For millions of families, agriculture was the only employment opportunity left.

An agricultural project dealt with big problems in miniature. Still, even with credit and technical assistance, a family with 10 hectares of potatoes is not in the market for a Maytag. For shoes, clothing, bicycles, and radios, however, a rise in disposable income makes a difference. And these are the manufactured goods that are still relatively labor-intensive and create jobs in the cities. Add to this assorted tools, containers, pesticide applicators, and farm equipment, and what at first is a production strategy has its consumption aspect as well. The small farm, in fact, does not preclude the tractor. In Costa Rica, cooperatives rotated machinery among their members for plowing and harvesting.

Compared to high-tech industries, where the jobs created and the income distributed benefited the affluent, agricultural projects were inexpensive and generated income where it was most needed. In Latin America, agriculture can still yield returns for the majority.

Solutions

At Plan Sierra, one trip with Iván Scarfullery gave me twenty pages on coffee production and reforestation. During an afternoon with César Villamizar at Pamplona, I learned about the potato crop and credit. Terraced fields, nurseries, and cooperatives conveyed accomplishments.

A health project, by contrast, countered adverse conditions in only a limited way. After a morning with Lucía Laverde in Bogotá, I had notes on rabid animals, rats, and garbage. Work was a community affair, but it did not change a family's income. Whether in Minuto de Dios, Sabaneta, or Venda Nova, the struggle seemed endless and inconclusive.

For these reasons, I spent more time at health projects. They acted on principles very different from my own assumptions about poverty. I wanted solutions on a large scale that could be applied immediately. To me, a valid social program left behind not a single hungry child, illiterate adult, or jobless worker. Because that had not happened, the world was wrong and had to be set straight. To do that required a frontal attack on global inequality. This event was highly unlikely, but my theories often disregarded probability. I explained myself in more or less these terms to Dr. Alfredo Aguirre in Cali. "The only flaw I detect," he said, "is that you analyze the problem so as to preclude a solution. Better to forget solutions and work on problems."

That solutions must come in big packages is a premise so ingrained it is hard to counteract. If a country has "infrastructure bottlenecks," it sends in the engineers. The result is superhighways, telephone lines, and dredged harbors.

For depression there is always a New Deal, for entertainment there is TV, for intelligence there is the IQ. Modern life gives us a pattern, from designer jeans to the weight of our hamburgers. Whether New Yorkers or São Paulo sophisticates, we are standardized models. This is not a complaint, just an observation about disparate facets of daily life. The question is this. What happens when the penchant for big solutions and standard-gauge track does not fit the problem? What if the projects are right? It is worth considering.

My friend, Dr. Jimmy Sullivan, put it bluntly: "They would accomplish more twice as fast with sewers and chlorinated water." That is absolutely correct. No project health worker ever denied it. The reality, however, was different. Brazil's regime put roads through the rain forest, not sewage systems in favelas. That being the case, projects had to foster civic action and local participation. Promoting public health meant strengthening the community and distributing responsibilities. This was accomplished without the kind of incentive credit provided in agriculture. At harvest time, a potato farmer could tally up his results. For a health project, the effects of water filters, latrines, and lactation were not so easily demonstrated. The impact maternal-child care had on infant mortality took more than a season to register. As to motivation, health projects could not offer higher family incomes. Nonetheless, they worked out methods that were as ingenious as they were practical. And they made sense to the families, neighborhoods, and communities involved. Projects simplified things, reshaping how medicine, dentistry, and nursing were applied.

A project put people to work doing what needed to be done. At the clinic, community members handled health care, kept records, made home visits, promoted vaccinations, and provided first aid. In rural areas, midwives delivered children and rezadeiras helped control dysentery. The community itself took over services, relying as little as possible on outsiders. Training programs added to the skills the community had. Health teams rotated to the clinics, but they had ample backup. For every doctor, the community had five health workers of various types.

The approach taken had far-reaching implications: that development, like health, was not something done to people, but something people did for themselves. Health care acquired a name and a face in the community. How to adapt the principle to other aspects of a community's welfare was the question, and projects had some tentative answers. That the approach applied in agriculture we already know—even urban projects introduced the vegetable garden. Across the bay from Rio in Niteroi, health projects had day-care centers managed by block clubs. When I revisited the project in 1986, it included seven rural counties. Its work was no longer confined to health. Primary education and technical assistance were of equal importance. At Juiz de Fora in Minas Gerais, clinics had expanded into community centers. University rotations applied not only in health but also in physical education, teaching, and engineering. What started as a health project ended up with a youth program, technical training, and kindergartens. Engineers, for example, helped neighborhoods reroute drainage ditches and design soccer fields. When I visited the project with Dr. Gothardo Granato in 1984, a strike had closed down the university indefinitely. At the community centers, however, students kept to their rotations. In Buenos Aires, projects included cooperative housing in which families worked on construction and thus reduced costs.

From the solid base that work in health provided, projects added new characteristics relevant to the community's welfare. Whether athletics, drainage ditches, or day-care centers, such efforts brought new recruits, and not just in the community. When engineers enlisted for rotations, they worked with the same orientation that applied to health. A drainage ditch had to respect both squatters' rights and gravity, and that required the kind of compromise only reached at community meetings. Projects changed the mentality of participants, and that had consequences not only in neighborhoods but also in professional schools.

When I asked if the projects were right, I meant whether they were right about development. Forget superhighways and computerized data banks. Neither Brazil nor the United States will let its highways deteriorate. Countries will get their Itaipús and Saturn plants come what may. The projects considered a different type of problem, one that corporate and state enterprise left untouched. In poor neighborhoods, statistics on GNP are meaningless abstractions. Development has to have a face people can recognize, and, most of all, people have to recognize each other. In Fortaleza, communities built clinics because they respected the midwife's role in childbirth. At Plan Sierra and Pamplona, farmers participated because friends and neighbors had done so to advantage. Projects took the everyday world of people as their starting point. This made them small-change affairs.

For modern times this is not satisfactory. We expect results of the instant variety: just add water and shake. When the roads go bad in the United States, Congress jacks up the gasoline tax and it all takes care of itself. The problems in poor neighborhoods, whether in Colombia or the United States, are less tractable. This is not to deny the importance of public sanitation and food supplements. They are antidotes to some of the worst conditions. As solutions, however, they are only a down payment. The United States is exemplary in this respect. Despite a safety net of food stamps, public health standards, and income subsidies, the ranks of the poor have not dwindled.

Although not opposed to standard features of a U.S.-type safety net, the projects I visited had a different vision. They defined development as the steps communities could take on their own behalf. People learned by doing. Projects started on a small scale, worked out an approach people understood, and then expanded. The lesson was that a country needed more than a health budget or funds for credit. It needed local organizations with a plan for action that brought results.

Plan Sierra needed funds for credit, training, and technical assistance. Health projects had a budget for supervision, community education, and support for the clinics. Projects, however, took a decentralized approach to spending money. At Pamplona, the budget came from the production plans of each township. In El Valle, the budget each health region submitted depended on the work done at the clinics. With centralized agencies, by contrast, funds follow the most expedient path, ignorant of which regions and districts match words with deeds.

Projects did not have five-year plans to banish poverty by decree. But they knew how to get things done: at El Rubio and Juncalito, at Roldanillo and Pamplona, at Cotia and Fortaleza. Neighborhoods organized civic groups, farmers joined associations, and women formed clubs. This is not income maintenance, but it is self-respect. The vision of development projects had was putting people to work on behalf of what they valued most: the health of their children, their crops, training, recreation, and better housing. Projects got results because they learned as much as they taught.

Big development considers the state an ally. Governments invest in petroleum exploration, build dams, and give new industries a tax break. Projects operated on a different premise. Whatever merit the state had as entrepreneur, it was not considered a dependable agent locally. Excessive centralization stifled the originality and participation that projects thrived on. Problems had to be narrowed down to specific districts and addressed within a community context; this was a project's strength, and precisely where centralized agencies came up short. As to growth, whether around the corner or not, it was simply irrelevant. So far it had not appeared in the favela, and that was the point.

• Home Again

Between 1981 and 1985, the United States spent over a trillion dollars on defense. That is enough to support a thousand projects for a thousand years.[70] The "necessary evil" is a truth the United States has learned to accept. That humiliation and misery are dangerous ways to build the future is a truth it argues about. Are the poor "good" or "bad"? Are they "lazy" or just "disadvantaged"?

We can manage collaboration in the national interest. Suppose we want Star Wars. Physics departments enter the research lineup, congressmen forget budget deficits, and defense contractors rally with wrenches at $600 apiece. On our farms, we have combined research and extension on behalf of productivity for decades, an approach that has involved land-grant colleges, the

Department of Agriculture, and local 4-H clubs. No problem. But talk about unemployment, functional literacy, or families below the poverty line and we lose our way. Pepsi and Coke know more about their patrons than the Labor Department does about the unemployed. Since my days in Vista, we have had a war on poverty under Johnson, benign neglect under Nixon, milk toast under Carter, and soup lines under Reagan. If IBM changed research and development strategies every time the U.S. government changed social policies, we would still be using the slide rule. We lavish our talents on the defense arsenal, hybrid corn, and Coke. We do not treat job training or substandard schools with equal determination.

According to the Census Bureau, the U.S. poverty rate dropped from 15.3 percent of the population in 1983 to 14.4 percent in 1984. On the basis of nine-tenths of a percentage point, the president congratulated the "free enterprise system." A White House aide called the figures a "triumph." "American capitalism," he said, "is the greatest machine ever designed for bringing people out of poverty."[71] What happened to those defined as poor in 1983 who found themselves out of statistical poverty in 1984? Did they move to suburban townhouses, outfit the kids in designer jeans, or buy new Toyotas? We all know they did not. We are talking about some marginal income soaked up by Krogers and auto repair shops.

In 1984, the United States had 34 million people below the poverty line: a Third World nation the size of Colombia within its boundaries. Disproportionately, they were children. For the United States overall, 25 percent of its children under six lived in households that got by on a poverty-level income.[72] In rural counties the number of poor families increased 40 percent between 1979 and 1983; the infant mortality rate (1983) was 16 per 1,000, compared to 11 per 1,000 in urban counties. Malnutrition was twice as high; 7 percent of rural children had deficient diets that stunted their growth.[73] In 1986, the Department of Education released the results of a Census Bureau test: 13 percent of the adult population was not functionally literate; young adults did worse than their elders. A prior study conducted by the University of Texas found that 22 percent of adults could not address an envelope so as to ensure delivery.[74] Between 1980 and 1985, unemployment averaged over 8 percent, the worst record since the Great Depression.[75] The jobs added to the economy paid less, and bunched up in low-productivity industries and services. Income distribution had deteriorated. In 1985, it was the most inequitable recorded since the Census Bureau started to keep track in 1947.[76]

Growth alone has not retired Brazil's social debt, and it will not retire ours. The "Great Machine" has accomplishments to its credit, but, when it comes to America's social agenda, it cannot do the work for us. Just as the Dominican Republic needs a Plan Sierra to invest in the future of its poorer citizens, so does the United States. We do have a safety net. But food stamps and welfare, however generous, are stopgap measures; they are not the building blocks of self-respect. To reduce America's social policies to budget debates over food stamps is counterproductive and demeaning.

Assorted programs applied piecemeal to a passive clientele have not been successful. The job for the poor is to work on problems of their own neighborhoods and communities, to work on an agenda they help set, to work on a project that makes training, health, housing, and recreation part of a common effort. America's cities and townships might accomplish more with small-scale pilot projects and community-based development.

I once asked Hernando Linero what his experience at Pamplona had taught him about development. He answered without hesitation, "Get to work and cut the crap." And I think Alfredo Aguirre is right too, that we have to stop defining problems so as to preclude solutions.

"Nobody cares," my friend Russ Carpenter used to warn me. In 1986, the 4.5 million Americans who paid $10 apiece to join hands against hunger did. If Colombia's barrios and Brazil's favelas are any indication, the poor may have more children than the rich, but they love them just as much. Why not start with the simple truth of Estevão, give it equal time, a face, and hands to do the work "God's greatness and man's goodness" have called us forth to do? Against evil cloaked in necessity there is a universe whose promise does not come by itself.

— NOTES

PREFACE

1. John Gunther, *Inside Latin America* (New York: Harper & Brothers, 1941), p. 11.
2. Elizabeth Hardwick, "The Teller and the Tape," *New York Review of Books*, 30 May 1985, p. 6.
3. See Albert O. Hirschman, "Out of Phase Again," *New York Review of Books*, 18 December 1986, pp. 53–57.
4. For this approach, see Michael M. Cernea, ed., *Putting People First: Sociological Variables in Rural Development* (New York: World Bank, Oxford University Press, 1985), and Warren C. Baum and Stokes M. Tolbert, *Investing in Development: Lessons of World Bank Experience* (New York: World Bank, Oxford University Press, 1985).

CHAPTER I

1. *Latin American Regional Report: Caribbean*, 10 May 1985, p. 5.
2. For the age structure, growth rate, and total population of the Dominican Republic, see *República Dominicana en Cifras 1985* (Santo Domingo: Oficina Nacional de Estadística, 1985), pp. 59, 76, 62. For the U.S. age structure, see *Statistical Abstract of the United States: 1986*, 106th ed. (Washington, D.C.: U.S. Bureau of the Census, 1985), p. 26.
3. World Bank, *Dominican Republic: Its Main Economic Development Problems* (Washington, D.C.: World Bank, 1978), pp. i–iii, 53–58, 61–63. GNP expansion slowed to an average of 4 percent between 1975 and 1981;

277

see World Bank, *Dominican Republic: Economic Prospects and Policies to Renew Growth* (Washington, D.C.: World Bank, 1985), pp. 1–3.

4. The estimate is for 1970. See World Bank, *Main Economic Development Problems*, data sheet, p. 1.

5. Ibid., p. 10.

6. World Bank, *World Development Report 1985* (New York: Oxford University Press, 1985), pp. 218–19.

7. World Bank, *World Development Report 1983* (New York: Oxford University Press, 1983), p. 190.

8. World Bank, *Main Economic Development Problems*, pp. 54–57. Figures on debt and GNP expansion are from Comisión Económica para América Latina y El Caribe (CEPAL), "Balance preliminar de la economía Latinoamericana 1985," *Notas Sobre la Economía y el Desarrollo*, no. 424/425 (December 1985): 17, 11.

9. World Bank, *Main Economic Development Problems*, p. 152; World Bank, *Economic Prospects*, p. 127.

10. For sugar prices, see James W. Wilkie and Adam Perkal, eds., *Statistical Abstract of Latin America* (Los Angeles: UCLA Latin American Center Publications, University of California, 1984), 23:503 (hereafter cited as *SALA*), and "Dominican Republic—Current Situation," mimeographed (U.S. Embassy, Santo Domingo, 17 April 1985), p. 3. On sugar's contribution to Dominican exports, see *SALA* (1984), 23:633. For sugar's declining share of the sweetener market, see *Nashville Tennessean*, 27 August 1985, p. 7-B.

11. Yearly interest rates are listed in *SALA* (1984), 23:507.

12. On urban-rural differences and agriculture's poor performance during the 1970s, see World Bank, *Main Economic Development Problems*, pp. 12–13, 19–23, 27. For rural unemployment and underemployment, see ibid., pp. iii, 10.

13. Ibid., p. 153; World Bank, *Economic Prospects*, p. 127.

14. World Bank, *Main Economic Development Problems*, p. 31.

15. On the country's hydroelectric development, see ibid., pp. 46–49, and World Bank, *Economic Prospects*, pp. 78–81. For food and fuel as a percentage of total exports, see World Bank, *World Development Report 1985*, p. 194.

16. For the number of families that rely on firewood and the Dominican Republic's wood imports, see "Propuesta para el plan de desarrollo global de la Sierra," mimeographed (Plan Sierra, San José de las Matas, 1982), p. 4. The document likewise cites statistics on dam sedimentation; see pp. 3–5.

17. The World Bank's most recent report notes the fragmented character of the countries' rural agencies; see *Economic Prospects*, pp. 81–83.

18. To be more precise, program supervisors were either agronomists with a

university degree or technicians with a diploma from an agro-technical high school. At Plan Sierra, the distinction did not mean much in practice, so I have not introduced it. The project's basic approach is outlined in Blas Santos, "Una experiencia de desarrollo rural en las montañas de la República Dominicana," mimeographed (Plan Sierra, San José de las Matas, 1980), pp. 1–21.

19. "Propuesta para el plan de desarrollo," p. 18.
20. Ibid., p. 10.
21. See Ramón Almonte, "Unos 300 mil quintales de yuca están a punto de perderse en la zona Sierra," mimeographed (Plan Sierra, San José de las Matas, 1983), pp. 1–2.
22. See "El rol de la mujer en el logro de los objetivos del Plan Sierra," mimeographed (Plan Sierra, San José de las Matas, 1982).
23. For a summary of the health program, see "Sierra Project Health Program," mimeographed (Plan Sierra, San José de las Matas, 1981).
24. See World Bank, *Economic Prospects*, p. 38.
25. See "The Dominican Republic: Foreign Economic Trends and Their Implications for the United States," mimeographed (U.S. Embassy, Santo Domingo, 1984), p. 8.
26. For a discussion of the sugar industry, see World Bank, *Main Economic Development Programs*, pp. 36–46.
27. Margot Hornblower, "Price Riots Imperil Dominican Government," *Washington Post*, 30 April 1984, xeroxed (Information Service on Latin America [ISLA], April 1984, p. 220).
28. The 1986 unemployment rate is noted in Guy Gugliotto, "Hope Replaces Fear in Dominican Vote," *Miami Herald*, 6 May 1986, xeroxed (ISLA, May 1986, p. 189).
29. María Elena Núñez, "La película E.T. establece record de recaudación taquillera," *El Caribe*, 13 January 1983, p. 1-A.

CHAPTER 2

1. Colombian Information Service (CIS), "Colombian Census of 1985," *Colombia Today* 21, no. 8 (1986): 1.
2. On the formation of party identity in the nineteenth century, see Helen Delpar, *Red Against Blue: The Liberal Party in Colombian Politics, 1863–1899* (University, Ala.: The University of Alabama Press, 1981). The persistence of party loyalty and how it crosscuts occupational groups is discussed in Jonathan Hartlyn, *The Politics of Coalition Rule: The Colombian National Front and Its Aftermaths* (Cambridge: At the University Press). Forthcoming.
3. On *La Violencia*, see Paul Oquist, *Violence, Conflict and Politics in*

Colombia (New York: Academic Press, 1980). For an overview of the National Front and its impact, see Albert Berry, Ronald G. Hellman, and Mauricio Solaún, eds., *Politics of Compromise: Coalition Government in Colombia* (New Brunswick, N.J.: Transaction Books, 1980); see also Hartlyn, *Politics of Coalition Rule.*

4. The 1970–80 growth rate is an estimate compiled from World Bank, *Brazil: Economic Development and Policy under Changing Conditions* (Washington, D.C.: World Bank, 1984), p. 9; for the composition of Colombia's exports, see p. 174.

5. Brazil's 1970–80 growth rate is an estimate compiled from World Bank, *Brazil: Industrial Policies and Manufactured Exports* (Washington, D.C.: World Bank, 1983), p. 5; for the composition of Brazil's exports, see World Bank, *Brazil: Economic Memorandum* (Washington, D.C.: World Bank, 1984), p. 254.

6. Samuel A. Morely, *Labor Markets and Inequitable Growth: The Case of Authoritarian Capitalism in Brazil* (Cambridge: At the University Press, 1982), pp. 233–65. For Brazil's income distribution, see text, Table 5.4.

7. See Miguel Urrutia, *Winners and Losers in Colombia's Economic Growth of the 1970s* (New York: World Bank, Oxford University Press, 1985), pp. 52, 130–31.

8. The comparative figures on education are from Oscar Altimir, "Poverty in Latin America: A Review of Concepts and Data," *CEPAL Review* 13 (1981): 74. That Colombia was still ahead of Brazil is suggested by data from Magdalena, one of Colombia's poorest provinces. For the cohort that entered the first grade in 1972, 30 percent made it to the fifth grade. By comparison, for a 1978 cohort from Maranhão, one of Brazil's poorest states, only 18 percent ended up in the fifth grade. See Hernando Gómez-Buendia y Rodrigo Losada-Lora, *Organización y conflicto: La educación primaria oficial en Colombia* (Bogotá: Centro Internacional de Investigaciones para el Desarrollo, 1984), p. 55. For Brazil, see *Anuário Estatístico do Brasil—1980* (Rio de Janeiro: Fundação Instituto Brasileiro de Geografia e Estatística, 1981), p. 217, and *Anuário* (1984), p. 261.

9. For a discussion of how education influences fertility, see World Bank, *Population Change and Economic Development* (New York: World Bank, Oxford University Press, 1984). For comparative figures on the rate of population growth and infant mortality, see World Bank, *World Development Report 1986* (New York: World Bank, Oxford University Press, 1986), pp. 233, 231. In 1974, the estimated coverage on piped water, sewerage, and electricity for urban households in Colombia was 89, 80, and 92 percent respectively; see Marcelo Selowsky, *Who Benefits from Government Expenditures: A Case Study of Colombia* (New York: World Bank, Oxford University Press, 1979), pp. 171, 173, 170. Six years later, the comparable figures for Brazil were still below Colombia. Urban cover-

age on piped water, sewerage, and electricity stood at 76, 57, and 88 percent respectively; see World Bank, *Brazil: Economic Memorandum*, pp. 129, 306.

10. Comisión Económica para América Latina y El Caribe (CEPAL), "Balance preliminar de la economía Latinoamericana 1985," *Notas Sobre la Economía y el Desarrollo*, no. 424/425 (December 1985): 17.

11. World Bank, *Colombia: Economic Development*, p. 2.

12. This particular formulation is based on remarks by Fernando Cepeda Ulloa at an international conference on "Political and Economic Change" held at Vanderbilt University in November 1983.

13. For Colombia, see Selowsky, *Who Benefits*, p. 146; for Brazil, see World Bank, *A Review of Agricultural Policies in Brazil* (Washington, D.C.: World Bank, 1982), pp. 22–24.

14. In 1984, the respective figures were 48 per 1,000 (Colombia), 68 (Brazil), 19 (Costa Rica), and 16 (Cuba); see World Bank, *World Development Report 1986*, p. 233.

15. For Colombia, see Urrutia, *Winners and Losers*, p. 89; for Mexico, see World Bank, *World Development Report 1986*, p. 227; for Brazil, see text, Table 5.4.

16. A survey of low-income households conducted in Cali in 1970 and 1980 showed a dramatic improvement in public services and housing quality; see Urrutia, *Winners and Losers*, pp. 62-64. For Brazil, even optimistic forecasts were disappointing; see Peter T. Knight and Ricardo Moran, *Brazil: Poverty and Basic Needs* (Washington, D.C.: World Bank, 1981), pp. 81-84.

17. See Richard B. Craig, "Domestic Implications of Illicit Colombian Drug Production and Trafficking," *Journal of Interamerican Studies and World Affairs* 25 (1983): 325-50.

18. See E. J. Hobsbawm, "Murderous Colombia," *New York Review of Books*, 20 November 1986, pp. 27–30, 35.

19. For Colombia's 1970 population, see James W. Wilkie and Adam Perkal, eds., *Statistical Abstract of Latin America* (Los Angeles: UCLA Latin American Center Publications, University of California, 1984), 23:107 (hereafter cited as *SALA*). Figures on the country's age structure and the 1985 population are from CIS, "Colombian Census," p. 3. For the United States, see *Statistical Abstract of the United States: 1986*, 106th ed. (Washington, D.C.: U.S. Bureau of the Census, 1985), pp. 5–6 (hereafter cited as *SAUS*).

20. *SAUS* (1986), p. 39.

21. Rakesh Mohan and Nancy Hartline, *The Poor of Bogotá: Who They Are, What They Do, and Where They Live*, World Bank Staff Working Papers, no. 635 (Washington, D.C.: World Bank, 1984), p. 9. The study is based on data collected in 1977.

22. The infant mortality rates for Colombia and the United States are from World Bank, *World Development Report 1986*, p. 233. Mortality data by age for selected health districts in Bogotá are for 1977 and are taken from "Programa de atención integral en salud en área urbana," mimeographed (Programa de Atención Materno Infantil [PAMI], Bogotá, 1983), p. 27. On the contrasting disease profiles between developed and underdeveloped countries, see World Bank, *Health: Sector Policy Paper*, 2nd ed. (Washington, D.C.: World Bank, 1980), pp. 5–19; for comparisons between the United States and Colombia, see *SALA* (1984), 23:162–63. The contribution infant mortality made to the U.S. death rate is compiled from *SAUS* (1981), p. 58.

23. World Bank, *Population Change and Economic Development*, p. 179; CIS, "Colombian Census," pp. 1, 5.

24. See Richard G. Feachem et al., *Sanitation and Disease: Health Aspects of Excreta and Waste Management* (New York: World Bank, John Wiley & Sons, 1983), pp. 3–20. See also World Bank, *Health*, p. 13.

25. World Bank, *Health*, p. 15.

26. World Bank, *World Development Report 1986*, p. 233.

27. Urrutia, *Winners and Losers*, p. 87.

28. Eduardo Wiesner Durán, Chief of Mission, *Finanzas intergubernamentales en Colombia* (Bogotá: Departamento Nacional de Planeación, 1981), pp. 153–62. On fiscal federalism, see World Bank, *Colombia: Economic Development*, pp. 77–84; on health specifically, see pp. 81, 83–84.

29. For the U.S. figure, see Andrew Hacker, ed., *U/S: A Statistical Portrait of the American People* (New York: Viking, 1983), p. 244.

30. On the growth of Bogotá, see Rakesh Mohan, *The People of Bogotá: Who They Are, What They Earn, Where They Live*, World Bank Staff Working Papers, no. 390 (Washington, D.C.: World Bank, 1980), p. 30, and CIS, "Colombian Census," p. 1. Figures on the percentage of the urban population in each country's largest city are from, World Bank, *Population Change*, pp. 178–79.

31. "Bogotá: Una ciudad de nadie," *El Tiempo*, 12 June 1983, p. 3-B.

32. Figures on population, family size, coverage, infant mortality, and malnutrition within the project area are noted in PAMI, "Programa de atención," pp. 7–10, 26, 32.

33. Guzmán Barrera, *Lactancia natural: Una revisión de conceptos* (Bogotá: Asociación Colombiana de Facultades de Medicina [ASCOFAME], 1980), pp. 5–9.

34. Mohan and Hartline, *Poor of Bogotá*, p. 6.

35. Marcelo Selowsky, *Who Benefits from Government Expenditures? A Case Study of Colombia* (New York: World Bank, Oxford University Press, 1979), p. 173.

36. The 1960 estimate is based on a population of 15.4 million, approximately 48 percent urban. See *SALA* (1984), 23:107; World Bank, *Population Change and Economic Development*, p. 179. For population growth rates, see CIS, "Colombian Census," p. 4.

37. For an example, see Urrutia, *Winners and Losers*, pp. 62–64.

38. Nestor Diez M. et al., "Características generales del Municipio de Sabaneta," mimeographed (Instituto de Ciencias de la Salud [CES], Medellín, 1982), pp. 19–20, 31, 44–45, 63–64.

39. CES, "Definiciones, normas y procedimientos para la elaboración de la historia de salud familiar," mimeographed (CES, Sabaneta, 1982), pp. 1–100.

40. CES, "Subprograma de Colaboradores Familiares de Salud," mimeographed (CES, Sabaneta, 1982), pp. 1–5.

41. On Colombia's oil production and the GNP growth for 1975–81, see World Bank, *Colombia: Economic Development*, pp. 180, 3; for balance of trade figures, see *SALA* (1984), 23:535, and CEPAL, "Balance preliminar," p. 16. The growth rates for 1982–83 are also from CEPAL, "Balance preliminar," p. 11.

42. *El Colombiano*, 28 May 1983, pp. 1E–2E.

43. *El Tiempo*, 13 May 1983, p. 1-D; 23 May 1983, p. 1–2-E. In the case of textiles, exchange rates and the tariff on imported fabrics affected the industry more than the alleged "high taxes on production." See David Morawetz, *Why the Emperor's New Clothes Are Not Made in Colombia* (New York: World Bank, Oxford University Press, 1981).

44. *SALA* (1984), 23:133; CIS, "Colombian Census," p. 5.

45. See Durán, *Finanzas intergubernamentales*, pp. 158, 160.

46. Fundación para la Educación Superior (FES), "Una estrategia para la participación del sector privado en el desarrollo," mimeographed (FES, Cali, 1983), pp. 12–13, 1–30.

47. Grupo Asesor para la Educación (GAPE), "Proyecto para el diseño metodológico de educación continuada para Promotoras de Salud: Resultados de la primera fase investigativa," mimeographed (GAPE, Cali, 1980), pp. 1–56.

48. GAPE, "Diseño metodológico de educación continuada para Promotoras Rurales de Salud," mimeographed (GAPE, Cali, 1981), pp. 1–36.

49. Rejection of the hospital is not so characteristic of urban areas.

50. The GNP figure for Colombia is for 1982—see World Bank, *Colombia: Economic Development*, p. xiii; the U.S. figure is for 1984—see *SAUS* (1986), p. 431.

CHAPTER 3

1. See Albert Berry, ed., *Essays on Industrialization in Colombia* (Tempe: Center for Latin American Studies, Arizona State University, 1983), p. 31; Luiz Bresser Pereira, *Development and Crisis in Brazil, 1930–1933* (Boulder, Colo.: Westview Press, 1984), p. 22.

2. Inter-American Development Bank (IDB), *Economic and Social Progress in Latin America, 1986 Report* (Washington, D.C.: IDB, 1986), p. 125.

3. For an excellent overview of the region's agrarian policies, see Merilee S. Grindle, *State and Countryside: Development Policy and Agrarian Politics in Latin America* (Baltimore: Johns Hopkins University Press, 1986). See also Gerson Gomes and Antonio Pérez, "The Process of Modernization in Latin American Agriculture," *CEPAL Review* 8 (1979): 55–74.

4. Compiled from the rates in Luis López Cordovez, "Trends and Recent Changes in the Latin American Food and Agricultural Situation," *CEPAL Review* 16 (1982): 14.

5. Joint Agricultural Division, "The Agriculture of Latin America: Changes, Trends, and Outlines of Strategy," *CEPAL Review* 27 (1985): 121.

6. On the growth of the seasonal work force, see Carmen A. Miró and Daniel Rodríquez, "Capitalism and Population in Latin American Agriculture," *CEPAL Review* 16 (1982): 51–71.

7. IDB, *Economic and Social Progress 1986*, p. 125.

8. López Cordovez, "Trends and Recent Changes," p. 27; IDB, *Economic and Social Progress 1986*, p. 127.

9. Joint Agricultural Division, "Agriculture of Latin America," p. 120.

10. IDB, *Economic and Social Progress 1986*, p. 125.

11. López Cordovez, "Trends and Recent Changes," p. 14.

12. Ibid., pp. 37–38. See also Manuel Figueroa L., "Rural Development and Urban Food Programming," *CEPAL Review* 25 (1985): 111–27.

13. López Cordovez, "Trends and Recent Changes," p. 20.

14. Ibid., p. 26.

15. On falling per-capita food production, see IDB, *Economic and Social Progress 1986*, p. 74, and Joint Agricultural Division, "Agriculture of Latin America," pp. 121–22.

16. See Eugene Havens, William L. Flinn, and Susan Lastarria Cornhill, "Agrarian Reform and the National Front: A Class Analysis," in Albert Berry, Ronald G. Hellman, and Mauricio Solaún, eds., *Politics of Compromise: Coalition Government in Colombia* (New Brunswick, N.J.: Transaction Books, 1980), p. 357.

17. Salomón Kalmanovits, *Desarrollo de la agricultura en Colombia* (Bogotá: Editor La Carreta, 1978), pp. 73–78, 106–7. See also M. Taussig, "Peasant Economies and the Development of Capitalist Agriculture in the Cauca Valley, Colombia," *Latin American Perspectives* 18 (1978): 62–91.

18. Efforts to modernize coffee production are discussed in Marco Palacios, *Coffee in Colombia 1850–1970: An Economic, Social, and Political History* (Cambridge: At the University Press, 1980), pp. 231–58.
19. For the figures on rice production, see IDB, *Economic and Social Progress 1986*, p. 115. On the benefits, see Grant M. Scobie and Rafael Posada, "The Impact of Technical Change on Income Distribution: The Case of Rice in Colombia," *American Journal of Agricultural Economics* 60 (1978): 85–92.
20. See Merilee S. Grindle, "Anticipating Failure: The Implementation of Rural Development Programs," *Public Policy* 29 (1981): 51–74. For a more positive assessment, see Figueroa, "Rural Development," pp. 121–24.
21. The main conclusions are summarized in "Análisis del sistema de manejo de proyectos aplicado en el Distrito de Pamplona," mimeographed (Instituto Interamericano de Cooperación para la Agricultura/Instituto Colombiano Agropecuario [IICA/ICA], Bogotá, 1981), pp. 2–6.
22. For an outline of each agency's responsibilities, see "Marco de referencia para la formulación y ejecución del programa DRI en el Distrito de Pamplona—Norte de Santander," mimeographed (Programa de Desarrollo Rural Integrado/Instituto Interamericano de Cooperación para la Agricultura [DRI/IICA], Cúcuta, 1981), pp. 32–36, and "Normas y procedimientos del crédito con asistencia técnica para el programa DRI," mimeographed (DRI, Bogotá, 1983), p. 2. The background to PROPLAN is discussed in "Análisis del sistema," pp. i–iv. A precise definition of DRI's mandate can be found in "Normas," p. 1.
23. On capital flight in Latin America, see Pedro-Pablo Kuczynski, "Latin American Debt: Act Two," *Foreign Affairs* (Fall 1983): 36.
24. For further discussion of how districts and counties were selected, see "Diagnóstico microregional en el Distrito de Pamplona—Norte de Santander," 2 vols., mimeographed (DRI/IICA, Pamplona, 1981), 1:2–10.
25. The statistics are drawn from "Diagnóstico," 1:11–14.
26. Ibid., 1:10–11, 2:9, 22–23.
27. In the case of potatoes, of the 1,440 potato farms in the counties of Chitagá, Pamplona, Mutiscua, and Cácota, 71 percent had less than 20 hectares; 16 percent had between 20 and 49.9 hectares, and 13 percent had 50 hectares or more. See "Proyecto para la producción de semilla mejorada de papa en el Distrito DRI de Pamplona," mimeographed (DRI/IICA, Bogotá, 1981), p. 29.
28. "Diagnóstico," 2:18.
29. Totals are from "Veredas preseleccionadas en el Distrito de Pamplona," mimeographed (DRI, Pamplona, 1983), pp. 1–3.
30. Colombia currently has the highest yields in Latin America. See IDB, *Economic and Social Progress 1986*, p. 114.

31. "Diagnóstico," 2:9.
32. Ibid., 1:14, 19, 29–38; 2:78. On potato yields, see "Marco de referencia," p. 15, and "Componente de producción: Programación 1981–1985," mimeographed (DRI/IICA, Pamplona, 1981), p. 73.
33. "Diagnóstico," 1:50-52.
34. See "Componente de producción," pp. 9–20, 56–72.
35. Ibid., p. 22.
36. Ibid., pp. 16, 21.
37. On the counties and veredas covered for Pamplona and Ocaña, see "Veredas preseleccionadas," pp. 1–7. The 1983 budget allocation for DRI in Pamplona—Ocaña came to 283 million pesos. The original projection for Pamplona alone totaled 91 million pesos. On the number of counties covered nationally by DRI, see "Marco de referencia," p. 1. To estimate how many farm families benefited from DRI in 1983, I multiplied DRI's original 17 districts by 3,500; newly established districts like Pamplona and Ocaña, of which there were 14, I multiplied by 2,500. The total came to 94,500, about 20 percent of what my sources estimated as half a million small farmers in Colombia. My guess as to how many families a DRI district included is a conservative one and is based on data from "Veredas preseleccionadas," pp. 1–7.
38. The potato's many merits and the statistics cited below are from Robert E. Rhoades, "The Incredible Potato," *National Geographic* (May 1982), pp. 668–94. See also Earl J. Hamilton, "What the New World Gave the Old," in *First Images of America: The Impact of the New World on the Old*, ed. Fredi Chiappelli, 2 vols. (Los Angeles: University of California Press, 1976), 2:857–60; Redcliffe Salaman, *The History and Social Influence of the Potato*, 2nd ed. rev. (Cambridge: At the University Press, 1985).
39. On the district's marketing structure, see "Diagnóstico," 1:31–36.
40. On the Agrarian Bank's lending specifications, see "Normas," pp. 17, 23, 46–51.
41. *El Tiempo*, 3 June 1983, p. 8-C.
42. On the research centers, see Consultative Group on International Agricultural Research (CGIAR), *1985 Annual Report* (Washington, D.C.: CGIAR Secretariat, 1986). See also International Potato Center (CIP), *Annual Report 1985* (Lima: CIP, 1986) and Centro Internacional de Agricultura Tropical (CIAT), *CIAT Report 1987* (Cali: CIAT, 1987). I have visited both centers and the Secretariat.

CHAPTER 5

1. In 1980, the South American continent, including Guyana, Surinam, and French Guiana, had a total population of approximately 240 million, of

which 119 million were Brazilians. For population estimates of Spanish-speaking countries and Brazil, see James W. Wilkie and Adam Perkal, eds., *Statistical Abstract of Latin America* (Los Angeles: UCLA Latin American Center Publications, University of California, 1984), 23:103–4 (hereafter cited as *SALA*). The population of Guyana, Surinam, and French Guiana was calculated from *Times Atlas of the World* (New York: Times Books, 1983), pp. xii, xiv. For figures on Brazil's population size and its growth, see *Anuário Estatístico do Brasil—1985* (Rio de Janeiro: Fundação Instituto Brasileiro de Geografia e Estatística, 1986), pp. 60, 63, 122. The estimated growth rate for the 1980s is from World Bank, *World Development Report 1986* (New York: World Bank, Oxford University Press, 1986), p. 229. For Brazil's age structure, see *Anuário* (1985), p. 61.

2. Statistics on Brazil are typically cited with respect to the country's gross domestic product (GDP). Because this is not a textbook, I have used the more familiar term, gross national product. For the kind of information this book conveys, it makes little difference in practice. The footnotes indicate the specific measure the source has employed. For manufacturing's contribution to GDP, see World Bank, *Brazil, Industrial Policies and Manufactured Exports* (Washington, D.C.: World Bank, 1983), p. 154. On the industrial sector's growth, see Luiz Bresser Pereira, *Development and Crisis in Brazil, 1930–1983* (Boulder, Colo.: Westview Press, 1984), p. 163.

3. Pereira, *Development and Crisis*, p. 26.

4. The GDP figures are from World Bank, *Industrial Policies*, p. 5.

5. On GDP, see *SALA* (1984), 23:16; for Brazil's share of vehicle and steel production, see ibid., 23:335, 342.

6. For the percentage of Brazil's population categorized as urban and rural, see *Anuário* (1982), p. 116; for metropolitan São Paulo, see ibid., p. 86. Cities near the million mark in 1970 and 1980 are calculated from the municipal population for each census year rather than from the population of metropolitan regions; see ibid., pp. 86–87.

7. Andrew Hacker, ed., *U/S: A Statistical Portrait of the American People* (New York: Viking Press, 1983), p. 24.

8. World Bank, *Industrial Policies*, p. 164; *Anuário* (1982), pp. 506, 527; *Anuário* (1985), pp. 477, 485.

9. The estimate is from World Bank, *Population Change and Economic Development* (New York: Oxford University Press, 1984), p. 177.

10. See World Bank, *A Review of Agricultural Policies in Brazil* (Washington, D.C.: World Bank, 1982), pp. 7, 1–27.

11. Ibid., p. 24.

12. Ibid., p. 21.

13. On inflation see World Bank, *Agricultural Policies*, p. 19. The credit total for 1979 is derived by dividing the cruzeiro amount allocated to "produc-

287

tion credit"—see ibid., p. 225—by the year's average exchange rate listed in *SALA* (1983), 23:458.

14. *Anuário* (1982), pp. 132, 303.

15. See World Bank, *Industrial Policies*, p. 16; averages for 1967–80 are calculated from the table.

16. Calculated for males ages 18 to 59; see *Anuário* (1982), p. 132.

17. Peter T. Knight and Ricardo Moran, *Brazil: Poverty and Basic Needs* (Washington, D.C.: World Bank, 1981), pp. 20–21. The expansion of the labor force declined to 2.3 percent during the 1970s but is expected to average about 2.6 percent between 1980 and 2000; see World Bank, *Population Change*, p. 177. Separating out the unskilled labor force, which grew at a rate of 3 percent during the 1960s, and comparing it to the expansion of the modern sector, which grew at a rate of 2.2 percent, the unskilled labor force would never be absorbed. See Knight and Moran, *Brazil: Poverty and Basic Needs*, p. 21.

18. Rio's average minimum wage for 1980 is calculated from the data in *Anuário* (1982), p. 676.

19. Ibid., p. 135.

20. The GDP figures are from *SALA* (1984), 23:16.

21. For the U.S. figures, see *Statistical Abstract of the United States: 1982–1983*, 103d ed. (Washington, D.C.: U.S. Bureau of the Census, 1982), p. 435.

22. *SALA* (1984), 23:16.

23. Knight and Moran, *Brazil: Poverty and Basic Needs*, pp. 27–28, 30.

24. Carlos Mauro Benevides Filho, "Income Distribution in Brazil: 1970–1980 Compared" (Ph.D. diss., Vanderbilt University, 1985), p. 80.

25. Oscar Altimir, *The Extent of Poverty in Latin America* (Washington, D.C.: World Bank, 1982), pp. 82, 39–78. A subsequent study estimated that, for urban areas in 1980, "absolute" poverty varied between 16 percent in the South to 49 percent in the Northeast; "relative" poverty included 31 percent of all families in the South and 62 percent of those in the Northeast—see James F. Hicks and David Michael Vetter, *Identifying the Urban Poor in Brazil* (Washington, D.C.: World Bank, 1983), pp. 46–49.

26. This is an estimate; 60 percent of the labor force earned two minimum wages or less in 1980—see *Anuário* (1982), p. 135. The country's average minimum wage for 1980 came to 3,592 cruzeiros; over 30 percent of the labor force earned less—see Mauro Benevides, "Income Distribution," pp. 50–51.

27. For infant mortality rates, see World Bank, *World Development Report 1986*, p. 233. The proportion of infant deaths attributable to various diseases, mortality by age groups, and waste disposable facilities are presented in *Anuário* (1982), pp. 187, 184, 195, 263.

28. Figures presented by Hector de Souza, 18 July 1983. For verification, see *Anuário* (1982), p. 232, and Knight and Moran, *Brazil: Poverty and Basic Needs*, p. 50.
29. The figures are still essentially accurate. Of the students who entered the first grade in 1980, only about 40 percent were still in school for the fourth grade in 1984; see *Anuário* (1982), p. 214, and *Anuário* (1985), p. 214. One of the main reasons primary education is so deficient has to do with how it is funded. See World Bank, *Brazil: Finance of Primary Education* (Washington, D.C.: World Bank, 1986).
30. For figures on GDP, see Enrique U. Iglesias, "The Latin American Economy during 1984: A Preliminary Overview," *CEPAL Review* 25 (1985): 12; on inflation, see Andrew Whitley, "Tougher to Stay in the Saddle," *Financial Times*, 7 May 1985, xeroxed (Information Service on Latin America [ISLA], May 1985, p. 330).
31. *Anuário* (1985), pp. 69, 80.
32. *Anuário* (1982), p. 424. The income estimate is for the Southeast as a whole, which includes São Paulo; it compares the average minimum wage for the region in 1980 with the average income calculated for each decile of the Southeast's income distribution—see Mauro Benevides, "Income Distribution," pp. 52, 59.
33. *Anuário* (1985), pp. 344, 346.
34. World Bank, *Agricultural Policies*, p. 22.
35. *Anuário* (1982), pp. 125, 189.
36. Ibid., p. 214; *Anuário* (1985), p. 214.
37. Thomas W. Merrick and Douglas H. Graham, *Population and Economic Development in Brazil: 1800 to the Present* (Baltimore: Johns Hopkins University Press, 1979), pp. 91–92.
38. Knight and Moran, *Brazil: Poverty and Basic Needs*, pp. 40–45. For an excellent background study, see James M. Malloy, *The Politics of Social Security in Brazil* (Pittsburgh: University of Pittsburgh Press, 1979). Health care was but one aspect of Brazil's social security system. For a recent study of its funding and administrative problems, see Francisco Eduardo Barreto de Oliveira and Maria Emília R. M. de Azevedo, "Social Welfare: Diagnosis and Prospects," in Instituto de Planejamento Econômico e Social (IPEA), *Brazilian Economic Studies* 9 (Rio de Janeiro: IPEA, 1985): 189–235. See also Maurício C. Coutinho, "A Previdência Social em xeque: uma análise a partir de adequação dos mecanismos de financiamento," *Revista de Economia Política* 6 (October-December 1986): 116–30.
39. On industrial output, see *SALA* (1984), 23:334; for the automobile fleet's size, see *Anuário* (1973), p. 447, and *Anuário* (1976), p. 366. For Brazil's petroleum consumption in the 1970s, see *SALA* (1980), 20:232, and *SALA*

(1984), 23:375; on domestic crude oil production vs. imports, see *SALA* (1984), 23:359, 612. For petroleum prices, see *SALA* (1984), 23:503–4. The cost of Brazil's petroleum imports is from José Goldemberg, "Energy Issues and Policies in Brazil," mimeographed (Institute of Physics, University of São Paulo, 1981), p. 48.

40. Goldemberg, "Energy Issues," pp. 8–11.
41. Ibid., p. 11.
42. On production technology, see World Bank, *Alcohol Production from Biomass in the Developing Countries* (Washington, D.C.: World Bank, 1980), pp. 16–20.
43. *SALA* (1984), 23:307.
44. For background on Brazil's Alcohol Program, see William S. Saint, "Farming for Energy: Social Options under Brazil's National Alcohol Programme," *World Development* 10 (1982): 223–38, and Harry Rothman, Rod Greenshields, and Francisco Rosillo Callé, *Energy from Alcohol: The Brazilian Experience* (Lexington: University Press of Kentucky, 1983).
45. The above discussion draws on World Bank, *Alcohol Production*, pp. 16–30, and Rothman, Greenshields, and Callé, *Energy from Alcohol*, pp. 16–35.
46. On how the regime financed alcohol production, see Saint, "Farming for Energy," pp. 223, 226–28.
47. World Bank, *Agricultural Policies*, p. 98; liters are converted to gallons.
48. Goldemberg, "Energy Issues," p. 7.
49. World Bank, *Alcohol Production*, p. 6.
50. Rothman, Greenshields, and Callé, *Energy from Alcohol*, pp. 90–96.
51. See Goldemberg, "Energy Issues," pp. 12–15. On investment costs and the number of alcohol vehicles, see Rothman, Greenshields, and Callé, *Energy from Alcohol*, pp. 56, 162. For total ethanol production by type—hydrous vs. anhydrous—see *Anuário* (1984), p. 614. On alcohol-fueled automobile production, see Andrew Whitley, "Vehicle Industry," *Financial Times*, 5 November 1984, xeroxed (ISLA, November 1984, p. 385).
52. World Bank, *Alcohol Production*, pp. 32, 38–39, 60.
53. Rothman, Greenshields, and Callé, *Energy from Alcohol*, pp. 65–78.
54. Goldemberg, "Energy Issues," pp. 16–20.
55. The figure is for 1984; see *Anuário* (1985), p. 547.
56. *Anuário* (1985), p. 429.
57. For the 1975 figures, see World Bank, *Agricultural Policies*, pp. 183, 95; for 1982, see *Anuário* (1985), p. 332.
58. For Brazil's energy-use profile and electricity consumption by state, see *Anuário* (1982), pp. 496, 498. For industry's share of petroleum consumption and the decade's rate of growth for electricity use, see Goldemberg, "Energy Issues," pp. 8–11, 47.
59. As of 1979; see Goldemberg, "Energy Issues," p. 29.

60. Peter T. Kilborn, "Brazil's Hydroelectric Project," *New York Times*, 14 November 1983, xeroxed (ISLA, November 1983, p. 570).

61. For the fleet's size and gasoline consumption by type, see *Anuário* (1976), pp. 366, 455; *Anuário* (1982), pp. 596–97, 452; and *Anuário* (1985), pp. 547, 418.

62. The drop in petroleum consumption is noted in Fiona Thompson, "Campos Puts the Country in the Big League," *Financial Times*, 5 November 1984, xeroxed (ISLA, November 1984, p. 379). On total energy use by source, see *Anuário* (1985), p. 462.

63. Thompson, "Campos," p. 379, and Juan de Onis, "Giant Oil Field Discovered off Coast of Brazil," *Los Angeles Times*, 15 June 1985, xeroxed (ISLA, June 1985, p. 372).

64. For U.S. prime interest rates, see *SALA* (1984), 23:507. For the slipshod way banks made their international loans, see S. C. Gwynne, "Adventures in the Loan Trade," *Harpers*, September 1983, pp. 22–26.

65. Mimi Whitefield, "Amazon Highway: A Long Hard Road into Dusty Dreams," *Miami Herald*, 13 August 1984, xeroxed (ISLA, August 1984, p. 332).

66. Andrew Whitley, "Brazil's Enormous Gamble," *Financial Times*, 21 May 1984, xeroxed (ISLA, May 1984, p. 348). For the cost estimate on Tucuruí, see *Latin America Regional Report: Brazil*, 12 March 1982, p. 5.

67. For interest rates and Brazil's repayment schedule, see *SALA* (1984), 23:507, 688–89.

68. Marlise Simons, "Some Smell Disaster in Brazil Industrial Zone," *New York Times*, 18 May 1985, xeroxed (ISLA, May 1984, pp. 334–35). See also Ethan Hoffman, "The Valley of Death," *Rolling Stone*, 24 October 1985, pp. 29–34, 84–86.

69. The medical diagnosis is anencephaly, a birth defect in which the cranium has no neural tissue.

CHAPTER 6

1. *Anuário Estatístico do Brasil—1985* (Rio de Janeiro: Fundação Instituto Brasileiro de Geografia e Estatística, 1985), p. 76.

2. For a good account of the period, see Charles R. Boxer, *The Golden Age of Brazil, 1695–1750* (Berkeley: University of California Press, 1962).

3. *First Stories* is translated under the title *The Third Bank of the River and Other Stories*, trans. Barbara Shelby (New York: Alfred A. Knopf, 1968). Guimarães Rosa's masterpiece appears in English as *The Devil to Pay in the Backlands*, trans. James L. Taylor and Harriet de Onís (New York: Alfred A. Knopf, 1971).

4. For changes in the state's urban-rural balance between 1970 and 1980, see

Anuário (1982), p. 80. For the state capital, see "Metropolitan Region of Belo Horizonte," mimeographed (Faculty of Medicine, Belo Horizonte, 1983), p. 1, and *Anuário* (1982), p. 86.

5. *Anuário* (1982), pp. 402-4, 436, 390.
6. Projeto Fundação Lugar de Estudos Contemporâneos—Belo Horizonte.
7. See "Venda Nova District," mimeographed (Faculty of Medicine, Belo Horizonte, 1983), pp. 1–2.
8. *Anuário* (1982), p. 192.
9. On Chagas disease, see Tinsley Randolph Harrison, ed., *Principles of Internal Medicine*, 8th ed. (New York: McGraw-Hill, 1977), pp. 1081–82.
10. See Peter T. Knight and Ricardo Moran, *Brazil: Poverty and Basic Needs* (Washington, D.C.: World Bank, 1981), p. 24.
11. On schistosomiasis, see Richard G. Feachem et al., *Sanitation and Disease: Health Aspects of Excreta and Waste Management* (New York: World Bank, John Wiley & Sons, 1983), pp. 443–53.
12. For a discussion of the Medical School's changing mission, see Hélio Lauar de Barros, "Currículo e Poder," *Cadernos do Internato Rural* 1 (September/December 1982): 74–84.
13. See "Controle da Saúde Individual e Coletiva em Diversas Populações Infantis—Implantação e Avaliação de um Método," mimeographed (Internato Rural, Belo Horizonte, 1983), p. 3, and "Metropolitan Region," p. 8.
14. The program's organization is outlined in Departamento de Medicina Preventiva e Social, *Internato Rural*, mimeographed (Belo Horizonte: Universidade Federal de Minas Gerais, Faculdade de Medicina, 1981), pp. 1–21.
15. "The Northern Region of Minas Gerais," mimeographed (Faculty of Medicine, Belo Horizonte, 1983), pp. 1–2.
16. "Nosographic Aspects of Minas Gerais," mimeographed (Faculty of Medicine, Belo Horizonte, 1983), pp. 1–2.
17. Geraldo Cunha Cury, ed., "Jequitaí," mimeographed (Internato Rural, Montes Claros, 1983), pp. 1–12.
18. See "Controle da Saúde," pp. 1–6, 11–14.
19. Carlos Ernesto Ferreira Starling, "Análise do Estado Nutricional Infantil em Relação as Condições Sócio-Econômicas e à Prática do Aleitamento Materno em Jequitaí e Ravena, Utilizando-se o 'Cartão Controle da Saúde,'" *Cadernos do Internato Rural* 1 (September/December 1982): 29–30.
20. On applying the method, see "Controle da Saúde," pp. 16–17.
21. Starling, "Análise do Estado Nutricional," pp. 31–37.
22. Renato Samy, Luiz Fernando Pena, and Ricardo José Ferreira, "Relatório Dolabela," mimeographed (Internato Rural, Montes Claros, 1983), pp. 1–6.
23. See also *Internato Rural*, pp. 1–21.

24. "The Northern Region of Minas Gerais," mimeographed (Faculty of Medicine, Belo Horizonte, 1983), p. 19.
25. *Anuário* (1982), p. 74.
26. For the region's respective urban and rural populations in 1970 and 1980, see "Northern Region," p. 19.
27. Conducted in the early 1970s, the study is summarized in "Northern Region," p. 22.
28. The data for Northern Minas compile statistics from the following counties: Sanfranciscana de Januária, Serra Geral de Minas, Alto Rio Pardo, Alto-Médio São Francisco, Montes Claros, and Mineradora do Alto Jequitinhonha. For the 1970 figures, see *Censo Agropecuário: Minas Gerais* (Rio de Janeiro: Fundação Instituto Brasileiro de Geografia a Estatística, 1975), pp. 206–9—hereafter cited as *CAMG* (1970). For 1980, see *Censo Agropecuário: Minas Gerais* (Rio de Janeiro: Fundação Instituto Brasileiro de Geografia e Estatística, 1984), pp. 442–49—hereafter cited as *CAMG* (1980).
29. The figures on cassava, beans, corn, and rice are compiled from *CAMG* (1970), pp. 880, 862, 896, 818, and *CAMG* (1980), pp. 1798–1800, 1760–62, 1824–26, 1672–74. For sugarcane, cattle, the acreage devoted to pastures, and milk production, see *CAMG* (1970), pp. 846, 548, 186–87, 696, and *CAMG* (1980), pp. 1734–36, 1004–6, 526–29, 1438–39.
30. Compiled from the tables in *CAMG* (1980), pp. 26–27.
31. *CAMG* (1980), pp. 26–27. The small farm's contribution to production is compiled from tables as follows: tomatoes, p. 128; potatoes, p. 116; cassava, p. 122; beans, p. 120; and corn, p. 124.
32. For the big estate's share of milk production, see *CAMG* (1980), p. 95; for land devoted to pastures and the share of cattle production, see pp. 26–27, 62.
33. *CAMG* (1980), pp. 62, 26–27, 95.
34. *CAMG* (1980), pp. 21–22.
35. *CAMG* (1980): tomatoes, p. 128; potatoes, p. 116; beans, p. 120; corn, p. 124; cassava, p. 122; rice, p. 114; coffee, p. 99; oranges, p. 100; bananas, p. 98; pork, p. 80; and milk production, p. 95.
36. *CAMG* (1980), pp. 62, 126, 118.
37. The total came to 37.5 billion cruzeiros; see *CAMG* (1980), p. 52. This sum is divided by the exchange rate average of 54 cruzeiros to the dollar. The "average" is derived by summing the year-end rates for 1979 and 1980, and then dividing by 2. For year-end exchange rates, see James W. Wilkie and Adam Perkal, eds., *Statistical Abstract of Latin America* (Los Angeles: UCLA Latin American Center Publications, University of California, 1984), 23:458 (hereafter cited as *SALA*).
38. World Bank, *Brazil: A Review of Agricultural Policies* (Washington, D.C.: World Bank, 1982), p. 24.

39. On credit's contribution to output, see ibid., pp. 36–37; for the 1979 credit allocation figures, see p. 225. The conversion to dollars is based on the exchange rates noted in *SALA* (1984), 23:458—calculated by estimating year-end averages as explained in n. 37 above.

40. World Bank, *Agricultural Policies*, p. 225; *SALA* (1984), 23:458.

41. World Bank, *Agricultural Policies*: livestock credit, pp. 19, 230; crop credits, p. 20.

42. *CAMG* (1980), pp. 26–27.

43. *Anuário* (1982), p. 436; *CAMG* (1980), p. 175.

44. *Anuário* (1983), p. 480.

45. *CAMG* (1970), pp. 186–87; *CAMG* (1980), p. 2044.

46. "Pirapora," mimeographed (Companhia de Desenvolvimento do Vale do São Francisco, Montes Claros, 1983), p. 1. The total cost was 200 million cruzeiros; the estimate uses the average of the year-end exchange rates for 1976–77, which was 14. See *SALA* (1984), 23:458.

47. The conversion is based on a 1983 mid-year exchange rate of 671 cruzeiros to the dollar; see *SALA* (1984), 23:458.

48. "Pirapora," pp. 1–3.

49. "Irrigação transforma Norte de Minas em pólo agrícola," *Jornal do Brasil*, 6 June 1982, p. 34.

50. Ibid.

51. Total expenditures as of 1982 stood at 2 billion cruzeiros. Because work on the project had continued over several years, I converted the sum to dollars at the 1978 exchange rate of 21 cruzeiros. For projected expenses—1 billion cruzeiros—I used the 1981–82 year-end exchange rate estimate of 190 cruzeiros to the dollar. See "Irrigação transforma," p. 34; *SALA* (1984), 23:458.

52. *Informativo Rural Minas* (February 1982), p. 1.

53. "Irrigação transforma," p. 34.

54. See Alan Riding, "Brazil Moves to Distribute Land to Poor Families," *New York Times*, 14 October 1985, xeroxed (Information Service on Latin America [ISLA], October 1985, p. 328).

55. Charles Vanhecke, "Brazilian Land Reform Still in the Balance," *Manchester Guardian*, 2 February 1986, xeroxed (ISLA, February 1986, pp. 325–26).

56. See Antônio Márcio Buainain and Hildo Meirelles de Souza Filho, "A trajetória recente da agricultura," in Ricardo Carneiro, ed., *Política econômica da Nova República* (Rio de Janeiro: Paz e Terra, 1986), p. 92.

CHAPTER 7

1. For the story of Canudos and Antônio Conselheiro, see Mario Vargas Llosa, *The War of the End of the World* (New York: Avon, 1984); on Padre Cícero, see Ralph Della Cava, *Miracle at Joaseiro* (New York: Columbia University Press, 1970); and for Lampião, see Billy Jaynes Chandler, *The Bandit King* (College Station: Texas A & M University Press, 1978). On the Northeast's famed stories in verse, see Candace Slater, *Stories on a String: The Brazilian "Literatura de Cordel"* (Berkeley: University of California Press, 1982).

2. *Anuário Estatístico do Brasil—1983* (Rio de Janeiro: Fundação Instituto Brasileiro de Geografia e Estatística, 1984), pp. 446, 76.

3. Ibid., p. 446; World Bank, *Brazil, Industrial Policies and Manufactured Exports* (Washington, D.C.: World Bank, 1983), pp. 174, 19–21.

4. Carlos Mauro Benevides Filho, "Income Distribution in Brazil: 1970–1980 Compared" (Ph.D. diss., Vanderbilt University, 1985), p. 9.

5. *Anuário* (1983), p. 78.

6. Mauro Benevides, "Income Distribution," p. 9.

7. Ibid., pp. 8–11; "The Challenge of the Northeast," *Latin American Regional Report: Brazil*, 8 February 1985, p. 2.

8. For an estimate of the infant mortality rate and the prevalence of schistosomiasis and Chagas, see "Challenge of the Northeast," p. 2; the nutrition study data are reported in Antero Coelho Neto, ed., *Anais do Seminário Sobre "Atenção Primária de Saúde"* (Fortaleza: Universidade Federal do Ceará, 1981), p. 62. The composition of the region's death rate is from *Anuário* (1983), p. 229; grade school enrollments are compiled from *Anuário* (1982), p. 214, and *Anuário* (1984), p. 265.

9. World Bank, *A Review of Agricultural Policies in Brazil* (Washington, D.C.: World Bank, 1982), p. 22.

10. Compiled from World Bank, *Industrial Policies*, p. 178; see also pp. 19–21.

11. *Anuário* (1982), p. 597.

12. "Challenge of the Northeast," p. 2.

13. Ibid.

14. *Anuário* (1985), p. 68.

15. The summary of the project's early years is based on field notes supplemented by José Galba Araújo, "Atenção de Saúde em Zona Rural," in Coelho Neto, *Anais*, pp. 17–21.

16. Ibid., p. 19.

17. A description of the project's organization, objectives, and strategies can be found in José Galba Araújo and Antero Coelho Neto, *Programa de Antenção Primária de Saúde* (Fortaleza: Universidade Federal do Ceará, 1981).

18. On how the project's experience in rural areas had changed the obstetric ward at the University Hospital, see Malcolm Potts, "Childbirth in Fortaleza," *World Medicine* 15 (May 1980): 75–78.

19. The results summarized below appear in José Galba Araújo, Lorena Araújo, Barbara Janowitz, Sylvia Wallace, and Malcolm Potts, "Improving Obstetric Care in Northeast Brazil," *Pan American Health Organization Bulletin* 17 (1983): 233-42.

20. Maria Auxiliadora de Sousa, "Saneamento Básico," in Coelho Neto, *Anais*, p. 53.

21. Galba Araújo, "Atenção de Saúde em Zona Rural," p. 21.

22. The project's diverse extension work is outlined in Galba Araújo and Coelho Neto, *Programa de Antenção Primária*, pp. 31–56.

23. Antero Coelho Neto, *Fantasias* (Fortaleza: R. Esteves Gráfica Editora, 1985).

24. On the region's ecological characteristics, see Selem Rachid Asmar and Maria Palma Andrade, *Geografia da Microrregião Cacaueira* (Itabuna: Comissão Executiva do Plano da Lavoura Cacaueira [CEPLAC], 1977), pp. 3–23.

25. *Anuário* (1985), p. 344.

26. For the rural to urban shift in Bahia, see ibid., p. 78. The cacao region's population was 57 percent rural in 1960; the figure had dropped to 51 percent in 1970, but had increased to 55 percent in 1980. See Salem Rachid Asmar, "Crescimento demográfico da Microrregião Cacaueira," *Jornal do Cacauicultor* 10 (January 1982). For cacao production by size of farm, see *Censo Agropecuário: Bahia—1970* (Rio de Janeiro: Fundação Instituto Brasileiro de Geografia e Estatística, 1975), p. 84 (hereafter cited as *CAB* [1970]), and *Censo Agropecuário: Bahia—1980* (Rio de Janeiro: Fundação Instituto Brasileiro de Geografia e Estatística, 1983), p. 94 (hereafter cited as *CAB* [1980]).

27. For a brief summary of how Brazil's agricultural research is organized, see World Bank, *Agricultural Policies*, pp. 65–69; the contribution small farms made to the region's exports is noted in Luis López Cordovez, "Trends and Recent Changes in the Latin American Food and Agricultural Situation," *CEPAL Review* 16 (1982): 26.

28. See also Robert L. Fowler and Paulo Alvim, *CEPLAC: Vinte e um anos de assistência técnica ao Cacau no Brasil* (Itabuna: Centro de Pesquisas do Cacau, 1979), pp. 3–24; World Bank, *Agricultural Policies*, pp. 160–68.

29. Fowler and Alvim, *CEPLAC*, pp. 24–25. Cruzeiros are converted to dollars using the exchange rates listed in James W. Wilkie and Adam Perkal, eds., *Statistical Abstract of Latin America* (Los Angeles: UCLA Latin American Center Publications, University of California, 1984), 23:458. The average 1976–77 rate is applied to the CEPLAC figures.

30. Compiled from the tables in *CAB* (1970), p. 84, and *CAB* (1980), p. 94. For prices, see World Bank, *Agricultural Policies*, p. 164.
31. Fowler and Alvim, *CEPLAC*, pp. 24–25; "Controle da podridão parda," pamphlet (CEPLAC, Itabuna, 1982), pp. 1–6.
32. The appropriate steps for harvesting, fermentation, and drying are outlined in CEPLAC, *Beneficiamento e padronização do Cacau* (Itabuna: CEPLAC, 1981), pp. 5–23.
33. Fowler and Alvim, *CEPLAC*, p. 33; World Bank, *Agricultural Policies*, p. 167.

CONCLUSIONS

1. Charles Vanhecke, "Brazil—The $100 Billion Debtor," *Manchester Guardian*, 25 March 1985, p. 14; Alan Riding, "Brazil's Hard Life with Austerity," *New York Times*, 12 August 1984, xeroxed (Information Service on Latin America [ISLA], August 1984, pp. 327–29).
2. The 1984 growth rate is from Comisión Económica para América Latina y El Caribe (CEPAL), "Balance preliminar de la economía Latinoamericana 1985," *Notas Sobre la Economía y el Desarrollo*, no. 424/425 (December 1985): 11. Brazil's 1981 import bill for goods came to $22 billion, compared to $14 billion in 1984; for 1981, see James W. Wilkie and Adam Perkal, eds., *Statistical Abstract of Latin America* (Los Angeles: UCLA Latin American Center Publications, University of California, 1985), p. 595 (hereafter cited as *SALA*), and for 1984, see CEPAL, "Balance preliminar," p. 14.
3. Alan Riding, "Brazil Recovers Despite Its Deficit," *New York Times*, 6 January 1986, xeroxed (ISLA, January 1986, p. 279); Tom Murphy, "Government Redefines Economic Policy," *Wall Street Journal*, 21 March 1986, xeroxed (ISLA, March 1986, pp. 440–44). The 1986 growth rate is from Fundação Getúlio Vargas, "Sinal de alerta na balança," *Conjuntura Econômica* 40 (November 1986): 13.
4. Murphy, "Government Redefines Policy," p. 441; Andrew Whitley, "Growth Rate Gains Priority," *Financial Times*, 20 December 1985, xeroxed (ISLA, December 1985, p. 362).
5. S. Karene Witcher, "Brazil Reaches Pact to Realign Part of Its Debt," *Wall Street Journal*, 20 January 1986, xeroxed (ISLA, January 1986, p. 281).
6. "Morre o cruzeiro e nasce o cruzado," *O Globo*, 1 March 1986, p. 21; "A semana que mudou o Brasil," *Veja*, 12 March 1986, pp. 20–66; Robert Graham, "A New Glow of Confidence," *Financial Times*, 7 April 1986, xeroxed (ISLA, April 1986, pp. 383–84).

7. Alan Riding, "Brazil's Inflation Fight: A Political Reawakening," *New York Times*, 26 March 1986, p. 8.

8. Murphy, "Government Redefines Policy," p. 440.

9. Compiled from the tables for gross domestic product (GDP) in Luiz Bresser Pereira, *Development and Crisis in Brazil, 1930–1983* (Boulder, Colo.: Westview Press, 1984), pp. 22, 140, 163. Brazil's closest competitor was Mexico; its GDP growth rate averaged 6.2 percent (1940–79). See *SALA* (1984), 23:405.

10. Carlos Eduardo de Freitas, "The Foreign Debt Viewed from Brasília," *Wall Street Journal*, 21 March 1986, xeroxed (ISLA, March 1986, p. 456).

11. Timothy E. Spence, "Saturn Dedicates Plant Site," *Review Appeal*, 9 April 1986, pp. A1–A2.

12. Peter F. Drucker, "The Changed World Economy," *Foreign Affairs* (Spring 1986): 778.

13. *Statistical Abstract of the United States: 1986*, 106th ed. (Washington, D.C.: U.S. Bureau of the Census, 1985), p. 744 (hereafter cited as *SAUS*).

14. This is Drucker's argument; see "Changed Economy," pp. 775–81.

15. For labor absorption coefficients, see World Bank, *Brazil: Industrial Policies and Manufactured Exports* (Washington, D.C.: World Bank, 1983), p. 17. In general, see Peter T. Knight, "Brazilian Socioeconomic Development: Issues for the Eighties," *World Development* 9 (1981): 1063–82.

16. Murphy, "Government Redefines Policy," pp. 440–43; Alan Riding, "Brazil May Soon Take Heed of Have-Nots," *New York Times*, 4 May 1986, xeroxed (ISLA, May 1986, p. 329).

17. Alan Riding, "Battling Brazil's Inflationary Fires," *New York Times*, 2 March 1986, xeroxed (ISLA, March 1986, pp. 434–35).

18. The GNP figure is for 1985; see *SAUS* (1987), p. 417.

19. CEPAL, "Balance preliminar," p. 11. Similar data through 1984 can be found in Enrique V. Iglesias, "The Latin American Economy during 1984: A Preliminary Overview," *CEPAL Review* 25 (April 1985): 7–44.

20. CEPAL, "Balance preliminar," p. 17.

21. Ibid.

22. See "Why PEMEX Can't Pay Mexico's Bills," *Business Week*, 28 February 1983, pp. 58–62. Much of what PEMEX borrowed the government diverted to other uses. On this point and for figures on PEMEX's debt, consult José Luis Manzo Y., "PEMEX: Una empresa generosa," *El Cotidiano* 15 (January-February 1986): 1–10. In 1981 alone, PEMEX borrowed over $15 billion; see Alan Riding, *Distant Neighbors: A Portrait of the Mexicans* (New York: Alfred A. Knopf, 1985), p. 145.

23. See Walter J. Levy, "An Agenda for the 1980s," *Foreign Affairs* (Summer 1981): 1079–1101; Hollis B. Chenery, "Restructuring the World Economy: Round II," *Foreign Affairs* (Summer 1981): 1102–20.

24. For 1981 oil revenues, see "PEMEX Can't Pay," p. 58; for 1986, estimates

ran as low as $5 billion—see *Latin American Regional Report: Mexico and Central America*, 21 March 1986, p. 7. Mexico's dependence on oil is noted by James L. Rowe, Jr., "Willingness of Debtors to Repay Now in Doubt," *Washington Post*, 19 January 1986, xeroxed (ISLA, January 1986, p. 294).

25. For Argentina's external debt in 1976, see *SALA* (1984), 23:687; for 1982, see CEPAL,"Balance preliminar," p. 17. Trade data are from *SALA* (1985), 24:593. On economic policy, see Edward Schumacher, "Argentina and Democracy," *Foreign Affairs* (Summer 1984): 1077–78.

26. *SALA* (1985), 24:807.

27. See William R. Cline, "Mexico's Crisis, the World's Peril," *Foreign Policy* (Winter 1982–83): 107–18.

28. CEPAL, "Balance preliminar," p. 17.

29. Ibid.

30. The debt relative to GNP is compiled from *SAUS* (1986), pp. 305, 431; for total 1980–85 deficit spending and the total national debt, see ibid., p. 305. For the 1986 figures, see *SAUS* (1987), p. 292.

31. See Robert Heilbroner, "Reflections on the Deficit," *New Yorker*, 30 July 1984, pp. 47–55.

32. *SAUS* (1986), p. 311.

33. Peter T. Kilborn, "U.S. Seen as a Debtor Nation," *New York Times*, 17 September 1985, p. 37.

34. The 1981 figure is from *SAUS* (1986), p. 797; the 1985 estimate is from "A Record U.S. Deficit in Trade," *New York Times*, 3 March 1986, p. 34.

35. Kilborn, "U.S. a Debtor Nation," p. 29.

36. For 1982 through 1984, see *SAUS* (1986), p. 807; for 1985 and 1986, see Associated Press, "U.S. Trade Deficit in 1986 Largest Ever," *Nashville Banner*, 30 January 1987, p. A–10. The manufacturing example is from Lester Thurow, "A Surge of Inequality," *Scientific American*, May 1987, p. 33.

37. Calculated from *SAUS* (1986), p. 305.

38. The estimate is from James Fallows, "Three Fiscal Crises," *Atlantic Monthly*, September 1985, p. 19.

39. Marlise Simmons, "Focus on Latin Flight of Capital," *New York Times*, 17 May 1986, xeroxed (ISLA, May 1986, p. 333).

40. CEPAL, "Balance preliminar," p. 10.

41. The region's 1983–85 trade surplus came to $104 billion; interest payments and profits remitted abroad totaled $105 billion. See CEPAL, "Balance preliminar," pp. 10, 17.

42. Gerald O. Barney, Study Director, *The Global 2000 Report to the President* (Washington, D.C.: U.S. Government Printing Office, 1980), 1:13–32.

43. See Drucker, "Changed Economy," pp. 773–74.

44. Drucker argues that "the primary-products economy has come 'uncoupled' from the industrial economy"; see "Changed Economy," pp. 768–75. The trend is also noted in "Brazil's Aluminum Hopes Fade with Weak Prices," *Financial Times*, 8 May 1986, xeroxed (ISLA, May 1986, p. 337), and James Bruce, "Brazil Loses Shine for U.S. Mineral Firms," *Journal of Commerce*, 13 May 1986, xeroxed (USLA, May 1986, p. 338).

45. See Dennis Avery, "U.S. Farm Dilemma: The Global Bad News Is Wrong," *Science* 230 (25 October 1985): 408–12, and Edward L. Morse, "After the Fall: The Politics of Oil," *Foreign Affairs* (Spring 1986): 792–811.

46. In 1980–81, before the debt crisis hit, the region's import bill for goods averaged $94 billion; for 1983–85, the yearly total averaged $57 billion; see CEPAL, "Balance preliminar," p. 10.

47. *SAUS* (1985), p. 816; *SAUS* (1986), p. 810.

48. Everett G. Martin, "Latin Debt Crunch Hurting U.S. Firms," *Wall Street Journal*, 8 May 1984, xeroxed (ISLA, May 1984, p. 356).

49. *SAUS* (1987), p. 792.

50. Peter T. Kilborn, "Oil Slump Delays 'Baker Plan,'" *New York Times*, 25 February 1986, xeroxed (ISLA, February 1986, p. 348).

51. See Cline, "Mexico's Crisis," p. 107; Pedro-Pablo Kuczynski, "Latin American Debt," *Foreign Affairs* (Winter 1982–83): 359.

52. See Richard S. Weinert, "Swapping Third World Debt," *Foreign Policy* (Winter 1986–87): 85–97. On Brazil and the banks, see Randall Smith, "Brazil's Debt Move Hurts Big Banks," *Wall Street Journal*, 24 February 1987, p. 59; Peter Truell, "Bankers Ask IMF Pact," *Wall Street Journal*, 24 February 1987, p. 33; and Eric N. Berg, "Brazil's Action Hurts Bank Stocks, *New York Times*, 24 February 1987, p. 33.

53. See Jorge G. Castañeda, "Mexico at the Brink," *Foreign Affairs* (Winter 1985–86): 287–303, and Jean-Claude Buher, "Mexico Is a Tinder Box," *Manchester Guardian*, 15 June 1986, p. 12.

54. Kilborn, "Oil Slump Delays 'Baker Plan,'" pp. 348–49; L. Ronald Scheman, "Latin Debt: The Global Problem," *Washington Post*, 6 January 1986, xeroxed (ISLA, January 1986, p. 293).

55. See Felix Rohatyn, "The New Chance for the Economy," *New York Review of Books*, 24 April 1986, pp. 20–23.

56. Christine A. Bogdanowicz-Bindert, "World Debt: The United States Reconsiders," *Foreign Affairs* (Winter 1985–86): 259–73.

57. CEPAL, "Balance preliminar," pp. 11, 15, 17.

58. Jeffrey Ryser, Lawrence Wippman, and Sarah Bartlett, "Alan García Is More than the Bad Boy of Latin Politics," *Business Week*, 30 September 1985, p. 64.

59. Riordan Roett, "Peru: The Message from García," *Foreign Affairs* (Winter 1985–86): 274–86.
60. Ibid., pp. 274–86; Marcel Niedergang, "Debts and Terrorism Preoccupy Peru," *Manchester Guardian*, 18 May 1986, xeroxed (ISLA, May 1986, p. 274).
61. For the 1987 growth rate, see Fundação Getúlio Vargas, "Sinal de alerta," p. 13. The 1986 trade surplus is noted in *Latin American Regional Report: Brazil*, 12 February 1987, p. 6; the 1987 projection is from ibid., 19 March 1987, p. 1.
62. See Mario M. Chaves, *Saúde, uma estratégia de mudança* (Rio de Janeiro: Editora Guanabara Dois, 1982).
63. For example, see World Health Organization, *Formulating Strategies for Health for All by the Year 2000* (Geneva: World Health Organization, 1979).
64. For a comparative study that includes Finland and Costa Rica, see World Health Organization, *National Decision Making for Primary Health Care* (Geneva: World Health Organization, 1981). That Cuba is a leader in community health is well known; see Ross Danielson, *Cuban Medicine* (New Brunswick, N.J.: Transaction Books, 1979). For China, see World Health Organization, *Primary Health Care—The Chinese Experience* (Geneva: World Health Organization, 1983).
65. The project's growth is noted in Dolly García S., "Enseñanza de Salud Familiar en pregrado, una experiencia innovadora," *Redes* 5 (1985): 16–21.
66. For Bucaramanga, see *Redes* 6 (1986): 7; for Barranquilla, see *Redes* 5 (1985): 9.
67. *Redes* 6 (1986): 8.
68. Edison José Corrêa et al., "Programa transectorial de ação comunitária," *Redes* 5 (1985): 22–27.
69. I visited each center; for a summary of recent work, see Centro Internacional de Agricultura Tropical (CIAT), *CIAT 1984: A Summary of Major Achievements during the Period 1977–1983* (Cali: CIAT, 1984), International Potato Center (CIP), *Potatoes for the Developing World* (Lima: CIP, 1984), and Centro Agronómico Tropical de Investigación y Enseñanza (CATIE), *Informe de Progreso 1983* (Turrialba: CATIE, 1984). CATIE is a regional center affiliated with the Inter-American Institute for Cooperation on Agriculture.
70. *SAUS* (1986), p. 311.
71. Robert Pear, "U.S. Poverty Rate Dropped to 14.4 Percent in 1984, Bureau Says," *New York Times*, 28 August 1985, pp. 1, 12.
72. Ibid.

73. Keith Snyder, "Hunger Found Up Among Rural Poor," *New York Times*, 26 March 1986, p. 9.

74. Ezra Bowen, Patricia Delaney, and Lianne Hart, "Losing the War of Letters," *Time*, 5 May 1986, p. 63. See also Jonathan Kozol, *Illiterate America* (New York: Anchor Press, 1985).

75. *SAUS* (1986), pp. 390–91. See also Alan S. Blinder, "A 7 Percent Jobless Rate Is Just Not Good Enough," *Business Week*, 3 February 1986, p. 16.

76. Thurow, "A Surge of Inequality," pp. 30–37.

INDEX

Alcohol program: and energy crisis, 162–63; gasohol, 164, 165, 167, 168; production steps in, 164–65; advantages of sugarcane, 165, 166; credit for, 166, 167; and pollution, 166, 171; alcohol vehicles, 167, 168; cost-effectiveness of, 168; pricing policy, 168; background to, 169–70; impact on agriculture, 170, 171; production in São Paulo, 170–71

Argentina, 45, 150, 157. *See also* Debt crisis

Belo Horizonte, 182, 192

Bogotá, 51, 56, 58, 100

Bogotá project: demography, 58; organization of, 58; vaccinations, 58; lactation, 59; malnutrition, 59–60; neural development, 60; neighborhood health committees, 61–64. *See also* Diseases; Infant mortality

Brazil: economic growth in, 46, 145, 153, 256, 264; income distribution, 47, 142, 150–52, 154–55, 256; politics, 132–38 passim; death squads, 135; education, 142, 153, 156, 160–61, 209, 231; demography, 144, 145, 228, 265; urbanization, 145, 182–85, 193, 208, 231, 248; employment, 146, 148–49, 182, 256, 270–71; wages, 149, 151, 152, 199, 202, 256; poverty in, 152, 158; immigration, 157; trade balance, 163, 175, 255, 256, 264. *See also* Debt cri-

sis; Hydroelectric power; Petroleum; Popular culture; and names of cities, projects, and states

—agriculture: and jobs, 145–46, 147, 148, 158, 171, 194, 199–200, 209, 270–71; export crops, 146, 156, 229; and food crops, 147, 170, 210–13, 227, 228; and land distribution, 147, 210, 211, 212, 228, 248, 258; and credit policies, 147–48, 166, 167, 209, 212, 213, 214–16, 231, 250; productivity of small farms, 211–13, 227; cacao production, 248, 250. *See also* Alcohol program; Cacao Research Center; Irrigation; Northern Minas; Projects

—health care: malnutrition, 151, 152, 196–97, 200, 231; sanitary conditions, 152, 183, 186–87, 194, 200, 201, 238, 240–41; National Health Service, 158, 161, 204, 247; medical schools, 158–59, 187–88; vaccinations, 161, 185. *See also* Cotia project; Diseases; Fortaleza project; Infant mortality; Projects; Promotoras; Rural Internship Program

—industrial sector: growth of, 97, 145, 162, 256; iron ore and steel, 142, 175, 176, 182; output of, 145, 148, 149, 162–63; automobile fleet, 145, 162, 169, 172; in São Paulo, 156, 169, 230; in Minas Gerais, 182; in the Northeast, 231